Praise for *Looking f*

"Imagine a personal tour through Buckingham Palace given by an aficionado with the erudition of Samuel Johnson and the irascible wit of Mark Twain, a tour that would avoid all the main rooms of the castle and focus on the hidden moat, the mousetraps, [and] the disused toilet, and you will have some idea of what Booth is up to. . . . In his thoughtful, funny, erudite, and endlessly entertaining travel book, Alan Booth gives us an insider's Japan most of us have never seen before."

—Alan Jolis, *The International Herald Tribune*

"I enjoyed *Looking for the Lost* enormously. To travel with Alan Booth is to travel in very civilized company indeed, but also close to the ground. He has a mind that illuminates and enlivens everything it encounters."

—Nigel Barley, author of *The Innocent Anthropologist*

"Booth transmits his fascination with life's small moments and the country's . . . details and thereby makes of his book a truly engaging, fascinating look at the Japan that doesn't make the headlines."

—Mary Ellen Sullivan, *Booklist*

"There are certain things in Japan that only Alan Booth had the ability to convey in writing. His controlled exuberance made for an inimitable style which, combined with his refusal to be taken in by appearances and his underlying compassion for the people he lived amongst, made him an exceptional writer."

—Karel van Wolferen, author of *The Enigma of Japanese Power*

"[Booth's] capacity for rueful, discerning observation will keep him in the front ranks of travel writers for years to come."

—*Kirkus*

"Although Alan Booth was a city person—having been born and brought up in London and spending most of his working life in Tokyo—one of his . . .

strengths as a writer was his ability to capture the anecdotes and atmosphere of present-day rural Japan, a world of farmers and fishermen, shopkeepers and school children, festivals and funerals. . . . This was a world far removed from the slick city life and corporate comforts of urban Japan. With sharp wit he criticised Japan's manic modernity and his sympathies always lay with people whose houses were pulled down to make way for new motorways."

—Derek A.C. Davies, *The Independent* (London)

"*Looking for the Lost* shows off a Japan most of us will never know. Alan Booth writes with an elegance that's alternately sweet, intimate, and powerful."

—Tom Miller, author of *The Panama Hat Trail*

"The narrative is both dense in the richness of its detail—its topography, mood, and sense of historical time—and sparse in that it merely documents in attentive detail his 'wandering[s] in towns and villages provoking conversations.' Ultimately, it is in capturing the sense of constancy and change which characterizes the 'ordinariness of things' that Booth achieves his greatest triumph."

—Ritu Vij, *The Bloomsbury Review*

"A fascinating study of the way a nation assembles the disparate elements of its own identity, transforming the past as it hurtles toward the future."

—F.G. Notehelfer, *The New York Times Book Review*

"Far more than a travel book, *Looking for the Lost* is a razor-sharp look at street-level Japan, alternately searingly funny and darkly insightful. This is a journey peopled not by politicians or businessmen but [by] peasants, surly innkeepers, gold-toothed old women, gangsters, dockworkers, and children. It is also Alan Booth's last and finest book."

—Lesley Downer, author of *The Brothers*

"Contain[s] Booth's customary blend of rich historical and cultural background with fascinating and often humorous anecdotal experience. Recommended."

—*Library Journal*

Looking for
the Lost

Looking for the Lost

Journeys Through a Vanishing Japan

Alan Booth

KODANSHA INTERNATIONAL
New York • Tokyo • London

Kodansha America, Inc.
114 Fifth Avenue, New York, New York 10011, U.S.A.

Kodansha International Ltd.
17-14 Otowa 1-chome, Bunkyo-ku, Tokyo 112, Japan

Published in 1996 by Kodansha America, Inc.
by arrangement with the Estate of Alan Booth.

First published in 1995 by Kodansha America, Inc.

This is a Kodansha Globe book.

Material in "Tsugaru" quoted from *Return to Tsugaru* by Osamu Dazai,
translated by James Westerhoven. Copyright © 1985 by Kodansha International,
Ltd. Quoted by permission from Kodansha International, Ltd.

Library of Congress Cataloging-in-Publication Data

Booth, Alan, 1946–1993
    Looking for the lost: journeys through a vanishing Japan / Alan
Booth
        p.   cm.
    ISBN 1-56836-148-3
    1. Japan—Description and travel.   I. Title.
DS812.B66   1995
952.04'8—dc20   95-6264

Book design and maps by Charles Davey

Printed in the United States of America

96 97 98 99 00   RRD/H   10 9 8 7 6 5 4 3 2 1

Dedicated by Su-chzeng and Mirai
to all those who loved Alan

Contents

❧

1 Tsugaru

2 Saigo's Last March

3 Looking for the Lost

A Note on Japanese Names and Usage

❧

Japanese names are presented in Japanese order, that is, surname first and given name second. Japanese words are italicized on their first, but not subsequent, usage (except for words generally familiar to the English-reading audience, which are not italicized at all).

1
Tsugaru

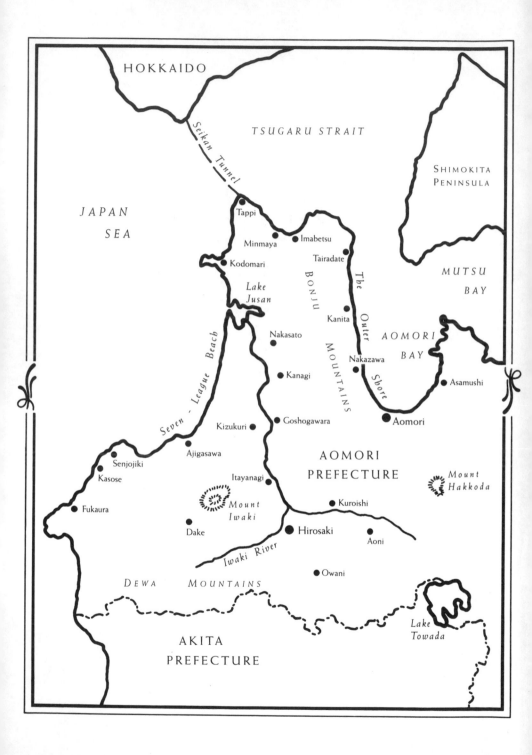

1
The Outer Shore

❧

The late spring rain in Tsugaru is a mixture of sleet and hail. All the puddles turn to streams and the streams swill with pachinko balls of ice. I felt a fool sloshing through them, with my nylon hood laced up round my face, soaked before I had walked for ten minutes despite the hood and the rest of my useless rain gear. It was mid-May, a time when up here in the far north, according to the book stuffed into my pack, "the apricot, peach, cherry, apple, pear, and plum trees all blossom together." The rain had begun at five the previous evening, two minutes after I stepped off the train at Aomori station. It had spat while I made the rounds of the hotels and been told in all of them that there were no rooms. It had turned into a regular drizzle by the time I stamped back to the tourist information desk at the station and asked the old man in gumboots if the hotels were all crazy or what. It was an off-season

Thursday. There couldn't be that many people wanting to sit and get sodden under the plum trees.

"No, it's always like this," the old man worried. "The trouble's the traveling salesmen. If you're a salesman with a northern route you're bound to pass through Aomori. We're full up every night of the year."

Outside the station the rain drove new arrivals toward the shelter of the covered arcades.

"What do the salesmen do when they get here and find that everywhere's full, then?"

"They've booked."

"But what if they haven't?"

"They—er—they share."

"All right."

The old man, who had looked fidgety and unwell from the moment I approached his desk, made small moaning noises under his breath.

"It's the same every night of the year, you see. . . ."

"I'll share if that's the only option."

"Well, it's just that . . ."

"What?"

"Well, it's just that it's cheap . . ."

I made him give me the name of a hotel where I might be able to share a room and tramped there through the thickening drizzle and the chill that had deepened with the early northern dark. The hotel was called the "New Yamato"; *Yamato* is a spirit-stirring name for Japan. The entrance was up a flight of dripping steps between a shop that sold plastic slippers and a pachinko parlor, and the girl at the desk looked as fidgety and unwell as the old man at the station had; perhaps it was the weather.

Well, yes, I could have one of the hotel's *furendorii ruumu* (friendly rooms), but there was no bath or shower in the room and no food at all and no lavatory on that floor and no service of any kind and there was a chance that someone would arrive later who would have to be put in with me.

"You mean there's no one in there now?"

The girl looked down at the register and said, "That's right."

"Do you think it's likely you'll put anyone in my room?"

The girl looked up, coughed quietly and said, "I doubt it."

So I had a friendly room to myself and went out for dinner to a restaurant near the fishing harbor where the owner told me that I was the fourth—no, fifth—foreigner to come into his shop in the twelve years since it had opened, and made me eat live whitebait in egg yolk. The whitebait squirmed between my chopsticks so I crunched them with my teeth to put them out of their misery.

For years, I told the owner over a beer, I had been attracted by the notion (which he found barmy) of taking a train from Tokyo to Aomori and then walking out of the city and on round the coast of the Tsugaru peninsula. Looking at a map, you get the impression that walking out of Aomori city will take you perhaps an hour and that, after that, you will pass through a succession of increasingly rustic villages of a kind conjured up by the word *Tsugaru* when it enters the urban Japanese imagination. Tsugaru is about as remote a region as you can still find among the habitable parts of Honshu, Japan's largest island, and therein lies its imagined charm. It is a place known for the hardness of its winters, the juiciness of its apples, the vibrancy of its folk music, the tenacity of its traditions, the drama of its summer festivals, the survival of its shamans, its impenetrable dialect, the dourly purposeful character of its people and, in general, for having preserved a way of life that most of Japan has tossed away but still likes to think is "truly Japanese."

This year Tsugaru was mounting a tourist campaign to mark the triumphant completion of the longest underwater tunnel in the world, linking Honshu with Hokkaido to the north. One end of it surfaces in Tsugaru, and there were posters and pamphlets about it everywhere. "The people up the coast are already complaining about the train rumbles," warned the owner. But I heard no complaints in Aomori. An Aomori Expo in honor of the tunnel was due to open in July and would feature, according to the brochure the owner showed me, a *meriigoraundo* (merry-go-round), a *gemu puraza* (game plaza), a *sukaishippu* (skyship), a *furaingu kaapetto* (flying carpet), a *baruun saikuru* (balloon cycle), and a *horaa hanto* (horror hunt).

"You wouldn't believe how fast Aomori is changing," the owner said, dropping another torture cell of yolk over a cluster of frantic baby fish. "There's the Sightseeing Center [a fourteen-story purple-lit pyramid] down by the old docks; there's the loudspeakers and boutiques in the shopping arcades, and the fancy craft shops and all the people talking la-di-da; and now the old ferries have gone to the wreckers and you can cross the straits on a railway train. . . . What are you expecting to find up there anyway?"

"I don't know," I told him. "Things I might not find in Tokyo."

I passed the purple-lit pyramid on my way back to the New Yamato. It looked like a gigantic advertisement for condoms. Next morning I sloshed off through the mid-May sleet, crossed the railway tracks on a slippery iron footbridge and then headed north, as I had dreamt of doing, up the coast that is called the Outer Shore.

"I had forgotten how cold it could be in the north," wrote Dazai Osamu, native of Tsugaru and author of the book stuffed into my pack, when he revisited Aomori on this day in May, forty-four years before me. "I pulled in my hands and feet as far as I could, until I looked like a turtle in its shell, and tried to tell myself that this was the way to purify my mind of worldly thoughts." It was later in the same book, in a different mood, that he listed all the blossoming fruit trees.

By eleven that May morning I was sitting in the Higashi Nihon ferry terminal three and a half kilometers up the road, my mind still mired in worldly thoughts, drinking hot sake to try and drive off the chill. The wind was blowing across Tsugaru from the west, the direction of Siberia, and it turned the rain into icy darts that punctured all my clothing. I had tried to get out of it twenty minutes after starting off by spending an hour in the municipal forestry museum. The two girls at the ticket office had hidden when they saw me and had had to be coaxed into selling me a ticket by a man I took to be the caretaker. But then one of the girls plucked up the courage to remark that I was very wet and helped me strip off my useless rain gear and hang it next to one of the two large oil stoves that the museum staff sat warming their hands at on this, by traditional count, the ninth day of summer.

Through the plate-glass windows of the ferry terminal the wind whipped the sea into thrashing grey porpoise-backs, and when I went to the lavatory and looked at myself in the mirror I was astonished to find my face a mess of dark purple blotches. Still, there was nothing to do except push on up the half-drowned coast, promising myself that I would fall into the first *ryokan*, or Japanese-style inn, that I came to and, for kilometer after kilometer, coming to none. The rustic villages of the urban imagination turned out to be an unbroken line of shabby suburban houses, occasionally interrupted by a shabbier beauty parlor or a dusty barber's shop that stank of pomade. Between the forestry museum and the municipal boundary I could have had a dozen haircuts and at least as many facelifts but I'd have had trouble finding a hot drink. I walked on the inland side of the road because of the fraction of shelter the squat houses gave me, but there was really no relief to be had. The rain clattered against the clear plastic doors of the Coca-Cola vending machines and hammered the cherry flowers that lay sodden along the pavements. At four o'clock, after about eighteen kilometers, I crossed out of the official limits of Aomori city into the little hamlet of Nakazawa, indistinguishable among the line of dowdy buildings that continued to stretch off to the limits of sight, except that one of the buildings was a ryokan into which I did not so much fall as dissolve.

The ryokan was presided over by a grandmother in a blue cardigan who hung up my wet things, shooed me to the bath, found me a dry woolly kimono, smiled and nodded whenever I said anything and called me Sensei, a polite term of address used by pupils to their teachers, publishers to their authors, electors to their parliamentary representatives, bar hostesses to their best-heeled customers, people wishing to be facetious to those they particularly despise, and by the general public to anyone who appears, or professes, to know something that they do not.

"A foreigner from Australia came here once, Sensei, and brought his little foreign daughter. You should have seen them! Such lovely foreign skin! And once, when my husband and I went on a package tour to Macau, we met a foreign family there—English foreigners, I think they were—and, well, we just had to ask them to line up and let us take their photographs. I've never seen anyone look so lovely as those foreigners. And you've got a daughter, have you, Sensei? I bet she looks lovely too—like a regular E.T."

At dinner, which was served in a small cluttered dining room next to the kitchen, the grandmother brought me a second bottle of beer and two of her grandchildren—a girl aged seven and another aged nine—stood in the corridor outside the dining room with their faces pressed to the glass door and shouted, "*Gaijin! Gaijin!*" (Foreigner! Foreigner!) at the tops of their voices whenever anyone came in or out. The grandmother in the blue cardigan poured my beer, and nodded vigorously and smiled.

"Yes, everybody commutes these days, so there's not much call for ryokans along here. You can drive into Aomori in twenty minutes if you want to. It's turned into a very settled life—not like years ago when all the young men had to go away for most of the year, except for planting and harvest time, to look for work in the towns down south. Now, what with the bus and the wider road, they can go in and out of Aomori every day. When they were building the tunnel up at Tappi the trucks were going up and down this road all day and night. You should have seen the dust! It was a regular nightmare, Sensei. But that's all finished now. Things have quieted down. We definitely can't complain."

The other guests at the little dining table, who had brought their own four-liter bottle of *shochu*, a potent liquor made from either rice or potatoes, were three workmen from across the bay in Mutsu Yokohama—still a part of Aomori prefecture, but not of Tsugaru, and this fueled their conversation.

"These Tsugaru people," the foreman whispered when the grandmother was out fetching beancurd soup, "can you understand a word they say? I'm blowed if I can half the time. It's not so bad near Aomori city because you get a lot of people who've settled here from other parts. But you go up to Goshogawara and round there and you'd think you were on another planet. Part of it is they don't open their mouths wide enough, because it's too cold in winter and the frost'll make their teeth drop out, and that's why they talk so quick too, so as not to let in the cold."

"But isn't it just as cold across the bay?"

The foreman considered this and was silent.

Then the grandfather, a bright, brisk gnome of a man, came in with a camera and insisted on posing us all for photographs. He made a great show of getting the three workmen and the grandmother and me all squeezed into the same shot, and then the grandmother fetched him his bottle of shochu while he marched round the table shaking our hands. His fingers were dark and very stubby and gave the impression that they had been sawn off at the knuckles, an impression reinforced by the dirty strips of plaster that were wound round both his thumbs.

"Dad likes to sing," the grandmother told us. "Do you like to sing, Sensei?"

"Yes, I do," I said. The grandfather jumped up and shook my hand.

"See that poster on the wall over there," the grandmother said. "That's a famous singer who lives round here and owns a bar called Charmant just down the road. You must have heard of her. She's famous in Tokyo too. That's a poster for one of her records. She's the mama of the bar and she's got three girls to help her, so it's a real big place, and it's got laser discs and everything, and we go there sometimes because Dad likes to sing."

"I bet it's expensive," grumbled the foreman, a stocky, red-faced man with hair like broom bristles. The grandfather jumped up and shook his hand.

"No, it's not so bad," the grandmother said. "You can generally get away for about three thousand yen a person."

"That's cheaper than you'd get away with in Tokyo," I said. The grandfather jumped up and shook my hand.

"Why don't you all go down there and sing?" the grandmother suggested. "We'll lend you umbrellas. You'd have a splendid time, I bet."

The workman sitting next to me, a hulking man with piggy eyes, began to bang the table lightly with his fists.

"No, not tonight," the foreman said, watching the workman carefully from across the table. "We can have a sing here. Go on, sing us a Tsugaru song."

The grandfather sang "Aya Bushi," his voice cracking on the high notes in fine country style. But the workman next to me stared down at the table and continued to bang it very quietly.

"And now, Sensei, you sing us a song," said the grandmother. So I sang "Ajigasawa Jinku." The first line was greeted with communal paralysis:

. . . the shrine at Takayama on the Seven-League Beach . . .

But during the second line, the grandmother began maneuvering with the camera, the workmen, except for the one with piggy eyes, started to clink their chopsticks against the neck of the four-liter shochu bottle, and the grandfather began to dance round and round the table, pausing to shake my hand at the end of each verse. Then I sang:

Old Jimmy Flanagan he had a little pig,
He hit it with a shovel and it danced a jig.

And all the workmen banged the table with their fists and the two grandchildren outside the glass door stood frozen to the spot with their thumbs between their teeth.

At eleven o'clock I was the last to leave the dining room. I counted six large bottles of beer I had drunk. The grandfather shook my hand as I mounted the stairs and I crawled into my futon feeling warm and full, as proper senseis ought to.

In May 1944, seven years after his fourth attempted suicide and four years before his fifth and successful one, Dazai Osamu, the man who wrote about purity of mind and blossoming fruit trees, was commissioned by a Tokyo publisher to revisit Tsugaru, where he had been born and brought up, and write a book about it. He arrived on May 13th, the day of my rain-sodden tramp out of Aomori, and traveled up this Outer Shore to Cape Tappi, where I was going too.

In the corridor outside my room at the ryokan in Nakazawa, where my pack and its contents, including the damp copy of his book, were laid out round an oil stove, Dazai was featured on a poster promoting Tsugaru's attractions to tourists. The poster showed a sunny blue sea with one of the last of the Hokkaido ferries, now made redundant by the new railway tunnel, turning a lazy circle in the middle distance. In the foreground, in sepia, stands Dazai, huddled in a cape, a half-smoked cigarette between his fingers, his hair whipped into a briar bush on the awkward flat top of his head, an expression of stoic misery on his face, staring out over the sea and looking, in sepia, like Jacob Marley's ghost. The caption was a quotation from his book: *Koko wa Honshu no kyokuchi de aru.* This is Honshu's North Pole.

Twice married and once a father, twice ambitious for Japan's most prestigious literary prize and twice thwarted in this ambition by the literary establishment, a university dropout, bedridden on and off with bouts of T.B. and drug addiction, once locked up for a month in a mental hospital and five times hauled in by the police on suspicion of being a political subversive, Dazai had spent twenty-three days in Tsugaru on that late spring trip during the Second World War, boozing with friends, visiting relatives, staying in the family house which, fourteen years earlier, he had been forbidden ever to enter again and, in the end, seeking out an emotional reunion with his nursemaid whom he thought he loved. The book that came out of all this is *Tsugaru*, regarded by the knowledgeable as one of Dazai's most touching pieces of work. Not quite a novel, not quite a travelogue, and certainly not the "gazetteer" that the Tokyo publisher had expected him to write, it is a book that mines the vein Dazai worked best—himself, at odds with fortune and the world—and, in inquiring into the nature of the land where he was born, it inquires also into other things that shape and nurse and crack the spirit.

"Not sure of myself as a man of the city," he wrote, "I hoped to find my true identity in Tsugaru." He was thirty-five years old at the time, six years younger than I was, and his house was in a part of Tokyo very near where I lived. I was twice married and once a father, never locked up or bedridden or questioned by the police, and I could afford to be as openly anti-establishment as I liked in a country, and an age, where a dissident stance was a fashion, not a duty, and where anyway I was a foreigner and so expected to hold odd and irresponsible opinions. I did not much care for Dazai, as a man or as a writer, but I planned to spend twenty-three days in Tsugaru too—the same twenty-three that Dazai had spent. And where Dazai had gone by bus and train and ferry I would go on foot. And what Dazai had seen here I would see or, equally likely, would not see, since I didn't know whether I was looking for a person, or looking for a country, or looking for the lost.

✌

The storm had blown over. It was a bright blustery morning and the barber's shops were doing unhurried business. In one a young man sat reading a pornographic comic while his hair was gradually smothered under a mess of pink and sky blue curlers. The road along the Outer Shore, though widened in places to accommodate the stream of trucks that had carted concrete and landfill for twenty-five years to and from the tunnel site, still ran between thin rows of squat colorless houses. The hills had begun to encroach on the backyards, so that the paper hamlets grew narrower and narrower as they butted one against another, squashed between hills and walled sea. If you could see these hamlets from the air, they would resemble the sloughed skin of a long, drab snake. When I found a gap between the houses on the seaward side I trudged out onto the concrete no-man's land that separated their back doors from the stony beach, where women in headscarves scraped the muck off bone-stiff nets. Across Mutsu Bay the Shimokita peninsula looked green and close enough to sink my teeth into. And if I glanced back the way I had come, round the long concrete curve of the bay, I saw the smoking chimneys of Aomori city, its absurd fourteen-story sightseeing pyramid visible for miles on up the coast and, soaring behind it into the pearl-colored sky, the pale ghost of Mount Hakkoda.

The Outer Shore—Sotogahama—seems an odd name for this, the more sheltered of the Tsugaru peninsula's two long coasts; the one washed by the ripples of a well protected bay, not the one that faces the wild Japan Sea. But the range of hills that now bore down on the backyards cuts this strip of shore off completely from the bulk of the peninsula's population, who live on the other side of the hills, on the west-central plain. When Dazai came here in 1944 there was still no road across these hills, though they do not rise much above four hundred meters, and the plainsfolk regarded this inaccessible shore as affording a pitiful living compared to what, with hard work and luck, they could glean from their own rice paddies. This shore was "outer" because it was shut off from the main source of local wealth, flat land. Proximity to Aomori city lent it precious little merit either, since in the past, as now for its procession of weary salesmen, Aomori was a city to hurry through, not to boast about, the prefectural capital through bureaucratic folly, while the real urban heart of the region lay south, and still does, in the old castle town of Hirosaki.

By noon I was in the little town of Kanita. The worst of squat suburbia seemed finally to have come to an end and, just before it entered Kanita, the road bumped into the first stretch of open beach that I had so far seen. Then, within a quarter of an hour, it had slipped back into its straitjacket of buildings to become Kanita's main street. Dazai had made Kanita the focal point of this first part of his trip because it was the home of an old schoolfriend who had done him favors. Being both a rice miller and a town councillor, the schoolfriend, whom Dazai calls "N," had managed to avoid being much inconvenienced by the wartime rationing of alcohol, and was thus in a position to do the visiting celebrity the only sort of favor he really appreciated— provide him with an unlimited opportunity to booze. Dazai spent four days and nights here. His account of these days and nights, and of N's accompanying him up the rest of the Outer Shore to spend a night at Cape Tappi, is one in which gazetteer-like matters are disposed of as perfunctorily as possible so that most of the sixty-or-so pages can be devoted to alternate bursts of celebration and stupor.

Kanita means "Crab Paddy," and Dazai had stayed sober long enough to record the excellence of the crabs he ate here. So I treated myself to an extravagant lunch of crab, scallops, raw squid and *shako*, a marine crustacean which my dictionary calls a squilla, and which looks like a giant woodlouse. While eating this I watched a lunchtime variety show on the most massive color television set I had ever seen outside an expo pavilion. Some Japanese comedians were causing a lot of hilarity by impersonating foreigners, which they did by donning ginger wigs and false noses a foot long and saying meaningless things in funny accents. I began explaining to the young man sitting next to me that, if a group of comedians on British television put on opaque spectacles and protruding teeth and said things like "We rike eat flied lice," there would be a God-almighty fuss in the letter columns of every Japanese daily newspaper as well as an orchestrated broadside of indignant editorials about Japan-bashing and the entrenched racism of Britain's Channel Four. But the young man cut me off with a hiss of breath the moment it sank in that I was British.

"Triumph!" he exclaimed.

"I beg your pardon?"

"Triumph!" he said again. "And Norton and BSA! I love them all! Yes, I love them all! But Lawrence of Arabia died on a Triumph!"

When I left Kanita a loudspeaker van was advertising the advantages of believing in Iesu Kirisuto (Jesus Christ), sometimes portrayed on variety shows hanging on a cross in a ginger wig. And a man spraying a car with a high-powered hose and not paying enough attention to where he was pointing it managed to soak me almost as thoroughly as the icy rain had done the previous day.

"Why don't you mind what you're doing?" I growled, but he only looked puzzled, wondering what had happened to my foot-long nose.

Now the hills and sea squeezed the road so tight that, for stretches of up to a kilometer, there was no room for any building along it but the occasional boat shed, and I could begin to imagine that I was finally in the countryside. Instead of telescoping one into another like the coaches of a crashed train, the grey specks named on my map as hamlets actually began to take on separate identities, though there was little in the way of architectural landmarks to set any of them apart from its neighbors. It is impossible to imagine a set of place mats depicting Japanese villages like the ones of English villages that Harrods sells to Japanese tourists: Castle Combe with its church and bridge, Woolpit and its green. Japanese villages all look so alike that I sometimes wonder how people know where to get off the bus. Hardly any of the buildings in most of them are more than twenty or thirty years old and if anything dates back before the war it is either the shrine, the rice shop, or the rusty fire tower. This has nothing to do with bombs or earthquakes—at least not in Tsugaru. Nor does it have much to do with the fact that the principal building material outside the centers of cities is timber; if you want to you can build to last in timber, as the survivors among Japan's old temples attest. It has to do, rather, with the Japanese passion for pulling things down and putting them up again, an activity which some observers have suggested reflects a Buddhist acknowledgment of the impermanence of the material world and others have thought a lunatic waste. But there are, according to the *Kodansha Encyclopedia of Japan*, 510,000 registered construction companies in the nation employing about ten percent of all workers in the industrial sector; so you obviously can't leave buildings standing about for much more than a generation without having to lay off a sizable part of the work force.

Another thing the hamlets had in common was a profusion of liquor shops—not the kind where you sit and drink, but the kind where you buy your booze and cart it away. The smallest community would sometimes have three or four of these shops, often next door to one other. Tsugaru people seem to do most of their drinking at home rather than indulging in the now more or less national pastime of going out to drink in tiny bars, or "snacks." (Later on I would overhear a conversation in Imabetsu between a weekend fisherman from Sendai and the owner of the ryokan where he was staying; the fisherman asked the owner if the town had any "snacks" and the owner repeated the word over and over again with his head cocked to one side, wondering maybe whether his guest meant packets of dried octopus and potato chips.)

Drinking in groups at home is a rural custom, born of a life in households where an extended family of many brothers and uncles and cousins all slept and boozed under a single roof. But in most parts of the countryside the migration of younger family members to the cities and the consequent breakup of such large households have led to rural customs giving way to urban ones, such as spending evenings in bars. Many country villages now have their traditional *nomiya* with its paper lantern hanging outside, or their "karaoke snack" with its microphones and surrogate mother. But Tsugaru seemed a notable exception. Near one or two of the larger villages I did pass a small shed-like building, always shuttered and dingy-looking, that advertised itself as a karaoke snack, and I was always struck by the siting of these sheds just outside the village proper, as though, like the bear pits and theaters of Elizabethan London, their popularity had not erased the stink of disrepute.

The widened highway bypassed a few of the villages on the seaward side, so that the piles supporting it gave additional protection to their little fishing harbors. The price for this protection, of course, was the ruination of any picturesqueness that the villages and their harbors may once have possessed, but this is a price that has seemed acceptable to coastal communities throughout Japan. Where a highway has not been built to spoil the view, the breakwater protecting the shore will almost always consist of a spiky ridge of concrete polyhedrons dumped there to be a permanent eyesore by the construction industry's floating cranes. Once or twice along this coast an attempt had been made to create a small area that might attract the odd holidaymaker, but the result was always half-hearted and artificial. A children's climbing frame or see-saw or slide would stand on a stretch of yellowing grass, its paint flaking in the wet, salt wind, looking as though it had been left there to mark the last settlement of vanished nomads. Once I saw a windsurfer struggling to fix his sail to his colored board and kicking both of them in frustration. And once I passed a car park that was ringed by three small restaurants but all three doors were boarded up and the car park was empty.

At four I reached the village of Tairadate. A funeral had just ended and the single main street of the village was littered with black-clad pensioners straggling home from the crematorium in the late afternoon sun, or being ferried home in a maroon jeep. The first ryokan I went to was hosting the funeral party but the second gave me an eighteen-mat room to myself and lit an oil stove for me and had the ten-year-old son of the owner serve me raw squid. He remarked with a serious face that I had blisters on my feet, looking at the burst one on the inside of my right heel. Perhaps he had heard me groaning in the bath. And on the wastepaper basket under the hanging scroll was a picture of a baby elephant on a skateboard, bandaged and unhappy and saying, "*Itaiiii!*" (Ouch!) in a bubble that came out of his trunk. Beneath him, the moral was printed in English: He keeps failing and failing. He will never learn. Oh, what a pain to practice!

❧

From a hidden shrine high up on a hillside came the faint, regular thump of a drum. Under the overcast a few ragged squid hung drying, and along the shore the seaweed gatherers plodded, wading over pitted lunar rocks and plunging their arms into pools clogged with weed, black and chalky white. In the sea itself floated seaweed that was green and feathery and bound up the wheels of bicycles that lay broken at the tideline. A signboard told me that I was entering a stretch of the Tsugaru Quasi-National Park and I looked for anything that might justify this fine-sounding designation. At the tiny fishing hamlet of Sunagamori I saw a pleasant stone-built harbor wall, and on the shoulder of road above this silent hamlet stood a flowering cherry tree, very old, with a smell that was heavy and sticky-sweet and with blossoms sprouting in crowds from its black trunk as well as from its branches.

Once or twice I came across monuments. Near Imabetsu there were two: a Daruma waterfall and a rock dedicated to Kannon, the Goddess of Mercy. *Daruma* is the Japanese name for Bodhidharma, the Indian sage whom legend credits with having introduced Zen Buddhism to China. He is said to have meditated for nine years in a cave and during that time his arms and legs atrophied; as a result the Japanese, being infinitely more comfortable with outward appearances than with inward illuminations, associate him not with piety, but with roundness. Thus a snowman in Japanese is a "snow Daruma" and a potbellied stove is called a "Daruma stove." One of the commonest talismans of good luck is an armless and legless Daruma doll, made of papier-mâché and sold at shrine festivals and fairs. The doll is eyeless as well as armless and legless (another legend credits Daruma with having cut off his eyelids in a rage because he had dozed off during meditation; they fell to the ground and sprouted as tea plants) and purchasers of the dolls—such as electioneering politicians—paint in one of the eyes when they make a wish and the other when the wish is fulfilled.

The Daruma waterfall near Imabetsu consisted of three or four thin trickles of water coming down a tall rock which, though it bulged slightly, could not have resembled a meditating sage except to a visionary or a drunk. And the Iwaya Kannon—the "Merciful Goddess of the Rock"—inhabited a lonely little cave that was invisible from the road but indicated by a wooden signboard, so I clambered round a sharp black outcrop of rock and boulders to look at it. The entrance was strung with grubby votive papers, and on the one or two flat patches of ground inside the empty cave worshippers had piled up pebbles as prayers, some sharp and flint-like, some worn and round and whitish pink. When I emerged, a car had stopped and two girls were setting conscientiously about the task of snapping pictures of each other in front of the Daruma waterfall. I hurried on, past another signboard that advertised the latest of Imabetsu's claims to fame—The Town Where The Seikan Tunnel Starts—and, as soon as I reached the first buildings of the town, began to look for a place where I could sit and have a drink.

Dazai found plenty to drink at Imabetsu. His friend N had persuaded a relative of Dazai's who lived in the town (the son of one of his cousins, a man Dazai calls "Mr. M") to go round his neighbors collecting up their sake rations so that he and the celebrity would have an adequate supply for the night they planned to spend at Cape Tappi. Then, having arrived at Imabetsu, they discovered that the boat to Tappi was not running that day, so they got themselves invited into Mr. M's house, suggested that his wife go and call him home from work, and set about polishing off his sake ration as well.

Dazai remembered Imabetsu as "a cheerful port," a judgment clearly colored by circumstance. Like the other small towns of the Outer Shore, it seemed to me, walking through it, to be three-quarters dead. Few coastal towns or villages in Tsugaru made any attempt to impress the arriving traveler, or even to put on a half decent face for the glumly returning resident, and in appearance Imabetsu was among the most dilapidated.

The first building I came to was that fixture on the outskirts of practically all Tsugaru towns: a cement factory. The next was an abandoned bowling alley, out of whose broken doors poured a dozen shrieking schoolboys. The corrugated plastic walls of the first houses were patched with peeling strips of rain-softened plywood. There were a couple of eating places on the town's main street, but they were closed and the doors and windows were boarded up. The whole town seemed to have been designed to serve as a backdrop for a funeral and, just as I thought this, I saw that a funeral was taking place. The three huge paper wheels on sticks that leaned against the outside wall of the bereaved house—white and black and gold and silver and studded with artificial flowers that rattled in the wind—were the liveliest objects I saw during my fifteen-minute tramp from one end of the town to the other. I was through Imabetsu and almost at Minmaya before I found a shed-like restaurant by the side of the road where there were no customers and the elderly woman who ran it sat knitting and talking to her cat.

I ordered a beer and a plate of fried noodles and soon four elderly travelers arrived. They parked their car, settled down at the table next to mine and, lacking my familiarity with shed-like restaurants in Tsugaru, they unwisely assumed that the menu posted all around the walls bore a relation to what the knitting woman could actually provide.

"Let's have something unusual," said one elderly traveler who came from Nagasaki, at the other end of Japan. The knitting woman listened without comment while the four travelers ran through the menu aloud. One entire window was plastered with colorful signs advertising the local specialty, squid.

"Squid! Let's have some squid!"

"There isn't any," said the woman. The travelers returned to the menu.

"All right, I'll have the meat stew," said the man from Nagasaki.

"That's a good idea," said two of his companions.

"And I'll have a pork cutlet," said the third.

"I'm not doing meat stew today," said the woman.

"We'll all have pork cutlets on rice then," said the man from Nagasaki.

"I haven't got any pork cutlets," said the woman.

There was a silence while the travelers ran sheepishly through the menu once again and, in the end, ordered four plates of fried noodles. The noodles came out of a packet and so did the bits of frankfurter that were mixed in with them, and the elderly adventurers in search of the unusual looked glumly at the four plates when they arrived on their table. Some dried black fish were hanging from the walls of the shed.

"What's that?" wondered the man from Nagasaki. "Mackerel?"

"It's cod, isn't it?" said one of his companions.

"That's right, it's cod," agreed the third.

"No, surely it's mackerel," said the fourth. The woman listened to this silently, knitting.

"What's that fish?" one of the travelers finally asked her.

"Mackerel," she said, shortly. "You can have some if you like."

They debated this.

"How much is it?"

"Nothing."

The woman stood up, still holding her knitting, reached up and took down two of the black fish from the wall and placed them on the scratched formica of the travelers' table. Then she sat down, put her knitting aside, folded her arms and watched them. The travelers took turns trying to tear bits off of the fish with their hands, and I took a turn too, but it was as tough as a suitcase. I brought out my sheath knife and tried to cut it with that, but the blade barely made a dent in it. After about five minutes of wasted effort, during which we shunted the two fish back and forth from one table to the other, the woman stood up with a satisfied grunt, took back the fish, went out into her yard, placed them one at a time on a block of wood, and bashed them for a minute each with a crowbar.

"There," she said. "Now they'll taste better too."

I began telling the travelers how to reach Kodomari. They had set off from Morioka that morning and they were aiming to drive round the whole of Aomori, Akita, and Iwate prefectures and be back in Morioka in time for supper.

"Whatever for?"

"For a trip," they beamed.

The woman paid very careful attention to what I was saying about Tsugaru roads and, when the travelers had gone, she rewarded me for the advice I had given them with a small dish of fermented squid guts and a larger dish of bracken. I spent most of the afternoon in her restaurant, drinking beer and nursing the cat. Just before I left a local workman walked in, plonked himself down at a table by the window that was covered with advertisements for squid, buried his nose in a three-inch thick comic book and said, with the voice of experience, "Fried noodles."

It had begun to rain and the light was failing. I stood in a doorway to pull on my rain gear and then walked quickly towards neighboring Minmaya, where Dazai and N had spent a night at a ryokan, having postponed their trip to Cape Tappi on account of the unavailability of a boat and the effects of a long afternoon spent drinking someone else's sake.

Imabetsu is a properly accredited township whereas Minmaya is only a village, but Minmaya has clearly copped most of the funds that have been allocated for local "development" so it must have a better-connected mayor. Most of its "development" appears to have occurred as a result of the building of the Seikan Tunnel. On the seaward side there is a new bridge, a new village office, and a new four-lane bypass, flanked by streetlamps whose dull orange globes turned the falling rain into clouds of plummeting maggots. Here and there houses and shops were being torn down (the most prosperous business in the village looked to be a lumberyard) and a huge muddy building site took the place of a village green. I asked about ryokans and was told that there were none, but I found a room in an obsessively clean lodging house that stood in a district called Shinmachi (New Town). Tumblers full of plastic flowers occupied all the available window sills, the Western-style lavatory seat had a pink electrically heated cover, and, when you used the toilet roll, it played "In Meine Haus." From the window of my room, beyond the artificial daisies, I could see the orange bypass lying eerily deserted, as it lay all night and doubtless all year, like an airstrip abandoned in a war already lost.

$\approx$

Dazai has several pages about Minmaya, parts of them devoted to ridiculing an earlier travel writer's account in which a fanciful local legend is presented as though it were fact—a practice not to be tolerated in grimly historical 1944. In the 1780s Tachibana Nankei, a doctor from the imperial capital, had traveled extensively throughout remote Japan and later published four volumes of his observations. In volume one of *Toyuki* (*Record of a Journey to the East*), the doctor records the slender claim to immortality from which Minmaya derives its name.

Minmaya (or, more properly, *Miumaya*, which is what the village used to be called) is written with two ideograms that mean "three stables," and Nankei tells how, during his long flight north in 1189, Japan's great tragic hero, Yoshitsune, arrived at Minmaya with two loyal followers in order to embark for Hokkaido. While he was busy pacifying the wind and waves by praying to the Goddess of Mercy, his followers sheltered their horses in three holes in a huge rock which stood on the shore nearby. Dazai is right to question this account, since it is unlikely that Yoshitsune ever came within two hundred and fifty kilometers of Minmaya, although legends recording his appearance crop up in many far-flung corners of the north, and there is even one which relates how he escaped to China and resurfaced there as Genghis Khan. (Aomori prefecture is well supplied with fanciful stories and among the other things you can see there if you have time is the grave of Jesus Christ.)

But at least the doctor's account ("one tall tale after another," scoffs Dazai) contains two undeniable truths. One is that, for centuries, until the rise of Aomori city, little Minmaya was indeed the port of embarkation for the island of Hokkaido, a fact which Dazai thinks accounts for the superior quality he found in the ryokans of the Outer Shore, the result of their long history of catering to travelers from all over the country. This was a quality which, forty-four years later, I looked for and missed. The other undeniable thing in the doctor's account is the existence of the rock itself. You can see it today, though time has wrought some changes.

For centuries the sea has encroached along much of Japan's coastline and, when Dazai passed this way, the waves of the Tsugaru Strait had crept close enough to pound Minmaya's rock and send great spumes of surf through its three gaping clefts; no horse could have sheltered there for a second. Today, though, the rock stands safely dry again, surrounded by pink paving stones and a municipal fence of concrete posts that simulate wooden logs, and a neatly flattened bed of grey stone chips to cover landfill dumped from the tunnel. The rock is tamed and signposted now like most of Japan's monuments, man-made or natural. Dazai says he passed it as quickly as he could: "There is something oddly embarrassing," he remarks, "about finding that kind of legend in one's native land." I passed the rock embarrassed, too—by its dumbness and its taming.

The stretch of road between Minmaya and Tappi offers an especially good opportunity to compare what Dazai saw with what exists today because it is one of the few stretches of road along which Dazai actually walked and on which he chose to exercise his talent for describing landscape, a talent that was not his forte any more than it is mine. Aside from the fact that the ryokan where he stayed had not been able to provide alcohol and had botched the cooking of his fish, Dazai seems to have found Minmaya an agreeable place, whereas I found it even more depressing than Imabetsu since I greatly prefer slow ruination to the sudden kind contrived by local authorities. In

Minmaya and Imabetsu, wrote Dazai, "I could see how serene life can be in the cheerful atmosphere of those trim, well-appointed harbors," and if any part of that sentence represents an honest description of what Dazai actually found here, then the change wrought upon these pitiful places in the forty-four years between our visits is hardly less than that wrought by an ice age.

Perhaps it was the sake talking. Once on the road—and the last thing on earth he revelled in was physical exertion—Dazai found a world less trim and cheerful: ". . . the scenery around us began to look strangely desolate and even, one might say, forbidding. It was no longer scenery. When you talk of scenery, you think of something that has been seen and described by many people over long periods of time. Human eyes have, as it were, softened it with their gaze, human hands have fed it and tamed it. . . . In all the steep and rugged places that have ever been celebrated in paintings or poems, without a single exception, one can discover a human element, but this extreme northern coast of Honshu has steadfastly refused to transform itself into anything resembling scenery. It even spurns that speck of a human figure that can often be seen in landscape paintings. . . . This landscape does not lend itself to picture or song. . . . There is only one word that befits the rocks and sea along Honshu's most far-flung road, and that word is 'frightening.' From then on I averted my eyes and kept them trained on the ground at my feet."

The notion that scenery requires human interference if it is to appeal to human sensibilities was one I pondered as I walked along that same road. I found myself much irked by this notion that has obviously found favor among the cement makers and development committees of Minmaya. But it received a sharper rebuke than any argument of mine could have supplied when I trudged through the little hamlet of Utetsu and, with an accuracy honed since the Tertiary period, a crow shat on my head.

The road up to Tappi is not what it was when Dazai stumbled along it with his eyes fixed on the ground, but on this dark morning of low cloud and misty rain, with the long low note of the cape's fog horn echoing off the grey-black sea, it recovered for stretches some inkling of its wildness. The road had been widened in recent years to allow truck access to the tunnel site and, from Dazai's account, it had already been improved in a small way by the time he used it in 1944. Six or seven years before that the waves had still crashed over it and in bad weather it had been completely impassable; Dazai remarks that it was still impassable at night. Now, in the several little hamlets, grocer's vans stood parked by the roadside, their loudspeakers shrieking endlessly in competition with the moan of the fog horn. At midday the loudspeakers were joined by Big Ben chimes that came out of the hamlets' own loudspeakers, reminding everyone that the moment had come to down tools and unwrap their rice balls. One or two dejected fishermen peered over the rowlocks of small dinghies in the offshore rain, and beyond Utetsu a taxi stopped, the driver got out, pulled on a pair of rubber boots, and waded into the drizzly rock pools to spend his lunch hour gathering seaweed.

I emerged from the last of a series of rock tunnels in which fishermen had hung their scrappy tackle and, just after one in the afternoon, found myself among the sheds of Tappi. "I was just thinking how narrow the path had become," says Dazai, "when I suddenly found myself with my head stuck inside a chicken coop. For a moment I had no idea what had happened.

" 'Tappi,' said N, his tone of voice different from before.

" 'This?'

"When I looked around more calmly, I saw that what I had imagined to be a chicken coop was really the hamlet of Tappi."

It has one narrow lane between the sheds, a tiny empty harbor, the usual concrete breakwater, and at the end of the sheds, where the lane runs out, there is a small stone monument to Dazai and his book. On it are chiseled the words which follow his discovery that the chicken coop was a community of people:

"This is Honshu's North Pole. Beyond this hamlet there is no road. There is nothing but a drop to the sea. This is Honshu's blind alley. Mark my words, reader: if you walk north following the road, ever northward, northward, you cannot fail to reach the Outer Shore Road; it will grow narrower and narrower, but if you carry on northward you will at last reach this strange chicken-coop world and there you will have come to the absolute end of your road."

This thought clearly occurred to Dazai because he had spent three uncharacteristic hours exercising his leg muscles. ("When you have to walk," he later complained, "Tsugaru is not as small as you think.") But if you did walk northward from the main body of Honshu, and if you reached Cape Tappi as Dazai insists you would, you would have to turn left instead of right at Noheji, otherwise you would go up the parallel Shimokita peninsula and reach the true end of Honshu, Cape Oma, which lies about eighteen seconds of latitude further up the globe than Tappi does. Still, what is geography to a writer, unless he is a gazetteer writer, which Dazai plainly wasn't. Besides, the Shimokita peninsula lacks Tsugaru's reputation, as it lacks its history, its language, its music, its pride, its festivals, its castle town. And when you consider that, until quite late in Japanese history, Hokkaido was not regarded as a part of the homeland at all, this lane running out into the sea at Tappi is as near the end of the world as any Japanese could want to be.

I climbed up through the freezing drizzle to the lighthouse, where visibility was down to about a hundred meters, and sat in the tiny restaurant nearby drinking beer and warming myself at a stove. Tappi has two communities now (it had three during the quarter of a century when the Seikan Tunnel was under construction, the third consisting of tunnel workers who were housed in jerry-built apartment blocks that have since been torn down). Now there are those who live in the chicken coop below, who fish and trade and gather seaweed, and those who work up here on the misty heights, where there are larger but equally scruffy buildings—a primary school with a damp, windswept playground; a "Tappi Hot Spring Hotel," which the woman at the restaurant admitted to me was not supplied by a real hot spring; a coast-guard station; the lighthouse; and what I took to be a radar facility with barracks-like huts to house the men who run it.

Throughout his book Dazai pretends a reluctance to describe the little hamlets of northern Tsugaru out of consideration for the sensitive issue of national security. No doubt in 1944 this issue was an obsession, although most of Dazai's references to it sound impishly tongue-in-cheek. But the Tsugaru Strait remains a strategic headache. It is one of three crucial straits that Japan is still pledged to blockade and defend for the Western alliance should there be a war. I sat with my steaming nylon clothes hung round the tiny restaurant's oil stove, shivering and gazing out of the window into a blank wall of white. Up here, close enough to be driven barmy by it, the fog horn sounded like a disoriented kraken, peering up into space from the bed of the ocean and wondering what had happened to the sky.

Just before three, with the drizzle still falling, I trudged back down to the chicken coop and looked for the ryokan where Dazai had stayed. It wasn't hard to find. On the wall outside was a sign that said, in letters large enough to be read from the end of the village, The Inn Associated with Dazai Osamu.

The night Dazai and N spent here forms one of the best-known episodes of his trip. On the road up from Minmaya, Dazai had been able to wrench his eyes off his feet long enough to discuss with N the possibility of their obtaining a fresh supply of sake in case the ryokan turned out to be suffering from the usual wartime shortage. At the last hamlet before Tappi N had managed to wheedle yet another bottle out of an acquaintance (N had emerged from the house "trying his best to stifle his laughter") and their relief had increased when it transpired that the ryokan at Tappi was suffering from no shortage at all.

"We would like to drink quite a lot," N had told "the elegant old lady" who had shown them to their room.

"Go ahead. There is as much as you like," she had said, smiling, not knowing what she was letting herself in for.

Soon N, in particular, was hopelessly drunk and began singing in a loud and tuneless voice. "He groaned," says Dazai, "he screamed, he howled; it really became rather disgusting." In short order the elegant old lady appeared, said, "Ah, I see you're singing! How about turning in by and by?" removed all their sake flasks and laid out their bedding. "She seemed genuinely shaken by N's magnificent roars," Dazai lamented. "I had intended to do a lot more drinking, but the whole thing had become very stupid. . . . Grumbling and complaining, I resigned myself to the inevitable." And so, with nothing else for it, they had slept.

It was the old woman's daughter, herself now getting old, who appeared in the entrance hall in answer to my shouts and, when I asked if there was a room free, told me they were all free. The place was cavernous and empty. We hung my dripping clothes over ropes stretched across the woman's living room downstairs, careful not to obstruct her view of the television. The room was curtained like a gypsy's tent, with kettles steaming on two huge oil stoves, and in the larger room opposite stood a dozen revolving electric lanterns, pink and green and blue and white, of the kind you see in bereaved homes during the summer festival of the dead. The atmosphere was that of a fairground from which all life has been expelled by an act of God, and from a dim back parlor came the only sound in the building, the ticking of a big invisible clock.

My six-mat room was on the second floor and overlooked the sea. But the rain doors were half drawn against the storm and to benefit from the view I had to pull the chair from the corridor into my room and push it as far back into the alcove as it would go and then sit and stare out of the slit of window at the ranks of gulls on the concrete polyhedrons, all facing seaward from where the storm was blowing, preferring the devil they knew. Up here on the second floor the rattle of the rain doors was sharp and loud and punctuated the long moans of the horn.

Dazai records that the room he occupied was well-furnished and that he had a charcoal brazier and a padded kimono to keep out the cold. But in the years that separated his stay from mine the ice age had come and gone and taken all the comforts. There was no brazier, no padded kimono, no heating of any kind in my room. I pulled on thick socks and wore my training suit under the ryokan's thin kimono and sat shivering in the alcove, staring out at the gulls on the concrete. The room was undecorated except for a single piece of no-nonsense calligraphy: five black ideograms on a white background that looked more like carpentry than brushstrokes. They were a quotation from a story by Dazai: *Sei Tei Dai Ichi Gi*, "One Must Turn One's Mind to Matters of the Spirit."

The maid came in to bring me a small green pudding in a plastic tub. She was grumpy from having been summoned out of her chicken coop to cook a meal for a solitary guest.

"Whose calligraphy is that on the wall?" I asked her.

"Ima Harube's," she said. "He's dead." And went away.

I shuffled down to warm myself in the bath and heard the maid clattering and grunting about the corridors. In the unlit party room downstairs the walls were hung with more Dazai quotations and with photographs of Dazai himself, one of them donated by the Dazai Society of Kanagi, the town where he was born. It seems he has been forgiven the disruptions of his stay here in the broader interests of commerce. I almost didn't notice the other fea-

ture of the room until I turned to leave and glimpsed it out of the corner
of my eye, pinned high up in the darkest part of the alcove: a Shinto charm,
yellowy-white and made of oddly folded paper, like a pine tree or a six-armed
creature with its forearms raised against some unseen evil.

I could still hear the maid grunting and banging as I climbed into the bathtub and felt warm for the first time since morning. The banging grew closer
and then suddenly stopped and the grunts changed to wheezes followed by
a long sigh. In seconds a terrible stink filled the bathroom and I composed
my only haiku of the journey:

> *A terrible stink*
> *I thought it was me*
> *Next door the sound of tearing paper*

When the relieved maid brought an ashtray up to my room before dinner
I said, "Dazai Osamu stayed here once, didn't he?"

"Umm," she grunted and changed the subject.

"I've talked to a foreigner before," she said. "It was twelve or thirteen years
ago, just before my husband went into hospital. I remember he had a cassette recorder and it was the first one I had ever seen. We don't have those
sort of things much up here. He was doing recordings of people speaking
dialect and he did one of my husband, and then my husband died. I don't
know what became of the foreigner."

I ate dinner by myself. The room was bitter cold and I drank as much sake
as I could to warm me, flask after flask of it. The maid came to clear away
the dishes and gave me a slip of paper to fill out for the register. She knelt
down with her fists on the table and watched me write my name and age and
address.

"You haven't filled in your occupation," she said.

"Sorry," I said and wrote *writer*.

She took the slip and peered at it and then stood up and went to the door.
Then she turned and peered at the slip again and looked at me and said
"Huh!"

I drank more sake, straining my ears to catch a friendly sound above the rattle of the rain doors; any sound would have done the trick, any raucous song. I got up and looked out of the window but there was nothing to see, so I crawled in my socks and training suit and kimono into the futon the maid had laid out on the floor and stared up at the wooden ceiling. In a corner of the room I hadn't looked into before the same six-armed creature made of yellowing paper raised its arms to ward off the intruder.

"One Must Turn One's Mind to Matters of the Spirit. . . ."

"You fraud," I thought, and rolled over and went to sleep.

2

The Rice Lake

❧

I left the gloomy sea and turned inland to the hills and plain. The day was warm, the sky pale blue, and in the flooded fields the rice planting had begun. I felt glad to be away from the shabby coast and surrounded for the first time by the sound of birdsong, in country where trees defined the horizon, not concrete pyramids and spikes.

Aside from his worries about sake rationing and his tongue-in-cheek nods at national security, Dazai is silent about the war, though in May 1944 its progress must have preoccupied many. Not until long after the war was over, of course, would anyone outside the government and high command be in a position to trace the march of Japan's fortunes across the battlefields of Asia and the Pacific unhindered by the increasingly spectacular fancies of official propagandists. Few people on the home front in 1944 can have heard, for example, of Imphal, the capital of the small Indian state of Manipur, although

what happened outside that town during the three weeks Dazai spent boozing his way round Tsugaru would arguably affect Japanese lives more completely than any event since Pearl Harbor.

Nine weeks before Dazai arrived in Tsugaru the Fifteenth Army under
Lieutenant General Mutaguchi Renya launched an attack from Burma, which
the Japanese had held since the fifth month of the war, across the border into
India, where a major build-up of Allied forces was known to be underway.
Imphal was the ultimate extent of the drive that, in Malaya and elsewhere,
had seemed unstoppable, and the battle for it turned into a massive reversal
of Japanese military fortunes. Negligently confident, its supply lines overex-
tended, with air support almost nonexistent and the onset of the monsoon
making impossible the outflanking tactics that the Japanese had employed
so smartly in Malaya and Burma, the Fifteenth Army ground itself into the
mud. When Mutaguchi finally quit his flooded trenches in late May, he left
behind 53,000 men dead, wounded, or captured (morale had sunk so low
that, for the first time in the war, large numbers of Japanese troops surrendered) and those that made it back to Burma were collapsing from starvation
and disease.

Imphal was the Japanese army's Stalingrad; it has been called the worst
disaster ever suffered by Japanese arms on land. True, battles had been lost
before, though in the islands, not on the continent, and it would be another
five months before real desperation set in with the defeat of the Combined
Fleet. But at Imphal the end lurched unmistakably into sight. In Tokyo the
Chiefs of the Army and Navy General Staffs both resigned; and in Tsugaru,
as throughout the archipelago, the village postmen in their khaki gaiters rode
their bicycles past these fields of young rice and into the yards of these darkened farms, and stood on the earthen floors at their doorways, cap in one
hand, flimsy envelope in the other, with a new and numbing regularity.

It may be that the war was nearer the front of my mind than it was Dazai's,
for each of the grocer's vans I kept coming across, parked by the roadside in
these little inland hamlets, had a loudspeaker broadcasting what sounded like
a tune of the early 1940s. One I definitely recognized as a march, but even
some of the ballads had that unmistakable martial thump which a Tokyo
dweller instantly associates with the sound trucks owned by patriotic orga-

nizations who tour the streets attempting to stir up the populace against the Japan Teachers' Union by destroying the populace's eardrums.

> *Japan is a great land! In the eastern sky*
> *Rises the glorious ensign of the sun!*
> *And ever at the first glint of daybreak*
> *The souls of all We Japanese*
> *By the glorious ensign of the sun*
> *Are dyed a single hue!*

You could hear these grocer's vans from miles away too; as though the proper way for a Tsugaru housewife to respect the glorious ensign of the sun was to rush out and buy a radish.

A woman had parked a small flatbed truck by the roadside and was spraying insecticide on her field. She had two large black dogs, one chained to the bed of the truck and the other prowling around its wheels and, as I drew abreast of them, they executed a classic pincer movement. The chained dog nearly choked itself trying to leap off the truck and bury its teeth in my face and, while I was thus distracted, the unchained dog skipped round to my blind side and nipped a small chunk out of my calf. I roared at the dogs and, across the field, their owner jumped, dropped her spray, tore off her headscarf, and began racing back towards us shouting, "Goro! Goro! Goro! Goro!" By the time she reached us she was incapable of speech. She stood in the road by the truck bent double, panting, "I'm . . . sor . . . ry . . . I'm . . . sor . . . ry . . . I'm . . . sor . . . ry," while Goro launched a kamikaze raid on my ankles. I limped away trembling. The woman hauled Goro onto the bed of the truck, clipped a chain to his collar, and began beating him with a heavy stick. For a full minute, as I walked quickly along the road, I could hear the thud of the stick on the dog's back, and when I came to the next hamlet and saw that it had a restaurant, I tumbled in, sat down, rolled up my jeans, dabbed at the blood on my leg with a paper napkin, ordered a bottle of beer, and fell to watching television.

Television is a useful indicator of the character of a region, not so much in the programs, which all over Japan are an unvarying blend of game show, song contest, variety (or "wide") show, "home drama," samurai drama, police drama, and baseball, but in the content of the advertisements. Granted, you can sit at home in Tokyo and see commercials for mechanical rice planters—an item not likely to figure high on the shopping lists of most urban consumers—but these are commercials of the "corporate image" type, aimed only at cementing a manufacturer's standing on the stock market. By contrast, advertisements for rice planters in the rural areas demonstrate practical virtues. Thus, on Tokyo T.V., an actor well-known for his appearances as a gang boss climbs out of the cab of a rice planter, lips tightly pursed, and thumps the chassis with the palm of his hand to show potential investors that, if a gang boss actually did this, the planter would not fall to bits. In Tsugaru, on the other hand, the mechanical rice planter is the center of a tableau vivant involving three excited young ladies in latex body stockings who turn their backs to us and bend over towards the machinery so that the camera can close in on their tight shiny bottoms. It is difficult to say how this image might affect the climate of investment at the Tokyo stock exchange, but on rural rice farmers its effect is electric.

For years now, farming families in remote areas have had trouble finding wives for their sons, a contributing factor to the population decline from which most rural regions are suffering. Young Japanese women nowadays do not want to marry farmers; they want to marry bankers. Farm wives have to get up at five o'clock on icy mornings and splash pails of nightsoil over bone-hard fields, and young women brought up on a diet of "home dramas," which are mostly set in big bright cities, and who have just spent two years having the time of their lives while pretending to study at a big city college, do not have much interest in pails of nightsoil. In some parts of the north, village authorities have tried to crack this problem. Some have encouraged young farmers to recruit wives from abroad, particularly from the Philippines, and have helped organize tours of fifteen or twenty young farmers at a time who have arrived at Manila airport intending to find spouses within the forty-eight hours or so allotted for this purpose by the tour group leader. "Brokers" have been commissioned, young women collected, fees handed over, marriages registered. But, alas, too often the relationship has lasted only until the first cold snap, or the first encounter with the mother-in-law, or the first collision with those eternal chimeras, "the culture barrier," and "the language barrier," or the first pail of nightsoil. It is no wonder that frustrated young farmers should be tempted to spend their inheritance on a mechanical rice planter that is known to figure prominently in the fantasies of latex-bottomed ladies.

Other indicators underlined Tsugaru's remoteness, the most obvious being that the television programs I watched in this empty little restaurant were all beamed across the straits from Hokkaido. Along the upper reaches of the Outer Shore and the inland areas that flank it, it is not possible for people to watch their own prefecture's broadcasts because the hills are higher than the transmitter. So the midday advertisements urge them to do their shopping in Hokkaido department stores, eight hours away; the weather forecasts are for Hokkaido; the phone-in numbers are all Hokkaido numbers; and the rapidly aging residents of this part of Tsugaru are encouraged (though not by latex-bottomed ladies) to have themselves buried in a new Hokkaido graveyard.

It was still a bright day when I left the restaurant and walked briskly into the low hills. The only people I saw were husbands and wives who had come to gather bamboo shoots and bracken and coltsfoot from the tangled banks by the roadside and were rooting about in the undergrowth, their little bottles of vitamin drink tied neatly in handkerchiefs to await them at the point where they had begun their scramble.

Just before the road started its spiraling climb, it crossed the railway track that, a few miles north of here, disappeared into the new Seikan Tunnel. By any standard this tunnel is a remarkable achievement. It is 53.85 kilometers long, took twenty-five years to build, including time spent coping with four major floods, and cost a bit more than a trillion yen as well as thirty-four workmen's lives. It had begun operating in March and, twenty-nine days later, to an even noisier spate of fanfare and celebrations, a similarly costly set of bridges had opened across a neck of the Inland Sea, linking Honshu with the fourth largest of Japan's islands, Shikoku. Thus, within a little month, two large islands had ceased to be islands, and for the first time in history you could travel from any part of the Japanese mainland to any other part without needing to set foot on a boat or an airplane.

Who, I wondered as I walked past an empty railway station, would reap the benefits of this much-feted linkage—construction companies excepted. The prime minister had called the Great Bridge of Seto "the pride of future generations," the crown prince had said that it would "enrich our lives," and the transport minister had told us that the Seikan Tunnel was "the realization of people's dreams." But whose lives and which people and what, exactly, had they been dreaming? It will now take a housewife from northern Tsugaru perhaps six hours instead of eight to reach the department stores in Sapporo that her television urges her to patronize. A Shikoku truck driver can now unload his tangerines in Osaka fifty minutes earlier than if he had taken them to Honshu on the ferry. And we must not discount the tourists, of whom both Shikoku and Tsugaru have been warned to expect a flood. On a small Inland Sea island there are plans to build a tower for visitors, 144 meters high, from which they can look down on the trillion yen's worth of bridge below them as they buy their souvenir T-shirts. Nor would it surprise me if the construction bosses in Aomori were at this moment poring over blueprints for more purple pyramids to be erected at intervals along the entire length of the peninsula.

The hills were bliss. The last of the bracken gatherers leaned out of her car window to give me a gobstopper. Then there was only the birdsong, the quiet trickle of the Imaizumi River, the beginning of a decent afternoon's sweat and, for a while, a bit of peace. The occasional timber truck grumbled past me as the road doglegged towards the crest but, despite its obvious usefulness and the time and effort and money it had cost to build it, no buses ran along this road, few cars, no grocer's vans at all, and I grinned to myself like a child playing truant as I walked along in fine solitude. The hills were still the new green of spring, not the heavy, brazen green of summer, and across them marched ranks of iron pylons, towering above the wild cherry trees that, here in the far north, seemed to cling more tenaciously to their petals and release them more grudgingly than the trees of the opulent south.

I was not a stranger to Aomori. It was the first prefecture I had visited after settling in Tokyo nearly eighteen years before. I had had a week's holiday due me and wondered where to spend it, so I opened a map and looked for a destination as far from Tokyo as I could get. Aomori jumped up at me like

a flea off a dog. North: that was where I would go; it never occurred to me
to go west or south, and even now when I think of taking days off to tramp
about the Japanese countryside, it is still the north I most often head for.
Besides, for that first week-long tramp, I had bought a thick old guide to
Japan, hopelessly inaccurate and out-of-date, and found from it that Osorezan
(Terrible Mountain) on the Shimokita peninsula was "reputed to be the
haunt of blind witches." So I caught the first overnight train. And though I
saw no blind witches at Osorezan (not that time anyway; years later when I
attended the annual festival there I found twenty-five spirit mediums, some
of them blind, sitting in rows of tents on the temple grounds telepathizing
busily with the dead), the attractions of Aomori for me have not paled. I have
seen the *nebuta* lanterns paraded through the summer streets behind their
massive drums, been out in a salmon boat on the autumn sea off Ajigasawa,
watched the Emburi dancers stamping about in the February ice at dawn on
Choja Hill, accumulated forty-six L.P. records of Tsugaru folk songs and
shamisen music, suffered diarrhea from eating raw deer meat, clapped my
hands to the gods at Takayama Inari Shrine and Iwaki Shrine and at other
shrines without names, and been told at Osorezan by one of the spirit mediums that I was born a foreigner in this life because of misdeeds committed
in a former one, but that three hundred or so years ago I had lived in
Hirosaki. All this happened to me in Aomori. In Tokyo I still look for bars
run by Aomori mamas and let them mother me while I speak halting dialect
to them and joke that I was born in their castle town. No, I wasn't quite a
stranger, and this journey through Tsugaru was stuffed with memories before
I began it.

The road over the unnamed pass I now approached was not completed
until 1976, and so Dazai never crossed these hills; instead he went back the
way he had come by boat and bus to Aomori city and then traveled up the
body of Tsugaru by train from the south. But in a rare gazetteer-like passage
he briefly discusses this natural barrier between Outer Shore and inner plain,
pointing out that the high-grade timber that is felled on these slopes has been
a source of pride and revenue in Tsugaru much longer than the crisp, juicy
apples for which the region is latterly famous. Apples only arrived in Tsugaru
towards the end of the nineteenth century, when seeds were acquired from

an anonymous American and tips on cultivation from a French missionary. But Tsugaru's timber, especially its *hiba* or arbor vitae, was planted as long ago as the sixteenth century and the forest, says Dazai, has long been regarded as one of the Three Great Forests of Japan. Dazai clinches his argument by pointing out that the name of the prefecture itself, Aomori, means "Blue-Green Forest," although it is misleading to think that Japanese place names invariably call to mind their literal associations. Mention of Chiba prefecture, for example, does not conjure up in the minds of Japanese speakers an image of "a thousand leaves" any more than Oxford calls to English minds a picture of bovines crossing a river. Chiba more likely suggests to those who live there a thousand drafty apartment blocks, and Kanagawa prefecture to the south of Tokyo, far from resembling "God's River," more nearly resembles His drain.

However, several of the place names you come across in Tsugaru are interesting, not because of their literal meaning but because they recall this region's long association with the aboriginal tribes who were here well before the arrival of the people we now think of as Japanese and who were driven off most of their ancestral lands by the genocidal campaigns which the imperial court mounted against them during the seventh, eighth, and ninth centuries. Scholars do not agree on whether the tribe or tribes variously described in Japanese historical documents as Michihase (hairy people), Emishi, Ebisu, Ezo, and Ainu were a single ethnic group from the beginning, or became identified as a single ethnic group once the hostile advance of the Japanese into their territory forced them to band together for protection. It is thought that these people once inhabited most of Honshu (some say, not very loudly, that the name of divine Mount Fuji is aboriginal in origin) but by the close of the eighth century they had been driven into Hokkaido (an island so outlandish that it did not even appear on Japanese maps until 1599, when it was called *Ezo*) and the far north of Honshu, including Tsugaru, where they are known to have remained until late feudal times.

Today, few Japanese people have heard of the Michihase or Emishi and school textbooks are entirely silent about them. The Ainu are well enough known because the 24,000 or so who survive on Hokkaido, few of whom are pure-blooded or can speak the Ainu language, have been parlayed into a tourist attraction and their "villages," such as the one at Lake Akan, consist almost entirely of souvenir shops that sell bookends, wall plaques, and carved wooden bears. Dazai mentions the rebellion of the Dewa Ezo in 878 and that the Tsugaru Ezo may have supported it. And one frequently heard explanation of the origin of the nebuta lanterns, which are annually paraded through the streets of Tsugaru in celebration of the summer Festival of the Dead, is that these huge trundled paper-and-wire contraptions were an invention of Sakanoue no Tamuramaro, commander of the imperial forces at the end of the eighth century, who used them to create fear and disorder in the Ezo ranks. History remembers Tamuramaro as the *Seii Tai Shogun*, the "Great Barbarian-Subduing General," prototype of all the other shoguns, including the one who sold millions of paperbacks.

But almost nothing else about the Tsugaru Ezo is remembered or surmised. Along the Outer Shore I had come across one or two towns and villages with names that sounded like place names in Hokkaido: Imabetsu, for example (the ending *betsu*, with its literal meaning of "diverging" or "different," is nearly exclusive to Hokkaido), and the double *p* sound of Tappi is a common feature of Ainu speech. But I saw no other sign that a separate race might have lived in this peninsula for more than a millennium, nor did I expect to. Today's Japanese are daily persuaded—by their prime ministers, their senseis, their game-show hosts, their "opinion leaders"—that they are a racially homogeneous nation and that this is a necessary and superior thing to be. Few people today are keen to believe that their ancestors might have belonged to a different ethnic group, particularly one associated with hairiness and other sorts of genetic "inferiority," so one finds no Michihase souvenir shops in Tsugaru, and the nebuta lanterns each summer recall not an Ezo tradition, but an Ezo defeat.

At half past two I reached the crest of the hills and began traipsing down towards the plain. The woods were blissfully dense and still and, next to a small wooden notice urging people to take good care of their forest, lay a rusting three-door refrigerator, five ripped-out sink units, an air conditioner, two kitchen stoves, three battered twin-tubs, eight dented oil drums, and three large blue plastic bags from which empty fly-spattered cans were spilling. Very often, walking through quiet hills like these, I have come upon this sort of rubbish dump—not the sort to which a municipal truck will come to cart everything away, but the sort where refrigerators and sink units and twin-tubs will rust till the last trumpet.

A little after four o'clock I found myself approaching the village of Imaizumi on the eastern hook of Lake Jusan, a twenty-square-kilometer lagoon that, for the most part, is little deeper than the newly flooded paddies surrounding it. On both sides the hills slid away to nothing and the lake and its dikes filled the dead flat horizon. It had been an eventful day—what with dogs, latex bottoms, and twin-tubs—so I stopped at the first little grocer's shop I came to and drank a bottle of beer. The owner stood with his hands clasped behind his back, rocking to and fro like a tipsy professor. He was very small and had no teeth and told me that all countries have their ups and downs. Korea, Singapore, and Taiwan, he admitted, were at present having an up. Britain will eventually have an up again but it may take a bit of time for it to climb out of its current down. I nibbled a sausage and asked him about the huge Japanese flag that was furled round a pole and stored in his rafters. Yes, he said, he always put it out on national holidays. He would feel *sabishii* (sad and lonely) if he didn't. Most of the other shops and houses in the village didn't bother to put flags out even on the emperor's birthday, so a down was definitely in the offing.

At a crossroads just before the lake I found a small restaurant and sat and had another beer. The youngish, healthy-looking man who ran it told me in broad dialect how proud he was that Lake Jusan was now a Quasi-National Park and that for most of his working life he had been a *dekasegi*—an itinerant laborer—of whom this lakeside village still sent out many. They would leave next month when the rice planting was over and be back in August for the Festival of the Dead, and in between these times the village would be a place of women and babies and old men. Dazai's house in Kanagi, in the middle of the plain, had been turned into a ryokan, the restaurant owner said, but not many people stayed there. A lot of Dazai's fans went to look round the building because one of the rooms contained glass cases full of important mementos. The restaurant owner himself had gone and been much impressed by a display of Dazai's underwear.

I stayed at the only ryokan in the village, a breezy place that the restaurant owner had phoned to prepare for the shock. Six years before me a middle-aged American had stayed here for about a week and, ah, what troubles had ensued! He was a geologist prospecting for offshore oil and had been given no choice in the matter of lodgings (not that there was any choice to give) so he had had a thoroughly miserable time. He couldn't eat Japanese food at all and hated sleeping on a futon and, it being October, had caught a cold. Could I eat Japanese food? Yes, I could. And did I want a bed? No, I didn't. And would I like to eat my dinner with the ryokan's only other guest that evening, a man who spent his life pumping sumps? Yes, I would feel privileged.

Pumping sumps, I concluded over dinner, was not the life I yearned for. The guest was a thin, precisely mannered man who knelt formally behind his lacquered tray and whose gestures and speech were so mincing that I anticipated an assault on my virtue. But he had two children and lived three hundred kilometers away in Sendai and spent all his working days driving a cramped little truck from petrol station to petrol station and pumping out their sumps. Only on Sundays was he ever at home. On Saturday evenings, after his last pumped sump, he would drive from whatever sump he had pumped to the tiny house where his family waited, taking an average of five hours to reach it. This had been a hard life while his children were small, he said, but now his children were in primary school and his wife could cope well enough without him, so he felt a little perkier as he drove between sumps wanting pumps. Sumps wanted pumps about once a year and he reckoned to pump three sumps a day. He never knew where he would end up each evening so he took potluck with ryokans, as I did. His boss growled if he spent more than five thousand yen a day on expenses, so he didn't drink beer with his meals and often went without breakfast or lunch. Yes, this seemed like a friendly place. He had stumbled on it quite by chance. And they had told him a hilarious story on his arrival. It seems that an American had stayed here six years ago who couldn't eat Japanese food and had caught a cold. . . .

When I got up at eight next morning the sump pumper was already an hour on the road. I ate a lazy breakfast and from my window watched the sun sparkle on the silver-grey of Lake Jusan, and on the vaster lake, the rice lake, that stretched to the end of sight.

❧

Very faint and very distant, like tiny gashes in the morning haze, the ribs of snow on the peak of Mount Iwaki dribbled into the lake of rice. Here and there along the road small trucks were parked, their canvas covers loose, their cabs empty, and their flatbeds stacked as high as hands could reach with seedling trays. In the fields the farmers steered their chugging planters back and forth and back and forth, and hooded women followed them, stooping to push fistfuls of young rice into the gaps left by the precise and wasteful machines. On the edges of the paddies tall metal screens had been erected to buffer the wind that blows in across Lake Jusan from the Seven-League Beach and the uneasy sea. I had not seen such screens before in eighteen years of wandering about Japan and I didn't know whether they were a testament to the ingenuity of Tsugaru farmers or the desperation born of wrestling the whims of so spiteful a land.

One of the most poignant pages of Dazai's *Tsugaru* simply reprints a table from a book that was shown to Dazai by N. It is a list of the crop failures suffered on this plain between 1615 and 1940. During that span of three and a quarter centuries, there were five "semi-disasters," thirty-three "disasters," and twenty-one "total disasters." In other words, there was a major crisis in the lives of the plain dwellers about once every five years.

The Tsugaru shamisen master Takahashi Chikuzan, who was born in 1910, a year later than Dazai, once told me about his childhood. His parents were Tsugaru farmers and they knew from bitter experience how fickle was the land they planted. So, like many other parents in this bleak peninsula, they planned to pull their son out of school when he was twelve or thirteen and have him learn a more dependable trade. In fact Chikuzan had to leave school much earlier. An epidemic of measles had struck his village when he was three and left him and several other children half-blind (his sight continued to worsen until by middle age he couldn't see at all). For half a dozen years after leaving school he had stumbled about the farm looking after his parents' few animals and then, at the age of fourteen, he had begun taking shamisen lessons from a neighboring musician who was himself blind. Like other traditional Japanese stringed instruments—the *koto*, for example, or the *biwa*—the shamisen has by long custom been one of the few sources of livelihood open to the blind and, by the time he was seventeen, Chikuzan was embarked on a life of *kadomawari*—tramping the icy lanes of northern Honshu and Hokkaido playing tunes in yards and at gates and on doorsteps in return for the odd coin or bowl of food. It was little better than a beggar's life and in early childhood, through his clenched eyelids, Chikuzan had seen these wandering musicians with their filthy clothes and ragged bundles and thought them "shameful."

"City dwellers," he remarked with some bitterness, "have a very romantic impression of what life in the north of Honshu is like. Life in Tsugaru was so hard when I was young that we used to say a dog couldn't stick it. People with money who come up from the cities to look around for a day or two might admire what they call 'a life lived with nature' but that's because they don't have to live it. They're privileged. They have the leisure to imagine. They're not forced to sink their hands into the stinking mud to earn their keep."

Dazai, too, had the leisure to imagine. "I am a Tsugaru man," he wrote in his introduction to the book I carried in my pack. "For generations my ancestors have tilled the land of the Tsugaru domain. I am, so to speak, of pure Tsugaru stock." Yet few boyhood memories from the same region could offer a more complete contrast than the somber recollections of Chikuzan, the son of real farmers, and the account of Dazai's early life that we find in his reminiscences and stories.

Dazai's family, the Tsushimas (Dazai's real name was Tsushima Shuji), were among the wealthiest landowners in the prefecture. Like the nouveau riche all over the world, they were extremely status-conscious and their huge house in Kanagi was—still is—a brick-walled marvel, much gaped at. Dazai's great-grandfather had amassed a large part of the family fortune, not by "tilling the land of the Tsugaru domain" but by lending out money at interest. When Dazai was three his father, Gen'emon, was elected a member of the National Diet. When Dazai was thirteen, Gen'emon was elevated to the

House of Peers on the basis of his wealth. When Dazai was fifteen, his elder brother, Bunji, by now head of the family, became mayor of Kanagi; later he was governor of Aomori prefecture. It was Bunji who provided Dazai with the money that saw him through high school and college, money that Bunji continued to send him long after he had opted out of formal education.

The hardships that Dazai dwells upon were sometimes genuine: his father died when he was thirteen, his mother was a semi-invalid, and two of his brothers had also died by the time Dazai went to Tokyo. But more often, like his suicide attempts, his hardships were the results of a conscious choice. For all his morbid sensitivity and his emphasis on the pains of being a misfit, Dazai lived a life elected; Chikuzan a life inflicted. Dazai fancied himself an outsider, while Chikuzan tramping the lanes in his rags was the living embodiment of that condition. Dazai had chosen to be a writer partly out of narcissism, partly out of a desire for recognition, partly because the "decadent" life of bars and hot-spring geishas attracted him and partly, he says, because he was "about to be consumed by a demon who eternally beckoned." Chikuzan's commitment to his art was more straightforward: "It was shameful but it was the only trade open. I was blind; what else could I be?"

By eleven o'clock I was in the little town of Nakasato, trudging up the single main street that, on this warm day, swirled with pale clouds of swiftly dying cherry flowers. All morning, despite the metal screens, the wind of the plain had filled my eyes with grit and dust and now it filled them with a ballet. In small back yards old women squatted, mesmerized by their azaleas. They would squat a whole day in front of these potted shrubs, their fingers twitching away the dead leaves and the cherry petals drifting in and out of their hair. Across the road a bent old woman was hobbling along with the aid of two sticks. She turned her head and caught sight of me and said "Ooooooooooo!" and fell flat on her face. Two shoppers on bicycles picked her up and I hurried into a restaurant where an elderly man stepped forward and slapped my back.

"Hello," he said.

"How do you do."

"Damn!" he gasped, or a Tsugaru equivalent. "How on earth did you understand what I said?"

I unslung my pack, sat down at an empty table and studied the complicated menu which was plastered all around the walls. Two men in overalls walked in, pulled off their shoes, climbed up onto the section of the restaurant that was floored with tatami mats and sat down cross-legged at a low table. I rarely sat in the tatami sections when I was having half an hour's rest because, for one thing, it was too much trouble unlacing my boots and, for another, it was far more painful getting started again from a position propped up on one elbow than from a stool three times too small for my bum. But today, after a quiet consultation, the overalled men invited me to join them, shyly ordering me a portion of intestines to grill on the hot plate in the middle of their table while I was struggling to prise my boots off.

I climbed up and sat down on the tatami and remembered another reason for not often doing this, which was the appalling stink that came off of my socks; in comparison the spluttering guts on the hot plate were an olfactory delight. The overalled men, who had been out gathering bracken and so had heads full of fresh hilly air, pretended to smell nothing amiss. What was I doing in Tsugaru? I was following the route taken by Dazai Osamu. Ah, then I must be the second Dazai Osamu. No, no, I hadn't married a geisha. We bantered on; more beer arrived. A seventy-year-old cyclist had come through Nakasato some days before and asked directions to Asamushi. Seventy years old, the men shyly marveled, and he was going to a town renowned for its nightlife! A man had once stopped his car outside this restaurant wanting to know how to get to Kodomari, and the old man who owned the place had explained the way to him but he hadn't understood a word the old man said. All the stories they had to tell me were about the oddity of strangers and of their own shy speech. We chuckled, munching the crackling guts, and the old man chuckled as he watched us.

On various pages of his book, depending on the mood he was in when he wrote them, Dazai describes the people of Tsugaru as "tempestuously welcoming," "bashful and sensitive," "obstinate," "rebellious," "pathetically honest," "complex," "headstrong," and "gracefully and delicately considerate of others." Chikuzan explained to me that they are a "competitive" people and that one sees this in the speed and energy with which they turn the six snow-less months of their year into the productive equivalent of twelve. He believed, too, that they illustrated the meaning of the dialect word *iifurikoki*—a desire to flaunt one's own accomplishments—and to this desire he attributed in part the breathtaking virtuosity of their shamisen masters. The sump pumper at Imaizumi had found Tsugaru people "less self-absorbed, more forthright and outgoing" than the people in his own city of Sendai.

Clearly, Tsugaru people make large demands on a man's store of adjectives. Once or twice my gut-chomping hosts cracked jokes against themselves—the old jokes about dialect and bumpkinness—and these jokes arose less from a sense of inferiority than from a deep and secret pride. I listened to them, chuckling softly as the old man chuckled, looking for the defiance and obstinacy and complexity that Dazai had itemized in his book. One man wore white overalls, the other blue, and they paid for all the beers.

The day had turned into a blistering one. The wind had dropped and I could feel my arms starting to burn. Eight days before I had been battling sleet; now I needed a pith helmet. I stopped to rest once or twice beside the shallow marshy ponds that had begun appearing along the margins of the paddies, each provided with a carefully lettered sign that told me they had been preserved in this semi-wild state as sanctuaries for the mountain cuckoo. Through the heat haze I could see Kanagi, the little town where Dazai was born, dominated by a tall, impressively roofed building that I guessed from seeing photographs of it was his family home. But I wanted to defer a close encounter until I had seen a little more of the other communities of the plain, so I switched to top gear and hurried on towards the small city of Goshogawara, whose department stores looked very close and, an hour later, looked hardly any closer. The Asano cement factory rolled into sight at about two o'clock, and beyond it, among the last of the paddies, the stands of stumpy apple trees were in powdery white flower.

Goshogawara appeared to have changed enormously in the decade or so since I had last been there and, like all the other sizable communities in Tsugaru, it would have been quite unrecognizable to Dazai, although he remembered it even from his childhood as being "lively or noisy, depending on whether you wanted to say something good about it or something bad." It did not, he said, seeing the place again in 1944, "have the smell of a farming town at all, but provokes the shudder of loneliness so characteristic of big cities, which is already creeping into small towns like this."

When I first visited Goshogawara, one late October ten or eleven years before, it had struck me as the quintessential farmers' town. The shops in the almost deserted main street had been full of gumboots and heavy oil stoves and along the quiet lanes between the shops and the river you could feel the emptiness left by the harvest and the dull approach of winter. When Dazai was growing up in nearby Kanagi, Goshogawara had a population of twelve or thirteen thousand. Since then its population has more than quadrupled. It is the third largest city in the region after Aomori and Hirosaki, but its industries are still nearly all primary—rice, mainly, and the huge red apples that it dispatches all over Japan. Dazai tells a story about falling into a meter-deep ditch in the middle of the city when he was seven or eight years old, and the Goshogawara I remembered from my first visit was exactly the sort of city where old women would be forever slipping on iced-up storm drains and falling into ditches clutching their sticks and going, "Oooooooooo!"

But the shopping streets were now roofed to make arcades; there were loudspeakers from which chirpy girls' voices urged me in nursery-school tones to patronize the boutiques; there were MacDonalds and Mister Donuts and boutiques and smart fake-rustic coffee shops with names like Labrador and their pedigrees painted over their windows: Since 1983. There was not a gumboot in sight, not a stove, not a ditch. The wooden station that I remembered with some affection had been torn down and replaced with a ferroconcrete one. And on this bright Saturday afternoon the entire population seemed to be strolling along the bustling arcades, the fathers in their Arnold Palmer sports shirts, the mothers permed, the babies scrubbed, the older kids in their black school uniforms ogling the racks of porn videos.

I was planning to stay the night in Goshogawara and, having several hours to kill, strolled across the road to one of the new-looking coffee shops. The peg-thin woman who ran it was in her mid-fifties—dressed in tight blue jeans and a spangled T-shirt—and gave me free gifts: a second cup of coffee, two sweets, and a stale Ritz cracker. A housewife came in with three shopping bags, plonked herself down at the table near the window and asked for coffee and a cake.

"I don't do cakes," the tight-jeaned woman told her. "How about a slice of toast and jam?" And the housewife, who had obviously been looking forward to a cake and who could see through the window a coffee and cake shop about thirty feet away across the street, blushed and looked down and fiddled with her bags and cleared her throat and ordered toast and jam.

She had only recently opened the shop, the tight-jeaned woman told me when the housewife had eaten her toast and gone, but it was clear that she had spent the best part of her life dispensing liquids of one kind or another from the way she kept experimentally dimming the lights. Ah yes, if I had visited Goshogawara in late October it was bound to have felt different from what it did in May. In May the dekasegi—the itinerant workers—were all back home for the rice planting and, on Saturdays like this, they would certainly be out with their families spending the money they had made on faraway assembly lines. But in late October, after the harvest, they would all have gone away again and the city would have slumped back into its more common condition of sober dreary manlessness. She spoke of this common absence of men with the air of one personally insulted by it, and I supposed it was why she had swapped more potent liquids for a housewifely coffee shop, whose lights she finally decided to leave full on.

Dazai had called Goshogawara "lively" and remarks elsewhere in *Tsugaru* that "the people of Goshogawara like their fun," but if their fun is compressed into two visits a year it can hardly form the basis of a stable economy. In most of Japan's major cities the bar owners regard *ni-pachi* (February and August) as slack times, February because it follows so close on the busy round of year-end parties that no one has any money left to lash out on drink, and August because many of the regular customers are away on holiday or visiting their home towns for the Festival of the Dead. But in areas where the migration of dekasegi is still a major demographic factor, the bar owners' calendar is presumably structured differently. May and September must be the busiest times and, as the winter lasts six or seven months in Tsugaru, ni-pachi lasts nine or ten.

Looking out at Goshogawara's busy streets at four o'clock on this Saturday afternoon, I decided not to spend the night here after all. Perhaps it had something to do with the loudspeakers, or the way the tight-jeaned woman kept telling me to stay as long as I liked while she hunted through her cupboards for another Ritz cracker. I have always preferred things out of season. I like fairgrounds in the rain and ski resorts when the snow has melted and seaside promenades in January. I left the shopping arcades, crossed the Iwaki river, and tramped a final five kilometers to the little town of Kizukuri. Mount Iwaki looked crisp and cracker-like in the late Saturday afternoon sun, the rich green meadows on its lower slopes a towel for the melting snow.

At Kizukuri a heavily made-up pharmacist with a squint pointed the way to a ryokan and, within seconds of arriving, I was being mothered by a coven of elderly women—one of my favorite pastimes. One mother in a dark red cardigan brought me tea, another with a black shawl fetched me a *yukata*, another on a broomstick showed me how to use the automatic washing machine. They were all clucking on about how hot I looked and how well I spoke Japanese and the state of my socks and several times I pictured them joining hands and hailing me Thane of Cawdor. For about ten minutes I stood watching my jeans and shirt and underpants revolving in a foamy soup the color of cat puke; "The earth hath bubbles as the water has," I hummed at them insanely. But when I put my head round the kitchen door to ask where the plastic buckets were kept, the mothers had vanished into thin air. It was half past five. I wandered through the corridors searching for them, in the bathroom, upstairs, but what seemed corporal had melted. I slipped into a pair of the ryokan's plastic slippers and looked for them in the yard. There was no one there. There was no one in the outhouse. I was growing nervous. There was no one on Kizukuri's streets.

I turned back into the ryokan's entrance hall and saw a large colored photograph of a man with a baby face looking blandly down from the wall opposite the door. Underneath was a handwritten notice identifying him as the sumo wrestler Asahifuji (Rising-Sun Wisteria) and explaining that he had been born in Kizukuri and was its most famous native son. From somewhere back in the depths of the building came the muffled voice of a *yobidashi*—the man who formally calls sumo wrestlers into the ring for their bouts. I looked at my watch. It was twenty-five to six and I knew exactly where the mothers had vanished to. I followed the sound of the yobidashi and found the entire staff of the ryokan, and one or two other people who had dropped in to watch, seated in the owner's living room before a twenty-nine-inch television set on which the penultimate day of the fifteen-day summer sumo tournament was being broadcast live from Tokyo. I found a space on the floor between two of the mothers who silently fed me rice crackers. The ryokan owner's wife, seated to the fore, stretched her hands out to the screen, clapped them in prayer, and bowed till her forehead touched the carpet. Behind me an incantation proceeded. Timidly, I nibbled a cracker.

Asahifuji entered the ring. From the opposite side his opponent entered, grand champion Hokutoumi (Northern Victory Sea), whereupon the ryokan owner's wife commenced a demonstration of the science of physiognomy:

"Just look at his face!" she crowed as Northern Victory Sea banged wet salt off his hands by thumping his belly with them. "You can see he's going to lose! Yes, Asahifuji's going to beat him! See those eyebrows! No doubt about it! Just look! Look at the way his mouth turns down!"

"He's from Hokkaido, isn't he?" I asked brightly.

"All the best ones are from the north," she hissed. "It's the cold that builds their spirit." And she craned forward, her eyes glued to the television, and continued to heap bad vibrations on Northern Victory Sea while one of the mothers moaned softly and clutched a dishcloth and another bit her nails.

Asahifuji gargled water from a wooden ladle and spat it out behind a paper towel. He stood half a head taller than his opponent but he had a reputation for collapsing in crises. Tournament after tournament his supporters had expected Asahifuji to clinch promotion to the highest sumo rank—grand champion—and, tournament after tournament, he had failed. In the last crucial days he would tense up, he would lose to a lower-ranked wrestler or else to one of the three current grand champions without appearing to put up much of a fight, and once again the promotion council would decide that he wasn't ready. But this time Asahifuji had the best chance of clinching promotion that he had had for many months, hence the twisted dishcloths and gnawed fingernails. A mathematically inclined mother explained:

On this, the fourteenth day, Asahifuji's win-loss record stood at eleven-two. The front runner, grand champion Chiyonofuji's stood at twelve-one. Asahifuji was scheduled to fight Chiyonofuji tomorrow. If Asahifuji lost today then Chiyonofuji would have to lose today and tomorrow to tie their records at twelve-three. If Asahifuji won today and Chiyonofuji lost, then they would go into the last day with equal records of twelve-two. If both won today and Asahifuji won tomorrow they would finish the tournament with identical thirteen-two records and so would have to fight again. If Chiyonofuji won today and Asahifuji lost . . .

I crunched my rice cracker, watching Hokutoumi's piggy eyes glare into Asahifuji's glazed ones, and knew that, ever since Asahifuji had won his eleventh victory at a quarter to six the previous evening, Kizukuri had been full of mathematicians. The computations, worries, talk, dreams, the offers of rice and salt and sake on the little restaurant god shelves, had all involved Asahifuji. If he won today a camera crew would arrive to film his supporters' faces before and after tomorrow's bout—possibly in this ryokan—and for a few heady seconds every sumo viewer in Japan would know that the nation contained a town called Kizukuri, an obscure town, a nothing town, a town whose name (which means "Made of Wood") Dazai turned into a joke. I imagined the mothers of the ryokan walking around all day sticking pins into Hokutoumi dolls, tossing bat's wool into bubbling cauldrons, distractedly scrubbing the lavatory with tea, stuffing dishcloths into the rice cooker.

The referee spread his feet and tilted his fan. The wrestlers crouched. All breathing ceased. And, to cut a short story shorter, Asahifuji won. There was a moment of pandemonium. Two mothers jumped up and danced round the room. The owner's wife upset the teapot. The brother who ran the sushi shop next door was heard dashing through the back corridors of the building, shouting like a maniac. And to conclude the short story with the benefit of hindsight, Asahifuji lost easily to Chiyonofuji the following day and was passed over by the promotion council once again. I was glad I was in Kizukuri on Saturday, not Sunday, and the wrestlers were barely out of the ring before the mathematicians were at work again:

Now if Onokuni beat Chiyonofuji, then Asahifuji and Chiyonofuji would both be twelve-two going into the last day, but if Chiyonofuji beat Onokuni he'd be thirteen-one, which meant Asahifuji . . .

Over dinner the mothers asked me to write my name and address for them on some pages of a memo pad. At first I wrote them in Japanese, which seemed to disappoint everyone, so I wrote them out several times in English and the mothers, seated in a circle round my table, folded the papers carefully, as though they were love charms, and tucked them inside their cardigans.

I went out for a walk. The moon and stars were very bright. And in my futon that night I dreamed I went back to my childhood home in London and found my father dying in his bed. My wife and child had gone away and no one knew where to find them. It was London but it was also Japan, and Leytonstone was a suburb of Tokyo. A boy I had known at school was in Japan too and I dashed about in a mad desire to see him; he was a boy I had hardly ever spoken to. I met a student from my university and greeted him like a long lost brother. He was someone I had never liked.

I woke up with a start at four in the morning. Beyond the flat roofs the sky was crimson. I told myself it was the husks in the pillow that were stopping me from sleeping.

At six A.M. the mothers began sweeping and polishing the upstairs corridor, making a frightful clatter. And when the time came for me to shoulder my pack and limp down the polished stairway, my double layer of greasy woolen socks kept slipping on the shine. It was a cool, windy, Tsugaru day, but the mothers gave me a rousing send-off, gathered in a magic circle on the mirror-like floor beneath Rising-Sun Wisteria, watching closely as I laced my boots.

"Come again," they called cheerfully.

"I will," I called back, and walked out of the gate onto the overcast road where a bicycle squealed to a halt beside me. The old man astride it barked, "What's the time?" and, before I could answer him, grabbed my wrists with fingers that were like charred bones, and stared down at my watch, his face tight with fury.

"A timeworn and tranquil town" is how Dazai describes Kizukuri, and I warmed to its single main street as soon as I started clomping along it. Its most obvious distinguishing feature is that the narrow pavements along one side of it are roofed and walled, turning them into extensions of the shops, so that pedestrians stroll down cozy little corridors just wide enough for two to walk abreast, protected from snow and wind and traffic, but exposed, as Dazai observed, "to the minor inconvenience of being stared at by the people working in the shops." To describe these walled and roofed pavements of the north, Dazai uses the dialect word *komohi* and remarks that "most of the older Tsugaru towns have them," but that is no longer true. I came across only the sketchiest remains of komohi, except in Kizukuri where they now line one side of the shopping street, not both, and where, apart from a short stretch that is still wood-framed, they have been rebuilt in aluminum and glass.

I don't know whether the shopkeepers stared at Dazai as intently as they stared at me but, by his own account, Dazai presented an odd sight during his three weeks of prowling round these intimate, out-of-the-way little towns. Several times in his autobiographical stories he displays a dandy's passion for describing his clothes, and he begins *Tsugaru* with a detailed account of the outfit he traveled in. It consisted of dark blue workman's trousers and tunic (the only officially sanctioned civilian alternative in wartime to khaki) which had been made and dyed for him by his wife but were "a puzzling, unrecognizable shape" and had turned purple when he wore them out of doors. To go with this purple suit, he wore green rayon gaiters, white canvas shoes with rubber soles, a rayon tennis cap, and a canvas rucksack and, in his own estimation, he looked "like a tramp," an appearance that must have brought him as much covert pleasure as embarrassment. (And, if embarrassment had got the better of him, he could—unlike the real tramp Chikuzan—have opened his rucksack and changed into "an unlined formal jacket embroidered with the family crest," "a lined kimono of fine Oshima silk," and "a formal *hakama* of Sendai silk," which he carried in case of emergencies. Few hobos are so well provided.)

Across the road stood the police station, a large ferroconcrete structure which in Dazai's time had been made of wood. "Of course, it's a wooden building," he had mused, perusing a sign that said Kizukuri [Made of Wood] Police Station, and then "smiled wryly" at his "mistake." That was his joke about the town's name. Afterwards he visited the pharmaceutical wholesalers where his father had been born, drank sake with the merry cousin called Mr. M who told him that Kizukuri's rice production was the highest in Japan because "we break our backs," and then, back unbroken, departed for the western coast. I, too, departed for the western coast, down roads that ran between apple orchards where the powdery blossoms were being pinched off the boughs, a cruelty I could not imagine being inflicted on the cherries.

I liked the dusty little towns of the plain. They struck me as having a certain dignity, a decayed grace, a grace without gentility, which the patched-up towns of the Outer Shore lacked. It is not correct to call Tsugaru's inland towns "attractive" because they are not—at least not in any sense that a person familiar with "timeworn and tranquil" towns in Europe might recognize. When we say, in the West, that a town is attractive, we usually mean that, viewed from a point of vantage, it presents a pleasing prospect; one in which each building, square, and spire contributes, by design or otherwise, to a whole. Few Japanese towns or cities do that. Bombs and fires and earthquakes and storms and the separate attentions of 510,000 busy construction companies have ensured that they do not. When a Japanese person tells you that Kyoto, the former capital, is a "beautiful" city, he does not mean that, if you climbed Mount Hiei and looked down at its roofs, you would be struck—as you would be by Florence from Fiesole or Oxford from the tower of the University Church—by a sense that the whole was magically greater than the sum of its parts. When you view Kyoto from any point of vantage, such as the elevated platform where the bullet train deposits you, its ugliness can make you weep. Its tangled, utility-cabled skyline is indistinguishable from that of any other Japanese city of comparable size, and every bit as jolting. The attractions of Japanese cities—if they have attractions—lie in what they contain, not in the prospect they present. Kyoto is "beautiful" because within it there are beautiful things; subtle, sometimes tiny details that resist the cacophony around them and may require a lifetime to unearth.

But that was not why I liked the towns of the Tsugaru plain. I liked them not for any postcard picturesqueness nor for the discovering in them of small resistant details. What I liked was the workaday imperviousness to anything resembling a philosophy of charm (which is not the same thing as an imper-

viousness to charm itself; I had seen enough of that along the Outer Shore).
Sometimes these inland towns contained resistant details—an old stone house
or something smaller: a sushi-shop curtain made of pale, plaited cords—
though even these could scarcely be called charming. But they gave you a
sense of being in a place that was built to be lived in, not just passed through;
that had formed an alliance with its residents in a way that the towns of the
coast had not.

Japan is an island nation, to be sure, and so the sea plays a towering role
in its historical and national consciousness (though hardly any at all in its literature). But there are two ways of looking at islands. Islands are either
fortresses or dungeons. Among people who are by nature outward-looking
and independent-minded, it is the fortress view that dominates, and that sees
in the surrounding ocean a source of great strength:

> *This fortress built by Nature for herself,*
> *Against infection and the hand of war . . .*
> *This precious stone set in the silver sea,*
> *Which serves it in the office of a wall,*
> *Or as a moat defensive to a house,*
> *Against the envy of less happier lands. . . .*

And even as Shakespeare was writing those lines, English adventurers were
busy founding an empire that encompassed half the known world on the
obliging highway of the seas.

By contrast, throughout most of its history, Japan has taken the dungeon
view, a view that combines the habit of gloomy introspection with the feeling of being confined, hedged in, deprived of innumerable benefits. For the
Japanese, the sea has been a barrier, moody, cruel, and dangerous—a barrier
you sense very clearly in Tsugaru, where the sea is moody, cruel, and dangerous.

When Japanese people attempt to account for what they perceive as fail-
ings in their national character they often dredge up their *shimaguni konjo*—
their "island-nation complex"—by which they mostly mean a narrow, exclusive, determinedly inward-looking cast of thought. The sea is a prison door,

never a highway; to cross it is to flirt with chaos and to dally with that frightful genie, the unknown. The sea is not an accomplice or a willing provider; it is an adversary against whom men must always be on guard, and its gifts are never given freely; they are torn out of it with muscle and prayer. Time after time I have arrived in a Japanese seaside town and looked in vain for an inn or a lodging house overlooking the water (that Western love of a prospect) and, time after time, I have had to make do with a place tucked up a backstreet somewhere, with a view of the bus terminal instead of the boats. You can live a lifetime in Tokyo, and quite forget that you are on a bay of the Pacific, so successful is the metropolis in keeping its back to the ocean. As a nation, Japan seems afraid of the sea. Perhaps that is why I found the little inland towns of Tsugaru so much more congenial than those of the moody coast, and why Dazai discovered nothing on the plain, for all its troubled harvests, to compare in desolation with that stretch of pounded Outer Shore whose "terrifying" rocks and waves no longer count as scenery.

With this thought in my head I rounded Mount Iwaki and came in sight of the sea again.

3
The Buddha Rock

❧

The fishing town of Ajigasawa has a folk song all of its own:

The Hachiman Shrine to the west guards the port,
And when a man's away his woman guards the home.

I've always liked that because it catches a quality I admire in Tsugaru people: an uncomplaining, no-nonsense attitude to the business of getting on with their often rotten lives. The Hachiman Shrine at Ajigasawa is nothing to write home about; shrines invoking the protection of this deity are often found on little hills overlooking villages or on cliffs that teeter above fishing harbors. But it's the woman guarding the home that I like, and the can't-be-helped, shrug-it-off acceptance of the man's absence—whether he's at sea with the herring boats or working the night shift at some Yokohama factory. Here's another verse from the same song:

She's an Ajigasawa girl so she's got dark skin,
But she tastes like the dried persimmons of Yamato.

The women of the north are fondly supposed by people in the urban south to be pale-skinned and beautiful. But many Tsugaru women are squat and dark, and dark skin has never been prized in Japanese women because it points to a life of manual labor and so to a lack of feminine grace and a supposed coarseness of manners. Also, though the song may not directly imply as much, dark skin can indicate (horror!) that its possessor is not a hundred percent racially pure. By "racial purity" is meant card-carrying membership of the Yamato race—the race that supplanted the aboriginal tribes and is nowadays regarded as being synonymous with Japanese nationality. Among many people who are not Japanese, mixed ancestry is likely to cause few sleepless nights. But so many Japanese people continue to fuss about their "homogeneity" and their "uniqueness" that the suspicion that one of them might have a drop of non-Yamato blood in her veins is not lightly dismissed with a chuckle and a shrug.

The girl in the song likely couldn't give a spit about her complexion. And there she exhibits another pleasant Tsugaru trait: an unwillingness to be cowed by any idea of a "proper station." I have to admit that I admired her. My mouth was watering for a dried persimmon. I looked for her on my way into Ajigasawa but saw only the homogeneous concrete polyhedrons, the sempiternal Asano cement factory, and a mechanical excavator demolishing what was left of the beach.

I had stayed a couple of nights in Ajigasawa seven years before and knew that there was no point in wandering along the coast road looking for a ryokan with a sea view because there wasn't one. Besides, the town trails on for miles. So I booked myself into the hot-spring hotel on the bank of the Nakamura River, not noticing (since the workmen were having a cigarette break) that one whole wing of the place was being reconstructed and I was committing myself to a Sunday afternoon of non-stop pneumatic drilling. The woman at the reception desk was squat and dark and seemed all too keen on her proper station, so I made do with the minimum intercourse required to get myself a room—name, address, age, occupation (I wrote construction engineer)—and then went down to wallow in the bath because the pneumatic drills were operating directly under my window.

Dazai makes no mention of Ajigasawa's being a spa, which is not surprising because the mineral spring only broke through to the surface the year before he came here, in 1943, when few Japanese people were giving much thought to developing leisure resorts. The temperature of the water as it emerges from the earth is 52 degrees centigrade, which is cool by the standards of the best Japanese hot springs and chilly compared with some of the mountain spas of the north (Tamagawa in Akita, for example, is 98 degrees). But it had balls of orange scum lolling in it to prove that it was genuine, and I had the entire bathroom to myself.

After dinner I went out for a stroll and found a little drinking shop called Yukiguni (Snow Country), where I spent the evening in the company of the master, his wife, and three male customers who reacted to me in different ways. The first, a fat respectable-looking man in a suit and tie and spectacles whom the master introduced as a teacher of Tsugaru folk dance and to whom he and his wife deferred on every topic of conversation ("Yes, Sensei; no, Sensei; is that so, Sensei?"), made a point of ignoring my existence. The second, a high-school teacher in a gym suit who lived in Goshogawara but was staying overnight in Ajigasawa to drive some of his pupils to an athletics meet, told me that one of the bars here employed a Filipina hostess who had mastered Tsugaru dialect in three months flat and was very popular among the more internationally minded of his school's third-year boys. And the last, with whom I spent most of the evening, was a steely-haired carpenter in his work clothes, who took endless pleasure in repeating, over and over, that although he could understand every word of my *hyojungo* (orthodox Japanese) he himself couldn't speak anything but broad dialect.

We kept the dialect joke going the whole evening and, in the end, it became a bit of a strain for all of us except the carpenter who, once he had shifted from beer to sake, illustrated everything he said by rolling his eyes, clenching his jaw, waving his arms and rocking backwards and forwards on his stool. *Igirisu no otosan* ("Our Dad from England") he called me, or sometimes simply *Papa*, a form of veneration I assumed was part of the joke. I said good night and spent the next fifteen minutes wishing I hadn't, sitting at the black formica counter of a modern bar-cum-coffee shop in which neither the young flouncy-shirted barman nor any of his sour-faced customers uttered a word. There were stainless steel executive toys and bottles inverted in foreign-style dispensers. A shot of Burnett's London Dry Gin cost five pounds fifty. Three youths came in, sat down at a table, and discussed the menu in nervous whispers. They ordered one glass of brandy between them.

"Remy or Hennessey's?" demanded the barman.

I went to bed.

Dazai found Ajigasawa "depressing." It is "a frightful straggle of a town," he wrote. "It is really nothing more than one street along the shore, one identical house after the other, without variation. . . . Ajigasawa has no center. In most towns the houses are clustered around a central point where even travelers just passing through without stopping can sense that they are in the heart of town. But in Ajigasawa there is nothing of the sort. It seemed to me to be dangling loose, like a folding fan with a broken pivot."

The town takes its name from the *aji*, a fish that my dictionary identifies as a "horse mackerel" or "scad" or "saurel," though it is much too small to be recognized as any of those things by the fishermen of the Atlantic. Seven years before, when I had gone out at dawn with a crew of five in one of the town's six-tonners, aji had formed a small portion of the catch. But it was October then and the principal mark had been the mature salmon on their way to the river mouths. Once in the rivers, the fishermen say, the salmon lose their flavor. Now, in May, the main catch was sea bream, a fish that occupies an important place in culinary lore since its Japanese name, *tai*, is pronounced in the same way as part of a phrase that means "congratulations," so tai is often served at weddings and other festivities and its presence on the table is supposed to signify good luck. In Dazai's time, it appears, the town was mostly known for its *hata-hata*, or sandfish, a lowly creature much mocked by city gourmets but which continues to be a winter staple in northern communities such as this. Once, on Christmas Day in Akita, I went into a restaurant that had nothing but hata-hata. I could eat it in a pot stew, or boiled in thin soy sauce, or grilled with salt, or deep-fried in batter, or even sliced raw, but if I wanted something different I would have to starve.

Though the hot spring has given Ajigasawa, at least for "travelers just passing through," a center of the kind Dazai found lacking, his description of the town as "tired" and "on the wane" seems as appropriate now as it was when he wrote it. In late feudal times Ajigasawa was one of Tsugaru's most thriving ports. Boats went for days, or sometimes weeks, to fish among the herring shoals off Hokkaido, and the people of Ajigasawa still pride themselves on having a longer and more adventurous history in the fishing trade than the upstart prefectural capital can claim. But there is little about the place today that can be called adventurous. The boat I had gone out in at dawn seven years before was back in port by eight A.M., the catch was weighed by eight-thirty (two boats in tandem had emptied three fixed nets), and most of the crew were back in their homes by nine. Hokkaido's famous herring shoals were fished to extinction long ago. And, at the furthest extent of Ajigasawa's straggle, a row of wooden sheds selling leathery grilled squid—each empty except for the woman who runs it, seated in front of her gas burner, one knitting, one playing with her cat, one staring out of the window beneath a large sign proclaiming that her dusty shed was once featured on national television—provides Ajigasawa today with its only visible remnant of a reputation born from the sea.

It was a cold day. I pulled on my sweater and tramped along the dull coast towards Fukaura. A low streak of black cloud hid Cape Gongen and the sea tore at the polyhedrons in dark, ill-tempered snaps. The storm drains along both sides of the road were clogged with leached cherry petals and the only figure on the dead street in the hamlet of Akaishi was an old man coughing his way to the hospital. After a time the polyhedrons gave way to craggy rocks. A train rattled by, a single coach plying between one unmanned halt and the next. The only building I passed on the seaward side was a solitary three-story clapboard house with "1984" printed in large black letters above its unnervingly English porch.

Halfway to Fukaura, at one of the unmanned halts called Senjojiki, I came upon the only stretch of this dark coast where an effort had been made to attract sightseers. At a bend in the road, on the seaward side, lay a wide ledge of surf-worn rock that, in summer, provides a platform for bathers, but which now, with the spume crashing up through its fissures, looked about as attractive as a seal slick. Dazai says that this rock platform "rose to the surface as if by magic" about a century and a half ago and was given the name Senjojiki (Thousand Tatami Floor) because it is large enough and flat enough for several hundred people to hold a banquet on. Near the wall that separates this platform from the road stands a tall grey rock which, viewed from a certain angle, is supposed to resemble the Great Buddha of Nara.

"Doesn't it!" shouted the master of the *minshuku*—family-run inn—where I had stopped to eat lunch and get out of the wind. And he showed me a matchbox of his own design, featuring a sketch of the rock and its Buddha face. I gazed from the master to the matchbox to the rock.

"You can see it better from upstairs!" he assured me. We went upstairs. I looked out of the window. The surf crashed over the bare rock ledge and the spray flung up like whale spouts.

"At any rate," said the master, "you could stay the night and make a proper study!"

So I stayed, and in the middle of the afternoon the master, whose name was Yamada, forty-eight years old and dressed smartly for this bleak part of the countryside in a black sports shirt and pressed white trousers, brought a tray to my table and pulled up a cushion and poured himself a cup of tea. Through the large glass windows behind Yamada's head I could see the rioting waves trying to smash the deserted platform of rock.

"In summer the kids all come to swim," he shouted over the roar of the sea, "though the waves get up sometimes, like they are now! My downstairs was flooded a while back. But in summer the sea's a lovely color. Look at it now though, grim and dark. That's because the rivers are all emptying snow into it. This time of year, never mind how blue the sky is, the sea's always the color of squid ink. And then we've got the Buddha Rock. And we've got good fish, especially me. There's four of us run minshukus here but I'm the only one who goes out in his own boat. We do all sorts of things to attract custom! We've organized a Let's Eat Fish Society and when all the members get together we entertain them with a few Tsugaru songs!"

"Who does the singing?"

"I do!"

"And is there anyone who can play the shamisen?"

"Yes, there's a young fellow called Araki, a fisherman. Why, do you like Tsugaru songs?"

I told him I loved Tsugaru songs and sang him the line about the Ajigasawa girl who tasted like a dried persimmon.

"My gawd, you should have said so!" he shouted. "Here, let's give Araki a ring. I'll tell him we're starting an international fan club!"

So I had a bath and changed into one of the minshuku's yukata, and when I climbed back up the stairs with a face the color of cooked lobster I found Araki and Yamada sitting side by side in the large empty matted space, with beer and fish on the table in front of them, and a thundering sea and the gathering dusk behind.

Araki was a young man, brawny and silent, his face almost as red as mine with shyness. He had taught himself to play from records he said, and then he picked up his shamisen and played "Jonkara-bushi." The dark came down. He played "Yosare-bushi." Outside the sea rose and fell with a hiss and clang like iron. Sometimes, when his plectrum skipped a string instead of striking it squarely, Araki would wince and smile and close his eyes. And once, in the middle of "Ohara-bushi," he stopped altogether and laid his instrument down and grinned and massaged his shoulder.

To a delicate accompaniment Yamada sang the throat-murdering "Aiya-bushi," his voice surprisingly mellow and high:

Aiyaa naa . . . Aiya . . . The songs flow, the songs of home:
Yosare, Jonkara, that's a good one. . . .

And then, while Araki massaged his shoulder, Yamada spread his arms and raised his face and addressed the empty beer bottles on the table as though they were a paying audience: "Well, I don't mind saying, we've played and sung for some interesting guests in our time. Yes, we have! But of all the guests we've played and sung for, I don't mind saying we've never played and sung for anyone as interesting as the guest we've played and sung for this evening. No, we haven't! That's a fact! And now let's hear from our remarkable guest!"

So I gulped down the last of my beer and sang an old English border ballad about a young knight who died in the wars and was eaten by crows and his golden hair used for nest-lining and no one would ever discover his bones because they were hidden behind a crumbling dike where the wind would blow through them forever. This song, when I had finished it and translated the lyrics, had a sobering effect on Araki, who was sober enough in any case, and he began quietly to pack away his shamisen; but it drove Yamada into the giddy realms of comparative musicology: "Well, I never! In all my years I must say I never heard aught like that before. On the other hand, we're bound to admit that it had a familiar ring to it. Yes, indeed! In fact, it didn't sound like an English song at all, did it? I think we're all agreed on that point. No, it sounded like a Japanese song! Why, it could have been made up right here in Tsugaru! Crows, we've got 'em by the bucketful. Yes! And that young samurai having his eyes pecked out; why, it's just like you'd see in a comic!"

Araki went home. I ate dinner downstairs. And no sooner had I sat down and picked up my chopsticks than an elderly man in a khaki jacket and a dark rollneck pullover came in, sat down at the same table as me, told me he had seen me that morning on the road, and offered to buy me a beer. He had thick lips wet with spittle, tiny slits where his eyes should have been, and a nose bent so far to the left that he looked, head on, like a cubist waxwork. He was drunk enough for Yamada's wife to come smiling out from behind the little restaurant counter and tell him that she was closing. But he was having none of that.

"Sake!" he shouted. "And I want the same dinner as this fellow here is having!"

Yamada's wife brought him sake and a bowl of nuts, and we talked for a few minutes about what I was doing here—wandering around the towns and villages provoking conversations.

Then, when he had yelled for a second flask of sake and Yamada's wife had brought it to him chuckling with embarrassment, the elderly drunk screwed up his little eyes so tight that he can't possibly have seen anything and asked me how many brothers and sisters I had. None, I told him. And straight away his eyes slid open and he started to abuse me.

That's what he had guessed the minute he saw me. No brothers or sisters. He could tell everything he needed to know about a man from the answer he gave to that question. No brothers or sisters. Yes. He'd known as soon as he saw me on the road that morning that I was a worthless, lazy, stinking layabout. In fact he'd only sat down at this table to confirm his intuition. A lousy, rotten shitbag, that was me. Spoiled to the core, with no thought for anyone but myself. Why else was I wasting my time and money wandering about the country indulging myself instead of doing something useful with my life? Something that would benefit other people?

Yamada crept across to our table, put his hand on the back of my chair and whispered, in a voice that must have carried out into the street, "Pay no attention to dad here! He's drunk!" But the drunk's eyes were locked on mine like two little poison darts at the ends of precisely directed blowpipes, and his spittle had begun to roll down his khaki jacket.

He could see from my face how much I detested Japan. Reading faces was his particular talent. Yes, look at me. I loathed Japan, rotten shitbag that I was.

He thrust his face forward till his spittle began to drip down onto my pickled radish and screwed up his eyes and opened them again and stared intently at my face. Then his eyes widened and his mouth shut and, as suddenly as it had grown abusive, his speech became hushed and respectful.

Here, wait a minute. What was that? Those lines there. Could he possibly . . .? Did I mind . . .?

He stood up from his chair and leaned further forward till his lips were almost kissing the tip of my nose and lifted my hair to get a better view of my forehead. Then his mouth dropped open again so that the accumulated spittle in it fell onto my plate in a round penny-sized blob.

There. Three lines. I had three straight, equally spaced lines across my forehead. What a mistake! In all his thirty years of reading faces that was the first time he had ever seen it. Two or three thousand faces he had read and never before had he had the luck to come across it. Only three. Did I mind . . . ?

He lifted my hair further and stared mesmerized at my hairline.

Only three. It was a sign of great wisdom. It was the highest sign of all the signs. The only historical personage he knew for sure to have had three such lines was—did I realize? No? The Buddha! He had read about it but never seen it. I would have to forgive him. He had made a terrible mistake.

He sat down and wiped the spittle off my plate with his sleeve.

I was a marvelous man. I could do anything I chose. Yes, he saw it all. He knew why I was journeying through this world I had come into. I was journeying through this world in order to discover it. That's why I was going among the people. . . .

I got up from the table but he grabbed the sleeve of my yukata, called for a memo pad, and asked for my signature as a keepsake. Yamada's wife brought a pad and a short stub of pencil and I signed a page, which the elderly drunk tore out and folded shakily and placed in his inside pocket.

He wished he could buy my dinner for me, he said. He wished he could pay my entire bill for lodgings. But he was a bit hard up this time of the month. I would have to forgive him. Truly. A marvelous man . . .

I said goodnight and went upstairs and from the window watched Yamada drive the elderly drunk out of the restaurant with wide sweeps of both his arms. Then Yamada came back inside and shut the door and drew a curtain across it, and the drunk spat loudly into the gutter and turned and stumbled across the road towards the Buddha Rock. He leaned on the guard rail and looked up at the rock for a few moments and then spat and began searching in circles at his feet for something he thought he had lost. All night the sea heaved like a human breast, crashing over the white guard rail and washing the stains from the street.

❧

Once upon a time there was a Tsugaru shamisen boom. It began in the early 1970s but by 1980 it was over. Another year there was a frilly lizard boom. You couldn't turn your television on or step outside your door without running into Chlamydosaurus Kingi, an Australian reptile with a membrane behind its head that it raises like a starched frilly collar when someone—such as a Japanese cameraman—creeps up on it and gives it a fright. Then it stands upright and scoots away on its bandy hind legs, a trait that so endeared it to consumers throughout the archipelago that for three or four heady summer months this lizard was more popular than Disneyland.

Chlamydosaurus Kingi advertised beer and cars and motor oil. It fled across hoardings twelve meters wide and was engagingly startled approximately twice during each prime-time commercial break. Toy shops stocked piles of Chlamydosaurus Kingi dolls and the actual creatures were begged or bought or borrowed from Australian zoos. Then autumn came, and Chlamydosaurus Kingi vanished from hoardings and screens and toy shops as abruptly as it had invaded them. Within hours, it seemed, not a soul in Japan had ever heard of the frilly lizard. The Japanese consumer turned his attention once again to latex-bottomed ladies and waited for another advertising executive to come up with a fresh definition of "cute." The creatures themselves expired in cages or were perhaps shipped back to Australia, and beer and cars and motor oil were once again the monopoly of the comparatively warm-blooded.

The frilly lizard boom, like all Japanese booms, was characterized by the twin qualities of fanaticism and brevity, and it died of a terminal illness made up of overkill, fickleness, and burnout. Compared with this and similar booms, the Tsugaru shamisen boom lasted an eternity: almost enough time for a person to actually learn to play the instrument, although not many did. Booms are a spectator sport; they amuse you but you wouldn't want your daughter to marry one, and your fan club membership always expires on the same date as everybody else's.

The Tsugaru shamisen boom owed a lot to the skill and blindness of Takahashi Chikuzan and, though it was not until the 1970s that the fans began lining up in earnest outside the concert halls, the boom had its roots in the more general folk-music revival that was kindled in the late 1940s by Japan's defeat and occupation. Defeat was the most devastating experience that Japan as a nation had had to face in sixteen hundred years of recorded history and the loss of national self-esteem was unparalleled and all-pervading. So much emphasis had been laid by wartime propagandists on Japan's divinity, its manifest destiny, the unique and unconquerable virtues of its people, that the sudden bankruptcy of these articles of faith left a yawning, seemingly unfillable void. Japan had never before been defeated by a foreign power (the received view of the abortive campaigns in Korea at the end of the sixteenth century is that they ended in a stalemate), let alone been required to surrender unconditionally and submit to the suzerainty of an enemy regarded as subhuman. The ensuing shock and depression could have presented large obstacles to economic recovery, and the swift establishment of new causes for national pride became a priority at all levels of society.

Many aspects of Japan's traditional culture—local festivals are a good example—had been suppressed during the war years because they were judged unseemly and lacking in proper martial seriousness. These events and entertainments were now energetically revived. Up and down the country old rites and ceremonies were dusted off and displayed to a public eager to congratulate itself on any achievement that did not stink of war; and where no local festival could be conjured from the records a new one was invented. The traditional arts (those that had not, like theater, fallen foul of the occupation censor) enjoyed a similar revival, and folk music was among the first to benefit. For one thing, folk music was a proletarian art. It had never been patronized or encouraged by the ruling classes and so was untainted by association with the discredited powers (or their feudal predecessors) that had led Japan to war. For another, folk music celebrated the regions, not the nation; and though national pride had suffered a devastating blow, the regions—Tsugaru included—had no local cause to feel guilty or ashamed. They could congratulate themselves, as they often had and would again, on being different from the mainstream, safely cocooned from its follies and excesses. And the more cocooned they now appeared the more likely they were, in this time of self-doubt and aching reappraisal, to earn the mainstream's regard and affection.

By 1951—the last full year of the occupation—the revived interest in folk music had grown so fast and spread so far that one northern folk song, "Mamurogawa Ondo," actually topped the Japanese hit parade. The songs that proved most popular during these difficult years were, of course, the liveliest songs; songs that celebrated in about equal measure the passions of ordinary peacetime life and the imagined uniqueness of Japanese sensibilities. "Mamurogawa Ondo" fit the bill perfectly. It had Japanese sensibilities oozing from every syllable:

> *I am a plum flower of Mamurogawa,*
> *You are a nightingale of Shinjo.*
> *You do not wait for my flower to bloom,*
> *You come while I'm still in bud.*

And it also illustrated a spirited refusal to be cowed by adversity:

> *Round the back there's a wooden fence,*
> *Round the front there's a noisy dog.*
> *Shhhh! Don't bark. I'm not a thief!*
> *I'm the daughter's fancy man!*

But the boom passed and, as Japan's economy flourished and the nation began grappling with the inebriating business of becoming "internationally minded," the urge to celebrate local achievements gave way to a desire to appear cosmopolitan. So folk music relinquished the limelight and was eclipsed by one foreign import after another. Where it survived, folk music became sanitized. The grubby-fingered local musicians who had kept the faith alive during the dark days were shunted into the wings and replaced by young "talents" from Tokyo and Osaka in crisp, neatly pressed kimonos, who were backed by large orchestras with prominent brass sections. By the end of the 1950s folk music had ceased to be a cause for renewed national pride and had become simply a minor branch of the entertainment industry: clean, slick, professional, and passionless.

Still, the postwar boom had altered Takahashi Sadazo's life. Plucked from his beggar-like obscurity and awarded the artistic name Chikuzan (Bamboo Mountain), he had found himself playing Tsugaru shamisen accompaniments on national radio. Even when the boom subsided he was able to make a more secure living than before by performing at the *minyo-sakaba* (folk song pubs) that sprang up in the fifties to satisfy the diehard fans—though Chikuzan always disliked the clublike atmosphere of these places and, in later years, refused to play for any audience that wasn't a hundred percent attentive. In the 1960s Chikuzan gave his first concert-hall recitals to groups of young urban workingmen under the sponsorship of an organization called the Workers' Music Council and by the early 1970s he had attracted an enthusiastic following not only among young workers but among young intellectuals and students, as well as among the fifty- and sixty-year olds who, then as now, provide Japanese folk music with its most faithful constituency.

The Tsugaru shamisen boom began in full earnest in 1973, the year in which oil prices skyrocketed, a Japanese resident of the United States won the Nobel Prize for Physics, and Chikuzan started giving regular concerts at the Jean-Jean basement theater in Tokyo's fashionable Shibuya district—an underground venue in both senses of the word, more used to staging avant-garde plays than shamisen recitals. No longer simply an accompanist, Chikuzan was now demonstrating to his young urban audiences something that Tsugaru people had long taken pride in—that the Tsugaru shamisen (unlike other, smaller forms of this three-stringed cross between a long lute and a thin banjo) is a perfect tool for the virtuoso soloist: perfect for embellishing a tune until it becomes a personal testament, perfect for showing off technical accomplishments and idiosyncratic inventions. Chikuzan had also begun showing off his talent as a raconteur. At his Jean-Jean concerts he would regularly launch into long accounts of his early life delivered with a sprinkling of earthy humor in a dialect so arcane as to sound avant-garde itself. By the mid-1970s he had achieved the most difficult double in any branch of the arts: he had become at the same time a cult figure and a household word.

How to account for this surge in popularity—especially among the urban young—of an obscure rural music, and why it happened when it did? A social historian might answer that, by the early 1970s, the educated young of Japan, like the educated young of other countries, were casting round for new directions in which to channel the energies and enthusiasms left over from the defunct struggles of the 1960s. The two great student activist causes in Japan during the sixties had been opposition to the U.S.–Japan Mutual Security

Treaty and the reversion of Okinawa from American to Japanese rule. But with the advent of the seventies both these causes died. In 1970 the Mutual Security Treaty was automatically extended and further protest became superfluous. The next year an agreement was signed with the United States to return the Okinawan islands to Japan, and in 1972 the last official vestige of American occupation came to an end. As elsewhere, the loss of such ringing causes resulted in a narrowing of focus among the young. The revolution, and along with it the greening and flower-powering of the nations, had failed or expired of old age. The urge to reorder the world had suddenly given way to an interest in macrobiotic food.

More to the point, Japan's postwar soul-searching had been drowned in the tsunami of the "economic miracle" and national self-esteem, far from requiring a boost, was flourishing as never before. Everywhere you turned you heard or read about the unique and superior virtues of the Japanese race. Only the Japanese possessed intuition; only they possessed a subtly ambiguous language; only they could appreciate the natural world; only they worked hard; only they had four seasons. So, as in the immediate postwar years but for completely different reasons, the climate was ripe for a celebration of peculiarly Japanese achievements, and the seventies and early eighties witnessed all sorts of cultural revivals, some spontaneous and some contrived. There was a revival of interest in Kabuki theater (like the Tsugaru shamisen boom, this was fueled in large part by charismatic personalities). The popularity of local festivals, spurred on by new affluence and opportunities for leisure travel, escalated at such a pace that travel agents could barely handle the volume of sightseers, and many of the more famous events began to resemble not local celebrations at all but vast theatrical extravaganzas. There was a sake revival and a sushi revival and a period when shochu briefly replaced whisky as the nation's favorite tipple. There was a boom in visits to hot-spring resorts, a brisk sale of ten- and twenty-volume encyclopedias on crafts and old roads and suitable subjects for haiku poems.

The Tsugaru shamisen boom was among the earliest in this wave of rekindled enthusiasms and it lasted as long as it did because Tsugaru folk music had several things going for it in addition to its being uniquely Japanese (*yuniiku*, adapted from the English word *unique* and applied only to Japan, was the buzzword of the times). It was also "ethnic" at a time when the first trickle of Japanese young were beginning to visit India and Nepal and Southeast Asia and discover in those places folk traditions that, unlike their own, had managed to avoid becoming slick and sanitized and "internationally minded." It was "exotic" because it sounded so unlike the more familiar folk songs that their uncles and fathers had occasionally embarrassed them by taking off their jackets to sing at weddings. It was, in fact, unsingable, just as the Tsugaru shamisen was unlearnable and the lives of its blind maestros inimitable. Chikuzan's popularity among the educated young was due as much to his blindness as to his musicianship and his skill as a storyteller. The shamisen is traditionally an instrument of the blind, and Chikuzan's blindness was solid evidence that he was the "real thing," like real ale and brown rice.

On his kimono tails Chikuzan had dragged into prominence several other Tsugaru shamisen performers and, though none of these ever matched Chikuzan's fame (all of them, in other words, could see), they released records and gave solo recitals, and it was in their work—particularly their records—that you detected the first signs of the boom's demise. Partly the demise was caused by the same tendency that was to scuttle the frilly lizard—the tendency to go so far overboard that drowning is the only possible result. Ah! said the producers, it's the young who are buying these shamisen records so we'll go all out to attract them. Let's have a record cover featuring Kida Rinshoei (a chubby, serious-faced, late-middle-aged performer, now dead) wearing a tight Levi's denim jacket. Let's do a record where Yamada Chisato plays shamisen arrangements of Hungarian dances and another where he plays a Tsugaru shamisen concerto with a Western-style orchestra which we will call the—yes!—the *Orientaru Fuantasuteikku Ookesutora* (the Oriental Fantastic Orchestra) and which will sound like all the Miklos Rozsa film scores you ever heard rolled into one. And let's do another record where we'll have not just one Tsugaru shamisen—or two or ten or twenty—but thirty, yes thirty Tsugaru shamisens, all playing together. . . .

✄

The sea was a summery blue for all Yamada's talk of snow-filled rivers. The wind had dropped, and in the still sky four jet fighters from the base at

Misawa screamed round and round in an endless dogfight, so low that I could see their pilots. The rocks along the shoreline were soft and porous, light green and grey and speckled with small hard-shelled creatures that scuttled for their lives as angry seabirds dived out of the path of the planes. I had made a late start and it was almost noon when I reached the lighthouse and the small harbor at Kasose where Yamada had been born and where he kept his boat, and found him spraying his nets with a high-powered jet like the ones repair shops use to clean a chassis. We went for a beer in the tiny restaurant that catered to the fishermen. A loudspeaker fixed to the wall relayed a day-long stream of boat-to-boat messages ("That's Araki!" shouted Yamada; "That's whatsisname from Kodomari!") and I ate the best raw halibut I'd ever tasted.

It might have been the halibut or it might have been the shortwave messages, but I felt eerily at home in this little shack with its pot of parsley on the doorstep and its one tired fisherman reading a comic book and its old lady sitting at a table in the corner carefully skinning the thin stalks of an edible grass she called *mizu*. In fact I felt so completely at home there that, just as a person might pinch his leg to stop himself from dreaming, I promptly mucked up the homeliness by talking about being a foreigner. Ten years before, I explained to the suddenly unsmiling wife of the shop's owner and the old lady who had stopped skinning her grass, ten years before, when I had walked the length of Japan, some of the ryokans and minshukus I had tried to get rooms in pretended they were full.

"Well," said the wife, "I'd do the same if it was somebody I thought wasn't going to fit in. I'd do the same if some long-haired Japanese hippie came to the door."

Yamada said, pleading: "But that doesn't happen nowadays, does it?"

No, I admitted to the silent little shack, it didn't seem to happen much nowadays.

The loudspeaker hissed and crackled with static, the old lady went back to her stalks of grass, and I said: "I'm not sure what that means though. Does it mean that Japan has changed or does it mean that I've changed?"

"I'm glad you like that halibut," the wife said. "I don't get it from a shop, you know. I get it straight from the boats when they dock. A lot of people think raw fish tastes best if you eat it the minute it's caught. But it doesn't. You want to keep it a day or two."

"Japan's changed." Yamada cried. "It's getting international!"

"Now with trout," the wife said, "you want to freeze it for forty-eight hours before you eat it. That way, you get rid of the oiliness."

"It wouldn't cross my mind to turn a guest away!"

"People who really go for raw fish sometimes phone and ask my husband the exact time a fish died."

"You wouldn't find anyone in Tsugaru turning guests away!"

"Not with squid though. Squid is different. You want to eat squid as soon as you can. Some people like it wriggling."

"And you've changed, I bet!" Yamada said. "You're more . . . well, you're more . . . more . . . I expect!"

The afternoon was warmer than the morning and I lay for an hour and dozed on a bank of grass overlooking the rocky shore. But when I woke the Tsugaru wind had sprung up and it buffeted me along the coast and into the port of Fukaura. The first ryokan I went to told me they were full and I could see that it was true. They were catering for a wedding. Dazai had stayed here in "a dirty room" and gorged himself on sea bream and abalone. Then he had gone to a restaurant to drink sake and had had a row with one of the staff. He had wanted a leisurely conversation with a waitress whose front teeth were missing, but a pudgy young maid kept interrupting the conversation to crack silly jokes and, when Dazai told her to go away, the toothless waitress had gone with her.

"I warn you, reader," wrote Dazai about this, "when a man goes into a restaurant he must never speak frankly. . . . I ended up drinking by myself . . . and I felt the loneliness of the traveler more deeply than ever."

Serves you right, I thought, and went to another ryokan a couple of doors up the street where, after I had banged about and shouted in the entrance hall for something like fifteen minutes, a dumpy, flowery-frocked woman bounced out from behind a screen, knelt down on the boards, bowed till her head almost touched the floor, smiled with delight at the sight of my rucksack, and reeled off her prices.

From the outside the ryokan had looked like a cramped little two-story affair, but the flowery-frocked woman led me up endless staircases and along sloping corridors that climbed the whole height of the hill behind the street till we reached a room that looked down on the red rooftops of the ryokan's six straggling wings and, when I opened the window and leaned out to see if the harbor was visible, the smoke from the bathhouse, giddy miles below, wafted past my nose bringing the smell of blanched cedar. The room was colder than the street, and so before and during and after dinner I drank half a dozen flasks of sake to keep off the chill. Then I went out for a stroll through the unlit town. There was no sign anywhere of life or drink or entertainment. I stood on a bridge looking up at the bright half moon and said to it, "I'll miss you when I'm dead."

I shuffled back past the shuttered shops and up the steep corridors to my empty room and spent much of the night wide awake listening to the drip-drip-drip of the leaking geyser in the corridor as it spilled water into the metal sink. Twice I got up to empty the plastic bucket I had placed under the drips to deaden the sound, and twice it seemed to me, lying in my futon, that I had smothered the heartbeat of the house.

✌

The only thing Dazai did in Fukaura, apart from eat and drink and feel sorry for himself, was pay a brief visit to Enkakuji Temple. So in the morning, after the flowery-frocked woman had knelt and made silent birdlike movements in her entrance hall, bowing and smiling repeatedly to cover the fact that, as I stood there lacing my boots, neither of us could think of anything to say, I visited the temple too. Dazai mentions having heard that one of its halls has been designated a National Treasure (but he had heard wrong; what he means is that the hall contains a lacquered feretory which has been designated an Important Cultural Property, these distinctions being the lifeblood of art). He also mentions that it has an impressive gate which houses two large statues of protective Buddhist deities. But what impressed me most about Enkakuji was the fact that the inscriptions on this gate, as well as on a wooden stupa inside the temple courtyard, were partly written in Sanskrit, a language no one in Fukaura has ever learnt a syllable of, including the priests.

Apart from the temple and its unknowable Sanskrit, there was not much to see in Fukaura. Dazai had found the whole southern part of the Tsugaru coast "knowing" and "cultured" and "tame" compared to the wild and stubborn north. "Northern Tsugaru," he wrote, "is like a half-cooked vegetable, but this region has been cooked till all the color has drained out of it." What fishing had been to Ajigasawa the coastal trade had once been here and, though both little towns were sadly run-down nowadays compared with what they must have been like a hundred and fifty years ago, you could still detect the hint of a class difference in their widely separate characters: workaday, straggling Ajigasawa with its grime and leathery squid and petrol engines; and pert, prim Fukaura with its concrete-sprayed, wire-netted hillside, its crescent-shaped harbor (one wall of which has been decorated with brightly colored murals), and its fading memories of ships' chandlers and wrapped packages and bills of lading. The people of Ajigasawa, if you got to know them, would be slovenly and blunt; those of Fukaura would be purposeful and nit-picking. In fact, the more I thought about them, the more the differences between these two little towns began to resemble the differences between Tsugaru's two major cities: Aomori, with its ramshackle markets and the smell of grease on everybody's fingers, and Hirosaki, with its cherry blossoms and Bach recitals and its complacent sense of a lapsed but lingering "culture."

Fukaura is as far south as Dazai came during his perambulations in 1944—and he clearly felt that, having come this far, he had wandered off the Tsugaru map. So, having been bored for an hour by the bay, I did what Dazai had done and turned north again, with no road to follow back up the coast but the one I had already walked along. I spent another night at Yamada's minshuku and scalded my foot so badly on the hot tap in the bathroom that Yamada's wife tied an ice pack round it with one of my long woolen socks. And I stopped a second time at the little fisherman's restaurant in Kasose to eat more raw halibut and listened while the wife, who was acting as go-between for a neighbor's son, expounded on the subject of arranged marriages.

Before the war, she told me, the principals were frequently not consulted. If the families decided they wanted a marriage then a marriage there would be and all else could go hang. I thought at first that she was explaining this to me in order to prove that it was not only foreigners searching for ryokan rooms who had a hard time of things, but then she got onto Americans and how, when they had come blundering in, the old ways started to change. So I said goodbye and forgot all about foreigners until, trudging into Ajigasawa again, I came face to face with a little boy about nine years old, with blond hair and blue eyes, dragging his satchel along the street on his way home from school. He was all by himself, as I was, and he was as surprised to see me as I was to see him. But as we came within speaking distance of each other he lowered his eyes and quickened his steps and passed me looking down at his shoes.

"Hi there," I said.

But he didn't reply, and his shoes were scuffed to pieces.

4
Spring and Castle

❧

The saga of Dazai's suicide attempts would read like a five-act comedy if it weren't that they cocked up other people's lives.

His first attempt occurred on the night of December 10th, 1929, when, at the age of twenty, Dazai took an overdose of sleeping pills. This bothered no one except his mother, who took him away for a month's recuperation, and whoever had to pump out his stomach. The attempt was attributed, by Dazai himself, to ideological confusion, class guilt, and literary precedent but, as at least one scholar has pointed out, December 10th was the eve of the final examinations at Hirosaki Higher School where Dazai was currently ranked thirty-first in his class of thirty-five.

His second attempt occurred eleven months later on November 29th, 1930, when Dazai, having recently been barred from the family house in Kanagi on account of his plan to marry a young Aomori geisha, took a divorced Ginza bar girl on a forty-eight-hour drinking spree and then, depending on the version you read, either threw himself into the sea with her near the resort island of Enoshima or took sleeping pills with her on the nearby beach. Either way, the girl died and Dazai survived to be charged as an accomplice in her death and then quietly released because of pressure brought to bear on the authorities by his brother Bunji, who was now an official of the prefectural government.

His third attempt occurred on March 16th, 1935, when, after failing to get a job with a Tokyo newspaper and blowing his entire month's allowance from Bunji on a twenty-four-hour pub crawl with a distant in-law, Dazai hanged himself in the woods behind the Hachiman Shrine in Kamakura but was up and about again the next morning "with the rope marks still round my neck."

His fourth attempt occurred two years later, in March 1937, after he had spent four weeks in a mental hospital during which time his wife, the former geisha, had been briefly unfaithful with the distant in-law of the twenty-four-hour pub crawl. Dazai escorted her to Minakami hot spring where they both took sleeping pills and both survived.

And finally, on the night of June 13th, 1948, four years after his trip round Tsugaru, one month after finishing his last novel, *Ningen Shikkaku* (*No Longer Human*), and fourteen months after his second wife had given birth to their third child, Dazai disappeared with a beautician called Tomie, a war widow who had twice already composed suicide notes of her own and whom Dazai had known for a little over a year. Six days later, on Dazai's thirty-ninth birthday, their bodies were dragged out of the Tama canal near Mitaka, about a mile and a half from my house.

"Mine has been a life of much shame," runs the opening sentence of *No Longer Human*, ". . . I have sometimes thought that I have been burdened with a pack of ten misfortunes, any one of which, if borne by my neighbor, would be enough to make a murderer of him.

"I simply don't understand. I have not the remotest clue what the nature or extent of my neighbor's woes can be. Practical troubles, griefs that can be assuaged if only there is enough to eat . . . if my neighbors manage to survive without killing themselves, without going mad . . . not yielding to despair, resolutely pursuing the fight for existence, can their troubles be real . . . ? The more I think of it the less I understand. All I feel are the assaults of apprehension and terror at the thought that I alone am different from the rest. It is almost impossible for me to converse with other people. What should I talk about, how should I say it . . . ?

"It was thus that I turned to clowning. . . ."

From Ajigasawa Dazai took the train back to Goshogawara to see his aunt, but I saw no point in going there again, nor in taking the train, and I had no aunt. So I began to walk along a little-used road that would take me up and over the foothills of Mount Iwaki, to Dake hot spring and Iwakisan Shrine and, finally, down to the old city of Hirosaki, where, three hundred years ago, give or take a life, I might or might not have been born.

It was a warm day and under the low cloud Mount Iwaki crouched without a head. I had spent forty minutes after getting up in Ajigasawa looking for somewhere to have breakfast. At nine o'clock, a small department store had opened and I had sat in its coffee shop eating "pizza toast." Now, at ten-thirty, the combination of fourteen consecutive days on the road, the prospect of a twenty-seven-kilometer climb before evening and the imitation Tabasco sauce that I had recklessly dribbled over my breakfast was causing my insides to feel much like Mount Iwaki's must about twenty minutes before an eruption. So I sat on a grass bank and groaned at a solitary duck that was threading its way carefully among newly planted rice seedlings. Between the rows of seedlings, already crushed and torn by the wind, I could see the ragged footprints that the planter had left in the silvery mud, and they moved me in an inward way, as the fake Tabasco was moving my bowels. The blossoms were all but gone from the apple trees. Young frogs in the paddies set up a commotion that crackled across the valley like the clacking of football rattles, and in a deep rain puddle swarmed thousands of tadpoles, fretting at the edges of their accidental prison and banging their heads against the three abandoned lunch boxes with which their prison was furnished.

A van stopped and two fresh-faced Canadians leaned out of the cab window and asked me where I was going. They were missionaries, one from the church at Goshogawara ("Come and stay! You must come and stay!") and one from Ajigasawa who had lived there for three years with his wife and five children and joked pleasantly about the size of his "parish" and the percentage of it that he had managed to convert.

"It must have been one of your children I saw yesterday," I told him. "A boy about nine, carrying a satchel."

"Oh yes," he said happily, "that was Donald. Donald speaks fluent Tsugaru dialect."

"How does he get on at school?" I asked. "Has he made a lot of friends?"

"Oh yes," said the proud father, "hundreds of friends. You never see him alone."

The day wore on. I passed a grocer's shop with a poster tacked to its wall advising me that The Kingdom of God was at Hand. An old man murmured, "*Gokurosama desu,*" as we passed each other in his village, an untranslatable greeting that older people sometimes use when they see me on a road near where they live and which conveys an appreciation for the effort I have made to get there. My effort was appreciated in a different way by two young men loading beer crates onto a delivery truck, who shouted "*Hai-to! Hai-to!*" ("Fight! Fight!"), a shout meant not so much to encourage me as to remind each other of the punch line in a television commercial for an energizing drink, whereupon they banged their crates down on the asphalt and indulged in a fit of giggles. Then the road rose briskly in sharp doglegs to a four-hundred-meter-high plateau from where I could look back towards the Japan Sea coast and see the creamy white of the Seven-League Beach bleed away into the mist of Cape Gongen.

At four o'clock I reached my destination, the hot-spring resort of Dake, halfway up the skirts of Mount Iwaki. Dazai never came here, but I had spent a night at Dake some ten or eleven years before and I strolled round the little circle of shops and shacks racking my brains to remember which of the three or four ryokans I had stayed in.

"Did it have a wooden bath?" asked the breathless old woman who answered my call at the first one I tried.

"Yes, I've got a feeling it did."

"Well, it must have been here! It must have been here! We're the only one with a wooden bath! And we've got an elevator too! I bet we didn't have an elevator when you stayed here before! Ooooooo, Missus! Missus! (to the *okami-san*—proprietress—of the ryokan who was rubbing her hands on her apron and frowning at us through her spectacles from the lobby). Here's someone who stayed here ten years ago!"

"Well, bring him in and stop fussing," said the okami-san. So I unslung my pack and unlaced my boots and rode the rattling elevator two floors to my six-mat room. Then, while the old woman was doing my laundry, I went down and sprawled by myself in one of the bathroom's two large wooden tubs, in water that was grey and stank of the volcano and was hot enough to put me to sleep.

Ten or eleven years before I had sprawled in this same bathtub. I was on my way home from Hokkaido where I had attended the wedding of a retired U.S. naval officer who was marrying a Japanese girl less than half his age. He had divorced his silver-haired American wife of twenty or more years after scribbling her a terse note which he left in their kitchen in San Diego. For the wedding Hank wore unseasonal dress whites with a dazzling amount of gold braid on the sleeves, and a saber which the pilot of his flight from California had smuggled through Japanese customs for him; and in the middle of the reception, just before the bride and groom made the rounds of their guests' tables lighting candles with a battery-operated fairy wand, the master of ceremonies announced that Hank had resumed his academic studies and was currently writing a dissertation on "Thought Control in Postwar Japan." I don't know whether it was this announcement or the dress whites or the cold lobster thermidor or something else that upset the president of the company that employed the bride's father. But when he rose in his pinstriped trousers and tail coat to propose the congratulatory toast you could have slit the air with Hank's saber.

"Well, what a splendid foreigner you are!" the president rasped into the microphone while several hundred guests stood staring at the tablecloths and clutching glasses of Suntory Nouveau. "And what a very impressive uniform! Yes! And a sword! Well, well! A splendid foreigner! I've been wondering how old you are. Still, never mind! Let's greet the era of international marriage! Yes, indeed! Foreigners coming over here and marrying Japanese girls, and sometimes not marrying them! How times change! How customs differ! I wish you happiness! *Kanpai!*"

After the ceremony I bumped into the tail-coated president in the hotel lavatory. He had a square Hitler-style moustache, which the half-dozen non-Japanese guests at the wedding had all quietly remarked on, and which was now dripping with water because he had plunged his face into the washbasin. I scowled at him in the mirror and his wet face broke into a charming smile. "Did I say too much?" he asked the mirror in a tone of sozzled triumph. So, a shade depressed, I had taken the ferry to Aomori next morning instead of flying straight home, and decided to spend a night in Hirosaki, a city I had never seen.

I remember the feeling I had when I got off the train at Hirosaki. It was the old station then, with its peaked slate roof, and a voice was chanting "Hirosekiiiii! Hirosekiiiii!" over the station speakers. A man from the northern city of Morioka told me once that he loved arriving back at his station because the cast-iron windbells that hung from the platform roofs made him feel that he had returned to a civilized and caring place—especially if he was arriving back from Tokyo. I had never been to Hirosaki before, but there was something in the chant of the station man—the northern tilt to his vowels maybe or the long whir of the last syllable—that gave me a sense of coming home. It was a chant for people who already knew where they were.

I found a ryokan and, after dinner, I went out for a drink. The place I wandered into had the familiar paper lantern and the counter and the wooden walls, but it was too new and too bright and too small and, while I drank two beers and ate five sticks of chicken liver, there were no customers in it but me. It was one of those places where, as soon as I'd sat down, I felt compelled to explain why I had walked through the door, but the master, a thin slow-moving man, showed no interest in my compulsions.

"I saw the name on your lantern," I babbled. "Torihachi, the same as the place I go to almost every night when I'm at home in Tokyo."

"Common name," the master grunted.

"There's a whole crowd of us who meet up there. A greengrocer, a taxi driver, a man who makes ballet shoes, a junior high school teacher who plays the mandolin."

"Friends, are they?"

"Oh yes. Good friends. That's why I dropped in. I saw your lantern."

We said nothing after that and I ate half an eggplant and drew a Christmas tree on the rim of a dish of soy sauce with the tip of my chopstick, and the master shredded cabbage into a plastic bowl. When he had finished shredding cabbage he put the bowl into the refrigerator and sat on a stool with a cigarette between his fingers and stared at the refrigerator door. I drank another bottle of beer. The froth vanished and the sides of my glass went dull so that I could see my fingerprints on them. As I was getting ready to leave, the door slid open, the master jumped up and burnt his fingers on his cigarette, and a customer strolled in.

It took perhaps six seconds for the customer's private bottle of whisky to appear on the counter, together with a glass, an ice bucket, a hot wet towel, and the pickled entrails of a sea squirt. The customer plucked a speck of wool off his crisply pressed trousers and sat down. He rubbed his hands and face on the towel while the master mixed his whisky and water. Then the customer rolled the towel into a neat tube, placed it on the counter in front of him, leaned forward, looked me over, nodded briskly, and made my acquaintance. His name was Matsuoka, he explained, and he selected one of his four or five varieties of namecard to present to me, taking back the first and swapping it for a second before I'd had time to read the small print. He was a stocky man, smartly dressed in a brown checked jacket and a dark striped tie, and very soon we slipped into a chat from which all of the ritual elements were missing: Where are you from? How long have you been in Japan? Are you married? Do you have children? Why not? Why did you come to Japan? What do you do for a living? Where on earth did you learn to speak Japanese? How old are you? How tall are you? Do you like Japanese beer? Do you love Japan? In encounters with foreigners these questions normally constitute a rite of passage through which the foreigner is obliged to pass before he is permitted to participate in ordinary conversation.

But Matsuoka asked none of them. Instead he sipped his whisky and ignored his sea squirt and we talked about the *neputa* festival, the cherry blossoms for which the castle grounds are famous, the price of land, the new planetarium, the shamisen, Tsugaru lacquer, the brief nine months or so in 1871 when Hirosaki had occupied its rightful place as the capital of the prefecture before that honor had been filched from it by the hole-in-the-wall upstart ferry port.

And what was I doing in Hirosaki? Oh, I was just passing through in no special hurry and I was thinking of spending the next night at a local hot spring. Could Matsuoka-san recommend one? So Matsuoka suggested Dake, but Dake, he warned me, had seen better days. In fact, the master, all attention now on the edge of his stool with his hands sandwiched between his thighs like a chastened schoolboy's, wondered aloud whether Dake was still in business. Not many people were interested nowadays in the old-style hot springs, where there were no floor shows or discotheques or pink-and-purple strip clubs. Dake had once had an open-air bath but they had drained it years ago and filled it in because there weren't enough visitors to justify keeping the pump running. And there were certainly no strip artists, unless you counted your fellow bathers. But Dake was there if I fancied it. And—no bother at all, don't even think about it—Matsuoka would run me up there in his car. So, late the following afternoon, I turned up at Matsuoka's rice shop and he drove me the twenty or so kilometers to Dake.

Matsuoka was good company. "*Soooooooo?*" he would say—a long drawn out "*sooooooo?*"—when I made an averagely mundane remark, treating it with the sort of seriousness and respect that most people reserve for revelations. "*So so so so so!*" he would say, breaking into a broad smile if he sensed that, in my sometimes imperfect grammar, I was leading up to a joke. He had a deep voice for a man his size and a slight growl when he spoke quietly, which was almost always. Only twice did I hear him raise his voice: once when he called out for the maid in the doorway of the ryokan at Dake and once when he spoke on the telephone, for he had the countryman's habit of regarding the telephone as a species of loud hailer and adjusted his decibel level according to how many miles of cable he was speaking down.

He didn't know the people who ran the ryokan at Dake, he told me, but watching through the car window while he fixed up a room for me I had the feeling that the people at Dake knew him. I wanted to give Matsuoka something in return for his kindness but the only thing I had with me apart from my wedding suit was a book about the neputa festival that I'd bought in

Hirosaki that morning and, when I showed this to him, he displayed such pride and pleasure in the fact that I had spent money on a book about his native city that I knew I mustn't give it away. So we had a beer in my room and then he looked at his watch and we said goodbye, and I went down to the bathroom—this bathroom—and lay in the yellowy-grey water thinking about the tail-coated president in Hokkaido with his wet face and Hitler moustache, and about Matsuoka with his thick slicked-back hair and the small black mole on the bridge of his nose and the way he growled when he was being friendly and how his eyes opened wide when he smiled.

Three young men from a Hirosaki sushi shop had come into the bathroom, briskly uncoiled their old-fashioned loincloths, twisted their towels in narrow bands around their heads, splashed water over their hairless bodies and climbed into the tub. What in the world was a foreigner doing here at out-of-the-way Dake? Oh, well, I wanted to try a Tsugaru hot spring. And who on earth had recommended this one? A man I met in Hirosaki. A friend of mine? Yes, a friend of mine. What was his name?

"Matsuoka."

"Matsuoka?"

"That's right."

"Matsuoka."

"I don't know his first name," I said. "His family owns a rice shop."

The young men looked at one another.

"Owns a rice shop," murmured the first.

"In Tamogimachi," grunted the second.

The third lifted his right hand off his crotch for the brief time it took him to draw his finger down his cheek in the scar sign that indicates a member of the gangs. Then he laid his knuckles across his crotch again, and the two other young men stared down through the yellowy-grey water at their kneecaps and said nothing.

After that none of us spoke at all until the three young men climbed out of the bath together and one turned to me and bowed lightly and said, "Please enjoy yourself at Dake."

I didn't see them again, nor anyone else except the maid. But in the early morning, about an hour before I had expected to be called for breakfast, the

maid slid the door of my room open and told me there was someone waiting to see me in the bathroom.

"You must have got it wrong," I said. "I'm not expecting anybody."

"It's all right," said the maid. "It's a friend of yours."

So I pulled my yukata round my hips and knotted the sash and picked up
my towel and made my way along the empty corridors. And there, in the
bathroom, sitting in the tub, with a large bottle of sake and two elegant porcelain cups floating on a red Tsugaru lacquer tray, was Matsuoka, who had gotten up at five o'clock and driven the twenty kilometers from Hirosaki so that
he could have a farewell drink in the bath with a foreign stranger he had met
in a bar and then drive him all the way to the railway station to save him the
trouble of taking a bus.

It was raining hard in the morning when I left Dake. I pulled on my rain gear
and procrastinated, hanging around the ryokan's lobby and chatting to the
brisk, bespectacled woman who ran the place. She gave me three Tsugaru
apples and told me that her husband's younger brother was a Buddhist priest
and lived in Berkeley, California, but that there wasn't much call for his line
of work out there, so he serviced computers part-time. Despite three long
hot baths, I'd slept very badly. Perhaps it was the sulfur but I'd woken twice
in the night with a mouth that felt as though a dentist's suction pipe had
teamed up with an electric sander and had been working it over from the
moment I closed my eyes, so I had slouched rattily about the corridors looking for the machine that sold canned apple juice. Then at eight o'clock the
construction noises had started. Business must have picked up at Dake in the
ten or eleven years since I'd stayed there last, hence the elevator. Certainly,
there had been a nationwide boom in hot-spring popularity, triggered partly
by endless appearances on late-night T.V. of giggling young female "talents"
sitting naked in outdoor bathtubs with artfully minuscule towels revealing
astoundingly minuscule breasts. And now, although it had no outdoor bathtub, Dake appeared to be gearing up for an invasion of the talent-seekers.
Already the view of Mount Iwaki from the window of the second-floor corridor was partly obscured by a new annex. And the skeletons of two more

buildings under construction bore witness that, within about a fortnight, the holy mountain would vanish altogether behind walls made out of aluminum sheets printed to look like planks.

The rain settled down into a steady drizzle. For a while I poked among the andesite boulders that the volcano had spewed out in its riotous days and that lay strewn about its lower slopes like pimples on an ogre's belly. The stepped watercourses that channeled the melting snow and rain off the mountain slopes gurgled and sputtered beside the almost empty road, and a huge flower nursery with a sign advertising irises was totally deserted. But the Tsugaru Country Club was doing brisk business despite the chilly drizzle, and a couple of dozen golfers accompanied by the club's white-hooded women caddies plodded round the greens under wide umbrellas trying to look sprightly.

At present Japan has under construction 315 new golf courses and is planning another 910—astonishing figures when you take into account the number of Japanese people you meet who still moan on and on about how small and overcrowded their country is and how land is at such a fearful premium and how all the poor young couples who marry will never be able to afford their own houses. What you hardly ever hear admitted—what the constant stress on the country's inconvenient geography serves to disguise—is the extent to which Japanese people have themselves to thank for many of their discomforts. Practically all the major developments that have characterized Japanese society since the war—the economic "miracle," the growth of demand for tertiary education and the intense competition at all levels of society from kindergarten upward that this demand has helped to fuel, the breakdown of large family units into "nuclear" ones, the decline of traditional values and norms and their replacement by the values and norms of soap opera—all these have conspired to ensure that a rapidly decreasing percentage of the ever-growing, longer-living population is willing—or able—to live and work in rural areas, and that more and more families from all corners of Japan prefer to squeeze themselves into rented city apartments hardly bigger than a two-car garage in pursuit of what television, peer pressure, and the Dentsu Advertising Agency have persuaded them to think of as "a better life." Once upon a time it was only the dekasegi who left the towns and villages of regions like Tsugaru to look for work in the big cities. Their wives and children stayed on in the countryside, looking after the family elders and preserving such links with the land as they could. Now, when a worker leaves the countryside he is just as likely to take his family with him, or to find a wife in the neighborhood of his city rooming house, and there will be no coming home for the harvest.

You can't, of course, blame the Japanese for wanting to live in condominiums instead of draughty old farmhouses and to sit at desks instead of push ploughs. People all over the globe who have found themselves faced with that choice have opted to do the same. But it is useful to recognize that the demographic upheaval, rural stagnation, urban congestion and other discomforts are in large part the results of this choice. Like almost everything else in life—whether private life or the lives of nations—the issue boils down to the ordering of priorities, among the highest of which is golf.

Golf, the current figures suggest, is the foremost preoccupation in the minds of those who decide how Japan's limited land ought to be utilized and to what sort of projects the nation's 510,000 busy construction companies ought best to be turning their attention. On the construction industry's priority list, country clubs easily outrank, say, sewage systems. Only about 40 percent of Japanese homes are at present linked to sewage systems; the smallest percentage of any industrialized nation. Nor does this appear to be the result of a cultural preference for cesspits since, in a recent survey, 96.6 percent of people living in homes without sewage systems declared that they would much prefer to have one and trusted that the Construction Ministry would shortly see its way to doing something about it.

Such is the enthusiasm of the construction bosses for golf, however, that many prefectures are reluctantly having to introduce statutory limits to the amount of land that can be used for this purpose, partly because some of their less sporting residents have begun pointing out that the large amounts of insecticide and weed killer needed to maintain the greens and fairways is having a more dramatic effect on things like drinking water than even construction bosses can ordinarily guarantee.

"Leisure!" I thought. "What a wonderful invention!" and turned in through the gate of Iwakisan Shrine.

It is hard to imagine a sacred place more perfectly sited than this one. The luminous bulk of Mount Iwaki rises directly behind a modest sanctuary that stands at the end of a long stone-paved avenue. The avenue is straight and slopes slightly upward, and every line of it draws your eye to the peak. As you pass under the *torii* gates and over a gently curving drumbridge with two great rows of black cryptomerias dimming the sky above you, you become aware that the peak is sinking slowly out of sight, until the steely grey roof of the enlarging sanctuary is capped by nothing but clouds. What you have come especially to admire vanishes as you approach it, and Mount Iwaki towers above the sanctuary again only after you have retraced your steps and are standing outside the gates, where you started.

As Iwaki is known as the Fuji of Tsugaru, so Iwakisan Shrine is sometimes called "the Nikko of the North"—an eloquent illustration of how the relatively unfamiliar needs a link with the instantly recognizable before it can expect to count for anything. Iwaki resembles Fuji in that they are both dormant volcanoes rising out of comparatively flat lowlands, but in every other way they are as different as two snowflakes. And the somber dignity of Iwakisan Shrine is about as similar to the brazen gaudiness of the shrine at Nikko as the charioteer at Delphi is like the sculptures in Singapore's Tiger Balm Gardens.

Like the Aw brothers' painted plaster figures, the shrine at Nikko is an exercise in excess. Where it sets out to awe it bemuses, and where it strives for other-worldly significance it ends up serving as a perfect emblem for the pedestrian forms of material ambition. It was built in 1636 to enshrine the spirit of the first Tokugawa shogun, Ieyasu, who himself laid down its specifications and forced his vassals to contribute the vast sums of money that funded its construction, so it is one of the world's great monuments to megalomania as well as one of its prime examples of architectural kitsch. But because it commemorates so important a historical personage, and because it is so crammed with colorful and exotic fiddle-faddle, and because it is so easily accessible to sightseers (a little over two hours by express train from Tokyo), the shrine at Nikko ranks as one of Japan's major tourist attractions. Guidebook pages and brochures devoted to it rarely fail to quote the famous saying, *Nikko o mizushite "kekko" to iunakare,* which the authors of these brochures always translate into English as, "Never say 'splendid' until you have seen Nikko," but which could just as accurately be translated, "See Nikko and say 'enough.' "

Iwakisan Shrine commemorates no dictator. Its ostensible deity is the mountain itself and its holy of holies is a four hours' hike away on the mountain's peak. It was founded towards the end of the eighth century and, as then, it serves not as a House of God but as a marker, a signpost, a way of demonstrating in wood and thatch that the numen is close. And, though it bequeaths you nothing and promises you nothing, the numen desires acknowledgment. It doesn't want bribes as the Chinese gods do; nor, like other gods, does it want your prayers; it won't answer them anyway, even granted that it could. What the numen wants is your ironclad guarantee that, come this time next year, the sixty-nine doglegs of the Iwaki Skyline Toll Road which already transports busloads of tourists to within a chairlift ride of the uppermost slopes will not end in three eighteen-hole golf courses, two ten-story resort hotels and the Aomori Club Med.

My guarantee—no guarantee at all—was a hundred-yen coin which I dropped in the collecting trough just before I rattled the bell and startled the numen into irritable wakefulness. Then I clapped my hands and bowed and prayed, knowing that this doesn't work. I said to the mountain, "Give me a happy home." And a young priest came out of the sanctuary and smiled to see me conversing so solemnly with a bellrope.

The rain had almost given up but the air was still heavy and the paving stones along the cryptomeria avenue shone green and dark and pewter. I waited while a busload of tourists photographed each other against a backdrop of the mountain tip peeking over the monochrome roof ("Look!" shouted a woman, handing her camera to another, "I'm going to pray to Mount Iwaki! Take a picture of me praying to Mount Iwaki!") and while they crowded round the shrine's little shop to buy fortune papers and travel charms. Then, when all the tourists had gone, I went up to the girl behind the shop counter, searched my pockets in mild embarrassment, and bought from her an *o-fuda*—a cardboard tablet blessed by the priests—which I transferred carefully to a pouch of my rucksack before going to eat a bowl of noodles and drink two bottles of beer.

✺

The rituals that the Japanese have instituted for the acknowledgment of the numen have been—and are—rigorously exclusive. Events such as the *shichi-go-san* festival when children of a certain age are taken to their local shrines to be blessed, or *hatsumode*, the first prayer of the New Year, are not so much religious celebrations as demonstrations of Japaneseness. They are gestures confirming membership in the tribe, which is why, when a non-member makes them, he not only lays his reasons open to question, but risks appearing flippant or comic or presumptuous or patronizing or loony.

Now, occasionally, you stumble across exceptions to this rule. In a few older rituals the outsider—the stranger—is actually credited with possessing some of the virtue of the numen; as in old Hollywood jungle movies where Cary Grant turns up among the cannibals and is suddenly proclaimed king.

One New Year's Eve, eight or nine years before, I was staying in a small village on the Oga Peninsula in Akita, not far south of Mount Iwaki. I had gone there to photograph and write about the annual ritual for which this peninsula is famous; a tribal event if ever there was one. The *Namahage* of the Oga Peninsula is an almost unique survivor of a type of ritual (some anthropologists call it a "visitors' ritual") that is thought to have been common long ago throughout Japan, but which nowadays, in its pure state—i.e., a state in which people take it seriously—is practically extinct. After dark on New Year's Eve a group of young men from the village dress up as devils. They wear huge horned masks and bulky straw capes and straw boots to make them look frighteningly larger than life and they carry weapons or things to make a clamor with, and they go from house to house in the village shouting and threatening and demanding gifts.

The main objects of their threats are lazy or disobedient children and wives newly married into the community—people, in short, who do not yet know their proper place and need to be taught it. The devils roar and stamp around the rooms of each house they visit, hauling the terrified children out of their hiding places, stuffing them into sacks, threatening to cart them off to the mountains and reducing the younger and more sensitive among them to fits of knicker-wetting hysteria. Then the devils are offered sake and other refreshments by the head of the house, who kneels formally in front of them. In some households the quivering children are made to approach the devils and pour the sake for them. After that, the devils leave for the next house on the street, getting drunker and more riotous at each one they crash into, and good fortune, good order, and all the good old Confucian virtues—wifely obedience, patriarchal tyranny—will attend the houses they have visited throughout the coming year.

Ordinarily, it is not easy for an outsider to observe this ritual because, for one thing, it takes place in private homes and, for another, the villagers go out of their way to discourage sightseers from turning up. They have managed, despite the best efforts of travel agents, to cling to the notion that their Namahage is a serious and important business. About six weeks after it is over each year, the same group of young men—their numbers sometimes swollen by people from the travel agencies—don masks and straw capes and boots and prance about in the nearby shrine, attracting large numbers of tourists and cameramen despite, or because of, the deep snow. Colorful posters advertise this prancing and it has been catalogued by whoever catalogues such things as one of the "Five Great Snow Festivals of Northeast Honshu." Certainly the tourists and cameramen go back to their cities under the impression that they have seen the Namahage. And certainly they have not. What they have seen is a theatrical concoction designed to fob them off, a cunning and courageous attempt to ensure that, for a few more years at least, the old visitors' ritual can go on being that, and not a peep show.

So I was prepared to be turned away. But I decided to improve my chances by turning up in the village not on New Year's Eve but four or five days earlier, and by spending those days hanging around the community centers where the straw capes were being made, chatting up the young men who would impersonate the devils, drinking sake with them, and jabbering on about nothing in particular until, finally, when New Year's Eve arrived, it was suggested, only half in fun, that I might impersonate a devil myself, since I was comparatively tall and wouldn't need a mask, my nose and other parts of my face being naturally arranged to provoke wilder shrieks from the village children than any fiend. In the end it was agreed that I could accompany the devils on their rounds, go into the houses with them, accept the householders' sake with them, take photographs of them if I wanted to, and frighten as many young wives as I liked.

Which I did, but by the time we had gone though six houses I had drunk so much sake (it being unthinkingly rude for numinous creatures to decline the hospitality of Japanese mortals) that I couldn't focus my camera. So at the seventh house, when invited to stay for the evening, I collapsed gratefully into an armchair, went briefly to sleep, and then woke up in time to watch the annual Red-and-White song contest on television. My host turned out to be the village policeman and, between nine o'clock and the pealing away of the hundred and eight sins upon which the nation's bells embarked at about eleven-thirty, we drank another large bottle of sake. As midnight approached the policeman rose unsteadily to his feet and told me that it was time for us to go and pray at the shrine, and that this was part of his official duty. Then he collapsed back into his armchair and we ended up crawling around on his carpet, among the potato chips and sake cups, trying to maneuver his legs into his uniform trousers without getting his balls caught in his zipper.

At the shrine I discovered another ritual underway. It was the village's *hatsumode*, the first prayer of the New Year, but, instead of visiting the shrine separately or in small family groups as people in the cities generally do, the entire village had turned out just after midnight to offer a communal prayer, the women hushing their grizzling children with threats of another visit from the devils, and the men staying on through the early hours of the morning drinking in the little unheated wooden sanctuary and warming themselves by the bonfire outside, where last year's ineffectual charms—the lucky arrows, o-fuda, zodiacal plaques—were being reduced, like the year itself, to a pile of incoherent ash.

The policeman and I joined the villagers in the sanctuary and drank a lot more sake. Then, at about a quarter to one, the priest came up and offered me his sake cup and, after a minute or two of priestly banter, told me that he would be very grateful if I would lead the communal prayer. This sobered me up quite swiftly, or rather it had the effect of making me feel sick instead of thirsty. Twice, with the utmost casualness and in completely incomprehensible dialect, the priest explained what I had to do. I must approach the altar with this branch, turn it that way, then this, then that, lay it here—not there—bow three times, clap like this—not that—and return to my place. Behind me—no need to worry about it—the villagers would all take their lead for bowing and clapping from me. In a deep silence I approached the altar, my head full of Cary Grant, and cocked it up. I turned the branch the wrong way, put it in the wrong place, bowed about nine times, clapped at the wrong moments, and returned to my seat. Everyone was immensely pleased. And then I went outside and threw up in the bushes.

Sometimes I have spared a moment or two to wonder why I was chosen to perform this rite and why I was admitted into those homes to see the Namahage when so many others have been refused. For instance, a Japanese television crew had turned up in the village at five o'clock on the afternoon of New Year's Eve and by five-thirty they had been sent packing. "Well, couldn't the devils do a little dance for us, then?" the director had moaned to one of the community center people. He was assisted onto his minibus. But I had crashed through seven front doors and sat at seven hearths and drunk approximately a hundred cups of free sake. And early the next morning I had led the villagers in wishing a happy New Year to their numen. Most Japanese people, hearing this tale, would claim that it demonstrates the kindness and consideration with which foreigners can expect to be treated in Japan, and the eagerness of Japanese people to introduce their "culture" to outsiders. I don't doubt that my being a foreigner—the ultimate outsider—had a great deal to do with it. The devils, too, are outsiders. They come from the barren mountain, across the lake; they are grotesque, brutal; they threaten and disrupt. And the treatment I was accorded was exactly the same as the treatment accorded them. They are invited in, fussed over, resignedly put up with, on this one night out of three hundred and sixty-five so that, for the other three hundred and sixty-four, they will promise to stay away.

. . . I finished my beer. The sun had come out, and I clumped off in the direction of Hirosaki to enact some vistors' rituals of my own.

❧

"Here resides the soul of the Tsugaru people," writes Dazai, confidently, about Hirosaki, and then his confidence trickles away. "There must be something [in Hirosaki]," he puzzles, "some unique, beautiful tradition you cannot find anywhere else in Japan. I can definitely sense it, but to show my readers what it is, or what shape it takes, is more than I am capable of, and this troubles me beyond words. It is utterly infuriating."

That is more or less how I feel about Hirosaki. When I am asked what my favorite Japanese city is I often say Hirosaki, though I have never lived here and am so infrequent a visitor that I am always struck more by the changes that have overtaken it—new bus center, new station building, new pink-walled Western-style hotel—than by any abiding character that might explain its special appeal. Kyoto and Nara are both cities in which I have spent more time, and they contain far more glorious and moving monuments to Japan's dead culture than does Hirosaki. But I also sense, definitely, that a soul resides in Hirosaki; something—perhaps, who knows?—unique; and I am less infuriated at my inability to describe it than gladdened by its refusal to be described.

Dazai, however, had an excuse all ready: "When you come to think of it, trying to convey the essential nature of your native region is about as easy as trying to describe your closest relatives, that is to say, almost impossible—you do not know whether to praise them or run them down." So, of course, he does both.

Hirosaki and its inhabitants are characterized, Dazai writes, by a "foolish obstinacy." They are "proudly defiant" and, he asserts with a hyperbole typical of a Tsugaru son, "the stubborn defense of their proud isolation makes them the laughingstock of the world." He can find in Hirosaki no meaningful tradition to boast of "and yet somehow the people of Hirosaki persist in holding their heads high in the air." When he was a student here, he remembers, the singing of *gidayu* ballads was popular among the citizens, and Dazai describes them at their hobby: "respectable gentlemen who, in their sincere attempts to master some insignificant form of art, go to such absurd lengths that the sweat flows in torrents from their brows. . . . In short, in Hirosaki there are still real fools left." In fact, the city is "a paradise of fools."

Then, with a change as swift as a cerebral infarction, he describes how, one spring evening, while still a student, he visited Hirosaki castle alone. "As I stood looking out toward Mount Iwaki from a corner of the open space in front of the keep, I suddenly noticed a dream town unfolding at my feet. . . . There immediately below the castle lay a graceful old town that I had never seen until that moment, its little houses huddled together just as they had been hundreds of years ago, its breath suspended. . . . It was as if I had come upon one of the 'hidden ponds' of which the *Manyoshu* speaks. . . . And it occurred to me that Hirosaki would never be commonplace as long as that old town was there."

Some years ago, in a four-month burst of rashness spurred on by a cerebral infarction of my own, or perhaps by the advance the publisher offered me, I wrote a guidebook about the whole of Japan, in which I had this to say of Hirosaki: "Hirosaki (population 175,000) is an attractive city, famous for its late-blooming cherries, for its apple blossom, and for the state of preservation of its small, elegant castle, completed in 1610. Hirosaki also stages a *Neputa Matsuri* in the first week of August, at once less spectacular, less tourist-oriented and more imbued with the solemn, warlike spirit of the north country than its larger counterpart in the prefectural capital. The Hirosaki festival features the appearance on the streets of the *Tsugaru Joppari Daiko* (the Drum to Rouse the Passions of Tsugaru), said to be the largest drum in Japan. Hirosaki is also the production center for a colorful and not inexpensive form of lacquerware."

Cerebral infarction or not, I find it embarrassing now that I could think of nothing more compelling to say about my favorite Japanese city—one where, three hundred years ago, I am supposed to have been born—than that smattering of gazetteerery which leaves out everything important. Not a word about Hirosaki's citizens, for example (the "solemn, warlike spirit of the north country" is as much hyperbole as Dazai's "laughingstock of the world"). And even its value as gazetteerery is diminished by the fact that I have managed to omit all the hotels and ryokans in the city, as well as Saishoin Temple (a five-story pagoda built in 1672), which has been designated an Important Cultural Property and is therefore formidably visitable. I could stretch a point and make Dazai's excuse—that my inability to describe the place properly has to do with my having been born there—though the numen might take a dim view of this. Or I could pretend to be fobbing the guidebook reader off—as the Oga villagers fob off the would-be intruder on their

Namahage—by misdirecting his attention in the hope that he will stay away and leave the place to me.

. . . I had crossed over the tracks by the footbridge and emerged from the old station, that first time ten or eleven years before, into a crisp October afternoon. Where the new pink-walled hotel now stands, there had been a wide pavement curving off to the left of the empty, dusty station square, and just before the curve had stood a little wooden shed with a notice on its roof that said Ryokan Information. So I squeezed myself through its tiny doorway and hunched over its cramped counter that was cluttered with pamphlets and slips of paper that had telephone numbers scrawled across them and asked the woman to book me a ryokan room. I wanted an old ryokan, I said. One with character. An old Japanese-style inn. Yes, that's right. No, I didn't want a business hotel. A ryokan. Just for a single night.

"Oh, and would you like a really nice place? A special place, with a big garden, right by Hirosaki castle?"

"That's exactly what I would like," I said.

So the woman wrote a name on a piece of paper and said, "All the taxi drivers know it."

And the driver of the taxi I got into didn't know it, so I directed him: "It's right by the castle."

As we drove slowly along the road, I saw a tiled roof and a high wall with clipped bushes and a carefully tended pine tree behind it, and said: "That's the place. Drop me there."

"You certainly know your way around," the driver had said.

This time, ten or eleven years later, I came into the city on foot from the west, but as always the castle was the landmark I made for and, as always, I seemed to know by instinct which of the narrow roads would take me there.

"Well, well, it's been a long time!" they said at the ryokan, smiling with pleasure as I sat in the entrance unlacing my boots.

"Not since I came up for the neputa. Five years would it be? Or four? Or six?"

"And that was such a fine piece you wrote about us in the—what was it?—the *Shukan Asahi*."

A while before, a weekly magazine had asked me to contribute to a series called "My Favorite Inn" and I had written about this one; or rather I hadn't. I had written about returning from the wedding in Hokkaido and the loud-speakers at the station saying "Hirosekiiiii!" and about the old blind spirit medium at the festival at Osorezan who, when I had given her my hand to hold, had stroked it and rocked from side to side and murmured:

". . . Ah, you're a foreigner."

"Yes," I'd told her, "but I can speak Japanese."

"Of course you can," she had whispered, her neck lolling forward in the heat and the midges settling in her hair. "You haven't always been a foreigner, you see. Three hundred years ago you were born up here in the north. . . ." She had stroked my hand and leant back into the dim tent and her voice had risen to a high sing-song. "In a town called Hirosaki . . ."

They had given the ryokan a page to itself when they collected the series into a book, though I hadn't even mentioned its name.

"Such a fine piece of writing it was!"

"Oh, that bit of hack work, do you mean?"

The old okami-san of the ryokan bowed and an elderly kimonoed maid led me past three younger maids who were standing in the long corridor waiting to serve at a plumbers' party, and showed me to a suite of two eight-mat rooms furnished with a lacquered table and screens, calligraphy on the walls, a kimono stand, and a television without a coinbox.

"Ooooo! Your hands are cold," the maid said, helping me off with my stinking shirt. "Do you want a beer?"

"Yes, I do."

"Your shirt button's come off," she said, picking it up from the tatami and placing it with care on the lacquered table. "I'll sew it on for you when the plumbers' party's over."

She brought me a beer that was cold enough to make my head hurt, and found me flicking through Dazai.

"Ooooo! You're a real scholar!" Our hands brushed again as she set a hot towel in front of me on its bamboo cradle. "And your hands are still cold. I'd better run your bath. . . ."

That night there was a violent storm, and I lay in my futon staring up at the ceiling and at the suddenly luminous screens that surrounded me. The scroll on the wall with its three curving ideograms looked jarring and white in the lightning, like a message flashed at sea: *Shin* something *Kei*, it said. The first ideogram meant "new." The third meant "to rejoice." But the second was so expertly written that it was almost impossible to read. The lightning sizzled, and the scroll turned so white for a second that it appeared transparent. *Gai*, was it? *Shin Gai no Kei*: The End of Life Is a Joyful Beginning. For some, I suppose. The numen would chuckle. The crash of the thunder made me think that all the rocks in the garden were erupting.

⁂

The last time I visited Hirosaki I had come to see the neputa. Nowhere in *Tsugaru* does Dazai mention this festival, perhaps because it was suppressed in wartime or because he couldn't think of anything rude to say about it. Matsuoka and I had sat drinking in a bar on the first night of that month of August and the huge lanterns—carnival floats the width of the street and the height of third-story windows, painted with pictures of heroes, demons, goddesses, furies, creatures out of legend and T.V.—had trundled slowly by in the rain, like a funeral procession on another planet.

Donko donko dondoko don. The drums had been muffled by the downpour but there was no mistaking their solemnity. In Aomori, where the largest such festival takes place (*nebuta* there; *neputa* here) the drums, it is said, are those that accompany an army returning victorious from the battlefield, which is why, in Aomori, there is dancing and whirling and shouting as the nebuta are wheeled through the streets: *Rassse! Rassse! Rassse! Raaa!* But in Hirosaki the drums are those that accompany an army on its way to war, when the outcome is far from certain and, if there is feasting, it is not for the living. So there is no dancing in Hirosaki and the haulers of the neputa shuffle by without speaking, their straw sandals sloshing in the rain, and the whir of the generators that power the bulbs inside the lanterns is like the hum-ming of absurdly bloated flies.

I had stood outside the bar with Matsuoka and watched them pass, cov-ered with vinyl sheets. We were drinking cups of Shiraume (White Plum) and the rain was slopping into them. The rain was the tail end of Typhoon 12 and it had been teeming down on the streets of Hirosaki for two days and nights. In Hokkaido, fifty miles away, four people had died in landslides and floods and another four were missing. *Yaaaa yadooo. Yaaaa yadooo.* That was Hirosaki's chant, sober and slow and falling.

"Look how different they are," said Matsuoka, "when they're coming towards you and when they're going away. When they're coming towards you, they hide the drums that follow them, so the sound appears to be com-ing out of the mouths of the painted warriors on them. Then, when they pass and the drums appear, you can see on the back of each of the neputa, very different from the front, a painted figure, sometimes a woman, perhaps a ghost, always alone. The approach of the neputa is very exciting. But is there anything sadder, I wonder, than the sight of the neputa retreating?"

The word *neputa* is usually written in the phonetic syllabary called *hira-gana*, not in tell-tale ideograms, so it is hard to say from what it derives. Some maintain that it comes from *nebusoku*, meaning lack of sleep—a curse of sul-try August—and the festival itself is sometimes called *nemuri nagashi*, the banisher of sleep. But I have also seen *neputa* written with three ideograms that mean craftiness, martial art, and great quantity, reinforcing the legend that it was Sakanoue no Tamuramaro who first employed these giant effi-gies to frighten and confuse the "barbarians" whom he had been sent by the imperial court to crush. Whatever the derivation, the drums are war drums; there is no more mistaking their purpose than if they were preceded along the streets by tanks. And if the celebrants shout and dance in Aomori city, it is because they have been spared, by someone's grace, to go on breathing for another year. When the festival is over, they say in Hirosaki, the mornings turn colder and autumn has come.

That year Matsuoka had driven me to Aomori to watch three of the largest of the nebuta floated out into the harbor at night on barges in a travel agency's version of the old-time launching of the lanterns of the dead. The harbor quays were crowded with sightseers and the police had erected rope barriers everywhere. But I had a press photographer's armband.

"Come on," I had said to Matsuoka. "We can tell them you're my assistant."

So he had slung my camera bag across his shoulder and we had stepped over one of the rope barriers and three uniformed policemen had descended on us like a rugby scrum.

"What the hell are you doing here?" an astonished policeman had said, recognizing Matsuoka.

"I'm assisting this photographer," Matsuoka had told him, smiling like a cherub.

Then there was the year I went up to Lake Akan in Hokkaido to cover an Ainu festival. A wind had sprung up in the late afternoon and the Ainu were reluctant to put out their canoe. They were supposed to drop some "holy" balls of waterweed back into the lake to mark the end of the celebrations, and the Japanese press photographers and television crews were beside themselves with rage at their reluctance.

"You'd better do it! Do it, for goodness sake! We haven't come all this way for nothing, you know! Go on, get on with it, I tell you! Do it!"

So one of the Ainu elders had clambered shakily into the small canoe, which was already a third full of water. And a younger Ainu had held the canoe by a short rope about a meter from the end of a wooden pier while it pitched and lolled in the choppy shallows and the elder, white-faced and expressionless, had pretended to conduct a religious rite.

"Get your hands up higher! *Oi,* shift your elbow! I can't see the balls of waterweed! Is that all there is to it, then? Do something else! Pray to the lake! Come on! Chant!"

When I couldn't stand this any longer I had wandered away and found a small bar in a back street by the lakeside and drunk a lot of sake with two bus drivers. Outside, all along the emptying quays, the wind tormented the green paper lanterns that were hung on wires for the festival, shaped like balls of waterweed. There were balls of waterweed in all the souvenir shops, too, in jars, in bags, in light bulbs like bottled ships.

"I wouldn't mind going to England, and then France," one of the bus drivers had told me. "Three days in each country would be enough. One for sightseeing, one for shopping, and one to do some serious drinking."

"D'you know, I've shot more then twenty bears in the hills around this lake," the master of the bar had said. "And just the other day I shot a deer. You're the first foreigner who's ever been in here, you realize. I bet you'd like some deer meat."

The master opened his refrigerator, which was packed from top to bottom with deer meat, and cut me half a dozen thin limp slices.

"Eat it raw. That's what we do."

So I had. And then I had taken the bus and ferry and train to Hirosaki and collapsed in Matsuoka's rice shop with a wrenching stomachache and been put to bed in an upstairs room by his wife and spent all night on his lavatory. . . .

"Do you remember the deer meat you ate that time?" Matsuoka would say to me next day when I saw him, laughing as he always laughed. "And the night we went and foxed the cops at Aomori harbor . . ."

. . . By early morning the storm had blown over and at seven o'clock the maid crept in, very quietly, to sew on my button.

At least my guidebook was right about the castle. Though much reduced in scale from what it once was, it remains unusually elegant and well preserved. The cherry blossoms had all fallen by the time I walked through the castle grounds, but their disappearance and the light rain that trailed after the night's storm did nothing to diminish the sense of permanence that the little keep of tiles and wood and plaster lends to its city. Two girls sat with their backs to me sketching a gatehouse in the rain. I knew they were sketching though I couldn't see their sketchbooks, because they were wearing berets. A taxi driver was explaining to some sightseers that only the walls of Japanese castles are made from large blocks of stone and that from earliest times Western fortresses were all built of concrete. A father, a mother, and their two sons were playing catch in the empty space where once a large dungeon had stood. "*Naisu* (Nice)!" the father shouted, not to his sons or to his wife but to himself. Underfoot, grey petals lay trampled, and several of the stalls that had served octopus and devil's tongue jelly to the blossom viewers stood shuttered and upended by the castle walls. But from a distance, this last Sunday in May, came the throb of the August drums being practiced, so I knew that, despite the drizzle and the dead cherries, all was more or less right with the world.

All was more or less right with Matsuoka too. The visitors' rituals passed off as I had expected. What a very long time I had stayed away! He was sure I'd left Japan and gone back home. Home. That was England, wasn't it? And look how his two sons had grown! Did I remember that night after eating deer meat when I'd slept upstairs with a stomachache? Ha ha! And how his younger son had played the festival flute to cheer me up? His elder son was helping with the rice business now. Yes, and—what a coincidence!—he was off to a rice millers' party that afternoon at the very ryokan where I was staying. Why hadn't I told them I was coming? Why wasn't I staying in the room upstairs? The younger son was still interested in music. He might become a piano tuner. And did I remember the little apple-shaped lacquer dishes I'd bought for his wife to thank her for putting me to bed? Here they were, look! She used them all the time. And where were the photographs I'd taken that night we'd gone up to see the nebuta at the harbor . . . ?

That night, as always, we went out to drink. First we went to Yamauta (Mountain Song), a place owned by Yamada Chisato, the shamisen player who, during the boom, had arranged the Hungarian dances and been a soloist with the Oriental Fantastic Orchestra. These projects, I was glad to see, had earned him the cash to open a pub in one of Hirosaki's prime locations, a two-minute walk from the station, just round the corner from the new pink-walled hotel. There, each night now, Yamada slopped around in his T-shirt and brown plastic sandals, his longish hair uncombed, his belly protruding over his belt, and played the large *taiko* drum or the shamisen, or nothing if he was feeling grumpy.

Matsuoka introduced me as a connoisseur and I was so excited (since I owned four of Yamada's records, including the Hungarian dances and the rotten concerto) that I spilt the draft beer I had just bought for Yamada all over a customer's spinach.

"No one wants to record me now," Yamada moaned. "It's not like the old days."

But he played. And Matsuoka, who was dressed in his usual nipping-round-the-corner-for-a-drink outfit of jacket just back from the dry cleaners, stiffly starched shirt, freshly polished shoes, pocket handkerchief, and impeccably knotted tie, pursed his lips and narrowed his eyes and five times during the course of the performance expressed outrage at Yamada's footwear:

"Sandals! Plastic sandals! It's an insult to his customers!"

"But he hasn't lost his touch. Listen!"

The clangs and purrs of "Jonkara Bushi" filled the pub with its empty tables.

"Sandals! Plastic sandals!"

Then we went to a karaoke bar called Kokoro ("Heart," "Soul," "Feeling," "Spirit") where the mama not only remembered me from my visit at the time of the neputa, but could recall every song she had ever heard me sing.

"Sing 'Journey in the Driven Snow,' " she demanded. "You're so good at the *Ahh-eee-yaaahhs*."

So I sang, to the accompaniment of throbbing brass:

When I play the shamisen,
I skin my hands to the bone.
When I have no plectrum,
I make do with a comb. . . .
Ahh-eee-yaaahh! Ahh-eee-yaaahh!

"And he was wearing plastic sandals," I heard Matsuoka tell the mama through grimly pursed lips. Matsuoka is a stickler for form. Watching the neputa one night, he had grown irritated that the flautists were playing the wrong melody. There are three melodies to accompany the Hirosaki neputa: one for setting out, one for resting, and one for coming home. And the flautists that night, Matsuoka insisted, were playing the coming home melody for resting and the resting melody for setting out.

"Perhaps his feet ache," suggested the mama, demonstrating very nicely the virtue for which her bar is named.

An old woman poked her head round the door with a basket of crabs to sell.

"She doesn't catch them," Matsuoka explained. "She buys them cheap when the market closes."

And while this was going on, a customer in a suit and tie made a large performance of clearing his throat and mopping his face and scrutinizing me out of the corner of his eye, and then picking up the microphone to sing "Going Along the Road":

Nightless and morningless, floating grass—
As tears of moonlight fall where I lay,
Though but in dreams, ah, take this hand,
And steal my sleeping breath away. . . .

The crab woman vanished; the mama applauded. So I took the microphone back and sang "The Izu Dancing Girl":

Bid me no more goodbyes as you weep,
Ah! my little dancer,
For my boat is set to sail;
I cannot stay to answer. . . .

The mama applauded louder, and gave me a dish of peanuts. So the customer took the microphone back and sang about a rainy night in Nagasaki. So I took it back and sang about the Straits of Tsugaru in winter. So the customer took it back and sang about how he had left his heart in a Kyoto bar. And watching the veins stand out like young bamboos on the side of the customer's neck, I couldn't help recalling Dazai's remark about the gidayu singers of Hirosaki who, "in their concentrated attempts to master an insignificant art form, go to such absurd lengths that the sweat flows in torrents from their brows." But mastering an art form was the last thing on anyone's mind that evening. All we wanted was the mama's praise. And in vying for it we were like spoilt twins contending for their mother's attention (that *mama* has become a generic term for female Japanese publicans is no sort of accident).

I drank two more bottles of beer and sang, "The East China Sea is a manly sea!" and thought, well, if this is a fool's paradise, there are worse things to be than a fool. Where else in the world can a forty-odd-year-old family man go and sit on a high stool and be bottle-fed, have a shiny noise-making toy thrust into his hand, be flattered and cajoled into showing off his musical talents even when they don't exist, be listened to with bated breath the moment he opens his pouting mouth, be showered with compliments, and—best of all—be nightly reassured that these are pleasures he can never outgrow. At home his wife may demand that he assume a sobering semblance of adulthood. He may be obliged to discipline his delinquent children, or say something other than *yes* to his boss, or perform once a month in the futon, or lay his pay packet, together with summer and winter bonuses, unopened on the kitchen table. But here in his favorite karaoke bar he can bask forever in his mama's affection. And his mama will never scold him or nag him or tire of him or pack him off to school. It's a fool's paradise. There's no doubt about that. I had quite a refreshing time.

Next morning I tramped out of Hirosaki along the busy road to Owani. The evening had ended on an uplifting note with Matsuoka, still a stickler for form, outlining the prodigious number of ways he knew of cheating at mahjong. And the morning had begun with the okami-san of the ryokan charging me for one night instead of two on account of the immortality I had brought her in the pages of the *Shukan Asahi*. So the day boded fine and, though the road to Owani crawled first through the truck-clogged suburbs and then along a bypassed but still noisy stretch of National Highway Seven, the rain had stopped, the morning was hot, and for a little while I followed a small elderly lady with a red-tinted bird's-nest hairstyle that increased her height by about a third, and wondered whose mama she might be.

Between Hirosaki and Owani bits of a half-formed, half-lapsed industrial estate sprawled in an unsightly fringe on the edge of the apple orchards and their *Appuru Rodo* (Apple Road), a boulevard touted to sightseers that curled away from the factories towards the smoky slope of Iwaki. In a school playground a marching band was practicing "Yankee Doodle" and from the loudspeakers in a car repair shop came the insistent refrain of a pop song posing the question that, for think-tank "Japanologists" and professors with Japan Foundation grants, has entirely superseded such hoary old chestnuts as: What is God? Why is war? Where do we go when we die? and so on. Like a singing edition of one of the scholarly volumes that clog the shelves of Japanese bookshops, it asked in a tone that brooked no ordinary argument: *Nihonjin-tte nan na no? Nihonjin-tte nan na no?* "What Are We Japanese?"

I had a lunch of grilled eel and draft beer in a restaurant where, once the midday rush of factory workers was over, the elderly master settled down to watch a week's worth of videotaped professional wrestling, fast-forwarding the advertisements and leaning closer to the screen with a quizzical smile whenever—as happened about every ninety seconds—a foreign wrestler dragged his Japanese opponent into the ringside seats by his hair. I wanted to pay my bill and get out onto the road again but it was more than the master could do to wrench himself away from his private mayhem. His eyes were glazed, his stick-thin knees and elbows and crotch were prickly with pleasure. So I paid his daughter and, when the door whooshed open, the song was still churning out of the repair shop speakers: "What Are We Japanese? What Are We Japanese?" It rang in my ears as I stood by the roadside releasing some beer from my think tank.

"Hello! Hello! O.K. everybody!" giggled some seven-year-olds in English when they spotted me crossing the railway track into their sleepy little hot-spring town. Then they vanished at full pelt down a back street in case I grabbed them and crammed them into my mouth, mistaking We Japanese for a foodstuff.

I found an elegant seventy-year-old ryokan that advertised itself as having a stone bath. The maids at the entrance were extremely polite and skipped away to inquire of the okami-san whether any rooms might conceivably be free. The okami-san appeared in a very expensive kimono with a jaw full of gold teeth and a pair of reading spectacles on a thin chain to match. She said:

"Yes, a room might conceivably be free but can you conceivably speak Japanese?"

"Oh, tell me What You Are?" I begged her. No, actually what I said was, "Yes, I can."

"Welcome, then," said the expensively toothed okami-san.

"And suppose I couldn't speak Japanese," I said, my think tank bursting as I sat on the doorstep removing my boots. "In that case wouldn't you have let me in?"

The okami-san frowned and smiled with her teeth and said, "Well, we should never get on, should we, if we didn't speak each other's language?"

Get on with what? I thought, hauling my rucksack up the narrow staircase and setting it down in a pleasant second-story room that overlooked a river. Each window frame and screen in the building, each visible cornice, each joint and plank had been carefully restored, the okami-san explained before I had had a chance to remove my stinking socks, in a style of carpentry which was all but extinct and which had strenuously tested her powers of discrimination, not to mention the extent of her bank balance. The okami-san had chosen all the wood herself and had personally supervised the carpenters and, clearly keen that I should appreciate what worlds would have been closed to me if I hadn't spoken her language, she gave me a guided tour of the whole ryokan, including the third story no longer in use, the other guest rooms, all of them empty (perhaps the guests had failed the entrance exam), and the bathroom, where a nude stone nymph stood cemented to a plinth above the gushing tap in a style which was all but extinct. Then, when I had finally taken off my socks and hung them next to the calligraphy, the okami-san sent me up a cup of instant coffee (a gesture that, at one stroke, reinforced my welcome, ensured that we "got on," and underscored my foreignness) and the maid who stayed to stir it for me advised me to stroll out and see the azalea festival, an annual twelve-day event of which this afternoon was the last.

The pathway that straggles across the beetling hillside which overlooks the little town had been hung with strings of pink and blue lanterns and, all along it, between trees bearing loudspeakers out of which came tape-recorded love songs, deep pink and purple azaleas were in bloom, some just beginning to fade. At the start of the path stood a secluded cluster of little shrines, once thatched, now roofed with tin. And at the other end, in a cage far too small for them, a couple of black bears shuffled and fretted, ignored by the two or three blossom viewers and abandoned by the stallholders who had all gone home.

Owani is a compact and drowsy town, and you can see all there is to see of it from up on the hillside. It stands unruffled in the curl of its river and looks both as though it had known better days and as though it didn't really give a damn. It was here that his mother brought Dazai for a month during the winter of 1929–30 to recuperate after his first suicide attempt. His family had made a habit of bringing him here as a child too, and he seems to have retained a comparatively nostalgic feeling for the place. Towards the end of *Tsugaru* he considers spending a night at Owani but gives up the idea, citing lack of funds and an itch to get the whole traveling business over with and be back in Tokyo as quickly as he can. At one point, early in the book, he worries that Owani may, like the more famous spa at Asamushi, have "coarsened itself by gorging on the stale leftovers of the city," but he finds cause for optimism by reminding himself that "the roads from Tokyo to Owani are far worse than those to Asamushi," that "the people here still cling to the old Tsugaru way of life," and that Owani's proximity to Hirosaki castle, so well preserved itself, must in some unspecified way guarantee the little town a form of metaphysical protection. "I like to imagine," he writes with no sign of tongue in cheek, "that were it not for Hirosaki castle, Owani would probably drink itself sick on the dregs left by the city."

If anything, Owani seems to have had the opposite experience. The ryokan where Dazai had stayed as a child and as a recuperating suicide had been pulled down, the okami-san told me in a tone implying considerable gratitude for his not having stayed at hers. The development of a ski resort does not seem to have had an excessive impact on the town's liveliness either. Nor, evidently, does the annual azalea festival, for all the pink and blue paper lanterns and tinny love songs and captive bears.

One of the things I've always admired about hot springs is the juggling act they play with their patrons' widely varying expectations. For example, Dazai's being brought to Owani as a child was on account of his mother's consistently poor health, and a fair number of Japan's hot-spring patrons, especially those over fifty, still take the waters because of their reputation for easing physical complaints. Dazai's recuperating here after his first suicide attempt illustrates the reputation that hot springs enjoy for easing mental complaints as well. In the past—Yamada, the master of the Senjojiki minshuku, had told me—Tsugaru fishermen would take their families to local hot springs at least twice a year and stay for up to a week. In their line of work, he explained, "the cold got so deep into their bones that they had to sweat it out from time to time or else it would kill them." And though the transformation of so many of Japan's hot springs from quiet convalescent centers to pricey pleasure spots has lessened the ability of ordinary working families to take advantage of their restorative powers, Yamada's story underlines the health-giving properties upon which a significant part of their popularity has rested.

Significant, but only a part. For the pleasure seeker has benefited from hot springs quite as much as the invalid or the neurotic or the bone-chilled seaman. Like most Asians, the Japanese have not traditionally seen much to entice them in the seaside. And the attractions of the mountains—skiing and climbing and hiking and villa-building—lay more or less unrecognized until the last few decades of the nineteenth century, when early Western residents began to exploit them. The traditional destination of the Japanese pleasure seeker has, more often than not, been a hot spring. So, side by side with their reputation for enhancing health has grown up a reputation for endangering it through various forms of overindulgence: financial, intestinal, and sexual. According to a famous folk song of Aizu, an apocryphal person called Ohara Shosuke lost his fortune due to three causes: "sleeping in the morning, drinking in the morning, and lounging about in hot baths in the morning"—precisely the modes of behavior that a spell at a hot spring encourages.

And there is a fourth mode. Long before the inclusion on the pleasure seeker's itinerary of purple-lighted strip clubs and darkened cabarets with hostesses who tweak their customers' penises under the tables, the place of these institutions was filled by a species of professional known, euphemistically, as a "hot-spring geisha." Geishas, the coffee-table books and up-market glossies and thoughtful T.V. documentaries never tire of telling us, have no truck whatever with crude fleshly pleasures. They are highly skilled entertainers who specialize in shamisen ballads, exquisite dances, elegant repartee, party games with matchsticks, and delicate liaisons with incumbent prime ministers. To confuse them with women who grant sexual favors to lesser mortals for money is to be as ignorant and misinformed as were the occupying American GIs who, shortly after their arrival in 1945, are said to have congregated on the Ginza and set up cries of "We want geesha girls!" Imagine the indignation of the local populace! Why, these barbarians wouldn't know a skilled shamisen performer from a hula dancer! Oh woe, the coarseness of foreign education! "Geesha girls" indeed! And then, to smooth their ruffled national pride, the more affluent among the local populace likely took themselves off to a hot spring for a bath, a drink, and a fuck.

But, yes, what I liked was the accommodating mix: the rural spa in the middle of a wood with its one old ryokan and outdoor bath; the cluster of inns halfway up a mountainside with a tub that stank of sulfur and a party room echoing to the claps and songs of a group of townhall workers celebrating their summer bonuses; the entire hot-spring town with its ryokan on every corner, its public bathhouses and sleazy alleys; the fifteen-story stuccoed hotel with its mirrored tub the size of a circus ring and its floor show staffed with Filipina dancers who might sit at your table between acts in order to make your better acquaintance. And the fact that to these stuccoed hotels and sleazy towns came families with small children to spend a Friday and Saturday night, and they would sleep in the room next door to yours and leave on Sunday perfectly innocent of any such acquaintances having been made. It is a marvelous and complex institution, the Japanese hot spring: livelier when the bathhouses and inns all encouraged mixed bathing, though that fine habit has been in decline since the end of the last century when it first occasioned the tut-tuts of stuffy Western missionaries. But you still find places where the habit survives; a bath for both sexes, for all ages, for most tastes, for every kind of reason . . .

I thought about these things while wallowing by myself in the chaste bathroom of my ryokan at Owani, peering through the steam at the nude stone nymph. After dinner a small old man in working clothes with the gruffest manner and roughest accent I had so far encountered, even in Tsugaru, came to lay out my futon and asked me if I liked hot springs. It's funny the number of people who ask questions like that. I've been sitting in the foyer of a Japanese cinema, ticket in hand, and been asked if I like films. I've been lounging at a bar drinking my way through my fifth large bottle of beer and been asked if I like beer. I've been slurping down my second bowl of noodles at a roadside stall and asked if I like noodles.

"No, I detest hot springs," I should have said. "That's why I'm paying to stay here." What I actually told the gruff old man was, "Yes, I like hot springs very much."

"Do you have hot springs in your own country?"

"Not really. The Romans tried to make a go of them about two thousand years ago. But once they'd left, the British went back to a quick splash once a week on Saturdays."

"If you like hot springs, you should go to Aoni."

"Where?"

"Aoni."

Matsuoka had mentioned Aoni. It was one of the last of the real ones, he had told me. One lonely ryokan right up in the hills and, why, they still used oil lamps. . . .

"Where's Aoni?" I said.

"I don't know," said the old man.

"How do you write the name?"

"I don't know. But I could find out for you. I could draw you a map."

I assumed he meant in the morning, and so I had come down to wallow in the empty bath. But after five minutes the gruff old man slid the bathroom door open and peered through the steam.

"I've drawn your map."

"I'll be out in a bit."

Two minutes later he slid the door open again.

"Aren't you out yet? I've drawn your map."

So I dried myself and put on my sticky yukata and followed the old man back to my room, where he spread a small crumpled page torn from a pocket diary on my pillow and pointed with a broken fingernail at two scrawled characters that meant "Blue Burden." I suppose they referred to the bunches of wild herbs and roots that a country villager might once upon a time have brought back from the hills on a pole across his shoulder.

I compared the old man's pencil lines with the roads and contours on my printed map and found "Blue Burden" in ideograms so small that I could scarcely see them. It was well off my planned route, through two valleys and across two high passes, maybe thirty kilometers away.

"Have you got a car?"

"No, I'm on foot."

"It would take you all day. Maybe it would take longer. I don't know anybody who's ever walked it."

"Is it worth it?"

"Oh, it's the real thing. It's one of the last. They don't have electricity. It's just a single ryokan in the hills. There's nothing else like it. They use oil lamps."

"It's off my route."

"You wouldn't regret it. I know you wouldn't. You'd want to stay there forever. I wouldn't mind staying there forever myself. It's just like. . . . "

"What?"

"It's just like home."

5
Home

❧

I t was a bright day and, once I had crossed the highway, the narrow road
began to climb sharply through the last of the apple orchards. All along the
highway the advertisements had been for apples, and the painted railings that
flanked the highway had iron apples wrought into them. The shops and
restaurants offered apples for sale, the factories all processed apples, and in
the smallest of the sloping orchards a man on a stepladder pinched the last
apple blossom from the branches. Beneath the steps of his ladder the orchard
grass had just been cut, and the smell of it, on this last day of May, told me
spring had turned to summer.

I sat and drank a beer on the bench outside a little grocer's shop where the
old shopkeeper had shifted his apple cartons to make a space for me. The
shop was in the middle of nowhere and the old man who kept it stood in his
doorway and told me that Aoni was at the end of nowhere.

"There's nothing at Aoni. Nothing at all. Although, in recent years, a lot of students and young people have found their way up there. Goodness knows what for. I suppose it's an Aoni boom."

I hoped not, I said, and shouldered my pack and tramped off up the steepening slope, but the old man chased me with the ten-yen coin I had forgotten to claim on the empty.

Then the apple orchards ended, and the high paddies ended, and beyond them stood a forest of pines. Higher still, what had looked from a distance like a mess of scrub turned out to be young firs and spruce planted like pegs in checkerboard holes on the logged and wasted hillside. Behind me, wreathed in white cloud, Iwaki squatted like a stump, and below it lay the hidden pool of whiter Hirosaki. At the first of the passes stood a signboard showing the hot springs of the region, but the plywood had rotted and come apart in the rain leaving a gaping hole in the center of the board, so that I literally stood in the middle of nowhere and all roads led to nowhere's end.

I crossed the pass and came after midday into the valley of Oguni. All along the road I heard the scuffling of animals, but it was always the hooded women of the villages foraging for bamboo shoots and bracken. Then I emerged onto the new highway that runs down to Lake Towada, and found a cluster of abandoned-looking shacks in a little glade set back from it, and in one of the shacks I stopped to eat a dish of cold noodles.

"Is this a restaurant?" I had to ask, hauling open the dusty glass door at the top of three crumbling concrete steps.

"Sort of," a woman replied, coming out of the room in which a grey-haired man lay sprawled on his belly on the tatami mats in front of a babbling television, sound asleep. The woman made me the noodles and sat at the formica-topped table with me and poured my beer. No cars stopped, no customers came in; outside, in the other shacks, nothing stirred, and in the little glade there was no sound but the growl of traffic on the new highway.

What was the name of this place, I asked.

"No one rightly knows; there are different names," the woman said.

Well, how did the post office know where to deliver letters?

"Oh, they'd been doing it for so long it never crossed their minds. Some people say it's called *Tsubakura* (Swallow) and some say the proper name is

Kiriake Yamashita (Where the Mist Lifts Below the Mountains). I've lived here all my life and I'm not sure of the right answer. At any rate, there's only three houses lived in: us, the shop, and the hot-spring lodge. The rest belong to city people who come out just for the summer weekends." She pointed to one. "That's Baba-sensei's. He's the medical doctor at Hirosaki University. Sometimes he brings his American friends, so we've gone quite international."

She laughed, the lovely self-deprecating laugh that I'd heard so often in Tsugaru.

"And now you've come. What are you doing here?"

I told her I was on my way to Aoni.

"I remember the old man who built the inn there," she said. "I saw him once when I was a child. He was a poet." She poured my beer and looked at me. "Have you heard the story?"

No, I hadn't heard it.

"He was a poet," she said. "And he was also a leper. He liked to get away into the hills by himself and one day, quite by chance, he discovered that the hot spring at Aoni seemed good for his disease. It didn't cure it; nothing would in those days. But it stopped it from getting any worse. So he built a house on the bank of the stream and, when he died, the house became an inn. They still use oil lamps there, you know. . . .

"This valley has changed so much in my lifetime, but they still use oil lamps at Aoni. When I was a child and you crossed the pass and came down into this valley you used to be able to smell the difference in the air. The air here was so fresh and clear. Now they've put the highway through and there's the bridge and the tunnel and it's all changed. And people would come from miles away to see the sunsets in this valley. They still come out from the city to see them—the people with the weekend houses—and they all say how wonderful the sunsets are. But the sunsets are not like they were when I was a child. It's all changed. But at Aoni they still use lamps. . . ."

I stood up and paid for the beer and noodles and then—I don't know why—I asked the woman if she had any children. She drew her shoulders into her body and looked down at the table and, with a tight, quick shiver, shook her head.

So that afternoon I walked to Aoni. And all along the twisting mountain road there were new signs advertising the inn there—*Rampu to Yukemuri no Sato* (The Home of Steam and Oil Lamps)—and each of the signs had a painted lamp on it and the exact distance remaining in meters. Behind me, far below in the valley of the highway, lay a grey-green river, clogged by a new dam with bulldozers clanging away on either side of it. And from the second pass of the day, which I reached at four o'clock, I could see Aomori's other great peak, Hakkoda, rising dead ahead of me, its summit tormented by nervous cloud and its slopes still patchy with snow. Then I turned off the empty road onto an unsurfaced track that fell away to follow a roaring, undammed river, and way below me, deep in the gorge that this river had taken millennia to carve, I glimpsed the rooftiles of Aoni.

By half past four I was standing in front of the lodge looking at the concrete foundations of a new building that was being laid out next to it. The tubby woman who met me at the door gave me a small glass of apple juice before I had unlaced my boots and told me off for not telephoning.

"I didn't realize you had a phone," I said, "I thought . . ."

"Of course we've got a phone. We could have sent the minibus to pick you up. Where have you come from?"

"From Owani. But I've walked. I thought . . . I mean to say, I wanted . . ."

"That's right. You've walked all the way from the bus stop."

"No, I mean I've walked from Owani."

"From Owani! What! You've walked from Owani." And while the tubby woman set off to tell everybody in sight that I had walked from Owani, a young man dressed like a trainee priest in dark blue baggy trousers and a matching tunic ushered me towards a hatch in the corridor wall, where another young man, identically dressed, issued me a yukata, a sash, a towel, and a pillow case—all of which I signed for—asked me what I wanted to drink with my evening meal, and then told me I would occupy room 203, to which billet I was smartly marched.

Aoni was not at all as I had imagined it. It was not old, it was not thatched, and, far from resembling the house of a poet, the main two-story building in which the guests were lodged reminded me of a cross between an army barracks and a reform school. But the ceiling of my room was stained in two places with soot from an actual oil lamp, my single unscreened window looked out onto an unmolested hillside, and, after changing into a yukata that was ten inches too short for me and tip-toeing along the undecorated corridor in case a warder should suddenly appear and admonish me for being improperly dressed, I saw that there was, after all, an outdoor bath set among rocks and palisaded with bamboo, so I picked my way towards it across the pebbles, grateful for large mercies.

I sat in the hot bath and watched the sun go down through the cracks in a canopy made of woven bamboo. One other bather was at the bath when I arrived, a man who didn't speak to me and looked the other way when I lowered myself in to join him, and then climbed out and beat a hasty retreat. Now there was no one, and no distraction but the splashing of the little river beyond the rocks and, churning through my sweaty head, the words of the song that I had seen a few minutes before on one of Aoni's specially printed chopstick covers which I had stolen from a used dinner tray in the corridor while being led under guard to my billet:

> *Just the two of us together,*
> *With an oil lamp in our hands,*
> *As we cross the hanging bridge,*
> *Ah, happiness complete!*
> *Come, let us cleanse our weary souls*
> *In water heated to perfection,*
> *At Aoni, in the north country,*
> *At the inn of the lamps.*

It is not such a feat to remember the words of a song like that after one reading, nor even to be able to hum the tune without ever having heard it. The phrases, melodies, and sentiments of such songs—and there are hundreds upon hundreds of them—are entirely interchangeable and, once you have mastered the basic pattern, you are set up for life. Change *oil lamp* to *mushroom basket*, *hanging bridge* to *mountain pass*, keep *north* as it is, change *lamps* to *mists* and you can register another copyright.

I stayed in the outdoor bath till the light had gone and the first mosquitoes began to whine and, when I arrived back at my billet, I found that the oil lamp had already been lit and my meager dinner had been laid out on a very small tray together with the two bottles of beer that I had been asked to order at the serving hatch when I arrived, an arrangement that saved both staff and guest the unnecessary bother of energy-wasting contact. So I ate dinner alone, listening to the river, and translating in my head the second of the three verses printed on the chopstick cover:

At the hearth—how good it smells!
The river trout are grilling.
Ah, must we say our fond goodbyes
To this mountain inn?
Two nights we've stayed here, man and wife;
Now all our future nights we'll dream
Of Aoni, in the north country,
Of the inn with the lamps.

Mmm, I thought, changing *goodbyes* to *farewells*, there doesn't seem to be any heat. I looked around and discovered that there wasn't. And this oil lamp, I thought, is too dim to read by. I opened Dazai and found that it was. So the best plan, I decided, getting to my feet and shivering, was to waste some energy going downstairs in search of family hearth and happiness complete. So I went downstairs, and sat on a bench by myself in the chilly hallway, sipping a beer that the tubby woman brought me, while in the party room next door the rest of the lodge's staff celebrated with a great deal of food and drink and chatter the successful conclusion of their "mountain vegetable fair," an event that had ended that afternoon with the departure of the minibus full of guests. I finished the beer, ordered another, and bent over my notebook to translate the third and last of the chopstick verses:

In his deep Tsugaru accent,
An old man gestures as he talks—
His eyes roll, his body sways—
Of how he hunted bears.

And as we raise our cups together
A human spirit warms my heart
At Aoni, in the north country,
At the inn of the lamps.

Or should it be *champs*? Or *damps* or *cramps* . . .

"You can come and sit in here if you want to," called the wiry white-haired owner of the lodge, who was dressed like his staff in the trainee monk's outfit. He was lying on the tatami propped on one elbow and picking his teeth.

"I don't want to intrude," I said.

"That's all right; we've finished dinner."

But huge dishes of sliced raw fish and whole cooked fish and mountain vegetables covered both long tables.

"Help yourself. There's plenty left over."

"You must be having a boom," I said.

"Oh, can't complain. Can't complain. How d'you like it here?"

"I liked the bath."

"There are only three outdoor baths in Aomori prefecture and ours is one of them. How d'you like the inn?"

" 'The Home of Steam and Oil Lamps,' " I said.

"Ha ha ha!"

" 'Happiness complete!' "

The owner removed his toothpick from his mouth and smiled a smile compounded equally of complicity and condescension, such as you might find on the face of an encyclopedia salesman.

"You know, I've studied philosophy," he said. "I've read Schopenhauer. I've read Socrates. I'm not an uneducated man. I ran my own business for thirty years. A construction business up in Sapporo. I was the boss."

He leaned over to fill my sake cup and said, quite loudly, "I was the boss."

"Are you related to the poet? The man who built the inn here?"

"Good grief, no," he said, leaning back on his elbow and surveying the eight male members of his staff who were drinking sake out of large glass tumblers and listening with half an ear. "I'm from Kuroishi, down the road. I went up to Hokkaido when I was young because there were more opportunities there. I came back here six years ago and I had it in mind to build a hot-spring inn. The place up here was falling apart. Ramshackle. There were no signposts or anything. It had been put up round about 1928 and virtually nothing had been done to it since. You can imagine the state of it, what with the years of wind and snow and total neglect. You can't leave a Japanese house to stand through that and expect it to be habitable. So, of course, I tore it down. And I built this lodge instead. Put in a phone and a generator. Got some young people up to work for me. Redid the bath. Started to advertise. But I kept the lamps. Ah ha, oh yes . . ."

It was his ace in the hole.

". . . I kept the lamps!"

One of his staff, a youngish man from Iwaki, thin and jut-chinned and fairly drunk, and dressed like everyone in the room but me in the dark blue trouser-and-tunic uniform that implied increasingly sinister things with every cup of sake I drank, dragged his cushion up to the opposite side of the table and said to me:

"What do you do for a living?"

"Oh, I write things," I replied, as uncomfortable as I always am when asked that rotten question.

"You write things. Oh yes? A writer, are you?"

"Umm."

"And what sort of 'things' do you write?"

"All sorts of things."

"Oh, all sorts of things! Well, what was your last book about? Or haven't you written any books?"

"Yes, I've written some books," I said. "The last one was a travel book."

"A travel book! Huh! That's the easiest sort of writing. That's not even writing; I mean not proper writing. You don't need any style or technique to write a travel book. You just jot down the things you happen to see."

"Wasn't Dazai's *Tsugaru* a travel book?" I asked.

"No, it wasn't, it wasn't," said the young man, confidently, as though it was a question he had pondered all his life. "That was a novel. That was real writing."

"O.K.," I said, and ate a slice of raw fish.

"And where do you come from, may I ask?"

"You may ask," I said. "I come from England."

"England! I see. And which country is easier to live in, England or Japan?"

"I can't really generalize," I said.

"I didn't ask you to generalize," the young man snapped. His face was red with drink and belligerence. "I just asked you a perfectly straightforward question."

"It's not so easy to sum up likes and dislikes."

"I didn't ask you about likes and dislikes. I asked you which country was easier to live in. Don't you understand plain Japanese?"

The owner, who had listened to all this smiling, giving his teeth an occasional pick, leaned across and refilled my cup and said, "You musn't mind; he's a little drunk."

"I don't mind," I said. "I came down for a chat."

The tubby woman who had served me the apple juice came in and plomped down on the cushion beside me, and for a second I thought the conversation might take a turn for the brighter: "You walked all the way from Owani," she might tell me.

But the owner rose with the toothpick in his mouth and bade me a very polite goodnight, and the tubby woman got up with a little puff of air and followed him to the door.

"Stay on and have your chat," the owner recommended.

"Goodnight," I said, and ate some bracken.

The owner disappeared. The woman followed. The jut-chinned man turned his back on me and began to speak broad fast dialect to a colleague; and a moment later they both rose, picked up the sake bottle and the plate of raw fish, carried them to the far end of the table and sat down to continue their celebration. So I took my cup and went to join the six remaining survivors of the party at the second long table, and for a while I listened, more or less ignored, and tried to pick up on the conversation. Twice I attempted a desperate tack.

"Don't you like songs?" I said chirpily, and "It must be nice living in a forest," and these prompts elicited about six syllables each, five of them grunts.

Two or three times we lifted our glasses in desultory toasts to international harmony.

"Kanpai."

"Umm, all right, kanpai."

But the magic circle had closed and, after twenty minutes, I rose and left and none of the commune said goodnight.

I turned the oil lamp down in my room and lay and listened to the crashing river. Once, I got up to use the lavatory and found that the river crashed directly beneath it, lending my squat the sensation of a balancing act, and inducing dreams in which the rocks and pebbles along the riverbed were all turds. In the morning I left earlier than usual and the tubby woman saw me off at the door. It was a bright day, Mount Hakkoda sparkled, and the checkerboard firs and spruces made the hills look as if they had been planted with bog brushes. I walked back down the long road to the bulldozers. From one of the spruces a cuckoo laughed.

Certainly, there are people who feel that Dazai's *Tsugaru* is more a "novel" than a "travelogue" or any other species of filed-and-labeled literature. And if you are inclined to regard autobiography as a sub-species of the filed-and-labeled "novel," you are pretty well bound to agree. But, of course, all travel writing in the first person is a kind of autobiography, the chief technical difficulty being to strike a manageable balance between the first-person seer and what he sees (or thinks he sees or pretends he sees), and the chief tonal pitfall being the too-overt transfiguration of a mundane trudge though the hills into a metaphor for something mind-popping and metaphysical: Zen and the Art of Wasting Boot Rubber.

There is a well-known photograph of Dazai taken in 1947, the year before his death. He sits in his usual author's get-up of kimono-cape worn over a thick work shirt and a thicker long-sleeved undervest at the heavy wooden table of a cheap-looking drinking place. On the table are two large bottles of beer and a small plate of food. A lighted cigarette rests on the edge of the table and is burning its way into the bare wood. Dazai's left hand hovers close to his half-full tumbler. The knuckles of his right hand support his cheek and he sits looking across the table towards a companion who is out of frame, with an appearance of listening attentively to what his companion is saying. We cannot see the whole of the table top, but on the part of it that we can see there is only one tumbler, one pair of chopsticks, one lighted cigarette. And this thought glides through the mind of the viewer as he contemplates the doleful eyes and pursed lips and uncombed hair: that the chair across the table from Dazai, upon which he has fixed his attention, is empty.

The same intense, often morbid introspection which led Dazai to cast himself, among his family and in his native region, as the eternal, ill-at-ease misfit-clown, resulted in a body of writing in which his own life is almost always the springboard of anecdote, character, and action, and the line between autobiography and invention—hazy at the best of times—disappears entirely. In this Dazai was, of course, not alone. Twentieth-century Japanese fiction has been characterized so strongly by a tendency on the part of authors to view themselves as the only legitimate objects of their readers' interest that the *shishosetsu* (the "I novel"), in which the author relates under the thinnest of fictional guises the doings, musings, and sayings of his all-absorbing self, might be said to represent its most significant and enduring form.

In *Tsugaru* Dazai makes no effort at all to hide the fact that the real subject of the book is him. Two of the book's most carefully treated concerns are Dazai's relationships with his family, particularly his elder brother, Bunji, and with the nursemaid who had cared for him until he was six years old and who had then vanished abruptly from his life. Much of the penultimate chapter describes Dazai's visit to his family house after a long absence enforced by Bunji. Bunji, having failed to dissuade Dazai from marrying his young geisha, had stipulated that if the marriage went ahead he would be barred from the house at Kanagi and, in November 1930, a few days before his second suicide attempt, Dazai's name had been removed from the Tsushima family register. Dazai had respected the arrangement for twelve years (it had been sweetened by his being set up as the head of a new family branch and by the regular dollops of cash that brother Bunji continued to send him) and had broken it only in October 1942 when he had taken his second wife and eighteen-month-old daughter to visit his mother who was seriously ill, and had found a warm welcome. Two months later he was in Kanagi again to attend his mother's funeral service. But the visit he describes in *Tsugaru* was the first in more than thirteen years that was not occasioned by an emergency, and Dazai felt—or pretended to feel—a good deal of uncertainty about how his elder brother in particular would receive him.

"About ten years ago," he remembers of Bunji, "we had walked down a rural lane in a Tokyo suburb, my brother silent and his back stooped . . . and I a few paces behind him, looking at his back and sobbing. . . . I doubt that my brother has ever forgiven me for that incident. Perhaps he never will, as long as he lives. A broken cup cannot be mended. No matter what you do to it, it will never be as before. The people of Tsugaru, even more than others, are a race of people who do not forget when their feelings have been hurt. I had thought at the time that I might never have another chance to go walking with my brother."

In the event, Dazai describes how, during this spring visit in 1944, he "burst in" on his brothers in an upstairs room at the family house and "apologized for not having kept in touch. They grunted and gave the slightest of nods," and then they became excessively polite, not to Dazai but to each other, which greatly increased his unease: "I felt," he says of his childhood home, "as though I were in the Palace of the Fairy Queen or on some other planet." Finally, they all set to and ate the crab that Dazai had brought them from Kanita, and his final comment on the reunion is a typical mixture of fatalism, melodrama, exaggeration, and self-pity: "The very thought of my Kanagi home makes me feel tired. True, but do I really have to put that down in writing? The gods spare no love for a man who goes burdened under the bad karma of having to sell manuscripts filled with details of his family in order to earn a living; they banish him from his birthplace. I'm afraid I am doomed to move from one drab Tokyo dwelling to another, wandering around aimlessly, longing for my native home in my dreams, until at last I die."

But even more crucial to the fictional-autobiographical interest of *Tsugaru* is the relationship that Dazai describes—and partly concocts—between himself and his old nursemaid, Koshino Take, a woman in her mid-forties at the time *Tsugaru* was written, who, in her teens, had looked after Dazai when he was between the ages of two and six. It was by no means unusual for a family as well-off and well-placed as the Tsushimas to employ a nursemaid for their child, particularly a tenth child—as Dazai was—born to a mother in poor health, and even before the arrival of Take he had been looked after by a succession of wet nurses. But the psychological effect of this policy on a child as imaginative and insecure as Dazai was bound to be a complex one, and the adult author, ever on the lookout for dramatic self-revelations with which to regale his eager readers, leapt at the chance offered by his sentimental journey home to develop the complications. The house into which Dazai was born had, counting servants, some thirty people living in it, and most of those people were women. They included—in addition to Dazai's mother—his great grandmother, his maternal grandmother, his four sisters, a widowed aunt, and the aunt's four daughters. The adult Dazai claims that he suffered from a childhood confusion as to which of the women in the house was really his mother, a confusion that grew at times, he says, into a belief that he had been lied to about her identity and that he was actually the son of someone else—his aunt, perhaps, or even Take, the two people with whom he had enjoyed the closest of his infant relationships. If such a suspicion really existed, the insecurity it wrought must have increased a dozenfold when, at the age of six, Dazai was deprived of both his aunt and his nursemaid within months of each other, his aunt to move in with a recently married daughter, Take to get married herself.

"Take disappeared without warning. She had found a husband in a fishing village and she must have been afraid I would try to follow her, for she left suddenly, without a word to me. . . . One morning I opened my eyes and called for Take, but Take did not come. . . . 'Take has gone! Take has gone!' I sobbed, feeling as if my heart would break; and for two or three days all I could do was cry. . . ." Now, says Dazai, "when I hear the word *hometown*, I remember Take. . . . I think of her as my own mother." And so, at the very end of *Tsugaru*, having postponed "the best thing until the last," Dazai sets out to find her.

Knowing only her maiden name and that she lives in a fishing village called Kodomari, "the last port on Honshu's west coast," Dazai takes train and bus—"in a ridiculous hurry. I felt as if I had not a moment to lose"—and arrives in Kodomari a little before noon. He is directed to Take's neat little hardware shop, but the curtains are drawn and the door is padlocked. Take has taken her children to the local school sports day and Dazai follows her there, producing, as he comes in sight of the festival tents, one of his most breath-stopping bursts of hyperbole: "I felt like the hero of a fairy story who has crossed seas and mountains and walked three thousand leagues in search of his mother, and who sees a beautiful sacred dance performed on top of a dune on the borders of the land to which he has been traveling. . . .

"As if possessed, I walked at least twice round the field, inquiring, 'Is Take here? Take of the hardware shop, is she here?' No one could help me. . . . Luck was simply not with me. . . . The gods had decreed that we should not meet. . . . Perhaps it was an outcome befitting the bungled life I have been leading all these years. The plans I make so ecstatically invariably end up in a shambles. . . . I was born under an unlucky star."

But then, returning past the hardware shop, Dazai runs into Take's teenage daughter, and this prompts a fresh outburst of affirmation: "I am Take's child. Even if that means I am the child of a maid or whatever, I don't care! I'll say it out loud: I am Take's child. I don't care if my brothers laugh at me. I am this girl's brother." The daughter takes him back to the sports field, to the tent where Take and her other children are eating lunch.

"I'm Shuji," he announces.

"Never!" says Take.

Dazai joins them and they sit together in the tent. "I felt utterly secure," writes Dazai. "My legs stretched out in front of me, I watched the games, my mind completely vacant. I felt absolutely devoid of cares and worries, without the slightest concern for what might happen next."

And suddenly he drops altogether the pose of bungler, hero, misfit-clown, and writes four sentences uncomplicated by hyperbole or self-derision:

"Is this the kind of feeling that is meant by *peace*? If it is, I can say that my heart experienced peace then for the first time in my life. My real mother, who died two years ago, was an extremely noble, gentle, and good mother, yet she never gave me this strange feeling of reassurance. I wonder, do the mothers of the world give all their children this rest . . . ?"

In later years, long after Dazai was dead, Take disavowed in a newspaper interview most of the details in his account of their reunion; in particular, the emotional intensity with which he loads it. Dazai, for example, has Take speak to him "in a flood of words, as if a dam had broken" and later stand dumbstruck "as if in a trance." Take died in 1983, not long after telling one of the English-language translators of *Tsugaru* that, yes, Dazai had visited her once and had written a book about it, and that everything the translator might want to know about the occasion was contained in the book. Perhaps Take had also reached the conclusion, via age or hindsight or other reflection, that there is a point where truth and invention collide, and that when they collide they produce a something that belongs wholly to neither; a something like peace.

✺

From the high pass, under early cloud, Mount Iwaki rose like an island out of a sea of pearly mist. The hills, as they jogged back down to the plain, looked ragged and accidental. They lay crouched like a dog that has bitten its master and forfeited all claim to his love. A crinkled snake, barely alive, lifted its head to me at the edge of the highway. It must have crawled out of the woods during the night and suffered some unspeakable torture. By noon I was being welcomed to the little hot-spring city of Kuroishi by a succession of increasingly fanciful signboards. The first said Welcome to Kuroishi, the Town Where Memories Revive. The next said Kuroishi, Birthplace of "Jonkara Bushi" (the most famous of all the Tsugaru folk songs). And the third said Kuroishi, Home of Hot Springs and Kokeshi Dolls. I chuckled at the cheek.

"Jonkara Bushi" is sung all over the Tsugaru peninsula and no town can be said with certainty to be its "birthplace." Kokeshi dolls are made and sold throughout the six northeastern prefectures of Honshu (and increasingly, where the tourist industry thrives, in other places). And hot springs are found practically everywhere in Japan. But the signboards were a reminder of that breezy Tsugaru trait which Dazai exemplifies so well in his "gazetteer"—a reluctance to be hindered by mere facts. It also exemplifies the nationwide consensus that advertisement and truth are not necessarily connected. And a slightly different sort of consensus—that history is irrelevant when inconvenient—was reflected on the signboard that pointed the way to the new Tsugaru Kokeshi Museum. *Yasashisa* (delicacy, gentility, tenderness, cuteness), it proclaimed, was the chief attribute of kokeshi dolls—an assertion that set me pondering, not for the first time, the question of what these now popular and collectable little souvenirs might really be.

Few Japanese people have any notion of where kokeshi came from or what they might originally have been used for, nor have they given the matter much thought. Partly this is because, like *nebuta*, the word *kokeshi* is usually written not with ideograms but in the purely phonetic syllabary called hiragana, so it is difficult to deduce an etymology. *Ko*, for instance, might mean "small" and *keshi* might mean "poppy," in which case the curators of Japan's doll museums would all be bouncing with joy. But it strikes me as more likely that the word is an amalgam of a different *ko*, meaning "child," and *kesu*, meaning "to get rid of," and that these cute, tender-faced little dolls, made from two simple pieces of wood, a sphere for the head and a cylinder for the body, may in origin have been fetish substitutes for children murdered at birth.

Infanticide was not an uncommon practice in rural Japan during the feudal period and it survived here and there into quite recent times. The American historian Thomas C. Smith suggests that, in the eighteenth and early nineteenth centuries at least, it was practiced in Japan "less as a desperate act in the face of poverty than as a form of family planning." In the towns, abortion was the commonest form of family planning (and, as the Japanese government persists to this day in refusing to permit the sale of oral contraceptives, it remains widely and lucratively practiced). But in rural areas, though officially prohibited by most clan governments, infanticide was the preferred choice. Moral questions aside, the killing of newborn babies rather than fetuses has the practical advantage of allowing a family—or a village— to exert a precise control over the ratio of the sexes, and it appears that, unlike in China and some other parts of Asia, the horror was not directed wholly, or even mainly, against female babies, but was used coolly and even-handedly to construct a gender balance that would ensure the continuance and stability of the group.

According to Mrs. Suzuki Fumi, born in 1898 in Ibaragi prefecture, not far north of Tokyo, and recorded on tape by the local doctor for a book of reminiscences called *Memories of Silk and Straw*, " 'thinning out' babies was pretty common" even at the time of her own birth. "It was considered bad luck to have twins," she explains, "so you got rid of one before your neighbors found out. Deformed babies were also bumped off. And if you wanted a boy but the baby was a girl, you'd make it 'a day visitor.' " The murder was often entrusted to the midwife. "Killing off a newborn baby was a simple enough business," Mrs. Suzuki remembers. "You just moistened a piece of paper with spittle and put it over the baby's nose and mouth; in no time at all it would stop breathing." But there were alternative methods, and another of Dr. Saga's informants, Mrs. Terakado Tai, born in 1899, describes two of them. One was "to press on their chest with your knee." Another was called *usugoro* (mortar killing), in which the murderer was usually the mother herself: "The woman went alone into one of the buildings outside and had the baby lying on a straw mat. She wrapped the thing in two straw sack lids, tied it up with rope and laid it on the mat. She then rolled a heavy wooden mortar over it. When the baby was dead, she took it outside and buried it herself. And the next day she was expected to be up at the crack of dawn as usual, doing the housework and helping in the fields. . . ."

One summer, about fifteen years ago, I went back to England to visit my parents and took two kokeshi to give as presents. These were new dolls with no history other than the days they had spent on the shelf of the shop where I bought them, but they were quite expensive specimens, painted in a traditional style and signed on their bases by the craftsman who had made them. The traditional kokeshi has no arms or legs; all it has is a cylinder with horizontal stripes on it for a body and tiny wistful, petal-like features inked into the middle of its broad, pale face. The absence of limbs might be disquieting, I suppose, if you had made the possible connection between kokeshi and child murder and had read Mrs. Suzuki's account of a midwife's attempt to quicken a death by wrapping an infant tightly in rags so that its arms were bound invisibly to its sides, or if you knew that one of the traditional attributes of Japanese ghosts is that they have no feet.

My parents, needless to say, knew none of these things. They were simple working-class people and I don't suppose they had ever heard of infanticide. My mother, then in her sixties, was born and brought up in Cockney London; my father, well into his seventies, was from the Derbyshire mill country. I never realized it until I thought about it after their death but there is a smattering of evidence that they were both slightly psychic. My mother, for example, had a premonition of her own death. I found her crying quietly one afternoon in the bed where she was assumed to be recovering from what we thought was mild influenza but which turned out to be fatal pneumonia. She was crying, she told me, because she could see the faces of Jesus's disciples in the pattern of the woodgrain on her bedroom wardrobe. On the day of her funeral, I was standing in the kitchen, alone in the house except for my father, when he suddenly appeared in the doorway and asked me matter-of-factly who the strange woman was that had just walked through the room where he was sitting. I later learned that as a young man my father had been briefly interested in spiritualism and a medium had told him that he was probably gifted. Before he died, he confided to me that my mother's ghost had visited him as he lay in his bed and brought him great joy. Anyway, my parents never liked the kokeshi. My father told me after my mother was dead that she had been very disturbed by them and had refused to let them stay on the sideboard where, at first, they had been displayed along with the china dogs. When my father died and I was going through his things, I found the kokeshi wrapped in newspaper, placed in a box with the lid taped shut, and locked in a cupboard. I gave them away.

If the original kokeshi were fetish substitutes for murdered children, how were they used? I suppose they were placed on god shelves, or perhaps in the Buddhist equivalent, *butsudan*, and the repose of the souls they represented was prayed for. The souls of children who have died without attaining a proper place in society have a special limbo in the obliging Japanese underworld, but this limbo is designed mainly to afford them an opportunity of belatedly thanking their parents for giving them life and caring for them. The victims of infanticide, I assume, do not go there. Their case seems more like that of the unborn cubs that Japanese whalers used to find when they cut open their harpooned mothers. There are monuments still in existence that the whalers erected for the souls of these fetuses. And as the unborn whales have their memorials in stone, so the murdered babies had theirs in dolls that they were never meant to play with.

I ate lunch in a restaurant next door to a nursery school that stood among the paddy fields, and through the window I watched the kids skipping about on their dusty playground. They looked extremely orderly. The girls were all in pink and the boys were all in blue, so if the gender balance was no longer adjustable at least it was color-coded. Across the road a grocer's van was parked, its loudspeaker summoning all the housewives of the neighborhood and, though the children ignored the van's appearance completely, it was obviously the high point of their mothers' day. Much more than a traveling shop to them, it was a combination music hall and conference table. They gathered behind it nudging each other, chortling and exchanging gossip, while the lanky grocer pranced about telling them jokes and trying to sell them carrots.

On the eastern approach to Kuroishi a colossal dam had towered over the hot-spring lodges like an alien starship. But once through the center of the little city and in its western outskirts, I came across some fine old wooden buildings, tile-roofed and large and dark, and the best preserved covered passageways that I had seen outside Kizukuri. Then lumberyards and woodchip factories, with the ripe, sweet smell of sawdust and dead trees; but soon I was again among apple orchards that stretched away to the ends of the plain. It was a bright late afternoon and there was nothing to see but the young trees and the pale, cloud-wreathed hump of Mount Iwaki. As I crossed into the precincts of Itayanagi a signboard welcomed me to the "Home of Apples," told me the town's population (19,500) and supplied me with the annual per hectare production figures for its orchards.

A very shabby ryokan stood at the town's main crossroads and the owner's wife looked me up and down and asked me if I was a biker. She was very quiet and nervous and I couldn't decide whether she was more afraid of me or embarrassed about the state of her inn. Everything in it seemed to be cracked or dented or coming unstuck. The concrete floor in the dining room was rutted and chipped like a go-cart track and the young woman who had just swabbed it down limped silently in and out of the kitchen with a hood over her head and a bandaged right foot wrapped in a plastic bag. But over dinner the owner's wife warmed to me, and when I came down to the dining room for breakfast the next morning she surprised me by standing to attention.

I praised her green tea and she bobbed her head and grinned. There was nothing special about the tea, she confessed, but perhaps it was the water. Was I used to drinking well water? No, she didn't think I could be. I was a city person, wasn't I? And every household in Itayanagi still drew its water from a well. But that would all change this year. They had built a dam above Kuroishi. Hadn't I seen it on my way through the city? And this year they would begin piping water to Itayanagi from the reservoir above the dam. They were going to put the rates up as a consequence. This was the last year that her guests would ever comment on the taste of her tea.

Was it wise to build such a dam, did I think? You see, Itayanagi suffers to an unusual extent from earthquakes. Not great destructive earthquakes that kill people and knock down houses, but little earthquakes, constant earthquakes. Often, you felt two or three a day. Was it wise to construct a dam in such a place and to pile up a weight of water behind it sufficient to supply a city and several towns? What if the earthquakes shook the dam, as they were bound to shake it over the years, and what if it developed little cracks (I looked down at the pitted concrete floor) too small at first for the eye to see? Ah well, she supposed they knew what they were doing.

And you couldn't escape the city ways now, could you? It wouldn't end with tap water, oh no. They had their apples, it was true. There would be no Itayanagi without its apples. But every day the city ways encroached. Why, not long ago, there had been two traffic accidents within a week of each other at this very crossroads, right outside her front door.

She glowed with pride. The world was cracking up. I finished the two apples from her orchard that she had peeled for me as I drank my tea. And it didn't surprise me to discover on my way out that the canary in the tiny cage that hung outside the stinking lavatory had a broken wing.

•   •   •

The time was right, I felt, to visit Dazai's home in Kanagi. So once again I raced through the city of Goshogawara, where a majority of the residents had just voted to sack their mayor because of doubts about the lawfulness of his dealings with the construction industry: those fillers-in of wells and flingers-up of dams. The mayor's immediate predecessor, too, had been forced to resign because of corruption charges and the deputy mayor had not long before been arrested for accepting bribes from contractors bidding for public works projects. In the towns of Tsugaru the economic miracle has entered an interesting phase.

But Kanagi, when I reached it, didn't feel like a Tsugaru town at all. It was easily the most prosperous-looking of all the townships of the plain and felt more like a resort on the Izu peninsula than an outpost of the bleak and bitter north. The plastic seats in the waiting room at the station all had little cushions on them and the coffee shop across the road was called—what else?—Dazai. Dazai's family name, Tsushima, appeared prominently on the signboards and nameplates of the town's more affluent professional concerns—the Tsushima Surgery, the Tsushima Dental Clinic—and one enterprising shopowner, clearly bent on milking the economic miracle for all he could get out of it, had divided his little premises up in such a way that he could concurrently rent videotapes, sell software for family computers, supply boxed sushi lunches, and run a pool table.

The house in which Dazai was born is one of the largest and most impressive of Kanagi's buildings, and it stands at one end of the town's main street. It was bought from the Tsushimas some years ago, converted into a ryokan, and named Shayokan (Inn of the Setting Sun) after Dazai's most celebrated novel. The choice of this name for an inn says much about the ways in which Japanese sensibilities and notions of attractiveness differ from, say, Chinese notions. No Chinese entrepreneur would dream of giving an establishment designed to attract the public so offputting a name, however useful its literary associations. In Chinese communities restaurants and inns are always called things like Prosperous and Happy and Lucky, and the name itself is viewed as a charm to protect the owner's fortunes.

But Dazai's title was a deliberate reference to the fall of Japan from prewar might, to the plight of his novel's chief protagonist, a woman from a formerly prosperous family now faced with dismal times, and to the general late-1940s climate of insecurity, impotence, poverty, and gloom. *The Setting Sun* was first published in 1947, two years after the end of the war and, though Dazai was in no sense a disciple of Nobel Prize–winning novelist Kawabata Yasunari, it perfectly reflects the spirit of that author's remark that, in the wake of defeat and occupation, Japanese writers had no choice but to compose elegies. Almost as soon as Dazai's novel was published the expression *setting sun* entered the vocabulary of common speech—particularly that of the hungry young who have always provided Dazai with his most faithful constituency—and was regarded by them as a metaphor for their society's depressed and depressing condition; a condition now commemorated on a large signboard at the end of Kanagi's bustling street of shops.

I stood in front of it and looked on the brighter side. After all, the new owners of Dazai's old house could have rummaged through the titles of his collected works and found worse names to call their inn. Shayokan is decidedly more agreeable—even to a Chinese hotelier—than Ningen Shikkakukan (No Longer Human Inn) or Kobutorikan (Inn of the Removed Wen) or Ubasutekan (Inn Where Old Women Are Abandoned to Die). Besides, decline, despondency, and helplessness in the face of uncaring fate are exactly the states and sentiments out of which the bulk of Japan's literary heritage, as well as a sizable chunk of its national character, are constructed, so a name riddled with all three is bound to impress paying visitors no end. I walked through the portals of the Shayokan humming "There Is a Happy Land" and came to a halt in the middle of a coffee lounge.

Revisiting his childhood home in 1944, Dazai was struck by how little had changed. "I sensed," he wrote, "that my brother must have made more than ordinary efforts to preserve the old house in its original state." The efforts of the present owners have not been expended in quite the same fashion, and in the remodeled entrance hall visitors can now sip expensive instant Kilimanjaro, buy postcards, books, and telephone cards with Dazai's portrait on them at the souvenir stand and—from the look of the large Wurlitzer jukebox that was parked at the bottom of the back stairs—engage in all manner of revelries undreamt of by brother Bunji.

From all the walls of the coffee lounge Dazai peered down at the absent revelers and for background music the proprietors had chosen to tune their radio to the American Forces Network, which as I entered was advising its listeners in English that if the sun could buckle a concrete highway, it could do wickeder things to their skin. I wandered past the jukebox and found, at the back of the building, a small museum. Most of the exhibits were photographs. There was one of Dazai's daughter, Tsushima Yuko, now a well-regarded novelist in her own right, attending a performance of her father's one and only attempt at a drama, an uninspired piece of work called *The New Hamlet*, and looking suitably embarrassed. And in a corner stood one of Dazai's trademark capes, propped up on an aluminum frame and looking like a raided mummy case.

It was a dreary Saturday afternoon. I went back to the coffee lounge and ordered a cup of Kilimanjaro which proved to be undrinkable. The revelers stayed absent. A plump woman whom I took to be the okami-san sat behind a glass partition by the open door tapping her fingers on a memo pad and looking as though she was there to sell tickets for a play that had not yet been written. The American Forces Network warned me in English against contracting AIDS. I sat in a wicker chair and slowly sipped the undrinkable Kilimanjaro and decided I would stay the night.

The okami-san behind the partition perked up. Yes, there was a vacancy. I could have a room called *Yuri* (Lily).

"*Yurei?*" I said. *Yurei* means a ghost. It was a joke. Solemnly the okami-san tittered.

A brisk maid conducted me to the second floor via the servants' staircase, and I found it in a much more careful state of preservation than the downstairs had been. Bunji would have recognized every wainscot. My room was small and I suppose it had been occupied by one of the younger and less important relatives. But it was high-ceilinged, had splendidly solid skirting boards (a great rarity in Japanese homes), a heavy polished wooden door in a massive wooden frame, and a hand-embroidered antimacassar on top of the coin T.V.

Five guests turned up for dinner, including me. The others were a young honeymoon couple dressed in jeans and an elderly mother and her middle-aged spinster daughter who had come down from Hokkaido through the new Seikan Tunnel. As soon as the honeymoon couple's lacquered dinner trays were placed in front of them on the tatami floor the husband began to take flash photographs with an automatic camera. The camera had a zoom lens with three settings and he took three careful pictures of his dinner, one at each available lens setting, warning his new wife to keep out of the way.

"I suppose you know all about Dazai?" the elderly mother asked the elderly maid.

"No, I don't know a thing," the maid said brightly. "I'm just filling in for the regular staff."

"I always thought Kanagi was at the south end of the Tsugaru plain," the mother from Hokkaido said earnestly, leaning forward across her lacquered tray and wrinkling her brow.

"Well," said the maid, looking at the mother as though she were a complete lunatic, "it's right in the middle, you see."

"I always thought it was towards the south," repeated the mother, shaking her head.

"*Maaaa. . . .*" said the maid, and burst out laughing.

"Do you want my oyster gratin?" the mother asked me. "You've got such a big body. I can't believe these little scraps of food can possibly satisfy an appetite like yours. What a big body you've got! Hasn't he got a big body?"

The maid said "*Maaaa. . . .*" again, and laughed so loud that another maid came in to see what was up. I caught the middle-aged daughter's eye and she stared furiously at the floor.

Throughout the meal the honeymoon couple spoke not a word. The husband sat cross-legged but the young wife in jeans was sitting *seiza* (literally, "correct-seat")—that is to say, kneeling straight-backed, her legs bent double under her with her bottom resting on her heels. It is the conventional way of seating oneself on tatami but nowadays it is considered very formal

and few young people find it comfortable unless they have spent years studying one or other of the traditional arts (in fact, in some schools and martial
arts clubs seiza is inflicted as a punishment).

The only times I have adopted it myself are on the rare occasions when I
have been invited to attend a tea ceremony and during the brief period when
I was in love with a girl whose hobby was playing the small hand-drum that
accompanies Noh plays, and I decided to take lessons in it too. Most of my
lessons were spent learning how to untangle the drum from its ornamental
cords while trying not to notice that my legs were about to spontaneously
combust. A British acquaintance of mine who was training to be a Zen monk
had the worst experience with seiza that I know of, and found that one of his
knees had locked solid and that he could no longer unbend it. This took place
during an important public ceremony at Eiheiji Temple, which involved my
acquaintance, together with about a hundred and fifty other trainee monks,
kneeling on a hard wooden floor for a long time early one morning and then
standing up smartly and processing round the prayer hall. When the time
came for them to stand up my acquaintance had to be lifted by three or four
other trainee monks and marched hopping round the hall with one leg stuck
up behind him like an actor playing Long John Silver. Not long after that he
became a salesman for a firm that manufactures baseball bats.

Anyway, the young wife had sat seiza throughout dinner—whether to
impress the foreigner or her new hubby or the ghost of Dazai I'm not sure—
and now she found that she couldn't get up. The mother and daughter from
Hokkaido made a hurried exit to spare her the embarrassment of an audience, but I lingered over my second oyster gratin and watched attentively
while she rolled about the floor. Her husband got to his feet without a word
and went away to photograph the jukebox. The young wife clawed her way
across the tatami, then up the door frame, then limped off in the direction
of the back stairs from which, eight or nine seconds later, came the sound
of her falling down them. The two maids practically choked themselves
laughing.

"Oooo, look at your feet!" said one of the maids as she knelt down to clear
away my tray. I had finished dinner and my legs were stretched out in front
of me, halfway across the room. The maid sat back and patted my feet.

"Blisters," she said, reassuringly. The Japanese word for a blister is *mame*. It always sounds reassuring. "And look at your arms," the maid said, chuckling. "They're all sunburnt. What have you been up to?"

"Walking."

"Are you a Dazai fan?"

"Not especially."

"Well, thank goodness for that."

Perhaps as a cure for my blisters and sunburn, the maid recommended that I visit the Shayokan's bar. It was in the converted storehouse but it had a separate entrance, round the back of the high brick wall. It had been open fourteen years now, a well-established spot, and it was directly managed by the ryokan so I had no need to feel uneasy about going there. All the guests visited it, the maid told me, making it sound compulsory. So I changed back out of my yukata, slipped into a pair of the Shayokan's plastic sandals and walked halfway round the block in the cool night air to get to the old storehouse beyond the kitchen. The door of the bar was set back amid a cluster of ivy and a lighted sign repeated the assurance that it was a directly managed (*chokuei*) establishment. The first ideogram of *chokuei* means frank, honest, cheerful, and upright. I marched smartly through the narrow door and fought my way round the velvet curtain.

Dazai, I saw at once, would have loved it, and brother Bunji would have died on the spot. His ghost must wriggle nightly, especially when one of the customers—and this was happening as I emerged from the folds of the curtain—stands spotlit on the little crescent-shaped stage in the middle of the bar and sings "I Left My Heart in San Francisco." I sat at the counter, its only occupant, and ordered a beer. The room was large and dimly lit and had bare wooden boards for a floor. The walls were painted to imitate half-timbering, the chairs were all upholstered in red imitation velvet to match the curtain at the door, the music to accompany the songs was provided by laser video discs, some of which were pornographic, and the stage on which the customers stood to sing was hung with pleated silk.

The elderly mama seemed disinclined to talk. She identified for me the slouching, dark-suited, dark-glassed, overfed figure in the poster above the bar. I had taken him for a local politician intimate with public works contractors but he proved to be Yoshi Ikuzo, a T.V. actor-ballad singer who lives in Kanagi. The mama assured me that he often dropped in. Most of the tables in the place were empty but the one in the corner farthest from the bar was occupied by a group of six young men and two attentive bar hostesses, so I decided to have myself invited over and placed in motion the process that would bring about this development.

"I'd like to sing a song," I say.

The mama passes me the song list, known in karaoke bars as the "menu," and points to the Elvis Presley numbers.

"What about 'Love Me Tender'?" she suggests.

"No," I say. "I think I'll sing 'Yosaku.' "

" 'Yosaku' is very difficult," she says. "How about 'My Way'?"

"No," I say. "I'll sing 'Yosaku.' "

The mama selects the laser disc. I mount the stage. A hush falls.

" 'Yosaku' is very difficult," she says.

I smile, take a sip from my beer glass, and sing:

Yosaku chops down trees with an axe.
Hey hey ho! Hey hey ho!
From far-off hills the echo comes back.
Hey hey ho! Hey hey ho!

At the end of the second chorus the *hey hey ho's* climax in a long, rippling falsetto, which I accomplish to sustained applause, tilting my face towards the spotlight so that the two hostesses at the far table will notice the manly concentration. I finish the song, look down at the music stand and see for the first time that a school notebook rests on it, and that it contains the words of several of the most popular Japanese karaoke ballads painstakingly transcribed in pencil into the Roman alphabet. "Yosaku" is not among them, so the notebook isn't for me. At the same instant that the penny drops I am invited, the applause having not yet subsided, to join the guests and the hostesses who are fluttering to make room for me at the corner table.

The six young men were all members of the Japanese Air Self-Defense Force, the imaginative name for the aerial branch of the nation's armed forces

which are supposed, under the constitution, not to exist. They were celebrating the approaching hospitalization of one of their number for the
removal of a nasal polyp ("Like Ronald Reagan," he told me, proudly). The
two hostesses, as I had guessed three seconds after seeing the school notebook on the music stand, were Filipinas, both dressed in red, both very pretty,
both almost totally incapable of speaking Japanese and not much more at
home in English, and both working illegally on three-month tourist visas,
their positions having been obtained for them by enterprising gangsters in
Goshogawara, dark-glassed like Yoshi Ikuzo, who had also thoughtfully
insisted on locking the young Filipinas' passports in their safe. I was glad to
see that the Air Self-Defense Force did not consider either the gangsters or
the illegal Filipinas a threat to national security.

Priscilla was thin and jolly. She was twenty-five, she told me, and this was
her third time in Japan. Lorraine, who had a round face and large, sad doe's
eyes, asked me to guess how old she was. I said I thought she was about the
same age as Priscilla. Lorraine was horrified.

"I am twenty-one!" she exclaimed, biting her lower lip. "I am twenty-one
only!"

It was the first time Lorraine had worked in Japan, but she was picking up
the customs. As soon as I sat down she put her hand on my knee, not to
arouse me or to express affection, but because it was part of her job and meant
that an extra couple of thousand yen could be added to my bill, none of which
would go to Lorraine but half of which would end up in the pockets of the
gangsters in Goshogawara. There were a lot of Filipina hostesses in
Goshogawara, Priscilla told me, but only three in Kanagi. Until last month
there had been four, but one had married a Japanese man and was going to
have his baby.

Priscilla explained that the man with the polyp was her "boyfriend." He
chuckled and raised his glass.

"He's got a wife and three children," Priscilla said, laughing in a wide-
mouthed, bright, un-Japanese way, and sipping a rum-and-coke.

"I want to sing a song specially for you," Lorraine said to me, holding my
knee and looking very serious.

"Thank you," I said.

Lorraine got up and mounted the little crescent-shaped stage, turned a page of her school notebook, and sang, at age twenty-one, "Love Is Over."

While she was singing, the man sitting next to me, who was thin and pale and spoke very quietly, told me how much he had admired my country's performance in the Falklands War. He also told me how proud he and his companions were to be defending their country, even though they knew they couldn't. His hobby was listening to jazz records and he envied Oscar Peterson the size of his hands. As we chatted, I saw that there were two other hostesses in the room, draped about chairs in the darker corners, their chins propped up on the palms of their hands, alone and half asleep. They were both Japanese, older than the Filipina girls, and they knew that they were out of the competition. They were no match for the Filipinas' looks and vitality. So they were trying to appear sophisticated, and ending up snooty.

"You like it?" one of them called out to me languidly as, from the stage, Lorraine lifted her doe's eyes and stared at me through the spotlight.

"Like what?" I asked, but the Japanese hostess turned away and lit a cigarette.

Lorraine came back and asked me to dance. We went to the area of bare floorboards in front of the counter where the untalkative mama was polishing chipped ashtrays, and Lorraine did her best to teach me the mambo, an exercise doomed by my blisters and the broken straps of the Shayokan's plastic sandals. She was like a little zoo animal whose keeper has forgotten to feed her and then remembers late and brings her extra scraps. She held me so tight that I couldn't move my hips.

"Are you Christian?" Lorraine said.

"No," I said.

She lowered her eyes and stared at my shirt button.

"What is your religion?"

I thought about the god shelf on my living room wall and said, "It would take too long to explain."

When we sat down at the table again I said to Lorraine, "Are you a Christian?"

"Yes, I am," she said very seriously. Her right hand rested on my knee.

Her left hand was stroking the thigh of the man sitting on the other side of her, who called himself Jimmy.

Later, I thought about Lorraine and her doe's eyes as I lay in my futon looking up at the high, blank ceiling. Perhaps she spent her nights as well as her evenings here in Dazai's home, the home that Bunji, mayor of Kanagi and governor of Aomori prefecture, had taken such pains to preserve from the buffets of a collapsing world, and from which he had expelled his erring brother for wanting to marry a young geisha. Perhaps Dazai had slept in my room after all and lay here thinking about the bar girl who had died next to him on the beach at Enoshima. Her name was Shimeko and she was nineteen. Within a month of her death Dazai had married his geisha. In later years the only thing that would interest Dazai about Shimeko was the footnote she provided to his own frustrations.

I slept easily. The heavy door in its frame, and the walls, and the skirting boards all stifled the night sounds of the old house. I couldn't hear "My Way" or "Love Is Over." I was troubled by no ghosts.

"... Is this the kind of feeling that is meant by 'peace' ... ? I wonder, do the mothers of the world give all their children this rest ... ?"

Dazai had traveled up to Kodomari "in a ridiculous hurry" to look for the nursemaid he thought he loved, but I would take my time. Over the next three days I walked the length of the Tsugaru peninsula once again, this time on the Japan Sea side, along the line of the Seven-League Beach. The leading edge of an early typhoon brought in from the choppy sea a string of smoke-like clouds that pressed down on the land and sheeted the sodden hills as if they were furniture in an empty house. The streets of the villages I passed through were deserted; everyone had fled the coming rain. The wild heathland in the north of the peninsula, with its stunted yellow pines and ugly scrub, stretched inland as far as I could see, crossed here and there by brand-new bypasses, wide and concrete, that bypassed nothing. A fat schoolgirl screamed *konnichi wa* at me, her arms held straight out from her uniformed sides like the wings of a threatened, angry bird. Another offered me her umbrella. The bone grey, ash grey palisades that protected the broken heathland from the wind were worn to spikes, and there were no paddies.

At Kodomari, where Dazai had searched for and found his Take, I arrived in the worst of the three-day storm and tumbled into a ryokan where they banished me to a corner room upstairs to get me out of the way of their fishermen's party.

"Can't I eat with the fishermen?" I asked.

"No," they said, and brought my dinner to my room. The window overlooked the street. The view was of concrete poles and wires stretched across a rainy blank.

But, leaving Dazai's house at Kanagi on Sunday morning three days before, I had had an urge to lie down and do nothing. I wanted to be, for one night, in a place where I didn't feel like an intruder. So I turned back south and tramped for half a day to reach the ryokan at Kizukuri where I had watched the sumo wrestling and the mothers in cardigans had made a fuss of me. They made a fuss of me again and gave me the same room they had given me before.

And in that room I woke up again from dreams that had nothing to do with Tsugaru. I was in a taxi with my mother on a hot road in Essex. The taxi stopped and we got out. There was no building in sight, no traffic, nothing. I turned to my mother and began slapping her face. By the side of the road my wife and daughter stood watching us; the taxi driver lit a cigarette. I slapped my mother again and again in the middle of the road and huge tears ran down her cheeks. Then I woke up. It was not quite six o'clock. And I heard a strange sound coming from a long way off. It sounded like a man's voice chanting something that I strained my ears to catch and couldn't.

"... *uunn.... gaaiiii.... mm ... uunnn.... gaaiiii.* ..." I got out of my futon and stood very still by the window and looked down into the empty street. There was nothing to see, no life of any kind. A light rain was falling on the neighbor's roof tiles. But the chant grew louder and I followed it with my lips.

"*Muuu ... nn gaiii. Muuu ... nn gaiii.* ..."

It meant nothing. It was beautiful. It made no sense to me at all. The sound of it began to recede. I listened until I couldn't hear it any longer. Then I went back to my futon and lay awake, hearing first the buzz of an electric shaver and then the rattle of a small earthquake, until a motherly maid brought my breakfast.

I asked the maid what the sound might have been. She hadn't a clue what I was talking about.

"It was like a man's voice chanting," I said. "*Muuuuungaiii. Muuuuungaiii.* From one end of the street to the other."

"I expect it was someone's television," the maid said.

"It was six o'clock," I said. "I looked at my watch."

"I think you must have been dreaming."

And I thought, too, that I must have been dreaming. It wasn't till I had pulled on my boots and was standing once more surrounded by the mothers in the doorway saying goodbye to them that I found out what the sound might have been. It was the okami-san who suggested it.

"I know what it was! It was the man who sells *shijimigai*. They're the small black shellfish that you find up in Lake Jusan. Sometimes he brings them round in his van and then he uses music. But if he's on his bicycle, as he is sometimes in the early morning, he just uses his voice. That's what he sounds like."

"Shijimigai?"

"Yes."

"How do you write it?"

"*Su, zu* . . . "

A man coming down the corridor laughed.

"You're spelling it in Tsugaru dialect," he told her. "It's not *su*, it's *shi*. *Shi—ji—mi*."

"Oh, *shi?*" the okami-san said, chuckling, unruffled.

I said goodbye and left for the second time. The rain strengthened almost at once and there was no one on Kizukuri's streets, as there had been no one at six o'clock to buy shellfish.

That chant still haunts me. It was very beautiful: a long, unwavering first note and a second note that died and left a hum behind it in the air. It felt as though it were centuries old. Perhaps that was why it struck me as lovely. Dazai must have heard it in his childhood, on his school trip to Takayama

Inari when he wore the wrong shoes and couldn't keep up and had to be pulled in the invalids' cart by his mocking classmates; or on this road up to Kodomari to meet the nursemaid who had left him one night without saying goodbye and whom he thought he loved. This road ran along the shore of Lake Jusan. I would pass the lake myself that evening and watch the rain spread and blur its edges until I couldn't tell the lake water from the flooded fields. And perhaps I'd hear the chant again, and buy shijimigai from the man who sang it. But it hadn't sounded like a shellfish-seller. In Kizukuri, in the early rain, it had sounded like an uncommonly lonely man crying for the moon.

2

Saigo's Last March

❧

Southern trees bear strange fruit;
Blood on the leaves and blood at the root.
　　　　—Lewis Allan for Billie Holiday

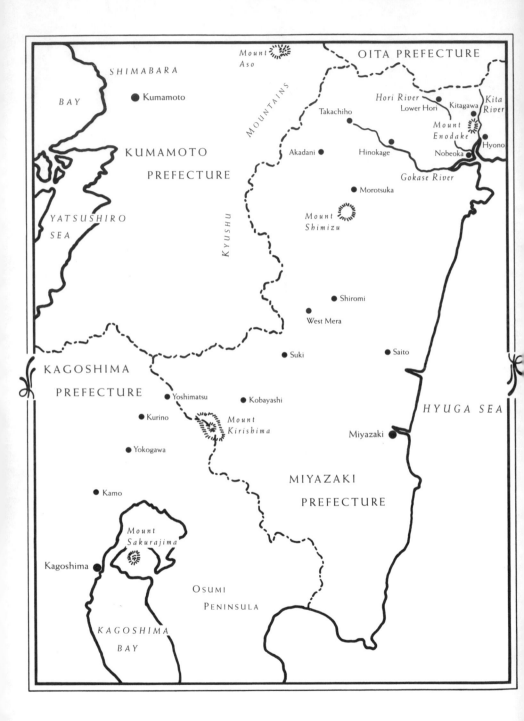

1
Enodake

❧

I went into a post office in the city of Nobeoka and an old man sitting on a bench there waiting to collect his pension bowed and said to me in a very loud voice, "Good morning." Then, through the glass door of the post office, he saw his wife approaching from across the street and the skin round his neck shook with fury. He stood up and bellowed, "My seal! My seal!" and banged his walking stick on the post office floor. His wife stayed on the other side of the closed door, staring in at her shaking husband through the glass, and the old man stood in the middle of the floor and waved his fist at her, roaring. He had come to collect his pension and forgotten his personal seal. She was in trouble now, the silly cow.

I walked through the streets of the little city, past the shops that were closed for the Festival of the Dead, dabbing my dripping face with a towel. The August heat was getting to everyone. I climbed the steep stone steps that led to Imayama Shrine and thought the sky would crack under the weight of the screeching cicadas. I had woken up early that morning and heard the cicadas and thought they were a vacuum cleaner. From the shrine I had a view that commanded the whole sweltering city: the hazy flats in the estuaries of the four rivers on which the city stands, the yellowtail hatcheries offshore in the shimmering sea, the waves breaking slowly and flatly on the beaches, the trucks whizzing across the distant bridges, the red-and-white chimneys of the plastic and fertilizer and pharmaceutical and synthetic fiber factories belonging to the Asahi Chemical Company, which is responsible for the livelihoods of about two-thirds of the 136,000 people who live in Nobeoka. The company has been here since 1923. It owns most of its employees' houses, the supermarkets and department stores they shop in, and an entire "Asahi" neighborhood on the south bank of the Ose River; and the city's northbound buses travel to a terminus called "Rayon."

In the compound of Imayama Shrine Japan's national flag was flying. Today was August 15th, the anniversary of the end of the Second World War. It is one of history's ironies that the war ended for Japan on August 15th because, when the lunar calendar was replaced by the Gregorian calendar in 1873, August 15th became an important date in the celebration of O-Bon, the Festival of the Dead, when departed spirits return to this world for a brief time seeking comfort.

An old man hobbling through the shrine compound told me that he was "seventy-three years and four months" old. He had lived in Korea before the war, when Korea was a colony of Japan, and he remembered his English teacher there and the presents she gave her pupils at Christmas. Park Chung Hee had been a great man; he had made the hills of Korea green again where once the loggers had stripped them bald. Seoul today was a fine city, indistinguishable from Tokyo except for the shop signs. . . .

"And forty years ago it was easy to tell a Korean from a Japanese just by looking at his face. Now it's not so easy, not with the young people. People under forty all look the same. But I can still tell a Chinaman, oh yes. . . . "

". . . and I can tell an Italian," the old man called back to me, shuffling away toward the shrine steps and mopping his face with a handkerchief.

I drank beer in a restaurant to get out of the heat. The cinemas had nothing on I wanted to see. There were all-night showings of *Space Invaders, Police Academy 3*, and Sylvester Stallone in *Cobra*. Along the roofed shopping arcades the loudspeakers broadcast a Japanese singer doing a Paul Anka medley. The only shops open were those selling watermelons, the pachinko parlors, the smart new boutiques with their black walls and carpets and their sparse, carefully hung collections of clothes in colors you might want to wear to a funeral, and the shops selling farming implements: hand-made scythes and hoes and rakes that one shopkeeper explained to me had been invented hundreds of years before, in Korea.

When darkness fell there was a Bon dance. The poster advertising it gave no indication of what time it was supposed to start; it said simply "evening." So at seven o'clock I turned up at the gravel space near the shrine steps where two paper lanterns and some bare electric bulbs had been hung. A small table in the middle of the space was draped with red-and-white striped cloth and on it was a taiko drum. But there was no one in sight; not a soul. I went away and walked around and had a drink in a little bar. A young couple sat at the counter, their arms round each other's bodies, the girl's head resting on the young man's shoulder. They ordered shochu mixed with Calpis. It was like a bad dream. I could hardly get my beer down.

I went back to the dancing circle at eight o'clock and found fifteen people there, three in yukata. A man as thin as a chopstick with an unlit cigarette butt stuck between his teeth banged out the taiko accompaniment to "Nobeoka Bamba Odori," which was coming from scratchy speakers hung in the wilting trees. There was no other music; no other song. It started and stopped and started again, and a lunatic with one eye and large khaki shorts jumped up and down in the middle of the circle as though he were demonstrating the Asahi Chemical Company workers' calisthenics. He threw his arms wide like a scarecrow's and looked at me out of his one eye and shouted "Dance!" When the taiko player changed everyone moved away except for the jumping lunatic. The new taiko player had no sense of rhythm and the lunatic was the only one who could follow the beat. Finally the chopstick-thin man with the cigarette butt came back and took the sticks away and started to bang the taiko again and the dancers wandered back onto the gravel.

A fat woman came up and gave me a slice of watermelon and two cold cans of beer. "I can't drink them myself," she said. And at twenty past nine everybody left. A man with a microphone pleaded with them to stay, but no one wanted to dance any more. Perhaps the August night was too hot, or shochu and Calpis had poisoned their passion, or perhaps there were no ghosts to dance for in this city, or such ghosts as had drifted back for the festival were made of synthetic fiber.

"They're dancing to this song all over Nobeoka tonight," the fat woman told me, taking "Bamba Odori" out of the cassette player. But I walked through the streets of the little city and saw and heard no other dancing. In the shuttered arcades the Japanese singer was still churning out Paul Anka songs: "You and I will be a flea as a balls up in a tree." And an oldish man in the Monochrome coffee shop told me that I would see "strange sights" if I went walking in the empty Kyushu hills. "Strange sights. You will see them. I hope so."

I stayed at Monochrome for an hour drinking Budweiser beer straight out of the can. The counter decor was a pyramid-shaped stack of empty beer cans: Budweiser and Heineken. One of the customers was a woman in her mid-thirties with serious-looking spectacles who was organizing a festival of Beatles films. And another was a bald young amateur photographer in a Clan Campbell tartan shirt who told me that Saigo Takamori had had the biggest balls on earth.

"They were massive," he said, gesturing with his hands. "They were so big that he couldn't walk."

"Do you mean he was diseased?" asked the Beatles woman.

"Diseased or not," said the photographer, gripping a Budweiser, "he was a rare man all over."

◈

I first came across Saigo Takamori some dozen years ago on a trip to Kagoshima, the city at the southern tip of Kyushu where, in 1828, Saigo had been born. My trip was a lazy one and had as its main objects the purchase of folk pottery, the imbibing of Kirin beer, and frequent immersion in the summer sea. In Kagoshima I saw Saigo's statue outside the Municipal Art

Museum. He stands there, a great bronze dunce of a man wearing Japan's first national army uniform (he was Marshal of the Army), with his hand on the hilt of his marshal's sword, his huge body leaning forward like a cairn about to topple, and his massive eyes popping out of his cannonball head like swollen olives.

The next time I came across him was in a shop in Kanda, the antiquarian book center of Tokyo, where I was wasting a winter's afternoon turning over a pile of late nineteenth-century woodblock prints, all fearsome grimaces and postures and chins. There was one of Saigo made in 1878, the year after his death. He still wore his army uniform, though now it had acquired so much gold braid that it looked as though it had come out of the costume chest for some Ruritanian operetta. A halo of swords and fixed bayonets surrounded Saigo, emanating from his body like the rays of the rising sun. According to the caption, the print commemorated his posthumous ascension to the planet Mars and his investiture there as the God of War.

Saigo's native province of Satsuma (the old name for what is today Kagoshima prefecture) was in his day—and some would say still is—among the most traditional-minded and reactionary areas in Japan. In the 1860s, it had been in the forefront of the moves to topple the shogunate (which, critics charged, had gone too far towards appeasing the "barbarian" Westerners who were clamoring for trade treaties) and to replace the shogun's government with one directly answerable to the emperor, the source of all unique Japanese virtues. Saigo himself—a minor clan official who, through sheer dependability, unquestioned honesty, and loyalty to his feudal lord, had risen to a commanding position in the Satsuma hierarchy—had been one of the prime movers in the eventual "restoration" of power to the Meiji Emperor in 1868, the event that ironically (considering the "expel the barbarians" rhetoric on the lips of many of those who promoted it) brought an end to Japan's feudal isolation and ushered in its modern age. Saigo had commanded the loyalist army against the diehard supporters of the shogun and defeated them. He had served in the newly formed cabinet, and played a major part in giving stability and authority to the new government.

But the methods and attitudes of feudalism survived the restoration, as they were meant to, and Saigo's loyalties and ambitions remained as entwined with the interests of his native Satsuma as with those of the newly "progressive" nation. The population of Satsuma contained an unusually large percentage of samurai—members of the old privileged warrior class (to which Saigo belonged) who neither tilled the land nor traded nor manufactured goods, but were maintained by taxes imposed on farmers, artisans, and merchants—and the time-honored business of the samurai was war. It was not long before the new government began debating measures aimed at limiting, and finally eliminating, the power of this privileged and dangerous class, ostensibly to create a more "egalitarian" society but, equally important, to reduce the likelihood of independent-minded provinces such as Saigo's acting against the central authorities. The wearing of swords and topknots, both important signs of samurai status, were at first discouraged and then prohibited (though it is said that both swords and topknots remained a common sight on the streets of Kagoshima long after they had disappeared elsewhere). And the annual stipends of rice by which the samurai had been maintained were reduced, then converted to cash pensions at a fraction of their value, then to a once-and-forever dollop of severance pay. The samurai were left without the badges of their rank, without lords to depend on or lay down their lives for, and without the means of support that they had enjoyed for centuries. Some moved to distant parts of the country—to Hokkaido in the far north, for example, still regarded in the 1870s as a "colony"—where they could settle down and learn new ways to earn their living. But discontent was rife among them, and nowhere were these developments viewed with greater suspicion and dismay than in Satsuma.

In October 1873, in a high fury at what he regarded as its despicable and self-serving pragmatism, Saigo quit the government and retired to private life near his hometown. His exasperation was in part the result of a born distaste for self-aggrandizement and duplicity, with both of which he accused his colleagues in the cabinet, and in part a reaction to the treatment that his own samurai class had received under the new order. Saigo had wanted to demonstrate how vital the maintenance of a trained warrior class was for Japan—even for a "modern" and "progressive" Japan—and, in pursuit of this project (say some of his biographers; others, who wish to portray Saigo as a modern-minded humanist, dispute it), he had urged the government to go to war with "insolent" Korea in order that samurai virtues might be dramatically revived and displayed. He had even offered himself as an envoy to Korea in the expectation, according to some, that he would be assassinated there and so provide an excuse for opening hostilities. But the government procrastinated and finally turned his proposal down. So, at the age of forty-six, one of the most admired and charismatic men of his time was to be found in self-imposed retirement among his native hills, farming, hunting with his dogs, and establishing a chain of private schools that aimed to keep alive the martial skills and authoritarian philosophy on which the privileges and strengths of the samurai class had always fed, bang in the middle of what was likely to remain the nation's most recalcitrant province.

For three years and three months resentments smoldered. Then, in January 1877, in the wake of two small regional revolts elsewhere, the central government determined to prevent the Satsuma malcontents from capitalizing on the ill-will that still simmered there and ordered that munitions stored in the huge Kagoshima arsenal be transported outside the province. To prevent this, a group of armed samurai students from Saigo's private military-style schools raided the arsenal and turned away the government-chartered vessel that had come to remove the stockpile. At the same time, along with some local officials and other Satsuma patriots, the students claimed to have discovered a plot against Saigo's life initiated by the central government.

Most historians believe that this plot was a fabrication; certainly, the "confession" upon which its credibility rested was obtained under torture—a fact that emerged at the eventual court of enquiry—although torture was normal for the times. But the combination of "plot" and armed challenge to the government struck a spark that no amount of conciliatory talk could now extinguish. If Saigo was a widely admired figure throughout Japan, then in Satsuma, particularly among the students at his schools, he was regarded less as a mortal than as a god. Most of his biographers agree that Saigo took no direct part in fabricating the assassination plot or in encouraging the raid on the arsenal. The most popular version of events has him out in the distant countryside hunting rabbits with his dogs when the arsenal is raided and his response, on being told what has happened, ranges, in possible English translation, from "That's torn it!" to "It can't be helped," "It wouldn't have happened if I'd been there," "The bloody fools!," and "Oh shit!" At any rate, with no alternative in view, Saigo took command of the situation. Within days a force of about fifteen thousand armed men had flocked to Kagoshima to join him and he had announced his intention of marching on Tokyo, a thousand miles away, to "demand an explanation" of the government.

Thus did Saigo Takamori go to war—the last civil war to be fought on Japanese soil. The war never spread beyond the island of Kyushu, but more than thirteen thousand men died fighting it and a further twenty-two thousand were wounded. It was a war in which a medieval-style castle was subjected to a medieval-style siege, in which arrow-borne messages were launched into opposing ranks and much of the fighting was old-fashioned swordplay. (At one stage, the government—though its infantry divisions were equipped with newly imported Snider, Mauser, and Enfield rifles—was forced to advertise in the press for skilled swordsmen.) And all this in the year in which Tchaikovsky wrote his fourth symphony and Brahms his second, in which Henry James published *The American* and Ibsen, *The Pillars of Society*, in which Walter Bagehot died, André Maginot was born, and the first All England Lawn Tennis Championships were held, with strawberries and cream, at Wimbledon.

It was on account of this old civil war—not the larger war whose end was being celebrated by the indolent dancers—that I had come to Nobeoka. In this city halfway down the east coast of Kyushu, in mid-August 1877, Saigo's campaign finally ran into the ground. On the morning of the 15th he came under heavy artillery and rifle fire in the thin coastal strip that I could see from the Imayama Shrine at dusk, beyond the rayon factory, and began retreating northward. By the night of the 17th, after three days of fierce fighting, he was well outside the city limits, dug in to the east of a 728-meter-high hill called Enodake. He had a force of fewer than three thousand men and was completely surrounded, cut off from supplies and further retreat by six brigades of the imperial army, about thirty thousand troops in all, whose positions ranged from the estuaries to the hills and pressed in on Saigo like the hoops of a barrel. All roads and rivers were denied him. His men had almost exhausted their ammunition. At a final council of war that night it was agreed that all but Saigo himself and the ringleaders of the rebellion must surrender. Saigo's war was lost. He was as good as dead. What followed is one of the most remarkable adventures in Japanese history.

◈

If I shaded my eyes against the heat haze and squinted towards the Hyuga Sea from the busy city bridge, past the solitary straw-hatted fisherman who stood crotch deep in the estuary of the Ose flinging out his weighted net to drag it slowly through the lazy weeds, I could see the overgrown sandbanks across which, that summer of the dead, the imperial army had advanced. It had pushed on through what are now the scruffy suburbs surrounding the rayon factory where from every window and door that I passed came the trumpets and drum thumps of the National High School Baseball Tournament being televised from Osaka. By the evening of the 17th, Saigo had built his last defenses near the tiny hamlet of Hyono. Five of the imperial brigades were deployed in a pincer-like formation to the south across both banks of the Kita River, and the sixth was dug in two miles to the north, above a bend in the river, to prevent his flight.

When darkness fell Saigo's council decided on surrender. But such was the loyalty of Saigo's troops that, so long as the great man remained to be protected, their compliance with this decision could not be guaranteed. So in the dead of night, with the moon sinking and a fog rolling down through the inland valleys, Saigo and those closest to him accomplished the impossible. They broke through the enclosing hoops of the enemy and escaped into the empty hills, leaving the remainder of their shattered force under the command of officers who had pledged to lay down their weapons when the dawn came. The council had determined that the escaping band would contain only men who faced a likely death sentence. But so indissoluble were the ties that bound the students of Saigo's old military-style schools to their sensei that those who heard of his planned escape could not be deterred from joining him. The eventual number who left the camp and advanced along the footpaths of Hyono toward the slopes of Enodake—the one route left half open to them because the imperial commanders had considered it impassable—was between six and seven hundred, almost all of them ex-students of Saigo's schools, all from samurai families, all resigned to their deaths.

By some accounts, the escape was a noisy one, with a heavy exchange of rifle fire and the small contingent of imperial troops guarding the approaches to Enodake overwhelmed and relieved of their weapons and supplies. By other accounts the escape was made in silence, in single file along a wild boar track that led in a steep, tangled climb to the summit of the hill, with word passed in whispers down the line to tread softly and to muffle all sounds.

Whatever the circumstances, Saigo escaped. Over the next sixteen days, pursued by the imperial brigades they had eluded, he and the last of the rebels fought their way first west, then south along the backbone of the Kyushu mountains, across daunting tracts of some of the wildest country in Japan, in a last-fling effort to reach their home city of Kagoshima and make a final stand there.

It was a journey that, in the dozen years since I had first seen Saigo's bullet-headed statue, had rattled about inside my head like a fly in a closed room. I wanted to make that journey myself, alone, on foot, as nearly as possible over the same mountain passes, down the same tracks, through the same forgotten villages, on the same days as Saigo had. I wanted to see how closely I could follow in his footsteps, how much the countryside had changed, what had gone, and what remained. I wanted to know what turns a man into a planetary, statued, woodblock-printed god. So on the morning of the 17th of August, a Sunday, with the Bon drums silent for another year and the baseball drums driving cats into the street, 109 summers after Saigo had done the same, I marched north out of hot Nobeoka, towards the sleepy hamlet of Hyono. . . .

It was the first overcast morning in days but the clouds had not dispelled the heat. And, as must have happened more than a hundred years before when the surrendered rebels and their captors began the long trek home from the battlefields, Miyazaki prefecture was losing people at a rate that animated the nightly newsreaders. The annual O-Bon holiday was over and the natives of Miyazaki who had come back for the three days of the festival now packed the buses and trains and planes that would return them by clocking-in time on Monday to their apartment blocks in Tokyo and Osaka and Kita-Kyushu, where they lived and would eventually die. Perhaps the ghosts that should rightly have been in Nobeoka for the dance already haunted those sprawling cities. The summers, like the hills, were growing emptier.

Close up, the patched and grimy walls of the rayon factory were like a prison's, topped by trees to give them the appearance of decency, just as the walls of the city jail in Kuala Lumpur are decorated with attractive murals to catch your eye and tease your fancy away from the thump of the gallows trap. The air of prosperity that had oozed from the boutiques in the roofed arcades of the city's center was absent altogether from its suburbs. They wound on, the road narrowing, past the Asahi Chemical Company's supermarket, until the drooping houses and the little shops that were falling apart bumped suddenly into the tangled hump of a hill, deliberately left in its wild state, flanked on one side by a primary school and on the other by lime-green paddies. At the foot of the hill stood the first of many remembrances of Saigo's war that I would come across on this five-hundred-kilometer tramp: a wooden plaque which recorded in stiff textbook prose that Saigo had paused here on the morning of August 15th and established the last of his rearguard positions. The hill was called Kashiyama (Oak Hill), but its slopes were covered with thickets of bamboo and its top was surmounted by a small wooden shrine and a handful of weathered graves.

By midday the overcast had dissolved into patches of lazy cumulus, and the sun was back out with a vengeance. I stopped for lunch in a small restaurant so run down and disorderly that it had no beer. The old man who operated it with his haggard wife trudged off to the liquor shop and came back with a single bottle. The place was called Akebono (Daybreak) and had a vending machine that sold *bikkuri suru* (shocking) pictures. You pressed a button to select the category of your choice: woman + woman, woman + man, or "open woman," all four hundred yen. Across the road, just outside the city limits, stood several love hotels one after the other—Akasaka, Hotel Fuji, Plaza House—with posted rates per hour for "resting." Going from Nobeoka to Kitagawa appeared to be much like crossing from Utah to Nevada; once free of the almighty chemical company's scrutiny you could debauch yourself in any number of ways.

My plan was to spend the night as close as possible to the foot of Enodake and then climb it, as Saigo had, the following morning, though not until after breakfast. So shortly after my disordered lunch I began looking for a place to stay. At Hyono, on a curve, stood the Hotel Kaabu (Hotel Curve), but this, like the Fuji and the Plaza House, offered small enticement to the solitary or the chaste. There were no lodging houses or ordinary inns in the little hamlet, just a grocer's shop where I drank a second beer and gave the old lady who owned it the jitters by asking her which footpath led up Enodake.

"Ooo, don't go up there. You'd better not. There's no telling what you'll come across. We don't let our kids go anywhere near those footpaths. There's wasps up there . . . "

I chuckled.

" . . . and adders. Hundreds and hundreds of adders."

Solemnly, I drank a third bottle of beer.

Then, across the railway track in a small compound full of sharp knee-high grass, I found a Zen temple with faded signs in English. One said "Priest's Quarters," another said, "Main Temple—worshipping," and a third said "It is prohibited to" but the rest had been washed away by the rain.

"What do you want?" said the woman who looked after the place, running out from one of the buildings with her hands and apron flapping. She must have been driven barmy by the loneliness and heat. "Do you want to pray? The priest's away. Are you studying something? There's nothing to see."

Who had put up all these English signs, I wondered.

"The priest's son," she said, hopping from foot to foot. "He works for the *Mainichi Shinbun*. He put them up in case Americans dropped in."

"What is it that's prohibited?"

The woman raised and lowered her hands, and made fists, and gripped the sides of her apron.

"There's nothing here," she said. "I'm sorry. I'm so sorry. You'd better go. There's nothing I can show you."

Finally, after five more minutes on the highway, I came to a much larger restaurant that doubled as a minshuku, and arranged to stay the night there. The place had two powerful attractions. The first was that there was nowhere else to go. The second was that it was called the Saigo Teahouse and contained several mementos of the hero, including souvenir curtains for shop doorways from Kagoshima and a miniature replica of the famous statue in Ueno Park, erected twenty-one years after the rebellion had failed, nine years after its leader had received a posthumous pardon from the Meiji Emperor, and funded by subscribers from all over Japan (who had originally wanted it to stand in the Imperial Palace Plaza). The statue depicted Saigo out hunting with his favorite dog, dressed so carelessly in a simple cotton yukata of the kind people sleep in that his widow had complained to the sculptor. There was also a framed picture on the wall in which the great man looked like a pop-eyed schoolboy who has stuffed himself so full that he is about to let fly a roaring fart, and a small notice to the effect that Saigo had rested here for about half an hour from 11 A.M. on August 12th on his way upriver to obtain supplies, before the hoops had tightened.

At nine o'clock the next morning, after two cups of bitter coffee, I set out back towards the village of Hyono, past the Hotel Curve where a single pale yellow lily had fought its way up through a crack in the asphalt and was being smothered to death by dust, then along what I assumed was the footpath to Enodake. Earlier the hills had been covered by a thick flat blanket of stagnant mist, but this had vanished in the gathering heat. The old woman at the Hyono grocer's shop poked her head out of the doorway as I passed to renew her warnings of the previous afternoon. There were wasps' nests every few yards. The hill was alive with adders. And now, at the height of summer, the track would be so overgrown that I was bound to lose it.

In fact I was lost before I got out of Hyono. The path had already forked four times and the branch I ended up following deposited me in the middle of the village graveyard. I called at the last house that stood on this path and another old woman gave me fresh directions, told me once more about the wasps and adders, and stood watching me suspiciously as I picked my way through the moldering headstones. The imperial commanders, I remembered, had considered this route impassable, but that was for a tired and disconsolate army. Whereas here I was, on a bright summer's morning, the better for a breakfast of raw egg and sweetfish, with nothing on earth to deter me and a consuming desire to put as much distance between me and the chimney of the rayon factory as I could before midday.

But if this route was impassable in 1877, little had happened since to improve it. Like most of the feudal-era paths—the paths that Saigo must have followed—there was hardly anything left to see of it. For the first few hundred yards it ran through a steep leaf-strewn gully, not much more than three feet wide, like a miniature railway cutting dug into the loamy earth. The gully walls were perpendicular and moss-covered, about a man's height, and exposed roots snarled out across the track and lurked there anticipating the rare approach of ankles. Not far up the track I found a grave on which it was still possible to decipher the name, Nakazu, and the date of the occupant's death, August 16th, 1877, the day before Saigo had begun his retreat. Perhaps he had been shot while reconnoitering or perhaps he was the victim of wasps or adders.

The main peacetime difficulty, however, was the immense number of spiders' webs that spanned the track at face height, many of them as resilient as rubber bands (the effects of the proximity of synthetic fiber factories on arachnid metabolism is a subject requiring study). Clearly, mine were the first boots to tread this track for many weeks. I lumbered along, slipping on the stones, tripping on the ankle-snaring roots, and holding a stick up stiffly in front of my face to collect the rubbery webs. Within minutes the stick looked like a dirty grey candy floss. I felt sorry for the spiders, but this was war. I suppose the advance guards of Saigo's party had been assigned to web duty, too; according to one account, the thirty men at the head of the column were armed with sickles.

All along the track the trees seemed petrified, until you looked up towards the invisible sky and saw that their upper leaves remained green, while everything below ten meters in height had shriveled and blackened from the long absence of the sun. In the early morning, outside the teahouse window, the cicadas had been as loud as the diesel trucks; but here in this forest there were no cicadas, and even the birds sounded eerily distant. It was, I think, the stillest forest I have ever had to clamber through. More graves appeared among the black trunks and logged stumps, like overgrown fingernails clawing their way out of the ground, but the writing on none of them was legible; the rain and mold of more than a hundred years had expelled their tenants from history.

The track emerged from the narrow gully and began to twist and swerve as the slope grew steeper. I came to a rock and swung my pack off to sit on it for a few minutes' rest, and when my pack hit the ground a couple of hundred wasps shot out from under the rock with a noise like a chainsaw. I flapped my towel at them and yelled and stumbled back the way I had come, leaving the wasps to punch holes in my pack. One of them—but only one— managed to punch a hole in my arm as well. I heard the puncture, like a tiny lead ball fired into stiff paper, and within minutes I had a bruise about four inches across. I stood on the track below the wasps' nest squinting, stamping, saying "bugger this," rolling my shirtsleeves down, tying a sky-blue towel tightly round my head and face, and recalling an article I had recently glanced at in a Japanese weekly magazine in which it was recorded that the number of people who died from wasp stings in Japan in an average year was thirty. Then I took several deep breaths, charged up the slope as fast as I could, grabbed my pack with one hand while in full flight, and didn't stop running for several hundred yards, not until I saw the adder.

The adder disappeared. And after another ten minutes (bugger this) so did the track. I poked about in the long weeds and found that, by climbing on a boulder, I obtained a wonderful view of the love hotel roofs and the red-and-white chimney of the rayon factory. The natural contours of the more accessible hills across the valley were broken by crisply regimented, dead straight lines of young trees planted in equidistant ranks like pegs in a cribbage board. I scooped a few mouthfuls of sweet-tasting water from a little brook that trickled among the cedars and then climbed on up towards what I took to be the summit, and reached it just after eleven o'clock.

One of Saigo's biographers speaks of a quarter-acre field on the summit of Enodake and a hut in which the great man and his rebels, having driven out a small, astonished garrison of imperial army soldiers, spent the last hours of darkness on this first foggy morning of retreat. The biographer appends a detailed account of everything Saigo found in the hut (fifty new Mauser rifles with ammunition, sixteen gallons of sake, a great many twenty-pound cans of beef, and a large supply of rice). But in fact there was hardly enough flat space on the summit to erect a scarecrow, let alone a hut. In every direction the slopes of the hill were a mad tangle of head-high shrubbery and I spent thirty minutes struggling about in it, looking for a way down into the valley of the Hori River where Saigo had taken advantage of the lingering fog to spend most of the next two days. But there was no sign of a track and, so far as I could see, no way down through the brambles and bracken that would not result in my suffering the Death of a Thousand Cuts. Nor was the ground visible through the tangle, nor was there any mapped landmark on which I could take a compass bearing. So, since the last thing I fancied was spending the night being devoured by wasps and adders and since, anyway, seven hours of daylight remained, I picked my way back down the slope I had climbed, rediscovered the track, skirted the wasps' nest, and an hour or so after midday unslung my pack once more at the grocer's shop in Hyono, where, to her everlasting credit, the old woman refrained from cackling and silently fetched me a beer.

My shirt was wetter from the morning's climb than it had been at any time since, several years before, I had become the first non-Micronesian since the Japanese occupation of the Carolines to cross the rain forest of Pohnpei on foot. I have done some very silly things in my life, but they have usually had their compensations. The compensation in Pohnpei was to arrive back at the Village Hotel with a sprained ankle (the result, my guide explained, of my having disturbed the forest ghosts), covered in grime and sweat and mildew and tottering along with the aid of a large stick, to discover Congressman Stephen Solarz of New York with a floral lei around his neck, a large whisky in his hand, and a fat cigar sticking out of his mouth, telling a dining room crowded with American politicians, their wives, and at least half a dozen secret service operatives how glad he was to be discovering the "real" Micronesia. In the background a small choir of island children under the supervision of an American missionary were singing to a guitar accompaniment, "We're Together Again Just Praising the Lord!," gesturing towards Congressman Solarz every time they sang the word *Lord*.

My compensation for having discovered the real Enodake was to sit in the little grocer's shop, naked to the waist, drinking two beers, eating a sausage, and entertaining the old woman's three fat giggling granddaughters (who kept staring at the bruise on my arm and going "Oooooo!") with tales of high adventure, while my shirt hung draped over my filthy pack drying in the hot sun. Masked, hatted women came in from the fields wiping their faces and bowed to me solemnly.

"He's been up Enodake," the old woman told them.

They bowed again and offered me cold barley tea. The delivery man who came to restock the sweet shelves guessed my age was twenty-three (I thanked him) and told me that when he was in primary school, his teachers had kept the track up Enodake in reasonably good condition but that in recent years nothing had been done about it at all, and the only people who ever went near it were "crazies who go up mountains."

The rest of the afternoon I spent in a restaurant that I found on the trudge back into Nobeoka, from where, next morning, I planned to make a fresh start by skirting Enodake to the south and west and following the Hori River up its valley. The restaurant was a great empty wooden shed with no chairs in it at all, just low tables and frayed tatami mats on which I lay propped up on one elbow sipping beer and watching the diesel trucks growl by and disappear into a filthy tunnel. There were no other customers in the huge, barn-like dining room, and so the owner—a muscular young man in a white vest who wore a neatly clipped Errol Flynn moustache—gave me an hour's free instruction in the gastronomy of the *ayu*.

The ayu is a small river fish, variously defined in my dictionaries and cookery books as a sweetfish, a Japanese river trout, a samlet, and an ayu. It was one of the first fish I ever learned the Japanese name for because it figures in a joke well known to Japanese students of English, several of whom were among my earliest Tokyo acquaintances. The joke is as follows: One student of English says to another student of English, "Are you a fish?" The second student either replies, "No, I am not a fish," or some variant of this, or looks at his interlocutor as though he were a fruitcake. Whereupon, the first student says, "No, no, *ayu*" (are you) "*wa*" (a)—subject particle—"*sakana da yo*" (is certainly a fish), and the second student's face clouds over with embarrassment or lights up with mirth as he realizes that he has been treated to a pun. That is a fairly typical example of Japanese humor and, in case it hasn't put you off cracking jokes for the rest of your life, here is another. One man says to another man, "When was the Great Buddha of Kamakura erected?" (The Great Buddha of Kamakura is an 11.4-meter-high bronze statue of Amida seated in meditation.) The second man replies something along the lines of, "Oh, round about the middle of the thirteenth century, wasn't it?" Whereupon the first man says, "No, no, it is still sitting down." This joke, also a pun (the staple of Japanese verbal humor), depends on the fact that the verb *tatsu* can mean either "to put up" or "to stand up." Get it?

But I didn't tell either of these jokes to the owner of the empty restaurant near Nobeoka because he looked a very serious-minded man, and this he proved to be, especially when it came to ayu. So much a specialty of his restaurant, indeed of the whole area, were these little fish that the man's menu didn't even mention them. It simply said *shioyaki* (grilled with salt) or *miso-yaki* (cooked in fermented soybean paste) and you were left to infer the object of these attentions. First, he took me to see the live ayu swimming about in a tank in his yard.

"See, that one's got something the matter with its neck," he said, pointing to a fish that I couldn't see anything wrong with at all. Would it make any difference once the fish was dead? "Oh, yes. We can't serve that to a customer."

Then we went back inside and he showed me the correct way to eat a grilled ayu. First you break off the tail. Then you press both sides of the body four or five times with your chopsticks to loosen the flesh. Then you pull the head away from the body and, if you have done the job properly, the spine will follow it in one clean strip. The tiny bits of flesh that cling to the spine are considered the tastiest parts. And a customer who after doing all this can detect that his fish, while alive, had something wrong with its neck is obviously a person of no mean gifts.

I conducted the dissection over dinner at my ryokan in Nobeoka and won glowing compliments from the maid. Then I did my laundry and was in bed and asleep by eight o'clock. Round one had gone to Enodake and the wasps, and Saigo had a thirty-four-hour start. But I knew that by skirting Enodake to the south I could reach Upper Hori in a single day whereas Saigo and his rebels had taken two, and I also knew (sweet dreams) that I would be going there along a road.

✼

There are two schools of thought among people who go on long walks and write about them. The more common school holds that you should stay away from roads as much as possible, take a tent and camp out whenever you can, and avoid human beings as though they carried the plague. To this school belong such luminaries of the genre as John Hillaby, who walked from Land's End to John o'Groats and wrote a book about it called *Journey Through Britain*, and Stephen Pern, who walked the length of the United States from the Mexican border to the Canadian border and wrote a book about it called *The Great Divide*. I have read both their books with pleasure and admiration, but I also found them frustrating, and this arose, I think, out of their being so noticeably short of encounters with people. Stephen Pern's most memorable encounter was with a bear and John Hillaby's was with Offa's Dyke.

As a matter of fact I had a correspondence with Stephen Pern who phoned me one day to say that he was planning to walk the length of Japan and did I have any advice about camping and provisions? There really wasn't much advice I could give him since, when I had walked the length of Japan, I hadn't camped or carried any provisions. But our correspondence provided us with an opportunity to air our opposing schools of thought. Stephen was all for trekking over mountain peaks, forsaking them for lower ground only in order to stock up on food, and then heading back to the forests and away from grocer's shops and restaurants and cold beer the minute he had done his shopping. My journey had been almost entirely along roads; not highways, of course—not by preference anyway; highways and their tunnels are a walker's curse—but along smaller, emptier, pleasanter roads that would, with luck, deposit me when dusk fell near a village or a town where I could eat and drink and sleep in comfort. I didn't carry a tent at all. I carried a sleeping bag, but on that three-and-a-half-thousand-kilometer journey I used it only twice (and both times it rained).

There is no way of reconciling our two schools of thought. But Stephen confessed to me in his last gloomy postcard that his feet had let him down among the Tohoku mountains and that he had reluctantly decided to go from Yamagata to Yamanashi by train and continue on foot from there; whereas, though my journey had lacked the challenge of his, I had maintained a very strict rule of not using any kind of land transport at all, not even on the "rest days," which I spent wandering about large cities. It is a rule I have kept on all my treks; I call it the Protestant Walk Ethic.

Some readers, I suppose, will scoff at my decision not to scramble down Enodake the hard way and blaze a passage towards Upper Hori through the brambles. But I travel to enjoy myself, not to test my eligibility for the Special Air Service. And I like meeting people. That is why I don't camp. I like roads, too. That is why, on this hot morning of August 19th, I was happier by far than I had been the day before.

What's more, the road to Upper Hori, all thirty-odd kilometers of it, was nearly ideal for solitary walking. Granted, there was not much shade and, for most of the day, there was nowhere to buy beer. There weren't many people along it either. But after the first hour, when it wound through a wide valley full of swampy rice fields and scarecrows made of blue-ribboned bonnets and black plastic raincoats and blue-frocked old ladies carrying pink parasols, the road clung tight to the Hori River, which alternated between fierce bursts of rock-strewn rapids and deep still pools of moody green. It was an uphill climb all the way and I think two cars passed me in seven hours.

Once out of sight of the last houses in the valley and beyond the frenzied noise of the televised baseball, I pulled off all my clothes and jumped into the river. It was flowing much too fast to swim in, so I waded out to a large boulder and sat with my back braced against it, immersed in water up to my neck, and let the cold, crisp current splash over and around me. Above my head reared the crags of Enodake and in all directions lay the summer hills. My skin tingled; I felt like a schoolboy.

I stayed in the river for half an hour. Then I pulled on my clothes and set

off again, passing a group of construction workers who lay on tables outside
their plywood huts snoozing or listening to the baseball with their tools all
around them.

"There's nothing up this road till you get to Lower Hori," one of them
called after me.

"That's all right," I said. "I'm not looking for anything."

"There's drinking water about a kilometer further on, though."

"Good."

"And if you're planning to walk all the way to Upper Hori you're an idiot."

Where the loggers had slung cables to haul trunks across the river, the valley looked as though it had been carpet bombed. It was a mess of sawdust,
dead rust-red pines, and scars torn into the hillsides by winches. I am told
that in Miyazaki prefecture the damage wrought by loggers is greater—or at
least more noticeable—than in any other part of Kyushu. An old man on the
train down from Kokura had described to me how, if you walk up into the
hills along the Miyazaki-Oita border, you can see the trees all standing
balmily on the Oita side and, twenty meters away on the Miyazaki side, nothing but a waste of stumps.

A kilometer up the road I found the drinking water, a thin torrent that
splashed down a cliff face and disappeared under the crumbling road surface.
Someone had directed part of it through a length of pipe and left a small plastic ice-cream tub upside down on a stick for a cup. I sat down for five minutes on an upturned fire bucket, gulped too much of the water too quickly,
and was thinking quite hard about vomiting when it started to pelt rain.
Twenty minutes later the rain stopped and the asphalt began to steam
so fiercely that half the gorge turned a smoky white as though filling with
Saigo's fog. I set off along the steaming road again and was tormented by a
swarm of flies that stayed with me most of the way to Hori.

There are two buses a day between Nobeoka and Hori and the afternoon
one passed me completely empty. My map showed a bus stop called
Hatsudensho-mae (In Front of the Power Plant Site), but the bus stop had
vanished and all that was left of the power plant was a shell of cracked con-

crete, twisted iron, and shattered glass. The gorge here was chock full of boulders that had tumbled down into it from the shifting hills and, as so often in Japan, huge stretches of the cliff faces had been sprayed with concrete or covered with wire mesh to prevent new landslides.

Throughout this nation of "nature lovers" the price of security has been ugliness, from the polyhedrons that clutter the coasts to the sprayed and netted cliffs and the breeze-blocked rivers. Miyazaki prefecture has a formidably heavy annual rainfall, much of it brought by the autumn typhoons. The danger of landslides and floods is real, especially in these narrow valleys, so you can't blame the local authorities for trying to take precautions. But between them, the loggers and the builders and the sprayers are changing the face of the Japanese countryside so radically that, within a couple more generations, I can't imagine anyone wanting to pay it a visit. There will always be the famous beauty spots, of course—the Pine Islands, the Floating Bridge of Heaven—all properly geared up for full-throttle tourism, oversupplied with hotels and cruises, and registered in order of attractiveness: the Three Most Beautiful Scenic Views, the Three Best Gardens, the Eight Best Prospects. But in a few more years the unregistered parts of Japan will be so safe from landslides and rockfalls and floods that you won't be able to hear the wind in the trees.

So I grumped to myself as I slapped away the flies, one of which had just died messily up my nose. But in mid-afternoon I found a way down the steep bank to one of the deep, lagoon-like stretches of the Hori River, tore off my clothes, plunged into it again, and had my faith in natural rejuvenation swiftly resurrected. If a river like this can restore my grumpy spirits, I thought, peering down through the dark translucent water at the small grey fish that were nibbling my toes, I suppose it can look after its own. It was, of course, an ecologically unsound conclusion. I dried myself on a rock, and when I set off walking again I felt as though I'd showered in shaved ice.

Fifty minutes later I reached the first patch of cleared ground that I'd seen for about five hours. It was not under cultivation, it had been burned flat. And lo! the first building I came to in Lower Hori—in fact practically the *only* building in Lower Hori—was a large and well-stocked booze shop.

I stood and drank a bottle of Kirin and chatted to the old man who ran the place. He wore a clean white shirt and learned-looking spectacles (I had actually caught him *reading*, not sitting in front of a television set) and he giggled hugely at the thought of somebody walking all the way from Nobeoka. Nobody to his knowledge had done that before, at least not in the seventeen years since they had built the dam.

"What on earth did you want to do a thing like that for? There's nothing here, you know. Nothing at all. In Lower Hori there's me and four other houses. Hardly what you'd call a village. And in Upper Hori, four kilometers up the road, there's a grocer's shop and an inn for the people who come to fish for carp. And that's it. That's all there is. What on earth are you supposed to be looking for?"

I told him about Saigo Takamori and asked him if it was likely that the old track over the hills from Upper Hori to Shikagawa was still usable.

"To where?"

"Shikagawa," I said, pointing to it on my map. The two ideograms mean "Deer River."

"That's not Shikagawa, that's Shishigawa," the old man said.

I stared at my map.

"But it's written *shika*."

"I can't help that. We call it *shishi*."

So I folded my map and said "I see," and poured myself another glass of beer. This conversation could only have happened in rural Japan, where it has often seemed to me that places have names deliberately designed to confuse any person not born within a radius of about five miles. But I couldn't complain; I was adding to my stock of country lore. In Hori, I now knew, *shika* is pronounced *shishi*. No wonder the imperial army had trouble locating Saigo. I opened another bottle of Kirin.

"If you're going up them old tracks," the old man said, "you want to get some decent footwear."

"What's wrong with the footwear I've got?" I asked him, looking down, miffed, at my Italian-soled boots.

"They're the wrong type," he said. "What you need is gaiters."

"Gaiters?"

"So as the adders can't get at your ankles."

When I left, the old man giggled again at the thought of my drinking two bottles of beer and still being able to walk without wobbling. But it was the flies who found the beer intoxicating. For the last four kilometers, all the way to Upper Hori, they fed in my armpits, swam in my sweat, flew into my mouth, and died in my hair. Beyond the dam, the hills ahead were a stage set for Lovecraft's *Arkham*. A thick mist rolled off them like ichor and above their dark humps a storm was gathering. To the south the craggier mountains, prussian blue and inky grey, were more like cut-outs in a ghost train, and five minutes later, when I looked for them again, they had vanished altogether in the mist.

At half past five I reached the first house in Upper Hori. A hooded woman stood outside it stoking her bath with firewood. I found the grocer's shop a few minutes further on, and took a room in what passed for a minshuku that the grocer operated above her storage shed. The room was bare and dusty and damp but the grocer's shop doubled as a diner for the carp fishers and I was halfway through my first mug of Kirin draft by the time the heavy rain started falling.

Rarely had I stayed in a lonelier community and never in one that, despite such isolation, still managed to operate a minshuku and a restaurant that dispensed draft beer. The more I drank the more I admired it. There was a large potted tree just inside the doorway decorated with empty three-liter Kirin cans and, behind the counter in a small glass case, a little furry koala bear with a sign round its neck that said, in cuddly Australian, "You be my Tootsie-Wootsie and I'll be your Fuzzie-Wuzzie." There was even a karaoke machine—a tiny red portable practice model called "Clarion Lesson"—into which the only other customer in the place, a young man wearing a "Manhatten" T-shirt, was croaking pop songs.

The place was run by a seventeen-year-old schoolgirl whose mother looked after the shop and the lodgers. When her mother was safely on the other side of the yard stoking my bath and clucking at her chickens, the daughter stole two cartons of instant noodles from a box wrapped up for the gift-giving season, and heated one for herself and one for the Manhatten T-shirt man who, judging from the intensity of their slurps, had more on his mind than karaoke.

"It's not such a bright life out in the country," the girl confided to me as she served me a plate of carp boiled until it was the texture of chewed tissue paper. I never supposed it was, I confessed. She showed me four small colored photographs of a local species of bamboo, with vertical yellowy-gold streaks on it, that was about to be registered as a protected species.

"But we've got nice things like this," the girl said. "Look. Don't you think this is nice?"

"I think it's very nice," I told her, and wondered where she went to school.

"I don't," she said. "It's too far away. I send reports in and they give me marks."

I hadn't realized you could do that, I said.

She picked up the photographs of the streaked bamboo, looked at them for a little while, and then arranged them carefully on top of the glass case that held the woolly koala.

"Yes, we've got some nice things," she laughed.

With an extra sharp slurp, the Manhatten T-shirt man finished his noodles and handed back the carton. The girl smiled sweetly and passed him the song list. I had two more beers and a bath and went to bed.

The men would know about the old roads, the girl had told me; I could ask them in the morning before they went to work. For most of the night the rain splashed out of holes in the drainpipe and clattered on the window panes. And when I went downstairs to the lavatory, I found it crawling with inquisitive, bright orange maggots.

The rain stopped at five o'clock but the maggots were still there when I finally got up. So twice in the space of a couple of hours I was glad that rural Japanese-style lavatories, which have no flush and normally no drainage, did not require my bum to come in contact with the porcelain. Hygienic-minded people have praised the arrangement on this account, though I can think of several drawbacks: the smell for one, and the pains and cramps that an unsupported squat must inflict on the elderly, the ill, the crippled, or the heavily pregnant. And here were a few dozen more little drawbacks, doing orange congas round the inside of the bowl.

What the girl had failed to tell me was that the men all went to work at half past six, and it was after seven by the time I dragged myself down the stairs and limped across the yard to breakfast. Would her mother know the old roads? No, she wouldn't have the faintest notion and anyway she had gone into Nobeoka on the early bus. Well, hadn't the girl played along them herself or gone up them looking for streaked bamboo? No, she hadn't. That is to say, she had. But she had no idea that any of the tracks (tracks they were really; you couldn't call them roads) went all the way to Shishigawa. She had never heard of anyone walking there from here. There were plenty of old tracks through the hills; loggers' tracks, hunters' tracks, foragers' tracks, charcoal burners' tracks. But so far as she knew, they all went up into the trees somewhere and stopped. The best plan she could think of was for me to sit here and wait until midday, when one or two of the men would be in for lunch. But if I did that, I pointed out, there would be no time left for me to make use of what they told me. That was true, she admitted brightly, and gave me a bowl of seaweed soup.

Eventually, I got her to telephone an acquaintance in Lower Hori who was supposed to know the tracks (it turned out to be the old man at the booze shop), and who offered me once again this recommendation: Don't go anywhere near them. They'll be totally overgrown in summer. The one you're looking for hasn't been used for at least a quarter of a century. And, what's more, all of those old mountain paths are alive with . . .

" . . . wasps and adders."

At nine o'clock, ignoring everyone's advice, I went in search of Saigo's vanished track. I knew (it is recorded in local history books) that Saigo had spent the night of the 19th, as I had, in Upper Hori and that he had stayed at the home of a Mr. Ono Kumayoshi, the whereabouts of which had been as unfamiliar to the girl as were the tracks that were supposed to start outside her shop. As the crow flies, Upper Shishigawa, which Saigo had reached by the evening of the 20th, is not much more than nine kilometers away. The largest-scale map I had with me showed a faint dotted line connecting Upper Hori with Upper Shishigawa along the crest of a range of hills and over a peak 1,103 meters high. The dotted line was even labeled at this point "The

Shishigawa Pass," and the map had been published only nine months before, so I had no reason not to trust it.

The last person I consulted before leaving the little hamlet was a red, lumpy-faced old woman, who pointed airily in several directions. The map showed four different dotted lines fanning out from Upper Hori.

"Which is the path to Shishigawa?" I asked her.

"That one," she said, indicating all of them, one after the other.

"And is it possible to walk there?"

"No, not at all."

I decided that the most promising-looking path was the one that followed the heavy-duty plastic pipe which brought the hamlet's water supply down from the hills. This black pipe ran sometimes beside my feet and sometimes high in the branches of the trees, jerking and sighing like an injured animal whenever an unseen tap fed off its contents. But it wasn't long before my woodland track had merged with a loose-surfaced motor road of which my nine-month-old map showed no sign at all. I followed the motor road for forty minutes, as it curved and twisted round the sides of the hills instead of going straight up and down them as the old tracks had. Then it forked, one branch plunging steeply down and the other climbing steadily up. It was impossible to take a compass bearing on a road that twined and wound like this, since on average it doubled back on itself about twice every quarter of an hour. I took the upper fork and tramped on for another fifty minutes, until the road ended in a logged glade where two women in track suits and head-scarves and black splay-toed rubber boots sat boiling a charred kettle over a log fire and eating tomatoes.

"No, this is not the road you want," one of them said. "And looking for it will be a waste of time. Once they've built a motor road like this, you can't even see where the old ones stopped and started."

"Mind you, there's no point in talking to us," said the other one. "We don't know anything; we're only women. If you want to know about roads, you see, you've got to ask the men."

"Aren't you a foreign person?" the first woman asked shyly, after I'd been standing chatting to them for about five minutes.

"Yes, as a matter of fact I am," I said.

"Mmm," said the other woman, and she gave me a mug of iced sugar water and a slab of crumbly cake. They were waiting for their husbands, they explained, who were away in the forest sawing up trees. If I wanted to sit with them I was welcome. The men would be back before evening, and they could give me a lift down from the hills in their truck.

Thanking the women for their cake, I trudged off back in the direction of Upper Hori.

By midday I was sitting in the restaurant drinking a draft Kirin and watching the schoolgirl hum busily to herself as she grilled me a trout. What was I going to do now, she wanted to know. I was going to drink two more draft beers, I told her, and eat another trout, and then I was going to put my boots on again and walk the thirty kilometers back to Nobeoka.

"Oh, yes?" she said, and gave me a lovely smile; the sort that psychiatric nurses reserve for the incurable.

"Take care of yourself," she chirped to me as I trudged away down the only route by which her shop now appeared to communicate with the rest of the world, the same paved, unshaded road up which I had trudged the previous day. I passed the well-stocked booze shop, cursed, muttered, sighed, swam, narrowly avoided treading on a three-foot-long snake, refused a lift in a loggers' van, passed the workmen sprawled out snoozing in exactly the same positions in which they had been sprawled out snoozing the day before, and the two grey uniformed security guards with helmets and walkie-talkie radios who were posted at either end of the road works to protect the snoozing workmen from nonexistent traffic. I met two junior high school girls who bowed to me and said *O-kaeri nasai* (the greeting which schoolchildren are taught to use when they meet their elders in this part of the countryside, and which, roughly translated, means "Welcome back") and two junior high school boys who giggled and yelled *Gaijin!* I drank one beer sitting at a plastic-covered table at the little grocer's shop in the hamlet of Myomachi, smelled the ripening rice till my mouth started watering, passed birds fishing in the silvery river and a man exercising his slavering dogs by making them run on leashes behind his scooter. By dusk, I was lurching once again through the narrow streets around the rayon factory. I had walked ninety-five kilometers in three days and arrived back precisely where I'd started.

I went out to a restaurant late that evening and was so weary that I stumbled against a pile of crates outside the restaurant's entrance and knocked a dozen empty shochu bottles into the street. At the table I dropped my rice bowl into the tempura sauce and the waitress who came to mop up the mess gave me a look that she had obviously been practicing in a mirror and that she saved up for difficult drunks. The arcade loudspeakers were still broadcasting Paul Anka songs and, in the coffee shop where I fell asleep over a cup of Kilimanjaro, the Percy Faith Orchestra was playing "Some Enchanted Evening." I would have no choice the next morning but to head directly for the town of Takachiho, fifty-five kilometers straight up National Highway 218 according to the road signs. Saigo had reached Takachiho by August 21st and, if I forgot about the old tracks and stuck to the busy highway, I reckoned that I could rejoin his route by the morning of the 23rd. Then the blisters on the balls of my feet and the smaller ones on the joints of my toes began arguing a case for the 24th. And my calves and thighs and ankles and knees chimed in to propose the 25th. What the hell, I shrugged as I stood up to leave the coffee shop, clinging briefly to a potted palm tree. Saigo was fifty-eight hours ahead of me and my legs had decided he could stay there.

2

The Highway of
Myth and Legend

≫

The lesson I had learnt about the old roads in these three frustrating days would stand me in good stead for the rest of my journey. Though the old roads appeared on my map as dotted lines, though the very elderly sometimes remembered them, and though they still played an important and widely acknowledged part in the life cycle of wasps and adders, they were nowadays practically all invisible or impassable.

The track up Enodake was still available to mountain-climbing crazies, and the road along the river bank to Upper Hori still furnished a trickle of a livelihood to one old man in a booze shop, one grocer and her seventeen-year-old daughter, and a handful of snoozing, local government-contracted workers and uniformed security guards who were charged with the task of maintaining it. But neither road went where it once had, and most of the rest went nowhere at all. The advent of motor transport was, of course, the heaviest nail in their coffin. They had struck out once, like old roads the world over, in straighter lines and up steeper slopes than motor transport could cope with. And besides, the wholesale exodus from the rural areas to the industrial cities—the most damaging and intractable of the social upheavals that affluence, or the search for it, continues to wreak on Japan—has meant that countrymen looking for work do not nowadays go into the hills where they once went, to collect mushrooms or burn charcoal, and so they do not need the steep, straight tracks. Instead they pile their families into trains and buses and go to Tokyo or Osaka or their environs, where about forty percent of the nation's working people now cram themselves into tiny two or three-room apartments that will never belong to them because the cost of the land would plunge them into debt for two generations, and maintain, for the sake of government surveys about "lifestyle," that they are "middle-class."

Coming down a now-vanished track—according to one of the best-known anecdotes about him—Saigo Takamori, near the beginning of his retreat, somewhere between Enodake and Hori, when his campaign had miscarried, the bulk of his army had surrendered or scattered, and his own death was a foregone conclusion, met two peasants also on their way down from the hills and these stood aside from the track to let Saigo pass. According to one of Saigo's biographers, the two peasants were a certain Maki and a little boy named Kawakami Takeshi.

"What is the matter?" the little boy had asked.

"We must get out of the way," whispered Maki. "Sensei is coming."

In later life, the little boy recalled that Saigo had been walking quietly, wearing a sword at his side and a uniform cap from one of his own private schools. His face had worn a benign smile. He had looked as though he were out hunting in peaceful hills, quite indifferent to the encroaching nearness of his enemies. The little boy remembered thinking then that Saigo was "the greatest hero that the world had ever seen."

"How great a man Sensei is!" he had murmured to Maki.

"Yes," Maki had answered, "he is a god."

Then Saigo had drawn level with the two peasants, they had bowed deeply, and he had acknowledged their bows.

That's all. That is the anecdote. Saigo was a doomed man, a samurai, a former Marshal of the Army and Counselor of State. And he had acknowledged the bows of two peasants who met him at the time of his defeat on a mountain track. Those peasants wouldn't have known what a "lifestyle" was. They weren't even "middle-class."

Interestingly, the little boy's recollection (as represented in this particular biography) continues to the point where the two peasants reach the valley and see Saigo once again, this time in a less benign mood:

"I have never forgotten the image of Great Saigo then. He was squatting with his elbows on his knees, the hilt of his sword thrust forward, his left shoulder a little higher than the right, his lips tightly pursed, his eyes glaring fiercely at his men who were following him down the track. The terrible glare must have been a reproof for their tardiness. A wild animal crouching ready to spring on its prey could not have looked more ferocious."

Together with the first anecdote, this exemplifies perfectly the two sides of Saigo Takamori or, rather, the two sides that subsequent biographers, apologists, patriots, and worshippers have beaten each other about the head with, some crying "Saigo the Humanist!" and others "Saigo the War God!"

The biographer who records these two childhood recollections is the well-known novelist, poet, and essayist, Mushanokoji Saneatsu (1885–1976), himself a man in whom contradictory natures resoundingly collided. During the 1920s, Mushanokoji, an aristocrat by birth, devoted eight years of his life to developing a Utopian commune called *Atarashiki Mura* (New Village), which he had founded only a few miles from the spot where the defeated Saigo met the peasants. This followed his publication in 1916 of a polemic vigorously opposing the First World War. The commune was idealistic and democratic in nature and, even after he himself had left it, Mushanokoji remained its guiding spirit. But his pacifist and egalitarian sentiments did not prevent him from publishing in 1942 a book called *Daitoa Senso Shikan* (My Feelings on the Great East Asian War), which, unlike his earlier work, expressed uncritical approval of Japan's World War II policies and actions, and which later resulted in Mushanokoji's being removed from public office (the House of Peers) under the Occupation Purge.

It was also in 1942 that an English-language translation (or, as the Japanese translator preferred to call it, an "adaptation") of Mushanokoji's biography of Saigo was published in Tokyo. No English-language book could have been produced in Japan in that year unless it had been regarded by the official censor, or someone with similar responsibilities, as contributing to Japan's war effort through the improvement of the Japanese image overseas. The translator makes clear in his own preface (and his own memorable English) how his work, entitled *Great Saigo*, accomplishes that aim. Saigo is to be regarded as exemplifying "the patriotism of the Japanese and the spiritual basis of the new Japan" (that is to say, circa 1942) and "foreigners who wish to understand the feelings and the dispositions and the views of life of those who are Japanese to the backbone, needs must know him." The translator then proceeds to disarm potential skepticism by falling over himself to emphasize that, out of all the many Saigo biographies available for the sort of "adaptation" he had in mind, he chose Mushanokoji's because it is "impartially written."

Actually, the resulting "adaptation" is worshipful sometimes to the point of absurdity. On the very first page of the introduction, the hero of *Great Saigo* is introduced to the foreign reader as "a great man," "every inch an Oriental-minded person," "shining and serene in every sphere of his activity," a man who exuded a "radiant impression," whose every utterance "possesses something appealing and inimitable," a man "who knew the secrets of the human heart." And by the time we reach page xi we are being invited to compare the sayings of Saigo with those of Jesus Christ.

But from the very beginning, too, though it is the altruistic, super-wise, spiritual qualities of the hero that the "adaptor," publisher, and censor are most anxious to purvey as "Japanese to the backbone," the contradictions are difficult to suppress. So on page xi the Christ-like Saigo writes, "Heaven loves all men without discrimination, and we must love others with the love with which we love ourselves." And on the previous page, the same Saigo has written, "if a government should fail to fulfill its duty out of fear of the word 'war' it might justly be called a commercial regulator, and should never be called a government."

Some of these thoughts flitted through my head as I ambled past a monumental mason's yard about an hour and a half along the highway from

Nobeoka, peering at a large stone bust of Saigo that stood, newly carved, among the miniature pagodas and the pristine graves. Mushanokoji describes the physical Saigo as "a large-sized child who appeared rather slow-witted," and that is precisely what the bust depicted.

It was another swelteringly hot day and the highway ran through a broad, unshaded valley. Already two people had stopped for me, a nut-brown truck driver with dazzling white teeth who had beckoned me up into his cabin and whose eyes and mouth had popped open in delight when I told him I would rather walk, and a motorist in a damp white shirt who crossed the road on foot to give me a can of cold Coca-Cola.

"No thanks," I told him. "I'm not that fond of it."

"Shall I buy you something else then? What would you like?"

Further up the highway a fish vendor with only one front tooth heaved herself off the pile of white styrofoam fish boxes that she was sitting on to buy me a can of a different sort of drink from the machine that supported her back. The drink she bought me was called Ambrosia, a brand I had never heard of, but that didn't surprise me. New drinks proliferate in Japan at the same rate as porn videos and religious sects, the chief recommendation of any product being not quality or price or usefulness, but the endlessly touted trinity of newness: *shintojo* (newly available), *shingata* (new style), and *shin-hatsubai* (newly on the market). Those three expressions form the basis, I would estimate, of about twenty percent of all the advertising copy written in Japan. I guzzled the Ambrosia cheerfully and washed the taste away with old-style beer.

"You're silly to walk along a road in heat like this without a hat," said the fish vendor, squatting back on her styrofoam boxes and probing her tooth with her loose upper lip. "If I were you I'd take the train. There'll be one along in twenty-five minutes. The station's down that little street. Don't take the bus; it's twice the price. And you should still get yourself a hat."

I explained that I preferred to walk.

"Well, in that case, go to the stations to sleep," she said, sounding the voice of experience. "You'll be safe in stations from everything except mosquitoes. Buy yourself a mosquito coil and a box of matches before you go to sleep.

And phone your family; they'll be worried about you. And get yourself a hat."

That conversation was a great deal more sensible than the one I had five minutes later, which consisted of an overalled young man who worked in a garage shouting "Hurro! Hurro! Hurro! Hurro!" in a high-pitched nasal whine that he must have thought sounded foreign and funny. Years ago, when I first went on long walks in Japan, encounters like this were a daily occurrence and I spent a lot of time thinking about what sort of response I was expected to make. On more recent walks this has happened less often, although one or two throwbacks have resisted progress just as a handful of Neanderthals survived the coming of Homo Sapiens. But I don't suppose they will last much longer. Foreigners in Japan have begun to lack the essential recommendations for this kind of attention (we are no longer new style, newly available, or newly on the market).

Ahead of me the mountains that separate Miyazaki from Kumamoto rose sharp and daunting, and I remembered being told that it was in the part of the countryside towards which I was trudging that Ground Self Defense Force personnel conducted survival training. Beside the highway old-aged pensioners smacked croquet balls under parasols. The scarecrows in the paddies were plywood hawks, each feather carefully outlined in black. And, at regular intervals, road signs told me that I was tramping along the *Shinwa Kaido*, "The Highway of Myth and Legend."

By five o'clock that afternoon I was sitting on a sofa in the vestibule of the only ryokan in the village of Kawazuru, wearing a light cotton summer kimono, sipping beer, pondering the fact that I had managed to trudge only sixteen kilometers since morning, and listening to the ryokan's washing machine whirl itself into a mechanical fury as it tried to cope with the encrusted mud that had got onto my jeans when, earlier in the day, I was clambering about the banks of the Gokase River looking unsuccessfully for a place to soak my feet. Were I to follow the Japanese tradition of writing seventeen-syllable poems about my journeys, a large number of these poems, I am afraid, would feature beer and washing machines:

Clink of brown bottles;
I limp from the twin-tub:
Late summer's evening.

In fact, the reason I had covered only sixteen kilometers and not my usual thirty-odd had partly to do with tiredness, partly with the thirty-four-degree afternoon heat, partly with the dispiriting realization that the meanders of the newer roads I was obliged to follow would likely double the distance that Saigo had had to cover on the old straight tracks, partly with the sheer unpleasantness of walking along any road as busy as National Highway 218, which I had no choice but to follow as far as Takachiho, still forty kilometers away, and partly with the fact that, just after scrambling back up onto the road after my muddy encounter with the river, I happened to discover the only liquor shop in the area to boast a draft beer machine and refrigerated glasses.

In the Japanese countryside many ordinary liquor shops follow the amiable tradition of allowing customers to consume their purchases on the premises (though they have no licenses to act as bars) and, more often than not, provide a place to sit and rest and gather a large amount of otherwise hard-to-come-by information. Dehydration is one of the most serious dangers faced by the long-distance walker and it is a danger that I have never flinched from confronting. But when my book about walking from end-to-end of Japan was first published, the literary editor of one newspaper described my journey somewhat archly as "a two-thousand-mile-long pub crawl," a description which, I must say, rankled. What that editor so entirely failed to appreciate is that my hobbling in and out of liquor shops, especially ones that boast draft beer machines and refrigerated glasses, is done not for epicurean reasons but solely in the interests of social and historical research.

In the liquor shop above the Gokase River I learned, for example, that the premises were very old—they had been there sixty years—and that the owner's wife's uncle was the mayor of the village of Morotsuka, where Saigo had stayed on the night of the 23rd of August at the house of a man called Fujimoto Tsuizaburo after an exhausting hike across the Nanatsuyama Pass.

This information was just what I craved. I took my boots off and had another beer.

The beer machine was giving trouble; it was spouting too much froth ("trouble" with a Japanese beer machine usually means the opposite; the head on a glass of draft is normally adjusted until it accounts for about a third of the total contents); so the owner's wife spent the next five minutes saying irate things to her supplier on the telephone. It was essential to have the machine in proper working order before evening, she explained, because that's when most of her customers came in on their way home from work. Four or five glasses some of them drank and frequently rendered themselves incapable of driving.

I ordered more beer and took off my socks.

The owner was a lean, bare-chested man with a deep scar below his right eyebrow who smiled a lot and joined the growing fraternity of local people who felt that I was improperly dressed.

"What you want is a pair of these," he said, pointing to his own black split-toed, rubber-soled, canvas working boots with clip-on leggings to support his calves when going up mountains. "They let your feet exert their natural energies."

Very sensible, I agreed. So as soon as his wife had stopped complaining to the beer supplier, the owner phoned the local workingman's outfitters to ask them what was the largest size of split-toed, rubber-soled, canvas working boots with clip-on leggings that they had in stock.

Twenty-seven and a half centimeters, they told him.

"That's no good," I said. "I'd need at least a twenty-eight."

"Can't you do a twenty-eight?" he bellowed.

Not in under a fortnight, they explained. It would have to be a special order. Immensely disappointed, the owner replaced the telephone receiver and sat with his shoulders hunched, staring at his split-toed feet. So to cheer him up I ordered another beer, stretched out my legs, and showed him my blisters.

He had been quite a walker in his youth, he told me. Twenty years ago he had climbed right to the top of Enodake on a school outing. Did I know where that was? And on weekends he had occasionally gone as far as the Nanatsuyama Pass looking for mushrooms. Yes, it was true that in those days the old tracks had been better looked after, and this was mainly because the schoolteachers had taken a proper interest in things. But education had changed for the worse, and he wasn't surprised to hear my account of the sorry state of the wilderness today.

"Mind you, in Saigo Takamori's day most of the traveling up and down these valleys was by river, not by road. You ask my father. He can remember when this highway was nothing more than a towpath and the villagers all went about in flat-bottomed boats. Things were a lot quieter then. Not like now with these blasted loggers' trucks thundering past every minute of the day and night within a meter of the door."

Other things had changed as well. In Saigo's day, everybody had had big square jowls like you see in the old sepia photographs, so it's no surprise that Saigo had had them too. All the men had been hefty then; nowadays the Japanese were a lot more *sumaato* ("smart," but meaning slim). And look at money; money had changed. When he was at school a hundred yen would have bought the family their evening meal. Now it would buy one can of Ambrosia. And not only here. It was the same all over. What did the British use for money? Pounds, eh? And what were they worth?

"Nothing," I told him. He nodded soberly, and grunted and sighed. And I ordered more beer.

In the end it was the owner of the liquor shop who booked a room for me in the ryokan at Kawazuru not long after I had finished my seventh draft, having insisted, for purposes of social and historical research, on a freshly refrigerated glass each time.

The ryokan was run by the liquor shop owner's relative and, when he phoned to book the room, he went out of his way to impress upon her my seriousness of purpose.

"He's studying Saigo Takamori," he insisted, as though the name would open Aladdin's cave.

And it did. I got a friendly reception. In fact, when I asked for a bottle of beer I was also served a large glass of Calpis, which brought to mind a recurring nightmare. I go into a bar and order a beer, but the bar serves nothing but Calpis. I try to leave but they lock the door. "We have ways of making you drink," sneers the evil-looking barman as he begins lining up glasses of Calpis in front of me. I wake covered in sweat.

A wag once remarked that the only thing the Japanese ever invented was the folding fan, but they also invented Calpis. Calpis is a soft drink made from milk, sweetener, artificial coloring, and lactic-acid bacteria. In the United States it is known as *Calpico* because, when the Dentsu advertising agency test-marketed it there under its original name, it was greeted with whoops of merriment on account of the phonetic similarity of *Calpis* to *cow piss*. About the same time, the Dentsu advertising agency began sending its middle-level account executives to English conversation classes.

As I sat listening to the ryokan's spin dryer, a thunderstorm broke suddenly and fiercely and lasted till the early morning. The loud rain and thunderclaps added to the sleeplessness that had plagued me the last three nights, and which I have found as inescapable on these long walks as washing machines and blisters. "I wish I had the head for work like yours," the liquor shop man had told me as I left. "It's not a head you need," I had groaned, "it's feet."

In the yard, in the rain, at three o'clock in the morning, a hen clucked miserably to the teeming gutters. And when I went to the lavatory at four o'clock I found a man in his underwear on the wooden floor of the vestibule asleep across the open doorway, like a sentry at the mouth of an army tent or a sleepwalker drained by the heat.

The rain had stopped and the heat was fierce again when I left Kawazuru the next morning, but as the river valley narrowed a breeze blew down it and the hills on both sides gave blessed patches of shade. My jeans were still wet and my shirt, though dry, was covered with bits of fluff from my socks. I peeled off all these unpleasant things at the first opportunity and plunged into a silent stretch of the river, green and deep and hidden from the truck-clogged highway. A few boats were out, mostly from the restaurants that I had passed a little while earlier, with customers in them fishing for *yamame*, a species of trout (or, according to one of my Japanese cookery books, a baby salmon) that in these clearer, upper reaches of the Gokase River were commoner than ayu. When the boats had drifted away I sat naked on a rock and let the sun tease me to sleep. A train passed high on the opposite slope of the gorge and I woke with a jerk to find the passengers in both coaches leaning out of their windows, waving cheerfully, and pointing at my penis.

My feet felt as though I had spent the last five days tramping over burning coals, so I stayed by the river till mid-afternoon swimming, sleeping, and entertaining rail travelers. Then I put on a burst of speed and arrived at half past four in the little town of Hinokage where I dropped into a restaurant for a beer. Opposite me at my table sat a thin-faced man in his late fifties, wearing a white shirt and a worker's cap with the ideogram for "sun" on it. The man had lived all his life in Hinokage (literally, "Sun's Shadow") and spent half an hour trying to persuade me to move there.

"I had to go and work in the tangerine orchards in Oita prefecture one year," he told me. "I was only there for two months, but I remember crying for joy when the truck brought me back across the border into Miyazaki and home to Hinokage. Come and live here! You'd never regret it. You could study Saigo Takamori as much as you liked."

"But what would I do for a living?"

"Oh, you'd have no trouble at all. Lots of people have come here over the years—from Shikoku or the islands in the Inland Sea—and they've all found they could settle down easy. You could gather mushrooms. You could open a shop. You could write your stories and send them off by post and then come here in the evenings and drink shochu with me."

I learnt from the man that the name *Hinokage* was interpreted by local people as an expression of gratitude to the sun for sending them warmth and light (*kage*—"shadow"—is part of a standard expression meaning "thanks to you" or "by your good grace").

"It's nice to be staying in a town with a name like that," I told the woman at the ryokan when she showed me to my room.

"It's nice for the town that you're staying in it," she replied.

Feeling perky, I went out for an after-dinner stroll and found an upstairs bar called Piipuru (People) where the master—a jolly, slightly paunchy man in a T-shirt that depicted two cartoon animals, a dog and a cat, rubbing their necks together to demonstrate the imperviousness of their affection to race or species—served me several different types of shochu and refused to let me pay for any of them.

"Now this one is made from barley and this one is made from *soba* and this one is made from pounded rice."

"They're all very drinkable," I concluded, so he set about cooking me a pizza.

The bar was large and smart and entirely deserted except for me, the master, and the girl who worked there in the evenings, so the three or four songs I felt obliged to sing to the accompaniment of very loud laser-discs echoed eerily off the lime-green walls and made me feel like the Phantom of the Opera.

When the master learned that I was interested in history, and in any part that his remote little town might have played in the career of Saigo Takamori, he telephoned one of his regular customers, a Mr. Ichimizu who worked for the municipal government, and within minutes Mr. Ichimizu had arrived, sung two songs, ordered four bottles of beer, and arranged to take me on a tour of the area's sights the following morning.

I left Piipuru liking people, and liking Hinokage. As with most Japanese towns, I doubt that the outward attractions of Hinokage would appeal much to a well-traveled European, although it is pleasantly enough situated at a point on the river where the gorge forks and the hills steepen into dense, undulating woods. It consists by and large of the same red- and blue-roofed houses, the same concreted river banks and breeze-block walls and aluminum window frames and television antennas that you would find in any of a thousand towns up and down the country. But the Japanese tend to be less discriminating than well-traveled Europeans when it comes to attractions, and the lyrics of one recent locally composed song proclaim Hinokage to be, like the walled cities of the Appennines, "as beautiful as a dream." A second song, partly in English, begins "The Gokase River and the blue sky. WOW! WOW! WONDERFUL HINOKAGE." And a third song contains a verse, also partly in English, that runs: "MY SWEET HEART! Because you are a dream town GET YOU! MY HOME TOWN! You make me dizzy HINOKAGE." These songs have all been recorded with orchestral accompaniments and are available on cassettes from Hinokage Town Hall.

Mercifully, the busy highway bypasses the town a kilometer or so to the north, soaring over a tributary of the Gokase on a 137-meter-high girder bridge called the Seiun ("Blue Cloud") Bridge, which completely dominates the landscape and which, since it opened in 1984, has been adopted by the town as its official *shinboru* (symbol), although there must be some among Hinokage's population of 6,700 or less who regard it as an official eyesore. But the bridge, too, has its own song, "The Song of the Blue Cloud Bridge":

> *Of all beautiful places and things,*
> *I treasure most the Blue Cloud Bridge.*
> *Look from below, it floats above the clouds;*
> *Look from above, you'll see Japan.*
> *It is here that these delights await you,*
> *In Hinokage, my own home town.*

I recrossed the older, deserted road bridge and in the light of its lamps saw cloud upon cloud of pale cream river moths swarming in the August midnight. Like tiny feathers, they covered my body and clustered so thickly on the ryokan windows that it was impossible to see past them into the darkness. But I could hear the splash of the Gokase River and, in my head, the songs praising Hinokage's beauty.

"It's nice to be staying in a town with a name like that."

"It's nice for the town that you're staying in it. . . ."

⁂

No photographs of Saigo Takamori exist; apparently he refused to have any taken, and he is conspicuously absent from important group photographs, such as those of the cabinet in which he served and for which he must have been pressured to pose. There was a brief fuss in June 1988 when an evening edition of the *Nishi Nihon Shinbun* published an old group photograph in which one of six kimonoed and topknotted figures was identified by a screaming headline as Saigo. The figure is bull-necked and stocky and has a relatively dozy expression on his face, but he is also of merely average height, or even slightly below, and most of the experts subsequently called in to comment pooh-poohed the whole affair. Nor did Saigo sit for painted portraits, and such portraits of him as exist were done from memory (or, in the case of the one by the Italian artist Chiossone, from photographs of two of Saigo's relatives).

A curious result of this very un-Japanese reluctance to appear in commemorative photographs is the lack of hard evidence as to whether or not Saigo had a beard. He seems to have had very bushy eyebrows, which suggests that a resplendent set of whiskers would not have been beyond his hormonal capabilities, but did he actually possess a set? One of the four Japanese portraits done from memory (by Hattori Eiryu, whose brothers had fought with Saigo in this last civil war) shows him badly in need of a shave, but the effect could hardly be called resplendent. Most of the contemporary or immediately posthumous woodblock prints in which he stars depict him heavily bearded, but these prints are fanciful in a thousand ways, and the artists may simply have reckoned that a set of bushy whiskers not only balanced Saigo's eyebrows but went nicely with his comic-opera uniform. All his more somber painted portraits and all his statues show him clean-shaven, and this is how he usually appears in modern dramas too, such as NHK's T.V. series, "The Age of the Lion." But beards and moustaches have generally been eschewed in postwar Japan, perhaps because they continue to be associated in some minds with now unfashionable military figures such as General Nogi, the hero of Port Arthur—the very reason why a bearded Saigo would have appealed to a print artist bent on depicting him as the God of War. In a print made shortly after his death Saigo appears in the guise of the Reclining Buddha, and even here he is furnished with a beard, as well as with so many hundredweight of heavy gold braid that he probably couldn't have gotten to his feet if he tried.

And now we come to a crucial matter, for it appears that, by the time he was halfway through this last long march from Nobeoka, the historical Saigo was also having trouble getting about on his feet. There can be little doubt that he was a big man. There is ample contemporary testimony to this (one of his nicknames at school had been *udo,* "big gawk") and a mimeographed pamphlet presented to me later in my journey by the seventy-year-old head of the Mikado Village Historical Association contains his actual statistics: Saigo, says the pamphlet, was 180 centimeters (5 feet 11 inches) tall and weighed 109 kilograms (240 lbs.) This would have made him hefty for his time even by European standards, but compared with Japanese norms he was a giant.

The ambulatory difficulties that Saigo was experiencing are hinted at in another eyewitness account quoted in the adaptation of Mushanokoji's biography. This is the recollection of a man called Nakao Jimbei, who had evidently followed Saigo on his retreat as far as the village of Mera, which the fugitives reached on August 26th. There they encountered a badly swollen river, and over this hung "a make-shift bridge, which swung and was so dangerous that we had to cross it very carefully one by one. . . . "

"Sensei's palanquin stopped quietly by the edge of the bridge, and he had come down heavily on his feet, and stood still for a while looking at the bridge, then taking off his overcoat, handed it to his servant, and had hardly begun slowly to cross the bridge, when suddenly he retraced his steps. The servant in his turn got across to the other side and again returned to the starting point. All this while Sensei fixed his large eyes on the bridge without blinking. When about twenty minutes seemed to have passed, he began to cross again. He laid his corpulent body obliquely on the bridge, took fast hold of the boards and was with difficulty able to reach the other side by crawling."

To this, either Mushanokoji or his adapter appends the comment, "it must have been a humorous sight," making one ponder, not for the first time, the Japanese idea of a joke. But several points emerge from this account that shed light on the great man's physical condition, and not the least of these is the palanquin.

What on earth was Saigo doing in a palanquin—especially on these steep, rough mountain tracks, overgrown at the height of summer? Why did a man famous for his "humanism" subject his poor faithful footsloggers, already in about as dismal a condition as they could possibly be, to the extra hardship of carrying his bulky person from village to village, as though he were the god in a portable shrine? If the testimony of the two peasants on the way down from Enodake is to be believed, Saigo was in no need of being carried at the beginning of his retreat and if, in the meantime, he had stumbled across a few too many wasps and adders, a palanquin still seems an unnecessarily fatiguing way of protecting him from their attentions.

The palanquin cannot have been the grand affair that the English word implies (the Japanese word for such a conveyance, *kago*, means, simply, "basket"). It was doubtless cobbled together on route out of whatever scraps of timber and other materials could be found in the villages and woods, and probably looked more like a stretcher with a box on it than a gilded carriage.

Was Saigo ill? Was he running a fever? Is that why he was wearing an "overcoat" at the height of the Kyushu summer? According to some sources not often quoted, he suffered from an uncommon disease called filariasis, which is related to elephantiasis and is transmitted by mosquitoes. Filariasis involves the invasion and blockage of the lymph system by nematode worms called filariae and results, in chronic cases, in the extreme enlargement of certain parts of the body, particularly the legs and scrotum. In his early years of Satsuma politicking, Saigo had on two occasions found himself sufficiently out of favor with his lord to be banished to a succession of remote southern islands noted, among other forms of gloom, for severe mosquito infestation, so it is quite possible that Saigo had contracted such a disease (especially now that I recall the tartan-shirted photographer in the Monochrome coffee shop and his eager description of the great man's balls). But the physical disability that filariasis causes progresses slowly and is cumulative. It is not easy to imagine nematode worms, even if they were in the pay of the imperial army, suddenly crippling a man who, seven days previously, had been fit enough to march up and down Enodake.

Neither Mushanokoji nor his adaptor mentions filariasis (it would not, perhaps, have enhanced the "radiant impression" that Saigo was meant to have on readers) or gives any other clue to the puzzle's solution, other than that Saigo was "corpulent," which seems to me a far stronger reason for his *not* being carried in a palanquin than otherwise. Besides, neither his corpulence nor his general state of health appears to have troubled him much in the years following his retirement from the cabinet. Between resigning in

October 1873 and setting off to besiege Kumamoto Castle in February 1877, Saigo had spent much of his time doing farm work, and on the eve of the rebellion itself he is supposed to have been out tramping around the mountains with his dogs. Even in retirement this man, who in his early days had been a noted amateur sumo wrestler, led a fiercely energetic life.

Others have suggested that he was carried in order to hide him from enemy spies (in samurai dramas palanquins feature frequently in attempts to smuggle fugitive celebrities past barrier gates and other obstructions). But these same sources must also acknowledge that Saigo was the last person in the world to have shrunk from facing the consequences of his actions or to have been keen to spend sixteen days cowering in a basket. And, in any case, with the rebellion all but crushed, he was thoroughly resigned to whatever fate awaited him. Perhaps the likeliest explanation of Saigo's ambulatory difficulties was furnished by Mr. Ichimizu of the Hinokage Town Hall.

"He had a hernia," he told me.

It was the morning after our night at Piipuru and I was in a car for the first and only time on this long summer march. With us was a more senior man from the town hall, a Mr. Sakamoto, and the master of Piipuru who had come along for the ride and had changed into a less philosophical T-shirt. I had left my rucksack at the town hall, and we were on our way to view a battlefield. Saigo had not passed through Hinokage on his last long retreat, but his troops had been involved in a major skirmish in the neighboring hills between July 1st and 4th, some six weeks before the disaster at Nobeoka, and the mementos of the occasion had been carefully preserved.

"The Satsuma-gun [Saigo's army] dug themselves in on top of that cliff and came under sniper fire from across the valley."

Mr. Sakamoto pointed. We got out of the car and scrambled up a grassy slope by the roadside. On top of the slope stood a small boulder set vertically in cement, like a grave, and in one side of the boulder could just be discerned the shallow dents made by five bullets shot from one or more of the imported rifles with which the imperial army had been equipped.

"Several years ago they decided to concrete over the whole cliff face to protect the road from rockfalls. There's not much of historical interest in Hinokage and so we decided to hack off this bit of the cliff with the bullet marks in it and preserve it for a monument. But look how close together the bullets hit! He must have been a crack shot, whoever he was."

"Except that all his bullets hit a rock."

There was a lull in the conversation and we got back into the car.

". . . Over in the valley of the Shishi River [the valley I had failed to find] there's a house where you can still see the bullet holes in the main pillar of the living room. During those four days of skirmishing in July, three men were killed. Only three. It was that kind of a war, you see. . . . "

"And do you really think Saigo had a hernia?"

Mr. Sakamoto was not so persuaded as Mr. Ichimizu, and harbored other doubts as well.

"If you ask me," he ventured cautiously, "I don't think Saigo was a very big man. Not much bigger than me. . . . "

But it was time to contemplate more recent history, as well as to view a more persuasive illustration of little Hinokage's eagerness to impress visitors than bullet marks in a chunk of rock. A twenty-minute drive north into the hills, during which we passed a total of three other vehicles ("traffic is heavy this morning," said Mr. Ichimizu with no trace of irony) brought us close to the site of the old Mitate tin mine. Tin had been mined in these hills since the early seventeenth century but, like other mining operations in Kyushu (for example, the coal mine on Takashima island, which was managed by the famous Thomas Glover whose mansion overlooking Nagasaki Bay is still pointed out to the credulous as the home of Madame Butterfly), the Mitate mine had only realized its full potential with the arrival of a foreign boss.

The boss was one Hans Hunter, the son of an English father and a Japanese mother (and himself a British national despite his given name), who was born in Kobe in 1884 and took over the running of the Mitate mine in 1924. Hunter recruited an entirely foreign managerial staff of eight and built a large and well-appointed villa near the mine, equipped with a tennis court and other amenities, which the foreign managers used as a clubhouse and which was strictly off-limits to all Japanese (a doubly disgraceful stricture, I thought, when you considered Mr. Hunter's own parentage). In 1940, with war in the Pacific growing likelier by the month, the foreign staff had quit their jobs and left the country, and both mine and clubhouse had fallen into disrepair. The mine closed altogether in 1946, reopened in 1951, but shut its doors for good in 1969. And the clubhouse stood abandoned in the encroaching woods, its tennis court completely ruined and its white enamel British bath ripped out and used by a local minshuku as a tank for keeping fish. Then, at about the same time as the Blue Cloud Bridge commenced its symbolic construction and the composers of songs about WONDERFUL HINOKAGE got busy polishing their exclamation marks, someone at the town hall had the bright idea of restoring the clubhouse to its former glory, and this the town had just finished doing at a cost to itself of twenty million yen.

I pieced together most of this story from conversation in the car as we traveled along the lonely, tree-shaded road up the narrow valley of the Hinokage River towards what the town now called the Eikokukan, "the England Mansion." But nothing prepared me for the building itself. Set in an almost inaccessible stretch of woodland, it gleamed like a newly polished monocle. The tennis court had disappeared; you couldn't imagine it ever having existed. But the long single-story timber-constructed villa, perched below a hill cleft like a clothes peg, upon whose buried wealth the discriminating Mr. Hunter had built his careful fortune, had been so painstakingly renovated that you wondered why it wasn't enclosed in a glass case. The floors were newly varnished; the old British water pipes and taps had been made to function again, and the white enamel bathtub had been re-requisitioned from the grumpy owner of the minshuku who now had to find alternative accommodation for the yamame he proposed to feed to his guests. There was central heating under the wooden floors (an innovation more Korean than British), but this had not prevented the builders from also installing a fireplace that made me itch for Christmas.

Being at a house built for Englishmen in the uncolonized back of the Kyushu beyond was an odd experience, and the oddness of it did not escape Mr. Ichimizu, whose Minolta camera and zoom lens remained in constant operation from the moment I took my boots off and began tip-toeing about the varnished floors, going "Ummmm" and "Whaaaa" and "Ahhhhhh." A visit to the Eikokukan by a genuine Englishman—the first, Mr. Ichimizu noted excitedly, since the departure of Mr. Hunter himself—was clearly the climax of the entire renovation. Never mind bullet holes in a bit of old cliff; here was history in the making. And shortly after I returned to Tokyo from this hot summer hike, I received a specially prepared album of photographs courtesy of the Hinokage Town Hall, which showed me sitting on the entrance hall step, sitting on a chair, contemplating a pillar, standing on a flight of steps, marveling at a mirror, and variously disposed beside every architectural feature of note as well as all three of my companions, one after the other.

From the Eikokukan we drove to another local sight deemed worthy of my attention, this time one that conveyed with fair clarity what life in these remote hills can be like today, rather than what it was like for a group of unneighborly expats in the 1920s and 1930s. The sight was a very thin, very rickety pedestrian bridge, made of greying planks and loose cables, that spanned a tributary of the Hinokage River and was the only link with the outside world for a single family that lived a further forty minutes' hike along a steep and otherwise unused footpath. At one end of the bridge a notice warned that not more than two people were safe on the bridge at one time and at the other end, where the footpath began, a can of beer lay wrapped in a plastic bag. This was for the postman, who every day clambered crabwise across the bridge and then climbed the footpath—an hour and twenty minutes both ways—to bring the family their newspaper and letters. Sometimes they rang down and asked him to bring them up their groceries as well. I inched my way to the middle of the bridge where Mr. Ichimizu's Minolta required me. It was so wobbly that it felt like something in a fairground and the resulting photograph, included in the special album, shows me gripping the cables with both hands.

But for all its remoteness, Hinokage had obviously inspired in those of its residents I ran into a measure of affection and pride not found in many larger communities with far greater treasures to boast of. It was not a fierce pride; just a pleasantly complacent one. Some of the illustrations of it—the cassettes and the brochures with their "Romancing Tour." and "Fantasia" captions— were amusing to a city slicker. But there was also the professionalism with which the clubhouse had been renovated, the eyebrow-raising welcomes I had had from people like the woman at the ryokan who told me that my visit was nice for the town, and the man in the restaurant who suggested I live here permanently, and the master of Piipuru who gave me free shochu and beer and snacks; and there was the guided tour I had received this morning of such attractions as the little town could tease out of history and the dense, mined-out hills.

We ate yamame for lunch in a small shed-like restaurant by the river. I was not permitted to pay. Yamame are found only in the clearest water, another attraction of the township and one which, Mr. Ichimizu explained, was reflected in his own name (*Ichimizu* means "Number-One Water" and his family is so called because, six or seven generations ago, when peasant and artisan families first acquired surnames, the house in which they lived was close to the spring from which the clearest river water gushes—not merely the clearest in Hinokage, Mr. Ichimizu insisted, but the clearest in Japan.) As in many parts of the country, a large measure of the local pride derived from the tightness of the community and the belief that its ways differed vastly from those of even its closest neighbors. Why, the dialect spoken in Miyakonojo, down near the Kagoshima border, was like a foreign language. ("Do they have dialects in your country?" I was asked for the umpteen thousandth time.) And the man who drove the local bus, but who lived in another town nearer the coast, had been completely at a loss as to how to eat the tiny river crabs that were a Hinokage delicacy. "Where's the meat?" he had kept repeating, peering at them and prodding them with his chopsticks, "How on earth do you get at the meat?"

"Won't you stay another night?" they asked me when we got back to the town hall.

"No," I laughed, and hoisted my pack, and tramped away in a gust of rain. Typhoon thirteen was approaching from the south and the hills that I had been driven through that morning were swiftly disappearing behind a descending curtain of mist. I trudged across the Blue Cloud Bridge, looked back at little Hinokage, and wished I'd stayed three or four more nights.

3
Home of the Gods

❧

Hours later I stepped over a dead fox and tramped into the town of Takachiho. It was to the hill on which this town stands that the grandson of the Sun Goddess Amaterasu Omikami descended from the High Plain of Heaven in order to establish his rule over the Central Land of the Reed Plains. His name was Ama-Tsu-Hiko-Hiko-Ho-no-Ninigi-no-Mikoto, the meaning of which (admits W. G. Aston in his 1896 translation of the *Nihonshoki*, the eighth-century chronicle in which these wonders are recorded) "is doubtful," so he was called the August Grandchild for short. He brought with him the Imperial Regalia, the sacred mirror, sword, and jewel which were to become the emblems of the emperors of Japan for generations unbroken. Then he built a palace, to which he fetched as his bride a young woman named the Princess of the Deer Reeds, but who was known in addition as the Princess of Upper Ata and who also answered to the name of the Princess Who Blossoms Like the Flowers of the Trees. After one night of intercourse this princess declared herself pregnant, a development which the August Grandchild stoutly refused to credit, saying, "Not even a god can screw that good," or words to the same effect. But the August Grandchild was mistaken, and the Princess Who Blossoms Like the Flowers of the Trees subsequently produced triplets who were impervious to fire.

Small wonder that the municipal authorities of Takachiho have outdone those of little Hinokage in striving to impress upon visitors the unusual pedigree of their town. As Hinokage has gone in for cassettes and Englishmen, so Takachiho has gone in for gods. The signs along National Highway 218 proclaiming it The Highway of Myth and Legend continue into the outskirts of the town (population 19,000), where they are superseded by mass-produced placards on the streetlamps outside all the shops that welcome travelers to The Home of the Gods. These were a brainchild of the works department. On many of the shops' metal shutters there are bright gloss-painted representations of the masked dances called *kagura*, which are intended as entertainments for the gods and which have been performed each evening for fee-paying spectators at the Takachiho Shrine ever since 1972. The shutters were all painted by the same busy artist a couple of years before my visit and were a joint project of the town hall's tourist bureau and the local retailers' association. The signs and shutters and posters and shops lend Takachiho a uniform air of prosperity. There is a ryokan with a sign that says English Speaking, a bar called Kagura, carefully lettered notices that identify all the trees in the vicinity of the shrine, telephone booths built like rustic log cabins, loudspeakers at the railway station that broadcast a tape loop of the town's most famous folk song, "Kariboshikiri Uta" (The Scything Song), played on a bamboo flute and, on the day I tramped in, the Takachiho High School kendo team had just won the all-Japan fencing championship at the Budokan in Tokyo. A victory parade and a fireworks display were being concocted for the team's return the following day, and I expect this famous victory will further enhance the reputation of the town, now visited by approximately one million god-fearing tourists a year.

I took a room, ate dinner, and went out to see the kagura dances, a nightly performance which, advised the master of ceremonies, is in the nature of a *daijiesuto* (digest). There are some twenty dances in the full kagura cycle, performed annually between the shrine's main festival in late November and the lunar new year, but tourists are notoriously busy people and are not expected to tolerate more than four. I and about thirty other spectators sat on the floor of a tatami-matted hall at one end of which stood a stage decorated with a sacred grotto made of cardboard. The grotto was furnished with real plants and hung with white paper cutouts representing various birds including cockerels, the heralds of the Sun Goddess's twenty-four-hourly reawakening. In the climactic dance two performers wearing the masks of an old man and an old woman, standard figures in the kagura repertoire, feigned extreme tipsiness, a state traditionally associated with the Sun Goddess's brother, Susa-no-Wo-no-Mikoto (the Impetuous Male), who, during one of his major impetuosities, smeared shit all over his sister's palace. The old woman tried to make the old man stand up by jabbing his prick with a stick. Then they both descended into the audience and lecherously groped several members of it foolish or holy enough to sit near the front. When the dance was over, the drummer delivered an advertisement for a neighboring souvenir shop and I repaired to the bar called Kagura, where the master showed me the flashlight he used for catching eels in the Gokase River and the owner of a pachinko parlor, unshaven and flabby in his undervest, told me that he was divorced and that his former wife had come from Kokura, about 130 kilometers away.

"We had nothing in common," he grumped to me. "We could barely understand what each other said. International marriage is a tricky business."

Despite which, since separating from his wife, he had made eight trips to Seoul, three to Taipei, two to Manila, and one to Bangkok.

"For work?" I asked.

"For pleasure," he grunted, and sank his teeth into a chicken thigh.

Then a round-faced man in tatty clothes came in and introduced himself as Mr. Yagyu.

"That's a coincidence," I told him. "I just stayed at a ryokan named the Yagyu Kaikan back down the highway in a place called Kawazuru."

"Oh, yes?" he said.

"Yes," I said. "There was a man asleep on the floor in the doorway."

"Mmm," said Mr. Yagyu. "That was my brother."

"Really? I'd been told about the place by a man who ran a booze shop near the Gokase River."

"Mmm," said Mr. Yagyu. "That was my cousin."

Mr. Yagyu ordered a large plate of the local delicacy, huge lumps of fatty chicken charred over a naked flame until the skin is blotchy black but the meat inside is still pink and dripping and nearly raw. He crammed these into his mouth one after another and blobs of fat spattered down onto his trousers and sizzled in his beer.

"I expect you find the people in these parts friendly," he suggested.

"Yes, I do," I said.

"Very nice and friendly we are. You see, the whole of Kyushu was once under the sea." (I spent minutes puzzling over the connection between these two statements and concluded that there wasn't any.) "People have found fossilized shellfish in these hills. Then the volcanoes rose and dragged the rest of Kyushu up with them, and here in the middle of the island we're still surrounded by volcanoes. We've got Yufu and Kuju and Aso and Kirishima. And not far from here there's a place called Kuraoka. It's supposed to be the first ever settlement in Kyushu. Maybe it was the first in the whole of Japan. The old folks call it *Kyushu no heso* (Kyushu's navel). Yes, you'll find we're very friendly."

I had never heard of Kyushu's navel and it played no part in my travel plans. It had not figured in Saigo Takamori's itinerary so it didn't figure in mine. But just before reaching Takachiho on the evening of August 21st, Saigo and his rebels had met the first sustained opposition to their retreat about eight kilometers to the northeast, near a village called Iwato, and had fought a hectic running battle with government forces over rough country between the village and the town. This skirmish provided me with a perfect excuse to tramp along the little-used road to Iwato next morning, since Iwato was a place that I very much wanted to visit. If Kuraoka can claim a greater antiquity and Takachiho can claim to have been the earliest repository on earth of the sacred mirror, sword, and jewel, first prize in the god-stakes still goes to Iwato, commonly called Ama no (Heavenly) Iwato, since this village is supposed to have hosted the best-known incident in the whole cycle of godly doings.

Not only had the Impetuous Male daubed the Sun Goddess's palace with shit (especially the floor under her throne, which had made her feel very sick), but he had peeved his sister in other ways. He had trampled all over her Heavenly rice fields and allowed his Heavenly piebald colts to frolic about in them as well. And when he saw his sister weaving one day, he flayed a Heavenly piebald colt and flung it through the roof of her weaving room, causing her to prick herself on her shuttle. Whereupon, at the end of her holy tether, the Sun Goddess retired to a cave and fastened the rock door, thereby plunging both heaven and earth into darkness.

Though Saigo's tracks had everywhere vanished, the cave into which the Sun Goddess retired has miraculously survived all these millennia. It is the very one now open to public view in the village of Iwato (a name that means literally "Rock Door") and it is to be found in the precincts of Amano Iwato Shrine, not far from the factory that makes Black Horse shochu, just behind the Heavenly Souvenir Shop.

The disappearance of the Sun Goddess into a cave distressed the eighty myriads of gods so much that they met together on the banks of the nearby river and racked their brains for a means of enticing her out. They tried getting cocks from the Eternal Land to crow, so that she would think the dawn had come without her. They tried hanging a mirror in a sacred sakaki tree so that, when the Sun Goddess opened the door of her rock cave and caught sight of herself in the mirror, she would think that heaven and earth had acquired a rival light and emerge from her cave out of jealousy. The only trouble with this plan was that they couldn't get her to open the door. So a canny goddess called Ama-no-Uzume-no-Mikoto (the Terrible Heavenly Female) made herself a headdress out of sakaki leaves and a pair of suspenders out of some moss and a spear out of eulalia grass and performed a merry dance, which most authorities believe to have been, like a lot of godly goings-on, extremely filthy.

But it did the trick. The Sun Goddess, intrigued by the commotion that the dance was causing, peeped out of her cave, whereupon the gods grabbed her and pulled her out onto the river bank and begged her not to deprive the world of light ever again. Then they plucked out all the Impetuous Male's hair, or, according to other sources, his fingernails and toenails, and banished him to Bottom Nether Land. This event, with its lewd dance performed to placate a deity, is regarded as the origin of kagura, and thus of all Japanese dances and dramatic performances, including those in which old women jab old men in the prick with a stick.

❧

It was an overcast day but the iron roofs of the pigpens along the road were being cooled by sprinklers. Not far from Iwato I passed a bus shelter that was decked out like a Buddhist altar, with seven stone figures seated in meditation; two bamboo flower vases; food offerings placed on a shelf before a red, faded, flower-patterned curtain; and posters on the walls urging passengers and worshippers to support their local railway and to take home their empty beer cans. No empty beer cans lay about, but in one corner of the shelter someone had dumped a cardboard box that had contained a portable word processor.

The Amano Iwato Shrine appeared to have been very recently rebuilt. Throughout the compound there was a powerful smell of freshly sawn cedar and brand-new gilded fittings gleamed on the steps and rails of the main hall. At the back of the hall, prominent on a stand, stood a small circular mirror like the one that was brought to earth by the August Grandchild eight kilometers away. And, behind this, open screens revealed a small grove of trees where the gods slept and sported and, invisible and silent, flayed piebald colts and flung them at one another.

The Sun Goddess's cave lay a little way beyond the grove, along a narrow path by a fast, boulder-strewn river. The floor of the cave was covered with neat piles of stones, each stone placed on top of the last by a visitor wishing to record his visit under the pretext of a prayer. Water dripped constantly from the roof as from a broken faucet, and a little altar with banners and lanterns and a tiny wooden torii gate stood inside the cave, but there was nothing else; nothing to indicate that the principal goddess of the Japanese pantheon, from whom the imperial line supposedly descends, ever shut herself away in here, or that the place was holier than the nearby bus shelter. I visited the Topkapi Seraphim once and, in the room that contains the arm of John the Baptist, I had to step over a mound of huddled pilgrims who were moaning in ecstasies on the floor. Here were no ecstasies. In fact, here were no pilgrims. The paths were very clean and well cared for and looked as though no one ever trod them. But from the restaurant next to the Heavenly Souvenir Shop at half past ten in the morning, two waitresses carried a smartly suited drunk towards a waiting taxi, and everyone—the waitresses, the drunk, and the taxi driver—grinned happily, participants in an ancient rite.

Saigo had reached Takachiho by late evening, and his men had entered the town, then merely a village, in something like triumph. Having fought off the imperial troops who had pursued them from Iwato, they seized, according to Mushanokoji, 2,500 straw-wrapped bales of rice and 7,280 yen in cash, then "shouted for joy at their good fortune and Saigo smiled, too." Mushanokoji estimates that, despite the hazards and hardships of retreat and the temptation simply to melt into the hills, the force still numbered around five hundred men, testimony to the iron loyalty that Saigo commanded and a definite advantage now that they had to hump so many bales of rice.

From Takachiho they headed south, their retreat aided by the spectacular lay of the land, for, in addition to its gods and painted shutters, Takachiho sits atop a celebrated gorge, where the Gokase River is narrow enough to jump across but has carved out a valley so deep that it could hide an army. By midday on the 24th, after I had walked back from Iwato and stood peering down into the gorge, the sky had clouded over and a thin grey dishcloth-like rain was falling. This rain had come suddenly, though not without warning. According to the midday weather forecast, Kyushu was at present sandwiched between two large and unusually wayward typhoons. Normally at this time of year, typhoons blow up through the South China Sea, soak Okinawa, take a bite out of Kyushu, and then glide as though laser-controlled towards Korea—a finale that always fills Japanese weather forecasters with a special delight. But Typhoon 14 had made a beeline for Honshu, soaking most of Japan in the process, while Typhoon 13 had busied itself doing delicate pirouettes not far off the coast of Miyazaki. Each evening, NHK's announcers assured their viewers that, by morning, both typhoons would have gusted off to darkest Asia, and each morning we woke to find both typhoons exactly where they had been the night before and, by the look of things, getting stronger.

I ate lunch in one of the circle of noodle shops that had been built for tourists beside the gorge, and which together formed a sort of rustic theme park, complete with thatched roofs, hanging lanterns, carp ponds, a custom-built waterwheel, and kimonoed maids who stood about in the drizzle under colorful paper umbrellas, bowing and beckoning to customers and getting wet. Faintly from loudspeakers in the thatch came the same folk song you heard as you got off the train at Takachiho station, "Kariboshikiri Uta" (The Scything Song), and over a bowl of noodles and several bottles of beer I had a shot at translating a couple of its verses, which I found printed on my chopstick cover. The verse that particularly intrigued me was this:

Autumn is over: on a path between rice fields,
Is that a bride with five fires to light her?

The more I looked at this as I slurped my noodles, the more I started to detect in it all manner of occult significance. The figure glimpsed in the darkening fields as winter approached—that was definitely spooky. And the odd fires that danced around her as she glided along—they were spookier still. And why were there five fires? Five of them! In China, from where Japan derived most of its old folk beliefs, five was a number of tremendous metaphysical importance. There were Five Elements and Five Seasons and Five Virtues and Five Tastes. The earth had Five Quarters and heaven had Five Kings. There were Five Sacred Mountains and Five Seers and Five Rulers and Five Poisonous Creatures and . . . My God! I ordered another bottle of beer. What had I stumbled onto?

"Look here," I said to a kimonoed waitress who was hovering around waiting to remove my noodle bowl, "Don't you think this is spooky?"

The waitress read it three times slowly, looked at me, said "Spooky," picked up my noodle bowl, and went away.

A minute or two later her mother came out, a plump old lady in a blue homespun kimono and an apron. She sat down on the bench beside me with a little puff of air as though she were a balloon coming in to land, and said, "What's all this about, then?"

"I think," I said, showing her the chopstick cover, "that this verse is about a fox spirit."

The old lady read it over once and said, "Actually, it's about a wedding."

"Ha ha!" I chuckled. "You mean you think the bride is just a woman?"

The old lady gave me a look that summed up much of the prevailing Japanese view of foreigners, which is that they ought to be locked away.

"What else would a bride be?" she wondered.

"Now, think," I said, "how many old folk tales there are in which young women—especially brides—turn out to be something else. Like the Snow Woman or the Twilight Crane."

"Well," said the old lady, "this isn't a folk tale. It's a song about cutting weeds to use as winter fodder for animals."

"In that case," I said, "why is the wedding taking place when autumn has just ended, a time"—I tapped the table with my finger—"when the hours of darkness are starting to outnumber the hours of light?"

"Because," said the old lady, unperturbed, folding her hands in her lap like a wolf pretending to be Red Riding Hood's granny, "the end of autumn is when farmers have finished their harvest, and they wouldn't have held a wedding before that because it would have interrupted serious work."

"So why does it take place at dusk?"

"Because, like most country weddings, the preparations for it went on all day."

"Well, where is this woman supposed to be going?" I said. "If it's her wedding day, what's she doing gliding about among the paddy fields?"

"At old-fashioned country weddings there are two celebrations," the old lady explained. "The first takes place at the bride's house. The second takes place at the groom's house. The second one usually starts in the evening and goes on for most of the night. Between the two celebrations the bride processes from one house to the other. And in the country," she added with a disarming smile, "there are often paddy fields between the houses."

"Look," I said, "you're missing the point. There are five fires, see? Five fires. What's that supposed to tell us?"

"It tells me," said the old lady, "that it was a medium-sized wedding. A bride is always accompanied by people carrying lanterns. A big wedding would have had seven and a small one would have had three. In these parts a lot of things are counted in sevens, fives, and threes. For instance, old farm houses have either three, five, or seven roof beams. Three is small and seven is big. Five is pretty normal."

I was quickly losing my patience with this unimaginative country lady.

"I think," I said huffily, closing my notebook and stuffing the chopstick cover into my shirt pocket, "that when you consider the mythology that surrounds Takachiho, like the fact that between this gorge and the shrine there is a place where a demon called Kihachi lived and that, according to your own local legends, that boulder lying beside the gorge over there was named Oni no Chikara Ishi (the Demon-Strength Rock) because it was flung there by Kihachi in a fit of pique—I think you will admit that the probability of there being supernatural preoccupations in a song composed by superstitious farmers in the middle of the eighteenth century is a strong one."

"Mah, what an awful lot you know!" said the old lady, standing up with another puff of air.

I put the notebook into my pack, zipped up the pocket, paid my bill, said goodbye, and stalked grumpily away, past a thin old man who was sitting on the pathway sharpening an axe and a prim old lady in a pink flowery dress with a picnic basket over her arm out of which stuck a huge long-handled scythe, as though she were on her way to commit mass murder. To hear some people talk, I grumbled, you'd think you were in Norfolk or Kansas or somewhere instead of in the depths of the Orient. Why, if you listened to such people long enough, you'd come away thinking that Japan was an ordinary place, just like any other.

●   ●   ●

The drizzle strengthened into a downpour that soaked through my thin nylon jacket until warm rain ran down my chest and back and crotch and thighs. I tramped past sodden camellias, past more bus shelters in which Buddhas sat with Burmese hairstyles—impassive, or with spare arms like Mother Kali—past an army of large black businesslike ants transporting half a sponge cake, over another huge suspension bridge of the kind I had grown used to seeing in the form of plastic and wooden miniatures on sale at the area's souvenir shops, past a restaurant called the Teahouse at the Peak that was shuttered and closed and nowhere near a peak, through a 947-meter-long trafficless tunnel that was at a peak, emerging in the late afternoon on the other side of the Tsubana Pass under a sky that had temporarily exhausted its rain and was filled with careening clouds.

A few kilometers short of the little village of Akadani a woman invited me into her house for a yogurt drink and pickles and watermelon and tea. I sat on the tatami with her four children who offered to show me their summer holiday homework. The eldest boy, about twelve, had been asked to draw a map of the world and had done this very conscientiously on a large square of thick white cardboard. The holidays were nearly over and the map was almost finished. Great Britain was beautifully drafted, about the same size as North America, while Japan had been rubbed out and redrawn several times over (you could see the gouges of many resharpened pencils), each time smaller than the last. It was now about the size of the Scilly Isles.

The woman offered to wash my clothes for me, but I saw no prospect of their being dry before night fell, so I thanked her and told her that I would walk the last few kilometers to Akadani and wash them at a ryokan there. Her husband had gone into Akadani, she explained. He was an auxiliary fireman. The auxiliary firemen were holding their monthly drill, after which they would get spectacularly drunk, so I was bound to run into him. This prediction struck me as odd at the time; perhaps I hadn't consumed the yogurt drink with enough appearance of satisfaction. But it turned out to be a reliable prediction because the only place to go for an after-dinner drink in Akadani was a karaoke bar called Shiki (Four Seasons), down some stairs and through a heavy door at the end of the village's one short street. I went down these stairs and through the heavy door and found myself among twenty-three grey-uniformed, very lively auxiliary firemen, one of whom was keen to practice his English.

"What's your name?" he asked me.

"Alan."

"Where from?"

"Tokyo."

"How old?"

"Fourteen."

"Where from?"

"Tokyo."

"What's your name?"

"Booth."

"How old?"

And so on, since these were the only three English expressions he knew.

Eventually I was rescued by two regular firemen in blue uniforms with smart caps strapped to their shoulders who had supervised the afternoon drill and now sat drinking by themselves in splendid isolation. Three very dolled-up middle-aged ladies came in and spread themselves among the customers. The firemen asked me which lady I wanted and I admitted that I wanted none. We sang. I danced with a dolled-up middle-aged lady. A younger hostess sat down beside me with two glasses and poured herself a beer. Why didn't we go for a quiet drink by ourselves, she suggested; just the two of us. Because, I told her, my feet ached; a lame excuse. So I finished my drink, said goodnight to the firemen, asked for my bill, and was charged for eight beers. I had drunk four, and three of those the firemen had bought me. Perhaps, when they left, they paid for them again.

Outside, above the village street, the sky was a dusty crimson, as though somewhere a distant fire raged. I hobbled back to my ryokan in the wooden clogs they had lent me, which might have fitted my infant daughter and would have interested the Inquisition, had they seen them on me. There were blisters all over both my feet and blood came out of them every day from now until my walk was over At my ryokan I slept in an extraordinary room that had an imitation parquet floor, a tatty green carpet, white plaster walls, a fake red-brick fireplace with a mantlepiece, a curtained king-size four-poster bed, and a hot-water jug on the bedside table that had printed on it, in capital letters, Happy Life in Good.

As I sat alone in the kitchen next morning, a thin, distinguished-looking, white-haired man turned up to give me his grandfather's brother's account of Saigo Takamori's passage through the little hamlet of Miyanohara, about three kilometers further along the road, where his family lived. He had come because he had heard from a fireman that a Saigo scholar was in residence.

"My grandfather's brother would have been sixteen or seventeen at the time," he told me, "and some of Saigo's men stopped at the house and asked him if he would help to carry the palanquin. Saigo's testicles were swollen something terrible and he couldn't walk. He was sitting waiting in the grounds of the temple. My grandfather's brother helped to carry him as far as the next temple at Sakamoto, another four kilometers down the road, where he was planning to spend the night. Saigo wanted to pay him for his trouble, but he had no money, so instead he gave him a pouch made of rabbit skin that he had used for carrying his tobacco. It was in such a filthy state after all the months of fighting and scrambling up and down mountains that my grandfather's brother threw it away."

The white-haired man laughed. It was the family tragedy.

"His name was Sakada Bunkichi. Sakada Bunkichi," the white-haired man repeated, standing over me as I scribbled in my notebook to make sure that I got the characters right.

I left Akadani in a deep morning overcast with too many kilometers ahead of me to worry much about the inconsistencies between Mushanokoji's version of events, in which the previous evening an army of five hundred men had "shouted for joy" at the acquisition of a large bundle of cash, and this eyewitness account, in which Saigo had been so strapped for manpower and funds that village youths had been recruited to help carry him and paid off with unusable tobacco pouches. Such, I suppose, are the vagaries of war, as well as of biography.

Less of a mystery is what happened to the 2,500 bales of rice. Four-fifths of them had been loaded onto carts at Takachiho and sent off up the road towards Kumamoto, eighty-five kilometers to the west on the other side of

Kyushu's spine, in an attempt to make the pursuing brigades think that Saigo had given up the idea of getting back to his home city of Kagoshima and was all set to make a last poetic stand near the battlefield where the back of his rebellion had been broken four months earlier. In fact, Saigo turned south after leaving Takachiho, into the Nanatsuyama Mountains, and it was here that I picked up his trail again, though I was still two days off the pace.

Before long spots of rain were falling. I reached Miyanohara about half an hour after setting off and stopped to see the large, well-kept temple where Saigo is supposed to have rested. A monument on the grounds records this event. But the temple's principal object of awe is a huge *shidare zakura* (weeping cherry tree), fifteen meters tall and at least two hundred years old, whose seed is said to have been brought from the Gion district of Kyoto, an area famous for its geisha houses, by the temple's ninth chief priest. In 1965 the tree was registered by the prefectural authorities as a Specially Protected Object, a fate from which geisha could also benefit. And in 1877, already elderly, the tree had wept over swollen-testicled Saigo, penniless or newly rich, as he clambered into a palanquin or onto a jerry-built stretcher, borne either by five hundred samurai or a sixteen-year-old youth who was fussy about where he kept his tobacco.

A woman I met on the road near Sakamoto asked me if I was an American, and explained that she could distinguish among different types of Caucasian people simply by looking at their faces. "I can tell English people from Americans," she said, "or Germans or Russians," although she refused to disclose the precise signs that gave us all away.

"Why did you think I was an American, then?" I wanted to know.

"Because you are a university professor," she said strangely, and vanished in the rising storm.

Typhoon 13, which had previously confined its energies to a few pirouettes, had in the night strayed inland over Miyazaki and was beginning to perform the meteorological equivalent of the Hokey-Pokey. On the T.V. satellite photograph that morning the storm looked enormous, and in the first feathery-light spittle of it I had to climb the 1,023-meter-high Iiboshi Pass. I met a young schoolboy who offered me a deep, silent bow, and I stopped at the last shop before the pass where it was possible to drink a beer. There a gloomy old woman with a blotchy face told me a muddled story in barely penetrable dialect about a sensei from Miyazaki city who had passed that way and stopped at a house to ask for a drink of water, but the people in the house hadn't liked the look of him and refused to give him anything. Whereupon he had taken one of their giant radishes instead, which is how there come to be so many—or so few—giant radishes in Miyazaki. I didn't understand this story at all and asked the woman to repeat it, but she silently washed a cucumber and wrapped some salt in a twist of paper and gave me these to take with me for the climb.

"In the temple at Miyanohara," she told me, "they will show you a spot where Saigo Takamori sat and rested and smoked a pipe. A bamboo pipe. Smoked a bamboo pipe. . . . "

By eleven o'clock the rain had thickened. A black mist was coming down on the hills, a wind had sprung up, and the sky was a blur of nothing. I reached the pass at twenty past twelve and sat in the rain and ate my cucumber under a stone tablet, identical to the one at the temple, which recorded, like the stations of the cross, yet another spot where Saigo had rested and possibly smoked a bamboo pipe. Two dogs, one brown and one black, met me at the pass and descended it with me, the brown one trotting along at my side and the black one following suspiciously at a distance. Both the dogs were wearing collars and gave every sign of knowing where they were, although it was a full hour before we arrived at the booze shop in Iiboshi and took shelter there together. The woman who ran the shop began phoning everyone she could think of to try and locate the dogs' owners, though in the event it wasn't necessary as they were soon joined by a very randy white terrier who chased them out onto the wet road where they started performing Hokey-Pokeys of their own.

Saigo had spent the night at Morotsuka, a large village on the Mimi River about twenty kilometers further on, where the booze shop woman's husband worked at the village hall. He had been one of the keenest subscribers to the Saigo monument at the pass, she told me. I asked her if there were any ryokans at Morotsuka. She replied that there were five and, wanting to give me something for my journey, offered me a large jar of honey, which I declined. So, although the rain continued to strengthen throughout the dreary afternoon, and although it was six o'clock before I limped to the end of the empty road where it forked by the river at Morotsuka, I was at least confident of finding a place to stay. The first ryokan I tried was full up with workmen who were shoring up the river banks. The second was in semi-permanent retirement. At the third there was no response to my shouts and a passing schoolboy told me that, since he didn't belong to the place, he couldn't say whether anyone was there or not, and walked off giggling merrily. At the fourth, the door was opened by a woman with a mouth full of rice who told me to go away because they were on holiday. The rounds of these four ryokans in the rain had added another two kilometers to the forty I had walked since morning and my feet felt as though they had been flogged with wire.

But at the fifth ryokan, which doubled as a restaurant, two chortling women received me with glee and served me a beer while I sat in the doorway stripping off my soaking clothes. They regarded this as the lark of their lives.

Outside my room, from the ceiling of the unlit corridor, hung a huge balsa model of a World War II Zero fighter. And while I was having dinner by myself the owner of the ryokan, a thin craggy man in a white shirt with a grubby collar, came into my room carrying a half-full tumbler of shochu, picked himself a cushion from the pile by the window, sat down opposite me across the low table, and regarded me with much curiosity while he smoked cigarettes one after another. He was not a talkative man but explained that he had felt obliged to come and have a gander at me because I was the first foreigner who had ever stayed at his ryokan and, so far as he knew, the first who'd ever stayed in Morotsuka.

I finished dinner and laid out my maps for his inspection. Yes, he knew the road that Saigo was supposed to have taken after spending the night at his village, although he'd heard conflicting accounts when he was young and they were studying history at school. By this stage of the retreat, his teachers had told him, the rebels would have been drifting about in small groups of no more than eight or ten, and these would likely have taken different routes to minimize the threat of capture. But the road over the pass east of Mount Shimizu to Mikado hadn't changed since Saigo's time and, especially if he was being carried in a palanquin, that was the one he would have used.

Was the road still usable?

It was usable in good weather, though it was loose-surfaced and slippery at the best of times. It would be a real bugger in this rain, he reckoned, and the rain showed no sign of letting up.

In the night it turned into a heavy thunderstorm and lightning flashed over the walls of my room until the dawn arrived to thin the flashes. I dragged myself up to watch the six o'clock news. The eye of the typhoon had reached the main island of Okinawa and there were flood and landslide warnings out for the whole of western Japan. The rain fell like a kettle-drum tattoo outside my window while I picked at a dried fish and a bowl of beancurd soup, and there was still no sign of a letup in the storm by the time I left the ryokan at ten o'clock, zipped tight inside my suffocating rain gear. The owner's wife stood at the door of the ryokan and gave me a completely straight-faced send-off:

"Just think what a wonderful memory it will be," she said, "to have walked thirty kilometers across a pass where no one goes in the worst typhoon of the year."

Both the coffee shops in Morotsuka that I had noticed the previous evening were closed, so my last chance to procrastinate fizzled soggily away. I tramped up the main road for a couple of kilometers and then crossed the Mimi River by an old bridge and started along the narrower, loose-surfaced track that followed an unnamed tributary into the hills. The rain slashed down like sheet steel and showed every sign of strengthening. My track clung at first to the bank of the tributary, now a river in its own right, swollen to a fury by the storm, and deep rust-red from the mud and clay that the typhoon had sent crashing into it off the logged slopes. It was faster than any river I had ever seen, apart from one going over a vertical drop, and loud enough to drown out two people trying to talk to each other on the track that ran beside it. I knew this because not far down the track I stopped a woman who was hurrying home with a bag of groceries to one of the outlying houses, and checked my directions for the last time, praying that Saigo hadn't come anywhere near these hills and this stream and its crashing banks.

But Saigo had, as the woman knew. This was the old road, she yelled at me, bent nearly double under her umbrella. Perhaps it was a couple of centuries old, widened and kept more or less passable by the loggers. And as I walked on in the stinging rain, and as the river went on pounding its banks with a noise like cannonballs smashing into the walls of a wind tunnel, I felt the slow return of something that, after a decent interval, I recognized as fear. I don't think I was so much afraid of the storm, or the river, or the mudslides, or the possibility that I might be washed off the track, though there were moments when that could have happened. Part it was an onset of loneliness. I can't remember a day when I have felt lonelier. But as I started to climb the twists of the pass, I found that I was beginning to reexperience an older and much worse dread.

With the leisure of hindsight and the urge to tell a moderately stirring tale, I can add that the peak towards which I was climbing, 1,205-meter Shimizu-dake, was on both my maps identified in parenthesis by what I took to be an older name that means "Mountain God." But, to be honest, I hadn't noticed that then; I didn't notice it until much later, and, though I have a vivid enough imagination and a healthy regard for superstition, I don't know how that odd bit of local lore would have affected the hollow feeling growing in my chest.

There are times in any countryside when the numinous slams into you without a scrap of warning, like a blow with an axe, or suddenly perceived mortality. Once on a snowy day in January I was walking alone near Hiraizumi in northern Japan on the hills that overlook the plain where the legendary hero Benkei is supposed to have died, and I startled a pheasant into flight, which made me cry till I rocked back and forth and my tears made holes in the snow. Another time I was on a high pass in the Shikoku mountains on a day when there was thunder in the air, and I saw a snake about to devour a baby bird that had not yet learned to use its wings. The bird was hopping in pathetic circles a foot from the jaw of the advancing snake and other birds were shrilling frantically from high up on the cliff face. I put out my hand to save the thing and it hopped once onto the back of my wrist and

then, with the same blind purposelessness, over the cliff edge, where it fell
into space and burst on a rock and died. The snake raised its head for a second
or two and then curled silently out of my way with what I know I am
right for thinking was contempt.

Moments like that—though I can't say what else connects them—stir in
me a conviction that there is a thing in the world we might call *god*, but that
it is a random thing, unfettered by meaning, and completely indifferent to
the world's condition. One of the cassette tapes available in Hinokage perpetuates
in a lyric the supreme folly: "After all," it burbles, "we are the children
of the gods!" On some roads we know that we are not.

And today the hollow feeling stayed in my chest and the rain strengthened
as I climbed towards the pass. For two hours I climbed and met not a soul. I
was riddled with a sense of helplessness, and of blundering where no help
was. The road dribbled out into mud, then rubble, then clogged itself with
brambles and weeds, and I thought it was going to vanish altogether. So I
cried out with surprise and relief when I rounded a steep twist high up on
this shaggy hillside and found two spattered cars, one white and one blue,
parked outside a shed with a corrugated iron roof and a door slightly ajar.
The cars blocked most of what was left of the road and to get past them I had
to squeeze by the door, pushing it open with my elbow. I pushed it further,
took a step inside, pulled back my nylon hood, spraying the plywood walls
and the dirt floor with rain, and blinked into the darkness. Seven men sat on
plastic mats round the embers of a dying fire and regarded me somberly.

"Do you mind if I sit with you for a little while?" I sighed to them.

"Not at all, help yourself," said one of the men, as coolly as though a trembling
Englishman were just the sort of apparition you'd expect to confront
on Mountain God Peak at the height of a typhoon. I set down my pack,
stripped off my rain gear and hung it on a wire that was stretched across one
corner of the hut, and felt as grateful for the company of these strangers as
I had felt for each childhood Christmas.

"Here, sit on this box. Never mind the drips. Could you drink a cup of
cold barley tea?"

Six of the men wore smart sports shirts and spoke clear, unfussy Japanese to me. They had been sent to investigate whether this road I had climbed might be improved to facilitate more access by loggers. And the seventh man, small and dark, was a villager whom they had hired as their guide. He was dressed quite differently, in blue plastic trousers cut and patterned with flowers like *monpe*, the traditional country pantaloons that are most often worn by women. He had cropped hair and stayed carefully silent, like a small child in a headmaster's study. Even when I asked him about local roads, to make sure that the one I was following didn't fork somewhere and leave me stranded like the path on Enodake, he was reluctant to speak until a question was addressed to him by one of the men he had been hired to guide.

I opened my maps. The men in sports shirts brightened.

"What scale are they? 1:25,000?"

But when I showed them to the villager, pointing out local landmarks in the dimness, he stared blankly at them as though they represented some distant galaxy. The problem was to get him to distinguish between what appeared from the map to be the major road and the several tracks, indicated by dotted lines, which branched away from it in unhelpful directions.

"There's lots of roads," the villager said slowly.

"You mean the one we're on splits up further ahead?"

He considered this for a long time.

"There's only one *major* road, though, isn't there?" I asked him.

"There's lots of roads," he said again.

"But are there any more like *this* one? Like *this* one?" asked one of the men in sports shirts who had grasped the problem but was at the same loss to communicate it.

"Like this one?" wondered the villager.

"Does this road continue on across the pass and down into the valley where Mikado is? Or does it fork?"

"Across the pass?"

"Towards Mikado."

"Towards Mikado? There's lots of roads."

"But are there any more roads *like this one?*"

"Like this one?"

And so forth, until all eight of us gave up.

The rain rattled like machine-gun fire on the iron roof and, while we sat with cups of cold tea in our hands, the embers faded from red to grey. The single 40-watt electric bulb in the hut had broken shortly before my arrival, so we sat in the dark while the generator whirred pointlessly and the villager in flower-patterned trousers nursed the dead lightbulb, turning it round and round in his black fingers and peering at it with deep concern. Occasionally he raised the bulb to his ear and shook it gently so that it tinkled.

"Don't you notice anything special about the Japanese spirit?" one of the men in sports shirts asked me.

"Special?"

He looked up from the embers and grinned.

"Everybody says the Japanese are the hardest-working people in the world, don't they? Only, here in Miyazaki we've got a reputation for not taking work very seriously. Some people would even say we're proud of it."

There was a chuckle from several of the other men in sports shirts, but the villager continued to stare at the bulb.

"Can you think of any great men who came from Miyazaki? Any at all? I'll bet you can't."

"Tochihikari," I offered, naming a retired sumo wrestler.

"Nah! Come off it! He never even made Champion. And in any case his family was from Okinawa."

"Weren't they from Korea?"

"Somewhere like that."

The villager put the bulb down on the dirt floor and solemnly pursed his lips.

"Besides," continued the man in the sports shirt, "you can't call sumo wrestlers great men. Except for their bellies, of course. Their bellies are big enough. And there's a good few bellies that size kicking around Miyazaki, make no mistake."

There were more chuckles. He poked the embers, warming to what must have been a favorite topic.

"No, I'm talking about really great men. You think about it. There's none from Miyazaki. But you start counting all the great men that have come from next-door, from Kagoshima, and you'll soon run out of fingers to count on."

"For example?"

"For example, Saigo Takamori. Perhaps you haven't heard of him. He was a hero if ever there was one. And Okubo Toshimichi [Saigo's ultra-pragmatic, ultra-authoritarian nemesis in the cabinet, Home Minister at the time of the rebellion, who survived Saigo by eight months and was stabbed to death in his carriage by Saigo supporters]. And Admiral Togo [who sent the Russian Baltic Fleet to the bottom of the Tsushima Straits in the war of 1904–05]. Isn't it odd? There's dozens of them. All from Kagoshima. Perhaps it's the climate."

The villager sat, moistening his lips.

"And do you know why the people in Miyazaki don't break their balls working? It's because in feudal times there were no great lords in this part of the country; just little ones. It wasn't the same as Kagoshima, where you had people like Nariakira [the lord who encouraged Saigo's rise to eminence]. My goodness, there was a lord all right! Talk about work, he didn't know how to stop! He built the first steam-powered warships in Japan, the biggest glass factory, a munitions foundry, and the first textile mill to use Western-style looms. He was the first man to set up gas lights in Japanese streets and the first to send messages in Morse code. He spoke Dutch and developed his own photographs. And on top of all that he found time to design the national flag [the *Hinomaru*—still the national flag]. No wonder they were all workaholics down there, with a lord like Nariakira to kick their asses. Whereas up here they took things a good deal easier. Their lands were small; they had nothing to prove. And neither have we. Have another cup of tea."

I drank another cup of their thin, cold tea, and the electric generator shuddered to a stop. The last embers of fire had died and the little hut was in near total darkness.

An hour later I left the seven men sitting on their dirt floor in the dark and tramped on towards the pass, feeling lighter despite the still-slashing rain. When the road finally began to turn down, the valley on the other side was an impenetrable white blank, as though the air itself had fragmented into tiny particles that hung suspended or congealed. More than ever, on this downward trudge, the broken road resembled a river, ankle-deep in rushing red water for long wearying stretches. Here and there the rock face had crumbled and blocked the road to a height of several meters. If the seven men in their hut didn't leave for home before dusk, I thought, with enough light to see the rockfalls and time to clear them out of the way, they would likely be stranded on this hillside for the night. Below the weirdly isolated and silent little hamlet of Matae, perched so high above a sharp dogleg of the road as to appear remote and completely inaccessible even as I passed it, the dreariness persisted. Trying to step round shin-deep ditches of rushing water on a twisting mess of rubble and mud covered with skull-sized rocks in blinding rain and still keep up a pace brisk enough to get me to Mikado before dark fell did nothing for either my blisters or my temper. But irritation is a fine exorcist and the hollow in my chest filled bit by bit with every stumble and curse.

4
Local Heroes

By the time—very late in the afternoon—that I finally trudged into the village of Mikado after thirty kilometers of typhoon-lashing with not so much as a vending machine to supply the indispensable beer, I was in no mood for the reception given me by the prim, disapproving woman at the first of the village's two liquor shops.

"I'd like a bottle of Kirin, please," I gasped.

She fetched me one in silence.

"And a glass, if you wouldn't mind."

"This is not a restaurant, you know," she said.

"That's all right," I said. "I don't want to eat."

It was clear from the way she set the glass down on the counter with a little sniff that the idea of my standing in her carefully dusted shop with a beer in my hand turned her delicate stomach. And it was just as clear, at least to me, that I wasn't going to shift until I'd had a drink. It would not have occurred to me to ask for a glass at a liquor shop in a large city. But in the countryside, most proprietors welcomed the chance to chat with someone unfamiliar. This was the first time I had ever been made to feel that, by staying to drink what I had bought, I was behaving like an oaf. Ah well, times change, things fall apart, and the worst are full of passionate primness.

I drank half the beer, slowly, and the woman lifted her chin and stared out of her polished window at the rain.

"If you want to drink, you should go to a bar," she said, pronouncing the word *bar* as though it meant spittoon.

"Look, I've just walked all the way from Morotsuka in this storm," I said, not thinking to mention God, "and I'm very tired and thirsty, and I'll pay you in a minute and get out of your shop. If you don't approve of people drinking, why don't you run a pharmacy?"

"From Morotsuka? But you haven't got a car," she crowed.

"That's right. They won't sell them to drunks."

However, the reception I got three minutes later at the Nango ryokan made up for this entirely. The ryokan, like the liquor shop (and like the coffee shop next door to the ryokan and the friendlier-looking liquor shop across the road which was built like an Alpine music box), was neat and clean and freshly renovated and the owner and his wife were so welcoming that I racked my brains to remember where I could possibly have met them before. The wife spent a long time helping me hang out the entire contents of my sopping rucksack on clothes hangers around my room, pick the half-dissolved vitamin capsules and the shreds of their cardboard box out of my spare underpants, and line my pack with plastic rubbish bags ready for the looming horrors of next morning. She also fetched me some ointment for the cherry red sores that had begun to form on my thighs and belly and crotch from walking thirty kilometers a day up and down mountains in soaking wet denims.

The maid who served me dinner had a pert face, dyed hair, and jet black teeth. She came from Hyuga, on the coast, and since her husband passed away she had lived alone, she told me, moving from job to job, mostly in hotels. She killed flies with more skill than anyone I had ever seen apart from Zatoichi the blind swordsman, Japan's favorite cinema swashbuckler, scooping them out of the air one-handed and not even pausing in her conversation. It was a breathtaking talent, especially for the flies.

"In the bar next door we've got laser-disc karaoke," she told me proudly, adding a fourth fly to the collection in the ashtray. "Well, I mean, you've got to have it nowadays, haven't you? No one wants the old hundred-yen-a-song-type cassette tapes any more, do they? Why don't you come and have a sing-song when you've finished your dinner? I'll bet you love a sing-song."

All the way through dinner I promised that I would. But when I had finished my last nibble of fish and drained the last drop of beer from my tumbler, a thudding weariness came down on me like a landslide and all I could do was lean back against the wall and think about going to sleep. The wife came in with a big dish of black grapes and wondered what I was doing in Mikado. I told her, fighting off four or five yawns. Two minutes later the wife was on the phone and five minutes later she had gone out in her car to fetch a retired junior high school history teacher who had written a mimeographed pamphlet about Saigo Takamori (the one that revealed his vital statistics) and who, she explained, was so anxious to give me a copy of this that he couldn't put it off until morning. I yawned four or five times more and eyed the futon cupboard, but at least I was spared the laser discs.

The history teacher arrived, a small, polite, soft-spoken, seventy-year-old sensei named Tsuchida, and a man from the shop across the street was summoned to photocopy Mr. Tsuchida's pamphlet. When he had finished doing this and had distributed copies to everyone in the building, he found himself a cushion and a glass and sat down to join the enlarging seminar. The owner arrived with beer and more grapes and settled himself enthusiastically at my table. The wife's sister was in London, she told me, otherwise I expect she would have turned up as well. We all sat drinking beer and peeling grapes and listening to Mr. Tsuchida, who in his soft, bronchial voice, for which he blamed the typhoon rain, outlined the brush that history had had with the little village where he was born, and where he was sure he would die.

"It rained heavily the day that Saigo came through Mikado, too," Mr. Tsuchida began, apparently under the impression that this would please me.

"In fact," beamed the owner, "it rains heavily in Miyazaki a great deal of the time. You might not know this, but Miyazaki has the heaviest rainfall of all the forty-seven prefectures in Japan; a total of about three thousand milliliters a year."

"I know that now," I said, glowering round at my belongings. "About two thousand of them have fallen into my pack."

"Ha ha," said the owner, and we drank more beer and listened while the rain lashed the roofs outside the window.

"The Satsuma men came down from the pass through Matae-no-hara, along the same road you took today," said Mr. Tsuchida. My map was open on the table, weighed down by the ashtray with the dead flies in it, and we all bent forward and studied the route. "Whenever they passed a house or a hut, the people who lived there came out and gave them shochu and pickled plums and anything else they could spare. This happened here in Mikado too, and all along the road to Kijino, about three kilometers further on, where Saigo stayed with a man called Shimada. I'll show you the place tomorrow if you like. I'll come and meet you on my bicycle. You'll have to come through Kijino anyway, and Kijino is where I live.

"The local people treated the rebels very kindly. But when the government troops came through later in the evening they turned their backs on them and ignored them. Partly it was because they admired Saigo so much, and partly it was because they felt sorry for his followers who were mostly just boys. But it's also because, at the time of the Meiji Restoration, the lord of Nobeoka and other smaller *daimyos* from around these parts had sided with the shogun. In fact the lord of Nobeoka was a relative of the shogun's. Then, of course, Saigo Takamori had led the imperial troops against the shogun's army so the people around here had opposed him. Not that they could do much about it, of course. None of the lords in Miyazaki had any power; most of them couldn't even send troops to fight. All they could do was fret and moan and observe these high events from the sidelines. But country memories are long, and now that Saigo had turned against the same government that, nine years earlier, had destroyed the relative of their lord, they gave their tacit support to the rebels, and their sympathies to Saigo in his defeat."

"That was how it was for most of Kyushu, I imagine," mused Mr. Tsuchida as everyone nodded their heads. "For centuries the other Kyushu clans had worried that Satsuma was too strong, too ambitious, too aggressive, that it could turn and gobble up their territories if it had half a mind. And, of course, it had. It had warred with its neighbors, and beaten most of them hands down. In the years before Hideyoshi came to power near the end of the sixteenth century Satsuma controlled almost all of Kyushu, and even after Hideyoshi stopped it from expanding north and east, it colonized the whole chain of southern islands, practically as far as Taiwan. No one in these parts had much of a reason to shed any tears for Satsuma. Until, of course, it became a question of Satsuma versus Tokyo. Then, as generally happens in Japan, local loyalties got the better of national ones. When it came to the push, Kyushu was Kyushu."

"Where did Saigo go after Kijino?"

"He went over the Teahouse Pass very early on the morning of the 25th. Local people still call it that, though there isn't a teahouse there any more. But you can follow the same road. And in the afternoon he went over the Goro Pass. . . . "

"Oh Christ, two passes in one day?"

"Ha ha. That's right. And he spent the night of the 25th with a family called Hamasuna in Shiromi. That's that little dot just there."

Mr. Tsuchida tapped a speck on my map that was barely larger than a pin prick. By peering at it through the lens of my Swiss army knife, I could see that it was identified by two ideograms that meant "silver mirror" and that, despite the dignity of its name, it was as near to the middle of nowhere as anyone might condemn a village to be.

"I don't suppose they've got a ryokan there, have they?"

"I've never heard of any," the owner confessed.

"I could find out for you if you like," said the obliging man who had made the photocopies, and he jumped up and went to use the phone. Two minutes later he was back with the news that, though there were no ryokans, a family in Shiromi sometimes took in travelers and that he had told them to expect me the following evening. The man was grinning like a Halloween pumpkin.

"And guess what! It's a family called Hamasuna!"

So the seminar recessed on a note of triumph, and the moment Mr. Tsuchida and the rest of the group had said goodnight and pulled the screens of my room closed behind them, I fell into my futon and closed my eyes and groaned and lay and listened to the rain. The red patches on my crotch itched like crazy and the rain crashed down bringing the odd rooftile with it.

Two passes to cross . . . One day . . . Oh Christ . . . Family called Hamasuna . . .

Saigo, for his sins, had been roused at midnight and was on the road again at one o'clock in the morning. At least that wouldn't happen to me. But the further I tramped into these god-ridden hills, the more I understood the great man's torments, and now I had a sore scrotum too.

By morning the typhoon rain was reduced to falling in fits and starts. In one of the starts Mr. Tsuchida telephoned to say that he could not come out in such weather. But half an hour later he turned up in a lull, riding a cream-painted lady's bicycle, carrying a floppy black umbrella and wearing a white shirt, a fawn cap, and rubber galoshes that would have been several times too large for Saigo. We walked together for three or four kilometers along the empty road that ran through a string of tiny hamlets, in the last of which, though we never reached it, stood Mr. Tsuchida's home. The air dripped like a squeezed flannel and sweat slid out of all my pores with every step I took. I was soon as wet zipped up inside my ridiculous nylon as I would have been with no clothes on at all. So I stripped my rain gear off and packed it away while Mr. Tsuchida, wheeling his lady's bike, coughing softly in his typhoon-battered voice, took up again the story he had spent his life retelling.

"By the time Saigo and his men reached Mikado they had started to come under sniper fire from the advance parties who had raced across the pass and spread out along their route, so they took cover among the buildings that are scattered through this valley. At that house on the right, from about four o'clock till about eight o'clock on the evening of the 24th, Saigo himself rested and had something to eat. That's puzzled the members of our local historical society for years, you know. One minute Saigo's under rifle fire and the next he's sitting having a snack. Perhaps one of his officers had been wounded and he was forced to call a halt whether he wanted to or not. Or it's just possible that a temporary truce was arranged, for even Saigo's enemies had the greatest admiration for him. Three Satsuma men died in the skirmish. You can see their graves here in the village, erected by the villagers, and one of the graves is still washed and tended at the equinoxes and during the Festival of the Dead. The family whose descendants tend that grave never knew the man alive. But they adopted his body and buried it out of respect for his commitment.

"In that place over there on the left," continued Mr. Tsuchida, wheeling his bicycle to a halt by the roadside, "Saigo spent the rest of the evening, until one o'clock in the morning when he left in the rain."

He pointed to a small, nondescript building which lay beyond some neatly tended paddies and which had been converted into a cowshed. Its old tiled or straw-thatched roof had been replaced with sheets of bright blue plastic, and these shone now under the dense, silvery sky that threatened every second a rekindling of the storm.

"There you can see a stone milepost that has stood since feudal times. We think it was probably at that spot that Saigo crossed the river. And in that small temple that you can see at the foot of the hill there one of Saigo's enemies stayed. There's a story about the night he stayed there that illustrates how the war was being fought in this, its next-to-last phase. It's a story that illustrates perfectly, too, the character of Saigo himself. . . . "

As the pursuing troops advanced down the valley Saigo's men had taken to the surrounding woods, and when dusk fell most of the houses in Mikado, and in some of the outlying hamlets, had been requisitioned by government officers for billets. But once darkness had taken hold, the rebels emerged noiselessly from the hillsides to converge on the house of Shimada Taniya, now the cowshed, where they knew their general was resting. On their way, a group of them passed the small temple that Mr. Tsuchida had pointed out to me, and discovered to their glee that a medical officer of the imperial army had been billeted there without sentries. So they seized him and dragged him before Saigo and asked their general if they should cut off his head.

Most of the rebels who had stayed with Saigo through this desolate retreat were still in their teens or early twenties, former students of the private schools that Saigo had set up during his retirement in Kagoshima to keep the old samurai disciplines alive. Saigo had a father's affection for these young men that neither their incurably headstrong natures (it was they, after all, who had precipitated the rebellion, and thus their idol's downfall), nor present defeat, nor wretchedness, nor the specter of death could diminish.

Saigo reproached them gently now and, when the young men had shuffled out of the cramped room, littered with farming implements, he apologized to the medical officer and invited him to sit down and share a small flask of shochu. Wars like this, Saigo observed, were hard on all whose lives they disrupted. He wished the medical officer well and hoped that he would soon be safe home with his family. They finished their drink and the officer returned to his billet. An hour later Saigo was gone in the rain.

And so was I, along the narrow road to the first of my two passes. I had stood at the parting of our roads with Mr. Tsuchida for another quarter of an hour, listening while he recounted the major events of his own life. He had been a Christian when he was young, he told me (Kyushu is, and always has been, Japan's most proselytized island), and for five years he had attended a Christian school. But apostasy had set him adrift and for many subsequent years he had floated restlessly from one new Japanese religious sect to another, staying longest with Tenri (the Divine Wisdom Sect), officially a nineteenth-century offshoot of Shinto although, in its doctrine of a single world-creating God who longs to delight in human harmony, it has clearer resemblances to the Old Testament teachings of Tsuchida's youth than to the unkempt numens of the mountains and fields whose principal attitude to human society is at best tolerance, at worst contempt. Now, Mr. Tsuchida professed himself a Buddhist, a faith to which many Japanese people discover a devotion once they sense their last years ticking away. He hated "the cult of shrines," he told me, by which he meant the "state Shinto" of wartime and the years of military conquest, and the whole spurious rigmarole by which the spirit deities of the natural world become the undistinguished cousins of the Japanese imperial tribe.

Oh, yes, and the other highlight of his life: he had been on a group tour of Europe. He had failed to see Buckingham Palace, he regretted politely, because the British trains and buses had been on strike, but he was mightily impressed by Big Ben. Twice on our stroll through the landmarks of war he had asked me shyly how to say "Bon voyage" in English. "Good luck," I had suggested; "Good luck," he had repeated. So now, with a measured intake of breath like that of a swimmer about to dive into a lake, a slow bow and a quiet smile, he wished me a carefully enunciated "Good luck" as I tramped away up the slope. Then he pedaled home on his lady's bicycle. The lull ended, the rain started to pelt down again, and I still had two passes to cross instead of one.

How little young people care for Saigo! Mr. Tsuchida had lamented in his bronchial voice. How many schoolchildren see in his single-mindedness, his courage, his refusal to compromise, his concern for his country, his humanity, his purpose, a model for their own behavior?

"None?"

"None. He is out of favor."

"And who is in favor with the young?" I had wondered. "What kind of a man are schoolchildren today encouraged to admire?"

Mr. Tsuchida thought for a long while.

"Perhaps a man like Noguchi Hideo . . . "

Hmm. There are plenty of children's biographies of Noguchi Hideo available in the shops, with large print and pronunciation guides alongside all the ideograms, and illustrations in pastel colors. Noguchi Hideo was a bacteriologist, born into a family of country peasants, one year old at the time of Saigo's rebellion, who succeeded in cultivating the causative agent of syphilis. For more than a decade following his receipt of an imperial award for that achievement he struggled in South and Central America to isolate the virus that causes yellow fever. In 1927 he went to pursue his research in Africa, and he died in Ghana the following year. It was yellow fever that killed him. There have been few enough genuinely international figures in Japanese history, but Noguchi was one of them. Even if his successes in the field of medicine tend to pale in comparison with those of a Pasteur, and the intellect and humanitarian selflessness that he brought to his work with those of a

Schweitzer, he is unquestionably a man to revere. But is he revered? And by the young?

Once I visited the Noguchi Memorial Center on the windy shore of Lake Inawashiro in northeastern Honshu where Noguchi was born, and I saw there a scroll on which the doctor had painstakingly written in a language that was obviously foreign to him: "*La patience est amere, mais son fruit est doux.*" (Patience is bitter, but its fruit is sweet.) Offhand, I could think of no sentiment less appropriate to the headstrong young men who had accompanied Saigo on his last adventure. But the scroll reminded me, as did Saigo's students, as did the rows of children's biographies in the bookshops, of an instructive difference between the heroes the Japanese admire and those who are admired in the West.

In the West a hero is presented to a young mind in the hope that he or she will inspire imitation. Japanese heroes, on the other hand, are meant to be admired from as safe and uninvolving a distance as possible. The question of imitating them, if it arose, would likely be laughed at. This is as true of the heroes of popular fiction as it is of historical figures. Take Kuruma Torajiro, or "Tora-san," the hero of the longest-running film series in the history of any nation's cinema. Tora-san has a heart of gold, a nature so guileless and charitable that one comes away from every episode wishing one's children, one's relatives, one's friends, one's colleagues at work were blessed with half such a heart. But Tora-san is a bumbler, a dreamer, a loser, a man by circumstance and temperament estranged from his family, lacking education, lacking foresight, lacking marital prospects or the remotest chance of achieving a settled life, completely incapable of understanding or occupying a place in what we like to call normal society. This is the source of his comedy and nine-tenths of the reason why audiences love him. But to wish such a plight on our children, relatives, friends, and colleagues—or on ourselves—would be tantamount to idiocy. Yes, we admire Torajiro. But should we strive to be like him? Don't be ridiculous!

The built-in alienation of audience from hero in Japanese cinema and fiction is the result of careful calculation. One finds it over and over again. An examination of Tora-san's case would disclose most of the means by which this alienation is achieved. A lot of them are obvious, like the unfashionable clothes and hat that he is made to wear and the frowned-upon nature of the trade he pursues (he is an itinerant hawker of trinkets). A few are buried deeper, like the fact that his unusual surname, Kuruma, was the hereditary name of the leader of the Edo *hinin* (literally, "non-humans"), a pariah caste consisting mainly of beggars that ranked below all the strata of ordinary feudal society, enjoyed none of society's benefits, and was subject to systematic persecution.

You could take most of the heroes of Japanese popular culture one after the other and show how their creators have sought to ensure that admiration and sympathy do not result in emulation. Often they incorporate into the hero's life some form of disability or anguish. We might wish we possessed Zatoichi's skill with a sword but that would hardly compensate for us being blind. We might envy the famous T.V. samurai Kogarashi Monjiro his courage, but to be that friendless, that rootless, that shunned—no thanks. And a similar attitude exists towards many of the real-life figures who attain hero status. Indeed, it often seems as though they are selected for their status precisely because they represent everything that Japanese society teaches its members to avoid. They are not models; they are cautionary examples, and sometimes they are scapegoats. In a conformist nation, they are misfits and sore thumbs; among a materialistic people they pursue impossible dreams.

This is as true of modern heroes like Uemura Naomi—who, in his solitary conquests of some of the world's highest mountains or his trek across Greenland with no company but huskies, was as unlikely a scion of "group-oriented," "consensus" society as one could ever hope to meet— as it is of older heroes like Saigo. Lead an armed rebellion for half a year and then flee up and down mountains for sixteen days with swollen testicles? Not likely! Spend the best years of your life in the jungles of America and Africa, surrounded by monkeys and foreigners, dying of fever, scribbling in French, and swallowing the bitter pill of patience? You've got to be joking!

There is, however, a further stage in the elevation of the Japanese hero. This occurs when his memory grows so exalted that he quits altogether the realm of common humanity and drifts in the ethereal spheres, apotheosized. Then it is no longer necessary to emphasize his disabilities and discomforts, his dreams, his hernias, his funny hats. We regard him then precisely as we regard the god who inhabits the next-door shrine, absolved of the need either to imitate or admonish, for the hero now inhabits a world in which imitation is beside the point. It is at this stage that society's attitude to the hero enters the realm of the thoroughly bizarre; and it is to this stage that Saigo Takamori was hoisted within weeks of his last defeat. Noguchi Hideo never reached this stage and I hardly think he will. He remains mired in humanity; indeed, it is in human mire that his memory has its only roots. But Saigo was residing on the planet Mars (which Japanese were calling "The Saigo Star") before he was even dead. By October of the year after his death his slimmed-down ghost had appeared in a spectacularly ghoulish woodblock print to haunt the government with a spectral petition. And within fourteen months of that he had been installed in Nanshu Shrine in his home town of Kagoshima as a fully-fledged, card-carrying deity.

After that it was all uphill. Where books about Noguchi intended for young readers have contented themselves with recounting known facts, those about Saigo have sometimes incorporated the most extravagant flights of fancy. Take a particularly bizarre example by a Japanese professor who lives in Kyushu, published as recently as 1990. This short book, written in English and entitled, quaintly, *The Truth of the Matter*, takes the form of a little fable in which Saigo is confronted on his last battlefield by an angel who has flown in from San Francisco.

"Hi, Buddy! How's it going?" enquires the angel.

Historically, it wasn't going terribly well, but we have passed beyond the stage where history need be considered, and within seconds the angel has whisked Saigo to the United States where, communicating in fluent English ("How come? Who is doing this?" "Heaven," replies the angel), he hails a taxi driven by a woman.

"Wanna ride?" the driver smiles. Her smile is irresistible.

"What the heck," replies Saigo, and introduces himself. "My name is Saigo Takamori."

"The Saigo Takamori I know," recalls the driver, "is the person who was born in Kagoshima and played a leading role in establishing the Meiji Restoration."

Needless to say, they get along famously.

"What a view!" exclaims Saigo, staring out of the window of his hotel suite. "Is this the America we have been afraid of? Are those the Americans we would call barbarians?" Evidently not. They are wonderful people. The taxi driver, for instance, is a gem. She can read Japanese and has made a close study of the life of her famous passenger, who urges her to call him "Taka." But she has one or two awkward questions to ask, for example: "Did you really want to conquer Korea, as most Japanese school textbooks suggest?"

"Heavens no!" exclaims Saigo, astonished. "Do textbooks say that? That's the last thing I would ever think of."

Saigo proceeds to outline his view that "Civilization should be the spread and completion of the 'Heavenly Way' which is full of mercy and love." All he had ever wanted to do was slip over to Korea in person and have "a peaceful discussion" with the suspicious natives. His suggestion to cabinet colleague Itagaki Taisuke, set down clearly in a surviving letter, that the Koreans would likely kill him and so provide Japan with a *casus belli*, was no more than a ruse to obtain the bellicose Itagaki's consent to Saigo's employment as an envoy.

As for the rebellion of 1877, it was all the fault of that infamous "conspiracy" of Home Minister Okubo Toshimichi's whereby Saigo was pegged for assassination. Saigo's decision to lead fifteen thousand armed men out of Kagoshima in February was purely the result of his desire "to talk with Okubo." He was "afraid there would be a fight on the way, and as it turned out, that's what happened." The retreat from Nobeoka was motivated by Saigo's concern for his followers and his desire that they be permitted to die in Kagoshima where their families lived. "It was our hometown, warm and friendly," he explains to the taxi driver. "There's nothing like home, is there? . . . I prayed that this battle was going to end and should be the last battle among Japanese people, and that the new Japan would sail along smoothly and peacefully."

The taxi driver has in her pocket a copy of the evening edition of the *Nishi Nihon Shinbun* for June 3rd, 1988, in which the headline identifies Saigo's photograph, and Saigo dismisses it as a case of mistaken identity. The taxi driver who, it turns out, has interviewed a former mayor of Kagoshima and a descendant of the feudal lord Shimazu Nariakira about this very photograph, concurs with Saigo's opinion. They have dinner together and in the bar afterwards Saigo is accosted by an American drunk who accuses the Japanese of unmanliness because of their "sneak attack" on Pearl Harbor.

"Well I'm sorry about that if it's true," says Saigo (or, as the taxi driver continues to call him, Taka), but that was not I. I have never thought of a sneak attack on anybody."

"Americans can never forgive and forget Pearl Harbor," snarls the drunk, pushing his luck.

"What about Hiroshima and Nagasaki?" shrieks the taxi driver. "What kind of an attack was that?"

"That was an attack of justice," thunders the drunk.

The drunk draws a knife. The invisible angel slips Saigo a Japanese sword. Outweaponed, the drunk opts for a wrestling match but Saigo tosses him out of the window. As the hero smooths his rumpled sleeves, the Americans in the bar break into applause. "Yeah, man," they say. It's a typical San Francisco night.

"You've been very kind and hospitable," says Saigo to the taxi driver when they are alone in the street. "You're free from prejudice. That's a noble state to be in. I admire you for that. I admire your beauty too."

"Taka, thank you for your compliments," replies the driver.

She kisses him on the lips. Saigo blushes. "Can you imagine," wonders the author of this fable, "how he looked when he was kissed by a beautiful American woman? This will be another mystery of Saigo in the next decade."

And there the fable ends.

It is striking how this author's purpose, otherworldly as his fable may appear, resembles the one that motivated Saigo's biographer Mushanokoji and his adaptor. Both have sought to ensure that Saigo makes a "radiant impression" and, once this impression has been established, to depict Saigo's views as mirroring their own and those of the times in which they live. Mushanokoji's adaptor, writing in the first full year of the Pacific War, wishes Saigo to exemplify "the patriotism of the Japanese and the spiritual basis of the new Japan." The author of the fable, writing forty-eight years later, wishes Saigo to exemplify an outlook so scintillatingly "international" that it would do credit to the Secretary General of the United Nations. The historical Saigo is as irrelevant to these figures as the historical Jesus is to the miracle-worker of the gospels. Both have quit humanity and entered a realm where the incredible outweighs the likely by a factor of thousands. That Saigo travels to America by air and does not walk there on water is a mercy for which we ought to be grateful.

⧖

I crossed the first of my two passes at about midday. All sign of the teahouse that had once stood there to refresh travelers had vanished. There was nothing at all at the crest of the pass and nothing along the whole length of the road that led to it, only the rain and the shiny brown frogs, much smaller than grasshoppers, that had come out to sit in the downpour, and beyond the dark woods the tumble of red water.

At two o'clock, in the valley between the passes, I found a lonely grocer's shop, well separated from any village, and sheltered there for three-quarters of an hour, nearly vomiting from the itch of my sores and the three beers I gulped as I stood in the doorway. The shop was run by an old couple and their shy daughter-in-law, whose eyes were large and dusky like a Malay's. The old woman sat in a chair in the middle of her living room with her neck held rigid by a leather harness that hung suspended from the cobwebbed ceiling. She spoke unintelligibly without moving her head and I felt as though I had interrupted some private ritual torture. The old man told me that the next pass I had to climb was called the Goro Pass, named after someone, but who . . . ? Who . . . ? He couldn't remember. The tortured woman muttered something from the harness. I left, and was accosted by a white-vested man in the only car I saw all day.

"Get in! Get in!"

"No thanks. I'm walking. I'm following the route taken by Saigo Takamori. . . ."

"Get in, I say! I'll take you where you want to go. I'll tell you all about Saigo Takamori."

"No, you don't understand. . . . "

"Get in! Get in! I know everything there is to know about Saigo Takamori. What's the matter with you? Get in, I tell you! Get in! Get in. . . !"

And gradually my replies grew sharper, and gradually the white-vested man grew rattier. He seemed unable to control his face. One second he was smiling, the next he looked as though he wanted to commit a murder. In the end I said an abrupt goodbye and the man drove away with the blood rising round his ears. The sweet fruits of patience had eluded us both. I set about crossing the Goro Pass and for five hours met no one.

It was long after dark when I came down near level ground again and saw the lighted doorway of a tiny shop.

"Hello," I groaned, blundering through the door. "Is this Shiromi? I'm looking for the Hamasunas."

"Hamasuna who?"

"I don't know Hamasuna who. How many Hamasunas are there?"

The thin old man pursed his lips and made a long mental calculation.

"Well," he said, "I'm Hamasuna, and so are three-quarters of my neighbors. We were all Hamasunas once, you know, until the newcomers came."

"I'm looking for the Hamasunas who put up travelers."

"Oh, the Hamasunas who put up travelers. It's another two kilometers through the woods before you come to the village and they're the third or fourth house on the left. Are they expecting you? I'd better phone them. It'll give me an excuse to have a chat. . . . "

I walked for another half an hour. There were no lights in the woods, or in the village, and I groped about, kicking over a bucket, and knocked on the door of what I took to be the third house on the left, stumbling against the doorframe from weariness. It was pelting with rain and a long time passed before the door opened a crack and an old woman said, with her hand over her mouth and her eyes wide and seeing nothing in the dark, that, yes, this was where the Hamasunas lived but they didn't take in travelers; no, that was the Hamasunas who lived up the slope between the fourth and fifth houses on the right, whose occupants were also Hamasunas. I found the slope and limped up it in the pitch black rain to find a woman standing silently at the top, waiting for me with an umbrella.

"We're here," she said. "He phoned from the shop."

"Are you Mrs. Hamasuna . . . ?"

"Hamasuna, yes . . . "

I half collapsed across her doorstep. Then I slowly peeled off my soaking clothes and hung them on a very wet clothesline, dragged myself across the yard, and squeezed into a scalding bath, from where I could hear two children called Hamasuna taking shamisen lessons from a man called Hamasuna. Dinner had been laid out for me in my room on a small lacquer table, but I couldn't keep my eyes open long enough to finish it.

"Don't pay any attention to the sirens that go off at five o'clock in the morning," said Mrs. Hamasuna when she woke me up an hour later clearing away the untouched dishes. "They're just for the workers. It's a village custom."

"Don't the workers have clocks?" I wanted to ask, as I always wanted to ask when sirens went off, but I hadn't the energy to do anything but nod.

"And here's a book that's been lent to you by Mr. Hamasuna the schoolteacher," said Mrs. Hamasuna the lodger-of-travelers, placing in front of me a thick clothbound volume called *The History of West Mera*. West Mera is the name of the administrative district next to the one that includes the hamlet of Shiromi. I picked up the book and put it down again. H. G. Wells wrote a history of the world in 520 pages and here were 1,170 on the history of West Mera.

"Mr. Hamasuna will come and see you in the morning," Mrs. Hamasuna promised. "I've told him you're studying Saigo Takamori and he's turned down the corners of the pages he thinks you ought to read."

I blinked and looked at the first page whose corner had been turned down. It was part of a chronological table showing that on the same day that Saigo had stumbled out of Kijino in the rain, lumbered across the Teahouse Pass and the Goro Pass in his palanquin, and spent a few fretful hours trying to sleep in Shiromi at the house of a man called Hamasuna, the last remnants of the Satsuma force that had remained behind in Takachiho were finally captured or driven away, and the main body of the imperial army had regrouped there and then turned south in force and begun pursuing Saigo's tracks through the Nanatsuyama mountains. Saigo was two weary days ahead of them, and the same two days ahead of me. I pushed the book away, pulled it back towards me, closed it, listened for five seconds to the rain, and woke up shivering in the middle of the night still bent across the table.

⁓

At eight-thirty the next morning two workmen in overalls rolled into the next-door room and began drinking shochu. I was sitting at my table, bleary-eyed, trying to catch up with my notes. The workmen passed my window as they crossed the yard and stopped and stared in at me through the insect netting. When I failed to look up, one of them clapped his hands sharply, as you would to summon a servant, or a god. I frowned at them. They nodded silently.

And at nine o'clock a seventy-seven-year-old retired headmaster called Hamasuna, the man who had turned down the corners of the pages for me, came to tell me about West Mera.

"There used to be an East Mera," Mr. Hamasuna said, answering my unasked question, "but it ceased to exist in 1962 when they incorporated it into Saito city, the year they finished the dam. The same'll happen to West Mera, mark my words. This area is already the most sparsely populated in the whole of Miyazaki. It's dying a fast death. When I retired as headmaster in 1969 there were more than two hundred kids at the village school. Today there are twenty-five. People from Shikoku used to come here in search of a living, would you believe. There's a few families like that who've settled in Shiromi. The other villagers call them newcomers, though they've all been here since before the war. We'd see them arrive on carts when I was a kid, and they'd stop and shout to us in the fields, 'Oiii! Any mushrooms in these hills?' 'Plenty,' we'd shout back. And they'd unload their carts there and then and start marking out a bit of ground for a house."

Mr. Hamasuna spoke in the celebratedly thick dialect of southern Kyushu, made all the more unintelligible by the amount of sonority he crammed into each sentence. "Oiii! Any mushrooms in these hills?" It was like Orson Welles saying "The crow makes wing to the rooky wood." He punctuated most of what he said by quietly pounding *The History of West Mera* with one of his mottled, lightly clenched fists. He was a distinguished-looking, sprightly man with silver hair, a white vest, and a head full of uncollected history.

"We've got a famous kagura dance in West Mera. They've sent people down from the University of Tokyo to see it. An Intangible Cultural Property it is now. One woman even came from France to have a look at it. We don't just do it for tourists though, like some places I could mention. And we don't shift the dates to the nearest Saturday or Sunday either, to suit travel agents. We do it like it ought to be done. But how many more years can we keep it up . . . ?

"When the telegraph first came through to Mikado, in the 1920s I suppose it was, they'd send runners over those two passes you walked across yesterday, any time of the day or night. Old men, some of the runners were. The young people today could never do it. . . .

"My mother was three years old when Saigo Takamori came through Shiromi. She had heard he was a big man, so she guessed who it was the minute he stepped out of his palanquin. They carried him in a palanquin, you see, to hide him from the government troops. Dusk it was when he arrived. He patted my mother's head. . . .

"This woman came all the way from France. Did I tell you? It lasts two days and she stayed for both. December it is; very cold. She sat and watched the whole lot of it. She came all the way from France. . . . "

I climbed into my wringing wet clothes and walked out of Shiromi in the dregs of the typhoon. Spots of mold had grown on my belt and water squirted out of my boots when I pulled them on. There was no one on the road, or in the fields, and for most of that day I saw no human figure but the lank black scarecrows. The mushrooms grew ungathered in the hills and there was no sound from the village school. But in cold December there would be kagura and a woman had come all the way from France to see it. She had passed into the history of West Mera, and so, before it vanished, had I.

•   •   •

The Shiromi River flowed brown and slow, clogged with the debris of the storm. By midday dams had broadened it into a lake, which I sat and contemplated through the splotches of rain and grime on the window of a workmen's noodle shop, under a poster that showed a white-suited Miura Tomokazu puffing sternly and butchly on a Cabin Mild. Before he married pop singer Yamaguchi Momoe, pop actor Tomokazu advertised chocolate. But marriage was a turning point in both their careers. Now Momoe spends her days laundering Tomokazu's underpants and Tomokazu spends his days touting cigarettes and booze.

The road along the twisting shore of the lake passed through long, unlit tunnels that dripped with water. The first of these bore a metal plaque which said that it had been opened in 1962, but it was one of few landmarks I encountered in the Miyazaki hills that looked as though it dated back to Saigo's retreat. The concrete had crumbled away from the sodden walls and the roof spouted water like a broken spigot. All day it rained, then stopped, then rained. And though Mr. Hamasuna the schoolteacher had assured me that the storm would lift by early afternoon, the typhoon clouds still scudded across the sky, looking like the smoke you get from burning garbage without bothering to take it out of its plastic bag. I sat for a while in a bus shelter next to a small sign that said May Peace Prevail on Earth, battered and dented by so many storms that it too might have dated from Saigo's time. Perhaps our Saigo had placed it there himself, our Saigo the Pacifier, Saigo of the Angels. By four o'clock a thick mist had hidden the hills. And at four-thirty, in the only grocer's shop I found to rest in that cold August day, I came face to face with one of the unlikeliest creatures you can encounter nowadays in the hinterland of Japan.

She was an unmarried college graduate, twenty-two or three, very bright and very pretty, who, despite studying for two years in Tokyo and working for another year at a day-care center in Miyazaki city, had come back to live with her aging parents on the shore of this lake in the middle of nowhere and help them run their shop. It was a move that almost anyone in her position, with her attractions, would have resisted, even though her mother was ill, she told me, and spent most of her time asleep. But the young woman looked content with her situation; or at least she looked more content than her father, who sat on the raised tatami of his living room, glaring suspiciously at us through his open screens for the entire time that I hung about his shop, which was as long as I could realistically make two large bottles of beer last, all ready to leap out and separate us at the first sign I displayed of committing aggravated rape.

"Aren't you bored here?" I asked the pretty young woman.

"Oh," she said, "I was born here, you see." Then she added, as though it explained the whole of life, "And there are fireworks in the summer."

Other attractions were posted on the walls. There were ink prints of three very hefty black carp that her brother had caught in the lake above the dam. The heftiest had been a contender for the local record and they had tried to keep all three alive in a tank until the newspaper could send a reporter out to see them. But the carp had died. What a shame. They had died. But her brother was also good at catching eels.

"What do you dislike most about this place?"

"The mosquitoes," she said brightly. "They're so big and black. Don't you think they are so big and black?"

I hadn't noticed any, I confessed, and she giggled. So I took my eyes off her face for a second and glanced around the shop for mosquitoes, and saw three of them, black and silent, feasting serenely between my knuckles.

I had better stay at the Fujiya Business Hotel, the pretty young woman told me. That's where she would stay if she were me. It was about three kilometers further up the road in the village of Murasho. Of course there was an old-fashioned ryokan as well, for men who came to fish in the lake. But a person of my tastes, accustomed to city life like she was, well, I should stay at the Fujiya Business Hotel. What on earth had they built a business hotel for, out here among these dams and mists? Oh, that was simply what they called it. It was more like a pension really, with a coffee shop downstairs and a few small bedrooms with showers. Sometimes she went to the coffee shop. There were no other coffee shops for miles and miles. Yes, sometimes she went to drink milk tea there. She would stay at the Fujiya, without a doubt, if she were me.

So forty minutes later, in a torrential burst of rain, I stamped into the

Fujiya Business Hotel, which stood at one end of Murasho's single street, and got myself a room. A business hotel is a hotel with practically no facilities or service and with rooms so small that you have to squeeze into them sideways. But this one had the coffee shop to which, that evening, the pretty young woman did not come to drink milk tea, and at whose counter I slumped, groaning and rubbing my thighs. It also had a woman who fed my laundry into a twin tub and brought it to my room all wet in a plastic bucket. She told me that when Saigo Takamori had spent the night in Murasho, he had hidden under the roof beams of the house where he had stayed, but I didn't believe a word of it. How on earth did he get up there? He couldn't even have got into one of the rooms of this hotel.

I fell into bed at eight o'clock with the rain still pounding on the panes of my window, and thunder and lightning to enliven my sleep. I had expected a short day from Shiromi to Murasho along the contorted shores of the lake, but it had seemed a punishingly long one. Perhaps it was the weather, or the redness of my spreading sores, or just the seeping weariness that the miles and miles of stagnating hills were marinating my bones in. At dinner, at the counter of the coffee shop, a truck driver told me that the road I planned to follow next day had nothing along it, nothing at all.

Nothing along it, nothing at all . . .

Nowhere to rest, nothing to eat, no one to talk to, nothing to see. . . .

What on earth, what on earth was I doing here? I turned over and smacked my face into the pillow and the night passed in one five-second gasp. But at least, since this was a "Western-style" hotel, there was a cup of hot coffee on the counter when I dragged myself down to breakfast, and a three-inch-thick slice of starchy white bread that the Japanese warm for twenty seconds and call toast. I had hung my laundered clothes on the curtain rail to dry but I still crawled into them wringing wet, and I had to apologize for the thousand-yen notes I fished out of my pocket to pay the bill with because if you tried to smooth them out they fell apart with damp.

As I lurched into my boots at seven-thirty, the manageress of the Fujiya Business Hotel, counting the loose change in her cash register, said: "It does you no good to sit all year round in air-conditioned rooms, you know. Get out and sweat a bit! That's the spirit!" She had giggled her head off the previous evening watching me trying to climb her iron staircase on legs that had ceased to function independently and been incorporated into someone else's body round about the same time as East Mera disappears. When I left, the manageress was busy adjusting her air conditioner. But, for a mercy, it had stopped raining; and this was an important mercy since today, August 29th, would not only be the longest day of my walk but the longest day I had ever walked.

5
Strange Fruit

❧

I had guessed it was going to be a long day from the map I had groaned over the night before, as well as from the truck driver's account of the road, which made it sound like a track through Antarctica. The map called it National Highway 265, which proves that cartographers have a sense of humor. All morning it wound alongside a river—not brown now, but loud and churning—towards the first of the two passes I had to cross, about nine hundred meters high. A strong breeze blew down the valley, agitating the river and shaking birds' nests out of the trees. The clouds had turned an innocent white, but the storm drains in Murasho still overflowed and the river was fed by impromptu waterfalls. I helped off the road a dazed snake that had been grazed by one of the six vehicles I saw that day and waved to an old woman at work in her vegetable patch, the last human I met for five hours. Sodden leaves and broken branches littered the road and the river bank, and the teetering mirrors at the dogleg curves were opaque with mold and cracks. A sign advised me to Love Wild Birds, and another warned me not to shoot at Japanese white-eyes. The pot holes in the road were as big as craters, and if there were any Japanese white-eyes in the trees they were too cowed by last night's storm to sing.

Beyond the first pass, at around midday, I found three khaki-trousered workmen, all stretched out fast asleep on the rubble. That brought the human count to four. An hour further on the doglegs uncoiled and the road, much narrower and rougher surfaced, rolled into what my map called the hamlet of Omata. Omata was a tiny dot on the map midway between Murasho and Suki, but I had still expected to find a shop there, or at least a machine to buy a drink from. The graves on the outskirts were the first giveaway; no one had visited them for years. Half the village houses had been torn down for their beams and tiles, and broken laths and chunks of plaster lay scattered among the rioting brambles. The buildings that still stood, mostly corrugated-iron huts, had been completely stripped of all they once contained. The old single-story school was in the best shape; it had been converted into the field office of a logging company, and the deadness of the village was perfectly matched by the desolation that the loggers had wrought on the hillsides.

I tramped on saying "shit"; there was nothing else to do. The only other human settlement I walked through that day, about ten kilometers further on, had no shop, no vending machine, and no inhabitants that I could see, although tacked to the wall of one of the dusty buildings was a pale pink sign for Coca-Cola and, below that, a faded blue sign for Sprite. My map called the place Tashirobae and, as I trudged morosely through it thinking that it must be the quietest living settlement I had ever been in, four fierce brown dogs sprang out from behind an empty hen coop and went with the precision of darts champions for my calves. I yelled at the windows of the nearest house for someone to come out and call the dogs off. An upstairs window opened; a bleary-eyed couple looked down and smiled. I drew my knife. The man said something to the dogs. The dogs slunk back with bared teeth to their hen coop, and the couple bowed, shut their upstairs window, and went back to manufacturing Hamasunas.

Just after three the road began to wind upwards again towards the second pass. At the crest, which I reached at about half past five, a postman on a motorcycle stopped to tell me that my feet were in a bad way and, since he found me sitting by the roadside trying to staunch the bleeding between my toes with cotton swabs, this was not a wild guess. In the late afternoon light the vista of the Kyushu peaks—Mount Kuju and the distant pale crater of Aso—made me long for legs I could stand on to gaze at them without closing my eyes and gritting my teeth. Signs were up for Men at Work, but the only laborer I saw was an elderly woman with a plastic helmet crammed down on top of her countrywife's hood painstakingly clearing a rock slide with her hands while the driver of a white minibus, the fourth vehicle I had seen all day, sat fidgeting and frowning behind the steering wheel, never dreaming of climbing out to help her.

The long descent took two hours. I could hear my own footsteps echoing across the valley. The sun set, the dark came down, and the evening star shone directly in front of me when I rounded the last dogleg onto level ground. Another hour and I passed the first lighted window. I tried to read my map by its light, but a dog barked and the light went out. Thirty minutes more to a liquor shop where I drank two beers in quick succession and asked the owner to phone the only ryokan in the village of Suki, which was another half hour's walk away. On the pitch black village road I passed a hut where an old man with a bald head sat crouched over a plastic tray sorting mushrooms by candlelight. He was the tenth human being I had seen since leaving Murasho. The batteries in my flashlight had died from the damp and I tramped the last three kilometers in the dark. At the ryokan two young boys skipped out to watch me come limping up the empty drive.

"It's arrived! It's arrived! It's a real one!"

Their mother saw the state I was in and shooed them away to play with their machine guns. I tried to phone my wife from the entrance hall but the line was so bad that I couldn't hear a word she said. I slammed the receiver down in tears. The bath was barely warm. "We've no other guests," explained the mother with an apologetic smile as I sank down alone onto the mats of a dining room built for a hundred people. At one end was a stage curtained with maroon velvet, where guests could sing to each other in amplified voices idylls of the Japanese countryside:

After all, we are the children of the gods. . . .

I fell asleep over the beancurd soup; it was getting to be a habit. As near as I could reckon, I had walked fifty-three kilometers since morning over the Omata Pass and the Kirei Pass, along an intermittently surfaced track called National Highway 265, and of the ten people I had seen three had been asleep. Not till the crest of the second pass, after ten hours of walking, had anyone spoken to me, and not till nine o'clock in the evening had I found a shop to sell me a drink. I went to sleep feeling a combination of pity and derision for myself. Saigo had reached Suki by a more direct track than mine that followed the tumbling Tsutsuki River, but like East Mera and that other dead hamlet impersonated by a dot, and like the country celebrated in the city-dwellers' idylls, Saigo's track lived nowadays solely in the memory and in the imagination.

But the next day's track was real enough to cry about. First, I spent two hours over breakfast, kneading my feet and catching up on my notes. Then I went to look at the little waterfall opposite my window, the only reason there is a ryokan in Suki; its splashing all night had filled my dreams with a horror of rain. Then I went to the Suki post office to draw some money out of my savings account ("We've only got big notes," worried the cashier) and ran into the postman who had met me the day before stanching blood. What time had I finally arrived in Suki? And had I been to see a doctor? And where was I born? And how old was I? And how long had I been living in Japan? Good grief! And had I spent all those years—what, *all* those years—walking?

My map showed an old road, marked by a bold double line and a couple of persuasive-looking twists, which appeared to be a viable alternative to the newer highway that wound over yet another pass to the small city of Kobayashi by way of a dreary kilometer-long tunnel. Tunnels are the bane of the long-distance walker, especially tunnels on highways, and the chance to avoid one is almost always worth adding a couple of extra miles to the day, even with a blister on your sole that feels as though a rusty nail is being driven into it. The postman warned me that the old road also ran through a short, dark tunnel but that, since it was now completely abandoned, there would be no thundering trucks or choking petrol fumes. In fact, there would be nothing up there at all. In fact, it would be an adventure.

I began walking up the road along which the postman had directed me and before long I fell in with four kids. Three were primary school pupils, two boys and a little girl; and the fourth, another boy, had just started junior high school, but he was no bigger than his younger friends and his eyes turned just as round at the sight of a foreigner tramping through his village on a Saturday morning. At first they followed me at a distance on their bikes, whispering and hissing, but they ended up conducting a full investigation. Where was I from? What was my name? Where was I going? Why was I walking? How long had it taken me to get to Suki from England and had I walked the entire way? At practically everything I said, the oldest boy exclaimed "*Sugeeeeii!*" (Wow!) and the little girl exclaimed "*Uso!*" (What a fib!)

"Where do you live?"

"Tokyo."

"Wow!"

"Have you got any children?"

"One daughter."

"What a fib!"

"Is your wife from England?"

"No, she's from Malaysia."

"What a fib! What a fib! Sugeeeeii! Uso!"

My family was a source of great agitation. The fact that I had married a person of Chinese ancestry seemed to strike the children as a sort of misdemeanor, like being out after dark without permission or cheating in a test.

"What's your daughter's name?"

"Mirai," I told them. *Mirai* is a Japanese word; it means "future."

"Wow!" said the oldest boy, "that's Chinese all right." And they fell to examining my Swiss army knife.

London was a very famous place. Even the people of Suki had heard of it. And Saigo Takamori was a famous man. The oldest boy's father had told him about Saigo. Saigo had stayed in Suki once, at the house of a man called Kawazoe, though what he was doing here goodness knew. And this one? Did what? Opened bottles? Sugeeeeii!

"Do people grow their own vegetables in Tokyo?"

"Not generally."

"Well, what do they have for dinner? Ice cream?"

We walked and talked for perhaps twenty minutes before it began to sink into the children's heads that I thought I was heading for Kobayashi.

"Kobayashi's the other way," said the oldest boy and they all wheeled their bicycles to a halt and pointed back the way we had come.

"I want the old road, not the highway."

"The one with the tunnel? It's full of spooks."

"Isn't it up this way?"

"No, it's the other way."

"Oh shit."

"Sugeeeeii!"

"Are you sure?"

"Yes. Hai. Ha. Um."

With serious faces, they turned their bikes round and began escorting me back to Suki, which we reached in another twenty minutes.

"We'll show you the way," the oldest boy said, and we walked out of the village in a totally different direction and began tramping up a much rougher road that, within a quarter of an hour, was so tangled with nettles that the children left their bikes by the verge and marched on beside me swinging their arms.

"It's very dark in the tunnel. There's no lights."

"Do you go there to play?"

"It's full of spooks."

Another ten minutes and they stopped and stood in a little group, scraping the ground with their feet and biting their lips and gazing at the slope ahead.

"Where's the tunnel?"

"Not far. Just round the next bend."

The little girl put her hand up to her chin.

"Aren't you coming any further?"

"No, we can't. Sayonara."

"What's the matter? The spooks?"

"No, we've got to get our bikes."

The children waved. The little girl giggled. The boys stood watching me, their cheeks red and puffy. At the bend I turned to wave goodbye but they were already skipping away down the tangled path, playing tag in and out of the trees. Thirty minutes later the path forked and I still hadn't reached a tunnel. I took the right-hand fork and within minutes it began to dip down again into the valley. I stamped back and took the left-hand fork. The map showed a road that ought to have been able to accommodate a four-ton truck but this path was now so overgrown that I could barely pick my way along it on foot, and my feet soon disappeared altogether. I gave up finally when I looked down and saw a brown snake slither across the path three inches from my right boot.

The sirens in Suki were sounding the noon lunchbreak as I trudged down the same street I had limped along the previous night, cursing all the children in creation. I ate lunch at a restaurant exactly opposite the liquor store where I had drunk my two beers sixteen hours earlier. Down the street came a workman in khaki overalls with two huge pruning knives swinging from his belt like something out of a time-warp, and I could just make out the words on a signboard in front of a temple across the street, which said: You can't alter your life but you can alter the way you look at it. I spent twenty minutes looking at mine from all angles and still couldn't work out what the fuck I thought I was doing with it.

I trudged for an hour and a half up the highway, reached the foul-smelling tunnel at half past two, and emerged from it choking into my shirt collar to see the cone of Kirishima pale on the horizon under a bank of lazy late summer cloud. I slept for an hour by the roadside on sweet-smelling grass and then tramped on through the ripening paddies. By five o'clock the valley had opened into a wide wet plain, stretching in bumps and rivulets toward the hazy grey squares of the city of Kobayashi, flat among black-green trees. I drank two beers in a grocer's shop, sitting in an armchair cooled by an electric fan which the owner's wife brought out for me together with a plate of pickles. Two workmen came into the shop and stood stretching and going "Aeeghhhhrrhh" "Uuggghh" "Ssssshhhhaaaa" to celebrate the end of their working week. "*Doko kara?*" one of them wanted to know—where from?—an everlasting, unanswerable question. London, Tokyo, Nobeoka, Suki. This time they settled for Suki. I passed a woman with a wheelbarrow full of mud and we giggled at each other in a conspiracy of folly. By six o'clock Kirishima had a feathered plume of cirrus streaming off it and the sun was sinking through a blotch of sky the color of a squashed persimmon.

By seven o'clock I was stamping through the cluttered streets of Kobayashi, the first city I had been in for ten days, past a shop displaying vast stocks for hire of white frilly sequined wedding dresses. I took a stuffy room in the Plaza Hotel, went out to eat at a nearby fish restaurant, and fell in with two Italian priests in tartan shirts who smiled shyly, beckoned me over to their table, and bought me a large draft beer.

One was Mario and the other was Flavio and Mario was treating Flavio to deep-fried prawns. They both belonged to the order of Saint Francis Xavier, the first Christian missionary to attempt the conversion of Japan, and Flavio had come on a visit from Kobe where he had spent a year studying Japanese and would spend another before his order decided in which part of Japan to incarcerate him. This was his last night in Kyushu. The prawns were good. Yes, very good. And Mario was the local parish priest. He had thirty parishioners, he told me, smiling, but only ten of them lived close enough to attend Mass every Sunday.

"I didn't realize I was in a parish," I said.

"Oh, all the world is parishes," laughed Mario, and ordered three more beers.

Ah, but it was hard to say Mass in Japanese, and harder still to hear confession. In the old days with Latin, well . . . And the bishop was Japanese. Yes, of course he was. That was Vatican policy. It had been policy since before the war. It was a solitary life with so few parishioners and a bishop who lived in Oita and was Japanese. But every week he saw two or three of the other parish priests at their get-together in Miyazaki city. That was something to look forward to. And after the meeting, if the other priests had business to attend to, well, he could always go to the cinema by himself. There was not much money to spend and not much to spend it on; the occasional film, the occasional beer. But hardest of all, yes, hardest of all was to win the confidence of his flock. Mario had been their priest for two years now and still felt like a stranger. Ah, and he would be the priest of this parish for eight years more. Eight years more. This was real country down here; real, deep country. The people were very conservative here, and very suspicious of strangers. All the restaurants were closed by nine; all the shops were shuttered and locked. Ah, if only they would trust him, he nodded, smiling all the while. If only they would talk to him. But they were so reluctant, so reluctant. If they would just confide in him a little. He opened his finger and thumb the breadth of a chopstick. A little would make all the difference in the world. Yes, he would be here eight years more. Well, well. And what about another mug of beer? Or coffee—what he missed most was good coffee. . . .

Celibacy must come hard to a man like Mario, a big, burly forty-two-year-old with a heavy beard and heavy eyes and a preference for draft over bottled. It was ludicrous to compare him with the Jesuits in Tokyo, chairing their comfortable committee meetings or sitting at their comfortable university desks composing score upon score of comfortable English textbooks for their polite and comfortable students. "Japan is a fairyland," one Jesuit-authored textbook taught, "so it is natural for the Japanese to act and to dance like fairies." I quoted this to Mario who laughed so loud that he probably imperiled his soul. Mario had studied for twelve years at a seminary in Glasgow, and I could imagine him preaching the rule of Saint Ignatius to the regulars at some dockside pub.

"What are the Japanese like then, Father?"

"Well, my son, they are fairies."

Xavier's Japan was not a fairyland. The missionaries who followed him here after the closure of the country to the West in 1639 were crucified, beheaded, burnt alive, or suspended by their feet for days over pits full of rotting offal until they died of suffocation or retched their innards up. One of Mario's "confrères," he told me, was now on Yakushima, an island south of the Satsuma peninsula highly favored by honeymooners. He had been there for the last three years researching the life of Giovanni Battista Sidotti.

Sidotti was the last missionary to penetrate Japan during the two and a quarter centuries of virtual isolation. A Sicilian, he had taken passage on a ship out of the Philippines in 1708 and, at his own request, had been landed alone on Yakushima, where he spent about two days. This was a great joke among the "confrères": two days' stay, three years' study; the order is nothing if not exhaustive. But it wasn't much of a joke for Sidotti. He was arrested as soon as he landed and taken via Nagasaki to Edo (Tokyo), where he was kept in prison for the next six years and managed to baptize two of his jailers. His last prison was a hole in the ground five feet deep with a small slit in the cover to prevent an easier death from lack of air. Food was thrown at him through the same slit. He stood it for twelve months and died in November, praising God and His works.

And if the beckoning fist of martyrdom helped fuel the zeal of Christian missionaries, did a similar impulse play any part in the career of Saigo Takamori? As evidence that the great man might have harbored such an impulse, commentators point to three events in his life.

There is Saigo's controversial stance during the crisis of 1873, in which he appears to have offered himself as a sacrificial lamb in the cause of sparking hostilities with Korea, whose government had recently forbidden trade with Japan and committed other inflammatory acts. At a cabinet meeting, according to Mushanokoji, Saigo expressed the view that the dispatch of a diplomatic envoy to the "obstinate" Koreans would be a better course of action than the immediate committal of troops (the course proposed by his cabinet colleague Itagaki Taisuke and others), but that "if they should go so far as to insult and kill our plenipotentiary without taking our reasonable advice, we can rightly denounce them publicly and subjugate them." He followed this up with a letter to Itagaki that is similarly unambiguous in content, although it lays more stress on the inevitability of conflict. "Is it not better to make the dispatch of an envoy precede that of force?" Saigo wrote. "In the event of their insolence, which will assuredly be inflicted on our envoy, we shall be able to go to war with sufficient cause." And then Saigo goes on to repeat in the letter the request that he had made at the cabinet session: "As they are expected to murder the envoy, I heartily entreat you to arrange for me to be appointed to this dangerous office. I may not be so well suited to the office as Soejima-san [the Foreign Minister], yet I think I am capable of managing such a matter as my own death."

Saigo's wording leaves little to puzzle over, but debate has raged about his motive. Although most historians place Saigo squarely among the hard-liners and attribute his stance to a desire to revive on a national scale the samurai spirit that had suffered such calculated eclipse in the five years since the overthrow of the Bakufu, the liberals and humanists remain adamant that their hero cannot possibly have believed that a solution to the crisis lay in armed conflict, even though he was Marshal of the Army. Was Saigo then (totally out of character) employing sophistry in order to trick hawks like Itagaki into agreeing to open a dialogue with Korea? Or was he urging, as on the face of it his letter suggests, a drastic means of provoking war? Or was he simply keen to seize for himself the opportunity presented by the crisis for conspicuous martyrdom and, if so, why?

"Saigo really wanted to die," declares Mushanokoji. Elsewhere his adaptor cites other moments in Saigo's career where he appears deliberately to have courted violent death. And there is at least one written hint that he regarded public service as an opportunity for self-destruction. In 1871 when he was finally persuaded to join the new national government, he wrote a poem comparing himself to "a sacrificial ox tied to the stake" who "awaits the next day when he will be killed and roasted."

The second pivotal event was Saigo's decision to assume responsibility for the hotheads who had raided the Kagoshima arsenal and to march off to war at their head, knowing for certain that the likeliest result of this action was defeat and death. Some commentators have stressed the reluctance of Saigo's decision, some the inevitability of it. But that the decision was suicidal is not open to much doubt.

The third pivotal event that suggests a persistent or recurring death-wish happened when Saigo was not yet a figure of national prominence, and is by far the most intriguing. In his early years of Satsuma politicking, Saigo had often been dispatched by Nariakira to Kyoto, the imperial capital, and had there fallen in with an influential priest named Gessho. Gessho was an ardent supporter of the restoration of nominal power to the emperor and was heavily involved in anti-Bakufu schemes. In 1858 he found himself a victim of a major Bakufu purge of imperialist activists and fled south to Satsuma where, as fate would have it, Nariakira had just died. Nariakira's successor decided that he could not risk openly opposing the shogun by harboring a notorious fugitive and ordered Gessho to be taken under guard to the frontier of his fief and expelled—a course of action that meant certain death for the priest. For reasons best known to the new lord, Saigo was assigned the task of expelling him. Gessho and Saigo set out late in the evening in a boat to cross Kagoshima Bay. Midway across they walked together to the prow of the boat, wrote the death poems that custom required, bade each other formal goodbyes, and jumped into the sea. Gessho drowned and Saigo survived.

Both the humanists and those more sympathetic to the ideals of the samurai have stressed the worthiness of Saigo's apparent desire to die with his doomed "friend." Subsequently the ghost of Gessho was to haunt Saigo all his life. Saigo regularly visited the priest's grave, celebrated each anniversary of his death, and, seventeen years after the event, addressed a poem to Gessho in which he pictured himself "standing before your grave, separated by death's great wall, while my tears still flow in vain." Others have suggested that Saigo may have been more moved by the recent death of Nariakira, who had encouraged and promoted him, and that his suicide attempt might better be interpreted as the conventional gesture of loyalty whereby a retainer immolates himself on the death of his lord (a gesture which had officially been proscribed for more than a millennium, but which continued to form, if only psychologically, an important part of the samurai code).

No one to my mind has adequately explained the nature of the friendship between Saigo and Gessho. Mushanokoji gives the impression that their relationship became close only after Saigo received news of Nariakira's death and Gessho undertook to persuade the younger man (Saigo was then thirty; Gessho forty-five) not to sacrifice his own life, a course that, according to some sources, Saigo had declared himself intent on following. Saigo learnt that Nariakira had died in a letter delivered to him on September 1, 1858, and the double suicide attempt took place on the night of December 19th. So a close relationship between the two men appears to have existed for less than four months, during five weeks of which they were apart. Saigo may have felt more compelled by responsibility than by friendship, since it was Saigo who had undertaken to conduct Gessho to a safe refuge and had suggested Satsuma. But it is stretching credibility to depict Saigo as laying down his life, Christ-like, for a friend when the friendship was of so short a duration. Four months is not much time for a death-defying bond of intimacy to mature, though it is ample for an infatuation.

If there was a homoerotic aspect to the relationship, Mushanokoji steers very clear of mentioning it. A woodblock print made years later depicts Saigo and Gessho leaping into the bay with their arms round each other's necks like two lovers going over Japan's most famous waterfall, the Kegon Falls, and the same poem in which Saigo describes himself weeping by Gessho's graveside depicts, too, the fatal leap—"clasped in each other's arms we leapt into the abyss of the sea"—but a man may hardly be judged by the emotions he feels and the gestures he allows himself to make at the moment he presumes will be his last. It is obvious that Saigo preferred the company of men to women, particularly perhaps the virile young men who flocked so worshipfully to his private schools, but that was normal for his time and class. He married three wives during the course of his life and seems not to have cared a fig for any of them. His first marriage was so perfunctory that we do not even know his wife's name. His second wife was a native of one of the southern islands to which he was exiled while out of favor following the Gessho episode. He had two children by her and left them all for good when he was subsequently recalled to Kagoshima, which, again, was normal behavior. He had three more children by a third wife whom he married at the instigation of a clan official. But once embarked on his career as national hero, he seems to have set no more store by his family than he did by the honors he consistently declined and the salary he often omitted to draw. He never sent his family money, made no provision for them after his death, and the tears that flowed so freely at Gessho's graveside do not appear to have been wasted on them.

But such speculation overlooks an aspect of Saigo's character which, it may be, rings the clearest bell in a head familiar with the European Romantics. From his deep-seated trust in the instinctive over the rational, to his preference for the untamed countryside over the city, to his consciously cultivated anachronisms such as the wearing of cotton kimonos and wooden clogs while on cabinet duty, to his disdain for anything that smacked of mercenary gain, to his Ruskin-like faith in the moral superiority of agriculture over industry and commerce, Saigo rubs elbows with a tradition many of whose practitioners were half in love with death: the easeful death of John Keats, the unquiet death of Percy Shelley in the night sea off Spezia, the glory-seeking death of George Byron and the burial of his heart at Missolonghi. Saigo had never heard of any of these men and would have loathed them merrily if he had. He was far more the master of his fate than they were, and the master of his posthumous reputation too, which may be what mattered most to him. By marching out of Kagoshima in the snow, and then stealing out of Hyono in the fog, he appropriated the power to do what every flirter with death, every martyr, dreams of doing: to sink into the flames a hulk of flesh and rise from the ashes an angel.

❧

And now my concern to root out Saigo's old tracks gave way to the simpler but equally tiring business of keeping up with his speed. For we were out of the high mountains now and on a long flat curving road that wound round the western foothills of Kirishima, crisp and dark in the late summer sunshine except for a little smudge of smoke that rose not from any of its cones, but from a fissure halfway up its slope. Saigo had fought the fiercest skirmish of his retreat just outside Kobayashi, where on the 28th with approximately two hundred men he had scattered the rearguard of a large force of imperial troops aiming to prevent his advance into Kagoshima. His exact whereabouts were therefore known, or would be known as fast as riders could communicate it, to the imperial high command. And with warships, troops, and artillery descending on him from the north like iron filings on a magnet, Saigo could not afford to hang about.

All along the road the smell of fully ripened rice in the fields on either side of me made my mouth water till the dribble trickled through my teeth.

Between the paddies were allotments of eggplants and signboards advertising grapes and pears. At one point there was a small stand of chestnut trees where I lay in the shade and snoozed for ten minutes until a group of hooded women arrived and started chucking chestnuts into plastic bowls with clunks that sounded like dud doodlebugs landing. A procession of loudspeaker vans came screeching through the little town of Iino, opposing at about seven thousand decibels a planned radar installation that was suspected by some of being a fin in the door for a U.S. nuclear submarine base. "We want peace! Peace!" the loudspeakers shrieked, destroying it for miles across the ringing paddies.

At Iino I walked up and down the main street looking for somewhere to have lunch, and found at one end a funeral in progress and at the other end a gaggle of wedding guests waiting with sweaty armpits and jackets slung over their shoulders for taxis to take them to the celebration, but there was no sign of a restaurant. As I made my second pass, a young woman came out of a closed fishmonger's shop, wiping her hands on her apron, and asked me what I was looking for.

"I'm looking for a place to eat," I said.

"We've got a place upstairs," she said, "only I don't know if dad wants to open it. It's Sunday."

"I'm only after something very simple," I said, eyeing the beer crates outside the door. In fact, it wasn't so much a restaurant as a large tatami-matted space, divided up by sliding screens and furnished with four sets of karaoke equipment, that catered less to casual custom than to properly organized musical rites such as those that attended matrimony and burial.

But I had a good lunch of raw fish there. And despite the matrimony and burial being attended under the scalding blue sky in the street outside, the tatami-matted space stayed empty. In the end the young woman's mother came up and flopped down on a cushion opposite me across the table, partly to keep me company, partly to give her something to do, and partly, she explained, because I was strange.

"Ooooo!" she said when she saw my large colored map of Miyazaki prefecture, staring at it as though it were a mandala, "This tells you everything! Everything you could want to know! You can go anywhere with this!"

"Aren't you catering for the wedding?" I asked.

"No," said the mother, topping up my beer glass and grinning broadly with teeth that were decaying like rainbows. "They're big shots, those lot. There's about two hundred of them. They'll throw some posh do in Kobayashi."

"What about the funeral, then?"

She grinned again, a wide slash of green and brown and black.

"Oh, I popped in to burn some incense of course, but we never had much to do with the sod."

The mother was a jolly, tubby woman, still dressed in the all-black outfit that she had worn for her three-minute incense burning, and it perfectly set off her wiry mop of dyed ginger hair. She spoke in a very thick Kumamoto accent, made all the more impenetrable by the gaps between her rainbow-colored teeth and, as soon as I mentioned Saigo Takamori, she began to describe for me, as though she had witnessed them personally, the great man's vexations at the battle of Tabaruzaka.

Next to the siege of Kumamoto castle and the final assault on Shiroyama, Tabaruzaka is the best-known engagement of the six-month war, and arguably the turning point of Saigo's campaign. Before Tabaruzaka there was a wafer-thin chance that the revolt might have ended in some sort of a parley, but after Tabaruzaka the only conceivable outcome was a rout. Around March 3rd, in an attempt to prevent reinforcements from reaching the castle garrison during their abortive siege, Saigo's men had built a seemingly impregnable defensive position some seventeen kilometers outside Kumamoto on the heights at Tabaruzaka, a place known to military minds as "Suicide Pass," and this position became the object of a two-week-long spate of attacks by imperial forces arriving from the north. Much of the fighting was done with swords, and the total losses on both sides for the week ending March 19th were some 3,000 dead and about 4,500 wounded. On the 20th the imperial army, now being reinforced almost daily, brought up artillery and drove the rebels off the heights.

But history poured out of the ginger head of the fishmonger's mother with a lot less brio than the words of the 1928 song which, somewhat eerily (it being midday, she all in black, and the funeral still taking place with florid ceremony across the sun-blotched street outside her fish shop), she proceeded to sing, clapping her hands, to her captive audience of one:

The rain rains down, rains down,
Drenching both mounts and men.
They must cross; they shall not cross
Tabaruzaka.

In their right hands bloodied swords,
In their left their horses' reins.
High and handsome in the saddle—
Ah, exquisite youth!

The hills are strewn with their corpses;
The rivers run with their blood,
Enriching, as it flows, the harvest—
Sad, wild autumn . . .

I left the singing mother in her fish shop to tramp on through the afternoon, and at four-thirty I coughed my way through the smoke of a fire burning chaff and crossed the prefectural border into Kagoshima—the original Saigo country.

In a minibus outside a little supermarket four children sat while their parents shopped. One child was examining a tourist brochure that bore a slogan which the national railways had recently commissioned from a well-known novelist for a fee that exceeded an average Japanese office-worker's annual salary. The slogan was designed to persuade Japanese holidaymakers to spend their vacations in Japan instead of going abroad. I expect it had taken the well-known novelist all of five seconds to compose and it consisted of two words, neither of which was Japanese.

"What does *Ekusochikku Jyappan* (Exotic Japan) mean, I wonder?" mused the child, pronouncing the two words in a tone of awe and turning the brochure round and round in her hands. Well, *Ekusochikku*, I badly wanted to tell her, referred to the act of paying a well-known novelist more than an office-worker earned in a year to spend five seconds composing a two-word slogan that was completely incomprehensible to anyone under the age of twelve or over the age of forty. And *Jyappan* referred to the fabulous place where such things were capable of happening. But I kept my mouth shut, bought a can of beer from a vending machine, and sat astride a fence waiting for my feet to drop off. The day was still scorching hot and the owner of the booze shop where I stopped for a further beer took one look at the state of my jeans and the sweat-worn holes in the chest and shoulders of my denim shirt, and suggested not unkindly that I wash my clothes there and then in the river that flowed past the bottom of his yard.

"Oh, I'll do them when I get to a ryokan," I said.

"The river's very clean, you know," he insisted, offering to lend me a basket.

In fact, the river must have been cleaner than the rust-brown bath water at the hot-spring town of Yoshimatsu where I—and Saigo—spent the night. The woman at the ryokan called her dingy little cubicles "family baths" but I wouldn't have advised my least favorite relative to wash in one. My legs were so tottery that, when I bent to take my laundry out of the twin tub in the yard beside the bathroom after climbing down a steep metal ladder with my blisters sticking to the soles of the ryokan's fairy-sized wooden clogs, my feet crumpled under me, and I put one foot into a drain, the other into a bonsai pot, and dropped my freshly washed underpants into a tank full of mosquito larvae.

The woman showed me each of her rooms in turn, all of them empty and all unmade. The one she finally decided to put me in had a futon still sprawled out in it from the night before and a large glass ashtray full of cigarette butts in the middle of the four-and-a-half-mat floor. "This will be the coolest room," she said. The sheets on the futon were stained with beer and the yukata she fished out of a closet for me (after I declined to wear the one that still lay on the futon where the previous occupant had chucked it) was stained with things that I would rather not identify. The light was a naked sixty-watt bulb, the tatami had cigarette burns in thirteen places, there was no mosquito coil anywhere in the ryokan, and the window overlooking the yard where the larvae tank was wouldn't close. All night the mosquitoes whined and dived but the stains on my yukata seemed to keep them away. And at midnight August turned into September. Ah, exquisite youth.

With every kilometer the traffic grew denser, the air more clogged with diesel fumes, and the sky with black ash from erupting Mount Sakurajima. Advertisements on televisions in the restaurants urged people in Kagoshima city to rent industrial vacuum cleaners so that they could clear the volcanic ash from their pavements, cars, gardens, and streets. At one restaurant the owner, who had cropped hair, checked trousers, and the obligatory white vest, gave me a great plate of fatty raw chicken that had just been killed and smothered with soy sauce, perhaps to hide the ash.

"Japanese is the most difficult language in the world, isn't it?" he asked me, turning away to swat flies before I could answer.

"Are you married?" demanded a haggard-looking woman in a tight knee-length pin-striped skirt. "Have you got a wife? Do you want one?" But she, too, turned away.

A truck driver from the north, in another white vest, told them both to stop speaking foreign languages (the Kagoshima dialect, like the Tsugaru dialect, is widely felt to be the most impenetrable in the country) and then went on to explain to me that, of all the Kyushu prefectures, only Miyazaki contained people who could speak proper Japanese. That was why all the T.V. newsreaders came from Miyazaki.

The restaurant owner nodded and swatted flies with a pink fly swatter.

"That's true," he said, more or less penetrably. "We've been right out of things down here in Kagoshima, ever since that botch-up at Tabaruzaka."

The stretch of road I was walking along had been badly jammed with trucks ever since Kagoshima Airport had opened, the driver explained, and truckers had found that by taking this route instead of the coast road through Minamata they could knock about a third of the time off the haul from Kagoshima to Kumamoto. The popularity of the route among truckers in a hurry was demonstrated at intervals by white wooden crosses: "30th May, Showa 49, two died," "4th August, Showa 56, one died," "6th March, Showa

59, three died." There's convenience, I thought, tramping down the valley and sniffing, through the fumes, the rich waving paddies.

Between the paddies neatly clipped tea bushes had replaced the vines and pear trees, and the virtues of these were proclaimed by huge signboards every hundred meters or so: Kurino Tea, Number One in the Nation for Fragrance and for Taste. Further along, near the little town of Kurino itself, the virtues of a love hotel were proclaimed with similar panache. A love hotel differs from a business hotel in that its rooms are rented by the hour instead of by the night and it makes no difference that you must enter them sideways since the whole of the rest of your brief occupancy will be horizontal. This one was called the Fashion Hotel Chestnut and looked like a Victorian fantasy of Camelot, or like London's St. Pancras Station, which is a Victorian fantasy of Camelot. It had red-and-white tiled turrets and battlements and plastic stained-glass windows blackened by ash and exhaust from the trucks that growled by every thirty seconds. Offhand, I could think of few places where I should feel less inclined to lie down and make love except, maybe, St. Pancras Station.

At four o'clock I tramped into Yokogawa, a dusty little trickle of a town with hardly any buildings in it above two storys. The growling trucks had turned a sunny afternoon into a noisy, dirty, depressing one and it was a relief to leave the busy bypass and trudge down the empty street of the town towards the railway station, past the body-building gym and the pet hotel and the schoolgirls at the bus stop giggling their heads off. I found a small restaurant in front of the station, unslung my pack, ordered a beer, and asked the tubby old woman who ran the restaurant where the ryokans were.

"Ooo, there aren't any ryokans in Yokogawa," she puffed. "There used to be one but they closed it down ten years ago."

"Well, where's the nearest place I can stay?"

"You could try the hot spring at Mizobe, about ten kilometers down the road. They're bound to have a ryokan there."

So I drank the beer, and then another to prepare me for two more hours of clogged road, and I had just paid for the beers and was shouldering my pack when another tubby woman, almost identical to the first except that all the teeth in her head were made of metal, walked into the restaurant, flopped down at a table, flapped a newspaper to and fro in front of her face, and said:

"Who's this?"

"I don't know. He's just drunk two bottles of beer. He's going to walk to Mizobe."

"What for?"

"He wants to stay at the ryokan there."

"There aren't any ryokans at Mizobe."

The second tubby woman nodded and flapped her newspaper. The first screwed up her face, chewed her tongue, and began carefully wiping the tops of her tables. I unslung my pack again and asked if I could consult the local telephone directory, which neither tubby woman knew where to find.

"There's that eatery place up in the hills."

"What place?"

"That one near the factory that makes whatsits."

"What whatsits?"

"You know. Those whatsits."

"That's not a ryokan."

"It's a minshuku."

"You said he wanted a ryokan."

"How far is it?" I asked.

"Ooo, not that far. Thirty minutes on a man's feet."

"We ought to have a ryokan here," said the second tubby woman, fanning her face.

"Yes, we ought," agreed the first. "We've got a sushi shop."

"And a pet hotel."

"Are you sure there's a minshuku thirty minutes away?" I asked.

"Oh, yes, quite sure," said both tubby women, nodding.

"It's not a ryokan though. It's just an eatery. It's run by outside people."

"Outside people?"

"People from Shikoku."

So I tramped out of the town down the same empty road by which I'd tramped into it forty minutes earlier, and the practicing brass band at the high school drowned out all noises except the shrieking of birds. As the road curled and began climbing into the hills the bird shrieks grew louder and more frantic. Perhaps Sakurajima was going to spew lava instead of ash and the birds had had a tip off, just as catfish are supposed to know about earthquakes days before they occur. I passed the factory that manufactured whatsits. The whatsits were integrated circuits. And next door to the minshuku-cum-eatery stood another factory that manufactured cement. The woman who ran the place was chubby and lively, and wore a pink T-shirt that said in English across the front of it, The Four Freedoms: Speech, Worship, Want, Fear. Hello, I thought, they're missionaries.

"Would you like a glass of shochu before you have a bath?" the woman asked me. "My husband generally has a drop. It's a habit he picked up when we first came to live here thirteen years ago. Shochu's the local religion."

All right, I thought, they can convert me. But after half a tumbler and a couple of minutes' reflection I decided that I would stick to beer. In the bath I recalled a fierce hangover that I had once got drinking *imo-jochu* in a fish processing plant at Makurazaki in southern Kagoshima prefecture. Imo-jochu is shochu made from potatoes (*imo*), and the genial fish processor who plied me with it kept referring to himself and all his neighbors as *imo-zamurai* (potato samurai). "We're all imo-zamurai in Satsuma," he would hiccup, sticking another kettle on his electric hot plate. It smelled like gasoline and tasted like I imagine hydrochloric acid would taste, and the first drop that reached my digestive tract ripped into it like an ulcer the size of a cabbage. In short, it is an acquired taste. But I still had fifty-odd kilometers to tramp before I reached Kagoshima City so I decided to delay acquiring it.

The husband was stick-thin, gruff, and jovial, and told me as I sat at the counter eating bonito that, in thirteen years of living in Kagoshima, he had still not deciphered the dialect. He was from Kochi in Shikoku, which explained the pennants on the walls depicting fighting dogs and long-tailed cockerels and other Kochi curiosities, and the cheap souvenirs that cluttered the counter, which included a pair of dolls, one dressed like a priest and the other like a nun, standing side by side, smiling coyly, in front of a sign that said Harimaya Bridge. The priest had his arm round the nun's shoulders, and in his hand he held an ornamental hairpin of the kind sold only at expensive shops that catered to the denizens of the floating world. I had seen this souvenir before. It is called *Bosan Kanzashi* (The Priest and the Hairpin) and it is meant to illustrate the first stanza of the Kochi folk song, "Yosakoi Bushi," about which two things have at odd times intrigued me.

The first thing intrigued me some years ago when I was asked to translate the words of "Yosakoi Bushi" into English for an educational magazine published by NHK. The first stanza presented no difficulty:

In Kochi in Tosa, on Harimaya Bridge,
I saw a priest buy a hairpin.

But the second stanza caused a furor:

Why shouldn't a priest buy a hairpin,
Or a cripple a pair of high-heeled clogs?

"No, no, no," gasped the horrified editor. "You can't use the word *cripple* in an NHK magazine. You can't use the Japanese original [*izari*] either. We're not supposed to print it, or utter it, or even let on that we know it exists. People would stop paying their license fees."

Luckily, the song has an alternative second stanza:

Why shouldn't a priest buy a hairpin,
Or a blind man a pair of glasses?

"No, no, no, you can't use the word *blind*," gasped the editor, horrified again. "And you can't use the original [*mekura*]. You can't print it, speak it, sing it, or think it."

"Well, it was you who asked me to translate the blasted song," I complained. "What do you want me to do?"

"Couldn't you translate the version that we sing on television?"

"How does that go?"

Kochi is a nice place,
Please come and visit it sometime. . . .

It was after this that I left off translating folk songs.

The second intriguing thing about the dolls concerns the way they are dressed. The incident celebrated in "Yosakoi Bushi" is supposed to have happened in 1855, thirteen years before the armies of Marshal Saigo sent the feudal era crashing into history's dustbin. Apparently the priest of Chikurinji Temple, the oldest Buddhist temple in Shikoku, fell in love with a girl who worked in a fix-it shop near the pleasure quarter (at the center of which stood Harimaya Bridge) and bought her an ornamental hairpin. He did this openly, perhaps as a public admission of his love or perhaps to precipitate disaster, since he must have known that the relationship was doomed. At any rate, the girl evidently liked the hairpin because she shortly attempted to elope with the priest, but they were stopped at one of the barrier gates and then exiled separately from different parts of the province so that there was no chance of them ever meeting again—a wonderful subject for a puppet play.

But what intrigues me is the transformation by the souvenir manufacturers of a girl from a fix-it shop into a Buddhist nun. Maybe they find the symmetry agreeable. Or perhaps the girl really did quit a cruel world for the cloister—a not uncommon postscript to doomed flings in the Japanese tradition. But to depict her in a nun's get-up before the elopement, standing side by side with her priest on the bridge, robs the tale's most potent symbol of all its drama. If she were a nun in the first place, what on earth would she have done with a hairpin?

I broached this conundrum to the husband but it did not seem to have taxed his imagination, nor did he show any sign that it would tax his imagination in the future. So we sat at the counter drinking beer and shochu until a car drew up outside and two slim, tanned, smartly dressed men breezed in and started quizzing the wife about her service. What sort of breakfast could she provide? Were her rooms quiet? Were they clean? Did she have beds or only futon? It turned out that the man asking ninety percent of the questions did not plan to stay at the minshuku himself but was merely concerned about the welfare of his companion. His companion was a professional golfer and was due to participate in the Kyushu Open, which would begin in three days time down the road at the Kagoshima Airport Country Club. While the man who had asked the questions was off inspecting the mosquito netting in the bedroom windows, the husband asked the professional golfer whether his friend was a hotel receptionist.

"No," said the shocked professional golfer, "my friend is a professional golfer."

"I see," said the husband, and poured himself more shochu.

And at eight o'clock three of the husband's cronies turned up from the factory next door to play mah jong. The first professional golfer had driven away after checking the supply of toilet paper, and the second had retired early. So I was left to my own devices, which included a book about Saigo Takamori lent me by the wife and published by the Kagoshima Parent-Teacher Association, which made much of Saigo's role in promoting a famous alliance between Satsuma and Tosa, the old name for Kochi. I went to sleep grateful that the alliance had held. Trucks rolled past my window all night and, through unquiet dreams, the mah jong tiles sounded like golf balls being tossed in a cement mixer.

Now that speed was essential Saigo's most obvious course was to follow the direct route into Kagoshima city, the route that dropped due south. But there were two things that prevented him from doing this. One was the massing of a large force of imperial troops under General Miyoshi, whose rearguard Saigo had surprised and scattered three days earlier at Kobayashi. This force had subsequently dug itself in north of Kagoshima with the aim of intercepting the rebels if they tried to enter the city directly. A second consideration was that the direct route would have taken Saigo along the northwest shore of Kagoshima Bay where he might have come under the guns of any government warships that lay at anchor there. Saigo's intelligence cannot have been very thorough and he probably had no way of knowing whether warships were converging on Kagoshima or not. But recent history had taught him the damage that warships anchored in the bay could do if their captains were in a shooting mood and, having come this far, he was in no mood to take chances.

In August 1863—when Saigo, out of favor with Nariakira's successor, was in temporary exile on the mosquito-ridden island of Okinoerabu—a squadron of seven British warships had sailed into Kagoshima Bay and demanded an indemnity of 25,000 pounds and the execution of some Satsuma samurai who had set upon four Englishmen near Yokohama, killing one and injuring two more, for encountering their lord's procession and not dismounting and bowing as custom required. Satsuma was, quite rightly, having none of this and the British demands were roundly ignored, whereupon the ships in the bay opened fire at more or less random targets and, within the space of a couple of hours, succeeded in panicking the city's population by starting several major fires. This single afternoon's activity is still referred to in Japan as the Satsu-Ei Senso (the Anglo-Satsuma War). Once in a Kagoshima bar I offered a jocular apology for it, which was received by my fellow drinkers with complete seriousness. My fellow drinkers ought to have apologized in their turn, since the Anglo-Satsuma War ended with the withdrawal of the warships in the face of a typhoon that killed sixty British sailors and greatly reinforced local faith in the saving graces of "divine winds" (*kamikaze*). Anyway, Saigo had reason to think twice before exposing himself and his weary men to a naval bombardment, so he chose a less direct route that took him in a long southwestern loop away from the bay and through the little inland town of Kamo, where he and his rebels spent the last night of August.

It was well after noon on a scalding hot day when I hobbled off the main road to follow Saigo round the houses. I had stopped to snatch a nap on the grass at the edge of a paddy, but there was no shade and the sun burned down and dried my lips and cracked the skin on the bridge of my nose until blood oozed out of it and dried the color of India ink. I had looked for a place to eat lunch in the villages along the last part of the truckers' route, but they all seemed oddly centerless, as though their buildings had been scattered by the bombardment Saigo feared. In any one of these villages I could have had at least three haircuts and died of thirst between barber's shops.

Crossing from Miyazaki to Kagoshima, I had come from a prefecture so depopulated that it figures in lawsuits charging that National Diet elections are unconstitutional. For example, the Osaka High Court ruled that, in the election of February 1990, one vote in the Miyazaki No. 2 electoral district, the least populous in the nation, was equal to 3.18 votes in the heavily industrialized Kanagawa No. 4 district. (It is no wonder that the ruling parties are still so reluctant to open Japan's markets to agricultural imports when the vote of a rice farmer is worth more than three times that of a teacher or an urban housewife or an engineer.) And yet, in Miyazaki, though I had trekked through rough country and sometimes met fewer than a dozen people a day, there had always been a minshuku or a ryokan—or even a business hotel—to stay in at the end of the trek, and there had rarely been a shortage of places to stop and sit down in for a snack. But in two days of Kagoshima prefecture, with its truck-clogged road, its integrated-circuit plant, its concrete factory, its Airport Country Club, and its crosses commemorating the accidental dead, I had twice been stuck for a place to sleep and at least half a dozen times for a meal or a drink in a village where I had confidently looked forward to finding both.

Ah, progress, progress, I hummed to myself. And I had trudged no more than fifteen minutes along my quiet truckless detour when I came across a huge complex of buildings, stuck like an elaborate mirage in the middle of nowhere, that combined a carp farm, a trout pond, and a restaurant designed like an aircraft hangar, each of whose tables was equipped with a cylindrical plastic trough round which whizzed streams of icy cold water for dunking noodles. For an hour I sat and happily dunked, letting the noodles go and then catching them again between the tips of my chopsticks with a little hiccup of glee. It was like a cross between sitting at some elaborate Lake Tahoe gaming table and playing with a train set. The only other customers were three businessmen dressed in suits and ties and chewing toothpicks, two of whom addressed the third as *bucho* (department head) and were careful to allow him twice as much time with the train set as they allowed themselves. Afterwards the bucho strolled away to contemplate the trout in their pond and then stood, still chewing his toothpick, at a safe distance contemplating me.

My road climbed away from the carp farm over bumps and curves into the low inland hills, and all afternoon the shrieks of the birds vied with those of the dying cicadas. Above the woods I could just make out the hazy cone of Sakurajima, topped by a billow of white summer cumulus and a higher overhang of dark drifting ash. Then the woods opened down into a valley of wide paddies beyond which lay the little town of Kamo. I already knew from a brochure I had picked up at the hangar-like restaurant that this little town's two claims to fame are the oak tree that stands in the grounds of its shrine (billed on the brochure as the largest oak tree in Japan) and the fact that the shrine itself was the location for a fatuous NHK television drama, a development which had quite eclipsed the claim of the tree in the minds of all the Kamo residents I spoke to. The brochure contains a photograph of a young mother and her little son playing happily among the giant roots of the tree, but when I hobbled into the shrine to have a look at it I discovered that its roots and trunk were now completely surrounded by a wire cage. A notice nearby explained that the tree had been designated a Specially Protected Natural Monument and protection had now reached such heights of efficiency that young mothers and their happy little sons were prevented from coming within peeing distance of it.

But this mattered little because the fascination exerted by trees of whatever size pales, for me at least, beside the lure of Kamo's two other specially protected objects—one of which I came across by chance as I trudged through the outlying paddies this September afternoon, and it brought me to so abrupt a halt that I stumbled over my boots and ended up on my knees. It was a stone statue of *Ta no Kami*, the god of the rice fields, and it stood by the edge of the remote path that I was following with an empty tin in front of it containing three freshly picked flowers. It was about eighty centimeters tall and stood peering out of a lump of rock from a niche the shape of a church door. The god was painted in bright colors and had the appearance of a Harlequin— yellow tunic, red and yellow pantaloons, and a pasty white face with red lips and puffy, rosy cheeks, making me wonder whether the influence of Francis Xavier and other god-touched Europeans had not seeped into the chisels of

Kamo's sculptors. In his hand the god held a large *shamoji*, the wooden ladle that is used to scoop cooked rice out of a pot. An explanatory plaque had been erected beside him on which was recorded the date of his carving, 1768, and the fact that he was a Prefecturally Registered Cultural Object.

A lean old woman who noticed me kneeling by the side of the road staring at this figure told me that there was another one about nine kilometers away in the neighboring village of Urushi and, sure enough, when I re-examined the Kamo tourist brochure (The Town That Exhales Historical Landmarks, Greenery and Romance), I found photographs of both. The other god was rougher, larger, and unpainted, but it had the same deceptive air of whimsy. It was a heftier figure, apparently a woman, made eyeless by the rain and riddled with lichen, and in its arms it was cradling what a man at the Kamo community center later told me was also a rice ladle, which in the recent past had been shortened by a sloppily driven motor car. Now the object in the figure's arms looked like either a newly bathed baby or a large excited penis. This Ta no Kami had also been registered as a Cultural Object by the prefectural office and a similar bureaucratically inspired plaque stood beside it to record the year in which it had been erected (1718). But the fact that there were flowers in the tin was a small sign that neither god had yet passed exclusively into the hands of the registrars, and that both remained the objects of an unembarrassed, if not very vigorous, respect. Sloppy motorists and prefectural officials had done their best to tame the spirits that these chunks of stone embody and placate. But if the motorists and officials had a fraction of an inkling of the random power of Ta no Kami, they would run away shrieking with fright.

I found the town's only ryokan, had dinner there, and then went out for a drink to a bar called Satsumaya, where the mama-san, though not specially protected, was at least carefully preserved.

"There were once five ryokans in Kamo," she told me, "and now there is only the one you're staying at. And we used to have two geisha houses as well. . . . "

She smiled, displaying a set of steel teeth.

"That was when I was a child and the gold prospectors were all over the place. Now people from Mitsubishi are in and out of the town hall debating whether to start prospecting again. Wouldn't it be nice if they put up a great big hotel?"

"With turrets?"

"Turrets?"

"Like Saint Pancras Station."

"No, no, not a station. We don't have a railway. A great big hotel in the middle of the fields . . . "

The mama-san leaned over and topped up my beer.

"You must get bored to death having an old woman like me pour your beer for you. Tomorrow you'll be in Kagoshima City. You'll have young girls then. As many as you fancy . . . "

She touched my arm. The hairs stood up like the bristles on a wire brush.

And when I got back, very late, to my ryokan the grandmother who ran it appeared in my room while I was undressing, silently, like a genie. She had grey hair and wore a grey dress.

"Where have you been?" she whispered. "Did you go to play pachinko?"

"No, I went to have a drink."

"Where? At Satsumaya? You didn't go to Satsumaya?"

She stood in the half-dark glaring at me with her sleeping grandson cradled in her arms. A baby, not a rice scoop, not a penis.

The last day of my walk was made easier by the discovery half way through it of a well-appointed hot-spring where I whiled away three hours, had two baths, a meal of noodles propelled again by jets of cold water round a circular race course in the middle of my table, four bottles of beer, and a run-in with five workmen, the senior among whom, steely-haired and grim, stood up, walked over to me as I was endeavoring to catch the noodles one at a time between the tips of my chopsticks, and topped up my beer from his bottle. He did this without a word and then returned to sit with his silent, grim companions. The waitress giggled happily. So I stood up, walked over to his table, and topped up his beer from my bottle. His eyes narrowed. His mates stared down at their smoldering cigarettes. The waitress turned her back on us with a little jerk and began dusting the souvenir keyrings. I went back to my table and sat down again. The steely-haired workman stood up, walked over to me with purposeful eyes, topped up my beer, and then returned to his table. Dead silence reigned. I stood up, walked over, and topped up his beer. The waitress took an uneasy step towards us, thought better of it, and vanished into the kitchen. The five workmen bowed stiffly, saying nothing, and after that we all ignored each other. I finished my meal by stuffing the noodles into my mouth a fistful at a time, aware that the Anglo-Satsuma War had just been refought and not having the least idea who had won.

The road wound over low hills, hugging a small sluggish river, and grew fouler-smelling and more congested the closer it approached the city. There was no shade, no place to sit and rest. Beyond the intermittently visible expressway, Sakurajima towered faintly through its own cloying curtain of ash, and the sides of the road, and the fields and trees, and the roofs of parked cars were thick and black with its vomit. At four o'clock I smelt the sea. At half past four I glimpsed Kagoshima Bay for the first time, hazy and pale and merging like spilled and watery ink with the grey hills of the Osumi peninsula away on the far side of it. At five-fifteen I slouched past the blunt, dunce-like statue of Marshal Saigo that stands on the grounds of the Kagoshima art gallery at the foot of Shiroyama (Fortress Hill) where the last act of his drama was played out, round the corner from the Hotel France and the Hotel Monte and the Hotel Versailles.

Saigo entered Kagoshima city late on September 1st. I entered it on the 3rd, having walked about 480 kilometers since leaving Nobeoka eighteen days before. To what must have been his own surprise Saigo found the city virtually undefended. General Miyoshi's brigades were still entrenched about ten miles to the north of it, waiting for the rebels to struggle down the coast, and Saigo and the bedraggled remnants of his army were able to occupy their old hometown with a minimum of difficulty, putting to flight the small bands of government troops and civil police who offered half-hearted resistance. Counting the men who had stayed with him through the march and the recruits (including soldiers still wearing their imperial army uniforms) who joined him for whatever reasons—reverence, bravado, nostalgia, desperation—now that he had reached his final goal, Saigo commanded at this last rally a force of about 370 men, but fewer than half of these were properly armed and some of the new recruits had no experience of fighting. Total casualties for the six months of the campaign had risen to more than twice the fifteen thousand who had marched out of the city with Saigo in February; and the number of live, armed government troops who now formed a ring around Kagoshima and began to close the vise on Saigo was about twice again the total of dead and wounded.

From the moment Saigo occupied the city it had come under bombardment from warships in the bay, as he feared it would, and fires had begun to break out among the close-packed mass of timber buildings, destroying the house where Saigo had been born and badly damaging the private school where, six months earlier, the spark of the rebellion had been kindled. Saigo and his lieutenants decided that their best course was to fortify Shiroyama, the great wooded, rubble-strewn mound that dominates the center of the city, where they dug trenches and erected bamboo palisades and scooped out or made habitable a number of small caves—barely depressions in the rock—to serve as their billets and last headquarters. On the 3rd, government troops began constructing a series of earthworks around the base of the hill, partly to protect themselves but mainly to contain the rebels and to ensure that no such daring escape as had taken place at Hyono would be repeated. As soon as the earthworks were finished on the 10th, naval and land-based artillery commenced shelling the hill day and night. But Shiroyama is a superb natural fortress and scaling it or flushing the rebels off it would be no easy task.

The siege of Shiroyama lasted three weeks, during the latter part of which the government infantry closed so tightly round the hill that they could smother the rebel positions with rifle fire as well as with fifty-pound artillery shells. The rebels had virtually no supplies left. For bullets they had taken to picking up spent government rounds and trying to recast them. They had dragged six cannon and two mortars up Shiroyama but had no shells for either, so they attempted to forge some out of kitchen utensils that they had looted from houses the owners had fled. They had no bedding, so slept on the bare rock; no surgical instruments, so made do with the makeshift tools at hand: a bayonet point for removing bullets, a carpenter's saw for amputating limbs, potato shochu for anesthetic. On the 19th Saigo moved into the last cave he was to occupy, a cave that has been religiously preserved and to which has been affixed a signboard that describes the actions of the great man and those closest to him on the night of the 23rd. According to the signboard, they played the biwa, danced Satsuma sword dances, and composed poems.

At 4 A.M. on the 24th the fiercest bombardment so far began, and under its cover seven brigades of government troops moved up the hill to make a massive onslaught on the rebel positions. At about 6 A.M. Saigo and his lieutenants began to descend Shiroyama along a narrow road that was already partly residential. In NHK's drama series, *The Age of the Lion*, the actor impersonating Saigo wore a comic-opera uniform for this scene and received a bullet wound in the chest, which he manfully clutched with his right hand while continuing his descent. The historical Saigo probably wore the loose informal summer kimono which he had favored even while a cabinet minister on official business in the capital. The bullet hit him in the groin (Mushanokoji's adaptor, being discreet, says the thigh and abdomen)—a final irony given the state that part of his anatomy was in already—and he called out to his closest associate, the young Beppu Shinsuke, in dialect thickened by the pain of the wound: "*Shin-don, mo koko de yokaro.*" (Shinsuke, this place is as good as any.) Beppu decapitated Saigo and a servant buried the head a certain distance from the body, causing consternation to the government troops who later that morning required several hours to find the head and dig it up. Immediately after the head had been buried, Beppu attacked a government rifle position with his sword and was killed at once. One hundred and fifty-seven of the last of the rebels died on Shiroyama; the rest fled or were prisoners by mid-morning. Saigo's war was over.

I climbed the 250-meter-high crag of Shiroyama on a baking hot day under a cloudless sky veiled only by the thin haze of ash from the volcano. The hill had been the site of a fourteenth-century castle and an eighteenth-century aqueduct, and was now, according to my tourist brochure, a sanctuary for more than six hundred species of subtropical plants and fifteen types of wild bird whose portraits appeared on signs along the pathways. All of the trees were neatly labeled and notices warned me to touch nothing, for the whole edifice was crumbling away. The base of the hill, behind Terukuni Shrine which houses the spirit of Nariakira, was already a wasteland of dust and powdery chalky-brown rubble propped up by straining fences. There is a society in Kagoshima dedicated to the preservation of Shiroyama, with a university professor as chairman, and the authorities have registered it as a Government Protected Natural Monument, so the hill is certainly doomed.

At the summit stood a line of souvenir stalls with bored women sitting behind them and very few customers. The ash has ruined the tourist trade and, except in March and November when the tug of seasonal tradition is too strong to be resisted, not even honeymoon couples now brave it. The stalls sold Saigo Takamori ashtrays, Saigo calendars, Saigo keyrings, Saigo letter racks, clogs, coffee mugs, money boxes, thermometers, barometers, plaques, pennants, wooden Saigo dolls, plaster Saigo dolls, Saigo dolls made of stuffed felt, and imitation bronze Saigo statuettes, some reduced to give-away prices.

I visited the cave, carefully burrowed, flat-floored, with tree roots growing out of its roof. Opposite stood the Satsuma Teahouse Restaurant, whose loudspeakers broadcast the Percy Faith Orchestra playing "Moon River." At the Arion Craft Shop next door I bought some cedarwood chopsticks and the woman gave me a bag with handles to carry my purchases in. The bag had English printed on the side of it: We Love Koala. My name is Ton-Ton and mother's name is Non-Non. We are friendly family. It's pleasure to meet you.

I visited the spot where Saigo died. There is a small stone monument there. It stands opposite the main railway line to Kumamoto. The trees, the bushes, the roots, the monument are inch-deep in ash that no one sweeps away.

I visited Nanshu Shrine where Saigo is worshipped as a god. It was destroyed by bombs during the Second World War and rebuilt ten years later. In the precincts stand slabs on which are engraved the names of 6,765 of Saigo's followers who died in the rebellion. The youngest of them was fourteen. A taxi driver was showing two businessmen round the shrine and one of them was reading the names of the dead.

"Miyazaki . . . Miyazaki . . . That's the name of the announcer on News Center Nine. . . . "

A smartly-dressed woman climbed the steps, threw a coin into the box and bowed in deep prayer, her car keys clinking lightly against the clasp of her crocodile-skin handbag.

I visited the grave.

It stood surrounded by the lesser graves of 748 Satsuma rebels, including Beppu Shinsuke and the fourteen-year-old Kodama. Saigo's grave had a wooden box for offerings placed in front of it, white-painted, the paint flaking. Ash lay thick on the graves and on the narrow pathways that threaded between them, and at the base of the stone steps that led to the graves stood a plywood cut-out of Saigo in his loose informal summer kimono with a hole for you to put your face through. But there were no photographers, no cameras, no customers.

I went to take a bath. The streets of Kagoshima were soft with ash and on a wall I found a poster advertising a concert to be given by the regimental band of the Coldstream Guards. I wandered around after my bath and finally went into a coffee shop called Coronet where I listened for an hour to Sonny Rollins. A man from the prefectural office explained that Saigo Takamori had been so hard-pressed on his retreat from Nobeoka that he hadn't had time to father babies on any of the unmarried daughters he was offered wherever he stayed.

"Their dads all wanted a hero's child," he told me.

Another man became excited when I told him that Glenfiddich costs more than White Horse.

"I've got a bottle!" he said to no one in particular. "I got it at the airport!"

And a third man reckoned that the reason so many people went to Nanshu Shrine was that the Japanese don't give a damn who they worship.

It grew dark. The lights went on in the Hotel France, the Hotel Monte, and the Hotel Versailles. A young office worker told me of his impending transfer to company headquarters in Tokyo, where he was afraid that he would be laughed at for his thick, uncompromising Satsuma accent. Sonny Rollins gave way to Billie Holiday, who sang, "Southern trees bear strange fruit. . . . " And through the thin September night the ash from the volcano trickled down on the coffee shops and on the graves.

3
Looking for
the Lost

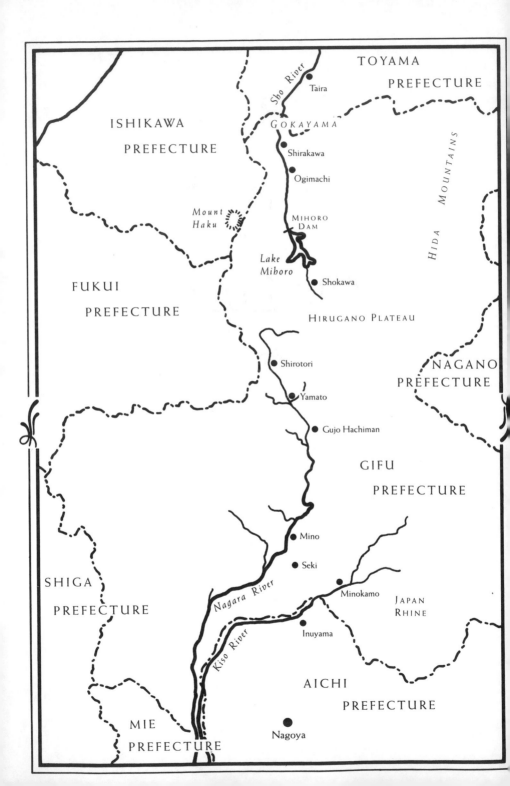

1
Dream

❧

The bell of the temple of Gion tolls into the heart of every man a warning that all is vanity and evanescence. At Nagoya's International Design Exposition, he is warned in other ways as well. On the "Narrow Road to the Deep North" pachinko machine the face of the wandering poet Matsuo Basho is replicated four times, each whiskered and wearing a conical straw hat, and each with a wide open mouth inside of which a red electric bulb lights up whenever a pinball strikes his tonsils. Next to Basho is a machine with a meditating yogi on it to demonstrate the importance to East Asian cultural development of mysticism and the Silk Road. And the machine next to that features space invaders with bleeping bulges and probing metal tentacles to underline the transience of earthly glory and the eventual destiny of the human soul: its explosion into tiny sky-borne fragments, each explosion scoring twenty points.

It has begun to spit with rain when I leave the Pachinko Pachislo Fun Hall (*pachislo* combines the *pachi* of *pachinko* with the *slo* of *slot* to mean a slot machine), so I wander over towards the covered rows of seats in front of the Rinnai Honmaru Stage, where two identically clad, identically coiffured young ladies are playing a duet on a digital piano and an advanced electric organ called a technitone (*techni* from *technology*, *tone* from *tone*). The duet is followed by a quiz in which the young lady on the technitone plays a couple of bars of "Sakura, Sakura" with the flute stop out, and invites the audience to guess what instrument's sound is being replicated. One man guesses it is a *shakuhachi*. A lady in a kimono thinks it is a pipe organ. The young lady on the technitone smiles, frowns, and switches from the flute to the violin stop. A very old man totters to his feet and says it is a harmonica. The young lady playing the technitone stands up, bows, and offers the old man an elaborate apology, while a person in a dark suit who has been standing near the back of the stage rustles some papers and vanishes into the wings. He is, we know, a technitone salesman.

The rain is getting heavier so I hold a plastic bag over my head and make a run for the Meitetsu Group Fantastic Aquapalace where the keynote is water. As the audience gathers in the rain with dozens of plastic bags held over their heads, video monitors treat them to views of ponds in the Belvedere and Tivoli Gardens. Inside the pavilion, identically clad, identically coiffured young ladies sport small green feathers in Tyrolean hats and a fairy with pointed ears made out of laser beams explains what we are about to see. We are about to see computer-controlled jets of water from 17 pumps and 758 nozzles form variously shaped and colored fountains before a backdrop depicting the Schonbrunn Palace while the audio system treats us to very loud renditions of "The Blue Danube" and "The Ride of the Valkyries" played on a technitone. These fountains are Dream Fountains, as the machines in the Pachinko Pachislo Fun Hall are Dream Machines, and the Rinnai Honmaru stage is a Dream Stage.

Outside the rain has stopped, so on my way to lunch I pop in to look at a Post Office of the Future ("Dream Plan For You") where automation will have reduced human contact to nonexistence. The afternoon I occupy with a visit to the dungeon of Nagoya castle, built between 1610 and 1612 by Hideyoshi's successor, Tokugawa Ieyasu, partly destroyed in the Nobi Earthquake of 1891, totally demolished in the U.S. bombing raids of May 1945, and rebuilt in ferroconcrete in 1959 at a cost of 600 million yen, which included the 18-carat-gold dolphins on the roof and the installation of elevators. The castle is now the temporary home of an exhibition dedicated to Gaudi and Modernisme Catala, which features large grainy photographs of the Sagrada Familia ("Barcelona's Dream Church"), a loudspeaker system that broadcasts a few bars of *The Rite of Spring* before switching to a digital piano, and a display of Catalan oil paintings, the most appropriate to its surroundings being a picture of a public garroting.

From the observation platform on the seventh floor of the dungeon you can look out over the hazy rectangular sameness of Nagoya's concrete buildings stretching away as far as the eye can see. It is difficult to conceive of any vista less allied to the eccentric architectural visions of Gaudi or to the spirit of whimsy with which so much of the International Exposition I am visiting is, by design or otherwise, haunted. Modern Nagoya is a city that would appeal hugely to Margaret Thatcher: a sprawling utilitarian testament to the Philistinism of corporate enterprise, ferociously workaday, mute, undreaming.

Perhaps to compensate for its own lack of appeal, Nagoya has collected four sister cities. In 1959 it acquired Los Angeles, in 1978 Mexico City and Nanjing, and it capped its collection in 1980 with opera-house-loving Sydney. I walk past photographs of these four cities on my way to the site exit, stepping on stars embedded in the pavement in the manner of Hollywood's famous sidewalk: Charlton Heston, Elizabeth Taylor, Julie Andrews, Sylvester Stallone. A Japanese sign says, with studied politeness, *O-te o furenaide kudasai* (Please do not touch the exhibits with your honorable hands). An English sign next to it says Hands Off! I leave by the front gate where two London Transport double-decker buses are disgorging more crowds holding plastic bags over their heads. It is raining again. I eat grilled chicken. I fall asleep. Day One ends.

•　　•　　•

Day Two begins with a stroll along the concreted banks of the Hori Canal, which are lined with lumberyards and love hotels. In an impressive demonstration of joint enterprise the hotels and yards have collaborated to enhance each other's assets. For example, one yard supplies the Fancy Hotel Seven with elegantly crafted wooden boards that fit snugly over the license plates of cars parked outside its cabins, their top halves hidden by bamboo blinds, so that passing wives and similar embarrassments cannot identify the patrons.

The canal plunges south, straight as a plumbline, towards shady Atsuta Shrine, said to have been founded almost two millennia ago as a repository for the Grass-Cutting Sword that, together with the sacred mirror and jewels, was entrusted by the Sun Goddess to her grandson when he descended to Japan from the High Plain of Heaven and forms the Imperial Regalia. The sword is called the Grass-Cutting Sword because it was subsequently used by the legendary Prince Yamato Takeru to slice his way out of a field that his enemies had set on fire. It was originally plucked from the tail of an eight-headed serpent by the Sun Goddess's impetuous brother, the same Susu-no-Wo-no-Mikoto who spread shit all over his sister's palace.

However, the visitor to Atsuta Shrine must not expect to see the Grass-Cutting Sword because it is too sacred to be placed on view. As early as the first century B.C., when it was in the possession of the legendary Emperor Sujin, the sword was replaced by a replica in order to preserve the original from the polluting gaze of humans, and this preservation order remains in force. The replica was lost at the sea battle of Dannoura in 1185 and was subsequently replaced by a replica of the replica, which resides today, according to popular belief, in a room in the imperial palace in Tokyo, together with the Sun Goddess's original jewels. It is the original sword, the one actually handled by the Sun Goddess, that is enshrined here in Nagoya, and the original mirror is supposed to be at the Grand Shrine of Ise, where it has reposed, so legend says, since 4 B.C. The visitor there will, of course, not see it. All three sacred treasures continue to be guarded from the profaning influence of human eyes with as much resourcefulness as license plates are guarded at the Fancy Hotel Seven.

Across the road from Atsuta Shrine, on a large parcel of land which until recently was another lumberyard, stands the main site of Nagoya's

International Design Exposition. It being an "international" exposition, one looks around for some indication that foreigners have been invited to participate on a meaningful scale. One of the sales booths has recently attracted the attention of the Aichi prefectural police for flogging fake Chanel jewelry, so Swiss design has been present in spirit if not in actual fact. But the corporate pavilions on either side of the site's main plaza, which the visitor approaches through an illuminated tunnel called the Dream Tube, do not present much national diversity. On the right are Mitsui, Toshiba, Matsushita, Morimura, Nippon Electric, and Sumitomo; on the left is Nippon Telegraph and Telephone; and straight ahead are Toyota, Toho Gas, Mitsubishi, Fujitsu, and Hitachi.

I queue up at the entrance to the Matsushita Pavilion, where I am treated to a journey through space. It is the year 2100 and, in company with my fellow travelers and a little robot with large ears who explains our trip to us using precisely the tones employed at less automated pavilions by impeccably attired and coiffured young flight attendants, I have lived all my life on the other side of the galaxy in a colony called Pana (after Panasonic, Matsushita's brand name) and am on my own very first trip to earth. The pilot of my spaceship is called Adam and his female co-pilot is called Eve. As we fly over a field of earthly sheep, co-pilot Eve exclaims *"Waahhh! Kawaaiiii!"* (Wow! Aren't they cute!) But no sooner have the sheep been flown over than we are trapped in a time warp which shunts us back to the year 8800 B.C. when earthquakes strike, volcanoes erupt, dinosaurs roar, and cavemen in hula skirts attempt to eat us, and then forward to the year of the Nagoya International Design Exposition, onto whose damp main site we disgorge when the spacecraft comes to rest and the auditorium doors swing open.

From the Matsushita Pavilion I wander over to the Toyota Pavilion, where I am taken on—a journey through space. This journey is made in a "Dream Adventure Vehicle" manufactured on a Toyota production line staffed by robots each of which, in case we are worried about impending layoffs, is stamped "friend." The vehicle takes us on a flight between skyscrapers, up to mother ships and space stations, across barren deserts and raging seas, and through meteor swarms and time warps, before landing us with a bump in

Nagoya again, not far from the factory where the friendly robots ply their trade.

I stagger out of the resurrected spacecraft and sit down on a bench to gather my thoughts beside the Collective Pavilion of Dreams containing the displays of small Japanese companies too impecunious to have pavilions of their own. The theme of the exhibit at this site is "Encounters with the 21st Century" and two of that century's major assumptions are beginning to emerge. One is that the world we live in is a grim, frightening, imperfect place that must be continuously improved through the application of advanced technology, preferably technology patented and owned by Japan's major corporations. The world in its natural state consists of barren deserts and raging seas, earthquakes, erupting volcanoes, meteor swarms, black holes, roaring reptiles, and child-eating cavemen. Only the far-sighted products of Matsushita, Toyota, Nippon Electric, and so on can render it fit for human habitation. And the second assumption is that, however habitable the earth becomes, much of our energy in the 21st century will be spent in getting as far away from it as possible.

The triumph of technology over nature receives more elaboration at the Theme Pavilion, the largest pavilion on the site and one of only two or three in which foreign artifacts have managed to wangle some display space. The triumph is announced by a series of introductory panels. "What does man see and learn from when beginning to design?" the first panel asks and then, with no pause for reply, rushes on, "The answer, of course, is the beauty of nature. These beautiful forms of nature have been reshaped by the hands of man into new appearances. This is the starting point of the creative power of man." There follow some photographs of microbes, mollusks, insects, fish, and leopards, all in their natural and unimproved state. A second panel takes up the story: "Man learned the workings of nature, sensed and realized its beauty; indeed with ceaseless passion he has acquired the technology to create a living culture." And then we are shown examples of the living culture that man has created: computerized metallic fish that change their shape in response to the clapping of hands, wristwatches with luminous plastic straps, a working copy of Gutenberg's printing press operated by a Japanese man wearing three-quarter-length rayon britches, vacuum cleaners through the ages so that we can keep nature tidy, scissors so that we can keep it trim, and, soaring above all this to remind us of our pressing need to leave the earth behind us, a replica of the U.S. light plane *Voyager*, which circled the globe in nine days without refueling, and the actual Soviet spacecraft *Mir* (Peace), which holds the record for the longest stay in orbit (366 days). The U.S. sent a scale model; the Russians sent the real thing. I ponder the implications of this for a free market economy as I queue up to poke about inside the *Mir* and am struck with a surge of reverence for the little refrigerator and the exercise machine and the grey utilitarian paint and the tiny packets of desiccated food that remind me of the snacks you used to get in the transit lounge at the Sheremetyevo Airport.

That, give or take a Hermés scarf, exhausts the foreign items on display at Nagoya's International Exposition. There is no IBM Pavilion, no ICI, no Apple, no Texas Instruments, and, of course, no General Motors. The rest of the day I spend sloping round the other corporate attractions. At the Fujitsu Pavilion an impeccably attired and coiffured young lady explains that the seasons, colors, and natural wonders of beautiful Japan can be revived by means of advanced technology and, specifically, that screen paintings of subjects from nature like cherry blossoms can be brought to life through the astounding magic of 3D computer graphics. Fujitsu's 3D isn't that advanced—we have to wear old-fashioned tinted spectacles with sky-blue plastic frames—but the effect of the computer-enhanced seasons and wonders is so stunning that it quite eclipses the real thing. At the Toho Gas Fantasy World we are taught about road safety and to say thank you when someone does us a favor, a habit which will apparently be close to extinction by the time we reach the 21st century. The roof of the Mitsubishi Pavilion, viewed from the outside, is the shape of a gigantic egg and the theme here is "Dreams on the Egg." The object, the English-language pamphlet explains, is "to have people discover a hint about designing future dreams, which is found by varying one's viewpoint while trying to match up various things." Third and fourth readings still fail to coax a meaning out of this sentence so I pass through the pavilion's Dream Tunnel into the World of Dream and

Color and from there to the Parades of Dream and Play. Our future dreams, I learn, will be about whales made of mirrored tiles and peacocks with winking Christmas tree lights all over their bodies and tails.

Finally, I visit the Mitsui-Toshiba Pavilion, which is dedicated to "Flying Dreams," particularly to "The Dream of Paul B. MacReady." Paul B. MacReady is an American professor who builds manpowered aircraft. On a large multi-screen display ("a world beyond time and space, a carnival of dreams!") we watch a group of children build a mechanical pterodactyl called Tera. On his maiden flight Tera is caught in that commonest of 21st-century mishaps, a time warp, and wafted back to prehistory where he meets a real pterodactyl whose name is not disclosed, contends with unpleasant natural forces (meteor swarms, earthquakes, erupting volcanoes), and experiences his own extinction. But, Tera, take heart! Technology—specifically, the technology of Paul B. MacReady improved by Mitsui, Toshiba, and the rest beyond his wildest, yes, dreams—can help you fly again. "Love, Love, Love!" sings a choir as we file out of the pavilion. "You can reach the sky, if you only try!"

The love hotels along the canal are busier now in the late afternoon and fresh wooden boards the size of license plates are stacked in the driveways ready for the evening. I stroll back to the shop that sells grilled chicken and drink four large draft beers in swift succession. The rain has blown over; it will be warm tomorrow. At my hotel I find that the lift is broken. I climb the stairs. So ends Day Two.

Day Three is bright and windy and it takes me two hours of walking in the wind to reach the Port of Nagoya where I stroll round the third and last of the International Design Exposition's sites, this one promising "A Journey Into New Pleasures." In the "Palpitating City" Pavilion, jointly sponsored by the Aichi and Chukyo Banks, we are promised an experience filled with "Dreams and Drama and Possibilities." What is a city, the pamphlet wonders, but "A Dream Designed By Man"? This particular dream has as its centerpiece a bank of color television monitors set on a hillock of pink silk on which a pop idol replicated dozens of times sings a song out of tune with her eyes focused significantly on the far distance. After this the bank of television monitors turns into a gigantic wedding cake that rises slowly to the applause of a collection of cuddly pink and sky-blue stuffed animals, while rainbows flicker round the walls.

Palpitating, I shuffle across to the L.A. Square Pavilion, where at first I make the mistake of thinking that I have stumbled upon a non-Japanese sponsor. But "Dream City" Los Angeles is one of Nagoya's four urban sisters, and this pavilion, whose sponsor turns out to be the Nippon Sharyo Corporation, provides a showcase for the new L.R.V. (Light Rail Vehicle) that the corporation is building to shuttle commuters between Los Angeles and Long Beach. On the screen the new train, not yet covered with graffiti, flies through the air above Disneyland, Universal Studios, "Dream Town Hollywood," and the HMS *Queen Mary* converted into a hotel, following which the mayor of Los Angeles congratulates Japan on its commuter trains and sisterliness.

That is the last of the corporate pavilions. The remaining attractions are the Japanese icebreaker *Fuji*, which was used by eighteen of Japan's Antarctic expeditionary teams between 1965 and 1983 and is now permanently berthed at Nagoya Port and so is not really a part of the exposition (although, like that of the *Mir*, its cramped, severely practical design prompts a greater surge of respect than anything I have seen in the corporate pavilions), and George Stephenson's *Locomotion*, which, like the light plane *Voyager* and Gutenberg's printing press and Nagoya Castle and the Grass-Cutting Sword in the emperor's palace, is a replica.

Lastly, I visit the converted warehouses where the entries for the exposition's two amateur design competitions are on display. The first contains the international Design Eye competition entries, which, as the catalogue emphasizes, have been submitted by design students from seventeen countries. But of the sixty-one students whose works have been selected for inclusion in the catalogue, forty-seven are Japanese; of the five judges two are Japanese, and of the ten prizewinners seven are Japanese. Japan certainly leads the world in design. A lot of the items are utilitarian. There is an example of computer software, a combined radio and cassette player called the Big Boom Box, a crash helmet, a prison, a wheelchair, a parking meter, a C.D. player that enables an expecting mother and her unborn child to listen together, and a color-coded aid for Japanese people wishing to learn the Korean Hangul writing system. The Grand Prize has gone to the computer software, a Judges' Prize to the Big Boom Box.

The entries for the other competition, the Design Masterpiece Awards, are all Japanese, as are all six of the judges. These entries are more whimsical. There is an airplane made out of a tea kettle, wooden clogs in the shape of alligators, a dachshund with wheels instead of legs, a set of blue and red penguins wearing black top hats that walk down a sloping wooden board, a machine that fills your home with jungle smells, and the Grand Prize worth three million yen has been won by colorful neckties that zip up instead of needing to be knotted. But my eye is caught by two creations that have not received prizes. One is a chair called *Suwarenai Isu* (The Chair That Can't Be Sat On) by 22-year-old Horikawa Kiyoto. It is a small red chair painted with bright yellow sunbursts, full of jagged edges, bumps, knobs and spikes. And the other is a wan flesh-colored music box by eighteen-year-old Maruyama Momoko which plays a pretty, tinkly little tune when you turn its wire handle. The four sides of the box are decorated with pictures of beer cans, a bottle of chili sauce, cogwheels, New York skyscrapers, a golf-playing salaryman, a broken mirror. And on top of the box stand two pale, plump, bare-breasted women with their hands bound above their heads, waiting to be whipped. "Good girl!" I keep saying under my breath as I stand here looking at Momoko's music box. "Good girl! Good girl! Good truthful girl!" Momoko has called her music box *Dream*.

2
Decline

❧

The bell of the temple of Gion tolls into the heart of every man a warning that all is vanity and evanescence," is the opening sentence of the fourteenth-century martial chronicle, *The Tale of the Heike*. Like the legends of Arthur or the Niebelungs, this long, episodic tale of war and defeat, struggle and sacrifice, ambition and decline, is in origin the work of no single author but grew through oral and literary traditions to become one of the great sourcebooks of its nation's poetry and drama.

The Heike (whose proper surname is Taira, this being another way of pronouncing the ideogram *hei*, which means, ironically, peace; but I will call them the Heike because that is what most Japanese people call them) were a military-minded clan, descended from the Emperor Kammu, and they flourished for three generations during the latter half of the Heian period (794-1185), achieving their ultimate pinnacle of power late in the twelfth century on the kimono tails of their ruthless head, Taira no Kiyomori. By 1160 Kiyomori had defeated his rivals in two brief and bitter civil "disturbances" and achieved an ascendancy over emperor and court that was to last almost until his death. But in securing power for himself and his family, Kiyomori had incurred the hatred of the other great military clan of the age, the Genji (or Minamoto, which is another way of pronouncing the ideogram *gen*), who were inspired by their own leaders first to bide their time, then to regroup, forming a league of warriors whose power base was the eastern provinces, far removed from the Heike-dominated capital of Kyoto, and finally in 1180 to rise up in force against the Heike.

So began a five-year war that was to change Japan more radically and completely than any subsequent event until the Meiji Restoration of 1868. The Genpei War smashed to pieces the refinements, the sensibilities, the wistful decadence of the Heian court, forcing the last vestiges of that aristocratic "golden age" to succumb in terror before the wall of flame that engulfed much of the country and to expire at last under a mountain of armored dead. The war ended the preeminence of Kyoto, of court and courtier, of concubine and emperor, and freed the fickle pendulum of power to swing east for the first time, to the low hills and flat swampy plain around Edo (Tokyo), where two successions of military dictators were to preside over a total of more than four hundred years of martial law.

The decline and fall of the Heike is the foremost epic and tragedy of Japan. Like many other tragedies that have found a permanent niche in the human consciousness, it is a story of ruin brought about, at least in part, by human folly—arrogance or insatiability or overreaching ambition. The prime mover of the tragedy, Kiyomori, died when the Genpei War was in its second year and so, though he dominates *The Tale of the Heike* like a brooding puppet master, it is his sons and nephews and cousins and heirs, the glittering young warriors in their prime, upon whom the axe of defeat and retribution falls. At the last pitched battle of the war, the sea battle of Dannoura, fought on the 24th of April, 1185, in the Straits of Shimonoseki between Kyushu and the southwestern tip of Honshu, the Heike were finally routed, and Kiyomori's eight-year-old grandson, whom the tyrant had placed on the throne five years earlier as Emperor Antoku, died when his grandmother leapt into the sea and sank beneath the waves cradling him in her arms. With the child emperor sank the Grass-Cutting Sword (or, according to other sources, its replica) and the sacred jewels that the Heike had taken with them on their long flight from the capital and which had embodied imperial authority in Japan since the Sun Goddess's grandson first trod upon these islands.

There. It is a stirring story. The more so for being (in its essentials) true. And yet, as with many other historical truths that have achieved their best-remembered shape at the hands of the makers of literature, it is less the facts that impel us than a sense of invisible wheels in motion, raising and dashing, propelling and crushing, revolving in the uncertain groove which we call Fate. The subsequent generations of Japanese poets, dramatists, and artists of all kinds who found inspiration in the Heike saga responded most readily to its illustration of the Buddhist view of earthly life: that, in the words of the tale's famous opening, "all is vanity and evanescence." Human splendor, human attainment have a career as brief as that of the cherry flower, Japan's favorite emblem of transient glory. And so, despite its heroic deeds, its panoply of warriors, its clashing armies, the tone of *The Tale of the Heike* is that of the speckled decline of late summer into autumn. The saga is tinged at every turn with what Japanese artists have called since the Heian period *mono no aware*, "the sadness of things." It is this sense of the brevity of human glory and the eternal sadness with which the world is charged that the poet Basho—he of the pachinkftargeted tonsils—sought to evoke five centuries after the defeat of the Heike in, for example, these two poems from *The Narrow Road to the Deep North*:

The pity of it—
beneath the warrior's helmet
cries the bush cricket

Ah, late summer grass—
all that remains
of bold warriors' dreams

The helmet that inspired the first of these poems was one that Basho found preserved in a shrine near the city of Komatsu on the Japan Sea coast. It had belonged to a warrior named Sanemori, who was killed in the Genpei War while fighting on the side of the Heike. According to *The Tale of the Heike*, his head was cut off, as was the custom, and presented to the victorious Genji general, who failed to recognize it as Sanemori's because the hair and beard were black. But when the general ordered his men to wash the head, the hair and beard turned white. Sanemori had been an old man—many had thought him too old to fight—who had dyed his hair in a vain attempt to stave off the ravages of time, and he had failed, as men—and grass, and crickets—must.

After the rout at Dannoura, the remnants of the Heike scattered. As to the precise directions in which they scattered, *The Tale of the Heike* offers no clues, but if you believed all the local legends that have sprung up in the eight hundred years since their diaspora, you would have to conclude that enough of them survived to populate half the country. If I had ten thousand yen for every hamlet I have visited in which I have been told that I am among descendants of the Heike, I should be rich enough to retire and start a clan of my own. I have been told it among the villages of central Kyushu, in the depths of the Shikoku hills, in the northeast, southwest, and center of Honshu, on Sado island, on the Oki islands and the Yaeyama islands, on the Goto islands off Nagasaki, on Tsushima island and Iki island, and at various places along the whole length of the Japan Sea coast. It is a claim one hears most often in remote, mountainous parts of Japan that boast of having preserved some vestige of an older way of life. It might be a tradition of kagura dances, of mask carving, of architecture, or some other craft or ceremony; or it might be simply a turn of mind that has shunned the more glaring encroachments of modernity and continues to cling to at least the semblance of a lifestyle that the urban dweller has lost.

That no village claims to have been founded by descendants of the victorious Genji is hardly a surprise. There is far greater resonance in defeat than in victory, as artists have known since Aeschylus wrote *The Persians* and Euripides *The Trojan Women*. If Saigo Takamori had survived his war to forge an accommodation with the Tokyo government and settle once more into peaceful retirement, he would have stood no chance of becoming a god. Most of the heroes of Japan are heroes because their careers exemplified what the late Ivan Morris called "the nobility of failure," a characteristic that runs from the legendary hero Yamato Takeru in the fourth century through the Heike in the twelfth, Saigo in the nineteenth, and the kamikaze pilots in our own. Not that the trait is unique to Japan. Spartacus and his rebellious slaves, King Harold at Hastings with the arrow in his eye, Roland at Roncesvalles, the men of Masada and the Alamo: all these share in the nobility of failure and in the awe of posterity that rewards it.

Poring over maps in my room late at night, I have often wondered how many of the Heike village stories are true. The Heike were a vast clan and had begun to scatter well before the final collapse of their warrior league at Dannoura, so they might have gone almost anywhere. The war boats escaping from Shimonoseki could well have fled to Tsushima or Iki. The women and children who watched the final defeat of their men from Kyushu's northeast shore could easily have turned inland and made their way south to find themselves, after weeks or months of wandering in the hills between Kumamoto and Miyazaki, near the little hamlet of Toji, famous for its haunting lullaby and now threatened with extinction by a dam. And they might have made a rough home for themselves further up where the hills turn into crags, at tiny Kajiwara, where I once watched an August drum dance with roots lost among the fogs of time and Asia, and wondered why anyone would want to live in a place so spartan and remote. And because the Heike who came to power under Kiyomori were originally from Ise, south of Nagoya on the Kii peninsula, they might have fled east toward their old home, but they would not have stayed there long. The Genji were in control of the capital, and the route between Kyoto and the Kanto area, where the new government had already opened for business, was suddenly the most important artery of communication in the country (as it was to remain into Edo times, when it became the celebrated Tokaido road, and into modern times, when its two ends were linked by Japan's first bullet train). The defeated Heike would, after the barest of breathing spaces, have wanted to put as much distance as possible between themselves and the Pacific shore.

With the exception of the great trunk roads that were to achieve such fame through the work of dramatists and song makers and print artists in the eighteenth and nineteenth centuries—the Tokaido, the Nakasendo and the rest—Japan's main routes of commerce and transport until quite recent times were its rivers. Three important rivers empty into the head of Ise Bay, just west of modern Nagoya. They are the Ibi River, 114 kilometers long, which flows down from the Ibuki mountain range that borders Lake Biwa; the Kiso River, 193 kilometers long, which flows down from the Japan Alps to the northeast; and the Nagara River, about 120 kilometers long, which flows the length of modern-day Gifu prefecture from the Hida Mountains due north. Any one of these rivers might have provided the Heike with an escape route that would have led them away from the roads and cities of civilization and danger into a remoteness that few pursuers would have wanted to penetrate. As I stared at my maps, following these rivers from their estuaries to their sources with a pencil or a fingertip, I imagined the Heike in their flat-bottomed boats, heavy with women and crying children and haunted by the echo of the Gion bell, moving slowly in the darkness and mists upriver, through forest and gorge towards the crest of Honshu, and then over it on foot to the Japan Sea–side of the island, to find hardship, poverty, loneliness, and peace.

There is no clue to the historicity of this vision, but there are things that prod the imagination. One of these is the name of a village that lies a little way beyond the source of the Nagara, on the other side of the watershed, across the border from Gifu in what is today Toyama prefecture. By *village* I mean here not a hamlet but an administrative area that contains several hamlets. These administrative areas have usually been carved out and named, or renamed, in modern times, so the resonance in a name can be an uncertain guide to the events of eight centuries ago. Still, the resonance in this name is difficult to ignore. The village is called Taira, written with the same ideogram as the *hei* of Heike. I decided to walk the length of the Nagara River, and on, until I reached it.

᪲

I walked out of Nagoya on a bright first of October morning feeling ashamed that I had been so rude about the place. It looked and felt quite decent under the cloudless autumn sky, and the fact that it was a Sunday lessened the sense of grim Philistinism that the weekday city exudes from all its flat concrete roofs and buzzing glass doors. In spite of the elevated expressways snaking everywhere, and perhaps because of the uncompromising grid plan on which its buildings are arranged (a result of wartime bombing so heavy that it necessitated a virtual rethinking from the ground up), Nagoya seemed a clean city, its main thoroughfares airily broad, and though there is a near total absence of what we normally mean when we talk about "culture" (Nagoya's best known cultural development is the pachinko machine, patented in 1948), life here has a softer feel to it than does life in Osaka or Tokyo. One Nagoya woman, hearing that I had lived in Tokyo for twenty years, remarked that I must find Nagoya a very *nonbiri* place by comparison. *Nonbiri* means relaxed or leisurely or happy-go-lucky. It wouldn't have been my first choice of word, or even among my first ten, although walking out of the city I caught a glimmer of what the woman meant. The traffic lights in Nagoya, for instance, take an eternity to change.

But people have been rude about Nagoya since feudal times, so I was only following a distinguished tradition. Here is what I wrote about it in *Collins' Illustrated Guide to Japan*: "Nagoya is a city that most visitors are likely to want to spend about as much time in as the bullet train does on its way from Tokyo to Kyoto (sixty seconds)." That was impolite I know, and I have since realized that Nagoya has attractions. I went back to one of them on three successive evenings following my days spent drooping round the Expo sites. It was an ordinary red-lantern grilled-chicken place a few minutes' walk from Nagoya Station, where beer and sticks of liver and plates of shredded lettuce were set on the counter in front of me by the most beautiful woman I have ever been served by in a red-lantern grilled-chicken place. I would guess that she was in her mid- to late-twenties, bright, smiling, slim, friendly, and apparently quite unaware of her own dumbstriking loveliness. I kept looking at her and looking at her and trying to find something wrong with her. Maybe her chin was just a touch too round. And she wore a ring on her fourth finger. The place was always very packed and each night it took me two draft beers before I could pluck up the courage to talk to her. The first night she asked me what I did for a living. It is a question I've never learned to answer with grace.

"I—er—write," I told her.

"Oh," she said. "What, you mean for magazines?"

"Yes, sometimes," I grunted.

"What magazines do you write for?" she asked.

"Well, some of my stuff comes out in *Shukan Shincho*," I mumbled.

When I went back the next night, she had bought a copy of *Shukan Shincho*.

"You write such fine Japanese," she said.

"Er—actually," I said, my face going the colors of the rainbow one after the other and then all at the same time, "I write in English and they get it translated."

"Oh," she said, "and I thought you were so clever." The concrete under my stool went crack and I fell through the floor into the underground mall.

"Do you really walk all those kilometers?" she asked.

"Yes, look," I said, grinning like a lunatic and lifting my foot above the level of the counter, about the height of my right ear, to show her my filthy boot.

"Oh," she said again, and went away to fetch a salaryman his intestine stew.

The third night I couldn't stand it any longer and in the middle of a conversation with a fat shopkeeper about whether the Seibu Lions or the Yomiuri Giants would win the Japan Series and whether Ochiai would be the league MVP, I said, "Look, look at that young woman behind the counter. Don't you think she's beautiful? I mean, really beautiful. I think she's beautiful. I don't believe her chin is a touch too round. She's beautiful. She's perfectly beautiful. I've come here every night the last three nights because I think she's beautiful."

"Oi!" shouted the fat shopkeeper at the top of his voice. The place went very quiet. "Oi, Kazuko! Come 'ere a sec! This gaijin wants to kiss ya!"

I never went back. I spent the whole of the rest of eternity in the underground mall with my feet in the air. There didn't seem any point in persisting. And there was nothing in it for *Shukan Shincho*.

But it was nice to be leaving Nagoya behind, even though it took all day. At first the quiet lane that ran alongside the Hori Canal had colored flagstones set into it to mark it as part of a sightseeing route. But here and there you could see from the sags in their roofs that the low wooden houses which are the designated canalside sights were slowly collapsing under their own weight. Little in Japan seems built to last, but in a land where the difference between an original and a replica is hardly noticed, or else the replica is preferred, this troubles no one. Around the replica castle moat four jogging courses of varying length had been laid out and marked in different colors on an explanatory signboard. Across National Highway 41, where I waited about ten minutes for the lights to change, the canal narrowed and hooked away towards the northeast suburbs, tree-lined on both banks despite its slopping along between ugly grey apartment blocks, and some of the trees were long pendent willows. A few of the older houses that lined the canal in the shadows of the high-rises had so many potted plants outside them that it looked as though their owners lived in greenhouses. Near its end the canal grew shallower, the weeds thinner and the water clear enough for boys to be wading in, barefoot with their tiddler nets. Then I left the quiet, willowed canal, and emerged onto a fiercely busy road that I would have to trudge along for the rest of the nearly thirty kilometers to Inuyama.

Alongside Nagoya Airport the road smelled strongly of spilled petrol and burning rubber, and I had begun wondering whether there had been an accident—some difficulty encountered during reentry maybe—when an All Nippon Airways Tristar roared over so close to the roadside buildings that, if its windows had been open, the passengers could have leaned out and plucked the grey laundry off of the balconies. For miles the shabby, five-story apartment blocks receded into the petrol-hazy distance, interrupted here and there by commercial enterprises like the Atomboy sushi restaurant, part of a chain that was trying to recruit staff by promising on its posters that "In three months you too can be making sushi" (or rather replicas of sushi, since the standard apprenticeship for a sushi chef until the advent of Atomboy had been six years), a cafe called Wimbledon, a poolroom called Tumble, a cake shop called Grindelwald, another cafe called My Pock, and a parade of glittering colonnaded pachinko parlors called President and Playland and Columbia and Diana, outside the last of which a little four- or five-year-old girl played quietly by herself at the stinking curbside while her parents amused themselves within, wasting her life as they wasted their own. Then came the first tiny suburban fields of ripening rice, surrounded by factories and corrugated iron sheds, and a used car dealer's where a string of plastic windmills spun surlily round with a squeak like an overwound spring.

Atomboy wasn't the only place having trouble recruiting staff. All the chain restaurants along the road, and most of the petrol stations, had notices in their windows offering *arubaito* (arbeit) or *paato* (from *part time*). In the past year a lot of restaurant chains had found themselves understaffed to the extent that they had raised the wages they pay part-timers by as much as twenty percent, but those wages had now reached their ceiling because, if they rose any higher, part-timers would be earning as much per hour as permanent staff.

Japan has a worldwide reputation for the efficiency of its service and other industries, but this efficiency is currently threatened by two related factors. One is the reluctance of younger Japanese people, persuaded daily by government opinion polls and advertising agencies that they are "middle class," to accept jobs—even vacation jobs—that are in any way dirty or demeaning. The construction industry was the first to suffer from this reluctance and the labor shortage there is now so severe that, despite newly draconian laws aimed at curbing illegal immigration, Japanese builders, often working in tandem with gangster recruiters, are increasingly forced to rely on the sweat of Iranians and Pakistanis who have entered the country on three-month tourist visas and whom one commonly sees slogging away on building sites with handkerchiefs tied across the lower halves of their faces in a pathetic token of disguise. The other factor is the draconian laws themselves. Japanese society as a whole is still very far from comfortable with the idea of foreigners settling in on a long-term basis. And whenever a crack has appeared in the fortress wall, it has more often illustrated entrenched forms of prejudice than provided evidence of Japan's much touted "internationalization." For example, a "special arrangement" makes it comparatively easy for people from South America to settle and work in Japan, but only people of Japanese ancestry. So when the draconian laws came into force the nation was treated to the edifying spectacle of thousands of foreigners called Khan being summarily shipped out via Narita Airport while authorities admitted thousands of foreigners called Fujimori to replace them.

"Internationalization" still tickled my thoughts when, at about four o'clock, I trudged into the little castle town of Inuyama, past the police box at

Inuyama Park where a large-lettered notice said in English, International Tourist Spot. I dropped in at the biscuit shop that doubles as an information center for people seeking ryokans, and the elderly man there stared at me, sighed, and shuffled with a careful display of reluctance into the little booth where he kept his pamphlets. He didn't show me any of the pamphlets. Instead he picked up the telephone, dialed a number, and said in a tone that was at once gruff, resigned, irritated, and apologetic, "You can manage one gaijin, can't you?" That is how I ended up in one of several tourist ryokans that line the concreted banks of the Kiso River, famous for its tradition of nighttime cormorant fishing.

"Is there any cormorant fishing tonight?" I asked the young woman at the ryokan desk.

"Oh yes," she said, "there's cormorant fishing every night."

"No, there ain't," snapped a man who was vacuuming the foyer. "It's the first of October. The cormorant fishing ended yesterday."

I went out for a walk anyway along the steeply built-up river, which at this season was, by Japanese standards, unusually wide and deep. The ryokan had lent me a pair of wooden sandals that were miles too small for me (and miles too small for most modern-day Japanese feet, so I can't imagine why such instruments of torture continue to be made) and I didn't walk very far. I hobbled down to sit as close to the river as I could and watched a young couple trying to take a double portrait of themselves with an automatic camera balanced on a fairy-light tripod that the evening breeze kept blowing over. When finally they got the timer to whir they both flashed little, half-embarrassed V-signs.

The sun sank, a perfect globe of gold, and as its rim touched the earth, the evening breeze strengthened. Mine was a large, empty, impersonal ryokan, neither friendly nor unfriendly, and I seemed to be the only guest. For the convenience of the staff they had placed me in the room nearest the foyer, so I ate my dinner of three cold fish to the accompanying blare of green-eyed monsters being reduced to tiny globs of plasma on the ryokan owner's television. Then, when I settled down to sleep, the fridge in my room began emitting the sound that an ANA Tristar's engines make when they are coping with reentry. Light from the foyer flooded into my room through a square opening in the wall above the screens, which I noticed were made not of paper but of semi-translucent plastic, and I discovered after three excursions that I couldn't find the switch. But nature, too, made its presence felt, as how could it not on the banks of the Kiso River? A mosquito got in and woke me up five times, but it only bit my toe.

Monday morning, and a bank of low dark cloud behind the mound of Inuyama Castle made it look as though the castle were a volcano erupting with the sound turned off. I climbed up to see it in my boots, having pointedly replaced the ryokan's wooden slippers in the shoe cupboard in full view of the woman at the desk with a little bow and a smile.

Inuyama Castle, though small and uninspiring as castles go, is interesting for two reasons. One is that it is the oldest surviving castle in Japan; it was built in 1537 by Oda Nobuyasu, the uncle of the great Nobunaga who was three at the time of the castle's construction and who was to become the first of the ruthless trio of military dictators (Hideyoshi and Ieyasu were the second and third) who unified Japan after centuries of civil war. Though extensively renovated in the 1890s and again in the 1960s, the castle was not knocked down and replaced by a replica. There are no elevators in it, no Spanish garrotings, and no background music played on a digital piano. The other reason why it is interesting is that it is the only Japanese castle to remain in private hands. In 1618 it was bestowed on Naruse Masanari as a reward for the support that he and his family had given Ieyasu, and it has remained the property of the Naruses ever since, with the exception of a brief hiatus following the Meiji Restoration when all the feudal lords were dispossessed. The Nobi Earthquake of 1891 damaged the castle so badly, however, that the fund-strapped government handed it back to the Naruses on condition that they repair it. Its present owner, Naruse Masatoshi, inherited the castle from his father in 1973 and, if lordliness had not been outlawed by pretended egalitarianism, he would be the twelfth Naruse lord of Inuyama Castle in unbroken lineal descent.

The Naruses must all have been dwarfs, I thought, smacking my head for the eighth time on a door frame installed about four feet six inches above the floor. A Japanese visitor of average height had warned me about the lowness of the lintels when he saw me taking off my boots at the dungeon entrance. Perhaps it was a ploy to delay attackers; and perhaps the local ryokans supplied them with wooden slippers on their way to the siege. From the top floor of the dungeon I had a hazy view of the surrounding land: Aichi prefecture stretching back the way I had come to the edge of Nagoya Bay, flat and full of pylons and factory chimneys; and Gifu prefecture across the river where I was going and where, beyond the thin, densely built-up residential strip that the commuter overflow from Nagoya has annexed, the hills rose almost at once, a cloudy leaden grey.

By a quarter past ten I had crossed the Kiso River into Gifu on a bridge that is shared, without separating fences, by pedestrians, two lanes of traffic and the double track of the Meitetsu railway line. Woe betide drunk drivers, or for that matter wind-blown pedestrians. I stopped at the first post office I came to to send the large packet of Expo pamphlets that I had accumulated back to Tokyo.

"It's printed matter," I told the woman at the counter.

"You mean it's not a letter?"

"No, it's printed matter. It's pamphlets."

"We don't count pamphlets as printed matter."

"But they're printed, look," I said, opening the packet and pulling out the one with the Dream Adventure Vehicle on it.

"They don't come into the category of printed matter, though," said the woman.

"What does come into that category?" I asked.

"Newspapers and magazines," she said, "and telephone directories."

I paid the full postage rate for the packet, which in another country would have been enough to send the twenty volumes of the Encyclopedia Brittanica twice round the globe by air, and then began tramping along National Highway 21 as it ran alongside the Japan Rhine. The Japan Rhine is what promoters of tourism call the stretch of the Kiso River between Inuyama and Minokamo, and it was first called this by a local geographer named Shiga Shigetaka who had a passion for Germany coupled with a hyperactive imagination. The scenery along this stretch of the river, though pleasant if you discount National Highway 21, is not what you would call Romantic, and for the most part the Japan Rhine runs between rocks and boulders that only an imagination as stirred as Professor Shiga's could mistake for cliffs and crags. But the main attraction is the rapids and the main tourist activity is negotiating them in long wooden boats piloted by two straw-hatted boat-men, one at the bow and one at the stern. The boatman at the stern steers the craft with a long wooden tiller and the one at the bow offers explanations through a hand-held microphone or plays folk songs on a portable cassette deck with a loudspeaker mounted on a post facing aft. The tourists sit between two long strips of green canvas fastened to the gunwales that they can pull over their shirts and ties and jackets when the rapids grow splashy. These boats headed down towards Inuyama at one- or two-minute intervals as I coughed my way up the truck-clogged highway past frequent signs that said Japan Rhine.

At half past eleven I drank two draft beers in a small shed-like restaurant that specialized in grilled meat, where I was served by a pretty, chatty girl with a bold and mistaken taste in lipstick. She had long hair that fell loose at the sides and was elaborately braided at the back, and she thought it was extraordinary to be walking along a road where there was nothing special to see.

"But what about the Japan Rhine?" I asked her.

"Oh, that," she said with a flick of her braids, "that's just for the tourists, that is. We don't pay any attention to it. I've never been in one of those boats. And I've never seen the cormorant fishing," she added with a defiant pout that emphasized her wrong choice of cosmetic. I told her that I had grown up in London and had never seen the Trooping of the Color or the Changing of the Guard and, though she confessed that she didn't know what those were, she acknowledged that we had a lot in common, which encouraged me to order another draft beer, some hot Korean pickles, and a plate of mari-nated liver.

While we talked her mother, or perhaps her mother-in-law, glared at us through the kitchen door like an ogre whose golden egg was being filched, and went on butchering already dead meat.

"What's this road to Seki like?" I asked the girl, pointing through the window at the small road I was about to explore, having come as far as I needed to along the fume-choked highway.

"Oh, it's just hills," she said with another toss of her braids. *Hills* meant a place where there was no sophistication and where no one in his right mind would want to go.

But all the way to the little city of Seki the landscape on either side of the road remained an uneasy mixture of countryside and industry. The paddies were broader and the houses lower but the pylons still stalked across the hillsides behind little factories and apartment blocks and chestnut orchards where orange-brown husks, split open, littered the ground among the trees, caked and muddied. From the stubble in the harvested paddies green shoots were sprouting from lopped stalks in the autumn heat. Near a pachinko parlor called Yodel (the Rhine was still only five kilometers away) I lay down on the bank of a small swift-flowing stream and went to sleep while the sun beat down on my sweaty face.

I approached Seki down a long, flat street called *Bunka dori* (Culture Road), where some of the shops sold scissors and kitchen knives and had posters in their windows reminding customers that, ever since the time of the Heike, Seki had been famous for its swordsmiths. Nowadays the stringently applied Firearms and Sword Possession Control Law, originally enacted by the American Occupation authorities, has taken the edge off its old trade, and Seki has been reduced to turning out about ninety percent of Japan's safety razor blades.

I wandered round the deserted town center till I found a pleasant little cherry-tree-lined canal with paths on either side intended for flower viewers to stroll along in spring. The paths, too, were completely deserted, but a large restaurant overlooked the canal, so I went there to drink some more draft beer and ask about places to stay. There were two places to stay, the shy master told me, interrupted and contradicted all the time by a customer with a set of teeth too large for his mouth, who did not live in Seki and so knew all about it. There was a cheap business ryokan in town and a more lavish Seki Sightseeing Hotel a couple of kilometers out of town on the bank of the Nagara River.

"Is it worth paying the extra for?"

"No, it isn't," said the customer with the teeth.

"Well," said the master, "it depends on whether you want to see the cormorant fishing."

"I thought the cormorant fishing was over," I said.

"Yes, it's over," said the customer with the teeth.

"No, it goes on till the fifteenth," said the master shyly, "if there are people wanting to see it."

"There's no one wants to see it," snapped the teeth.

"I want to see it," I said.

"Yes, you should," said the teeth. "It's wonderful. It's culture."

I borrowed the master's phone and rang the hotel. They told me that they had a vacancy and that there was cormorant fishing that evening and that I could see it if I wanted to pay an extra three thousand yen. So I said, all right, I would pay the three thousand yen.

"It's daylight robbery," said the teeth when I sat down again.

"It's a bit pricey," agreed the master.

"It's worth it, though," said the teeth. "It's culture."

The restaurant was echoingly empty and the master remarked that he was only ever busy at cherry-blossom time.

"The cherry trees must be beautiful along the canal," I said. The master nodded happily. The man with the teeth could not sensibly contradict this so he changed the subject and began to boast of how he had not been to see the Design Expo in Nagoya and didn't intend to go.

"I went to see it," the master admitted.

"Huh!" scoffed the teeth.

It was after five when I crossed the bridge over the clean, shallow Nagara River and found the Seki Sightseeing Hotel, a small posh white building with an illuminated floor plan displayed in the foyer and a receptionist behind the foyer desk who clapped her hand over her mouth and told me that she had forgotten to book me a place on the boat.

"What time does it start?"

"Six," she said, clawing for the telephone.

But the boat people had no shortage of places, and at a quarter past six the receptionist led me across a gravel parking lot to the pitch dark river bank where the boat lay moored. We sat, I and the other sightseers, on cushions along either side of the boat, and were each presented with a small hand towel in a cellophane packet to celebrate the boat company's thirtieth anniversary. To my surprise I found that I was seated opposite two Germans. They were wearing business suits and ties and sipping lukewarm beer from small green cans called Bavaria, and they were with two English-speaking Japanese associates, similarly dressed and similarly provisioned. At once I began to notice the stink arising from my shirt and socks which I hadn't had time to change. But this didn't matter because the Germans had decided to ignore me, and I sat trailing my fingers in the water, astonished at how, though night had fallen, I could see small fish gliding over the clearly visible shingle of the riverbed.

"Why don't you give your neighbor a beer?" suggested a Japanese associate after a while in fluent American English to one of the German businessmen.

"Uh?" said the businessman.

"Neighbor?" said the other.

The Japanese associate nudged him and pointed. The German businessman reached silently into his bag of Bavaria beers and handed me a can.

"Where are you from?" I asked him brightly.

"Germany," he said.

We sat with smiles welded to our faces.

Then another group of sightseers boarded the boat: an unattractive middle-aged man and three much younger women dressed in designer culottes and tailored jackets. They might have been three actresses with their manager, except that only one of the women was pretty enough to be an actress. But they all behaved with carefully rehearsed flamboyance, seating themselves fussily in the bow of the boat, smoothing down their pleated clothes, and smiling about at the air.

"Look," said the manager. "There's three foreigners; one for each of you."

"Hooo hooo hooo!" they went.

The last party to board consisted of two fat countrywomen who stumbled up the gangplank and set the boat swaying violently when they fell onto their cushions. The tillerman walked to the stern and raised a paper lantern to signal the cormorant boat which was moored in the wings that the audience had assembled. The curtain rose. We pushed off and caught a small wave that soaked the Japanese businessman who was fluent in American English, so he took off his shirt (he was wearing no vest), stood up and began to towel down his slim, tennis-player's torso, angling himself a little toward the bow for the benefit of the actresses.

"Showtime!" I said to them.

"Hooo hooo hooo!" they went.

"Yup," said the stripped businessman loudly in Japanese, "this'll cost you another three thousand yen!"

"Does that include consumption tax?" I asked. He didn't laugh. The Germans scowled.

"I wish there was karaoke," said one of the actresses.

In two minutes, the cormorant boat had drawn abreast of us, center stage, a bucket of blazing logs suspended from its bow, and the cormorant master in his apron of knotted string yanked at the leashes of a dozen flapping birds while his two assistants thumped the side of the boat with their oars and the sound echoed down the river valley.

Cormorant fishing on the Nagara River has been going on for more than a thousand years, sufficient time, you would have thought, for someone to have realized that it is not a very efficient way of securing your supper. The cormorants wear tight collars round their necks to stop them swallowing their prey. The bucket of fire slung across the bow attracts this prey and so, I suppose, do the thumps of the oars, although if I were a river fish they would frighten me all the way to the sea. The cormorants dive into the river and swim about with their heads sticking vertically out of the water like little Nessies. They dive below the surface as the mood, or hunger, takes them, and whenever one of them catches a fish in its beak the master yanks it in by means of the leash attached to its collar, forces it to disgorge the fish into a basket in the bottom of the boat, and then slings the hungry bird back into the water. Each time this happened the actresses applauded. The master yanked and choked and slung without any sign of tenderness, treating his captive cormorants like bits of mechanical equipment. The whole performance lasted ten minutes, and within a quarter of an hour we were back on land.

I wandered along the dark shore to the cormorant boat with the other sightseers to see what had been caught. The performance had ended with the cormorant boat drawing away upstream, stage left, offering the pretense that fishing would continue after we sightseers had retired. But the minute our boat touched the river bank, the cormorant boat swerved in towards the shore, its basket of fire was quickly extinguished, and by the time we reached it the catch had been sorted. Twelve small ayu lay on the concrete bank behind the white hotel.

"Are the cormorants males or females?" asked one of the two Japanese businessmen.

"Don't know," said the cormorant master shortly.

The other sightseers departed in their limousines and I strolled back to the hotel for dinner.

Dinner was served in a large tatami-floored dining room, which I had completely to myself. The food was brought in by a plump, pleasant woman and included the first matsutake mushrooms of the season, picked in the hills beyond the opposite river bank. Matsutake are nowadays a highly-priced delicacy; they cannot be cultivated and the only way of procuring them is to spend a lot of time in the forests hunting for them, ideally among forty- or fifty-year-old red pine trees. I was permitted about a tenth of one, sliced into tiny slivers which were mixed into my rice and which gave it a flavor not unlike Joyce's description of the flavor of mutton kidneys ("a fine tang of faintly scented urine"). Anyway, it went well with the grilled ayu, in which I might otherwise have spent a lot of the meal trying to detect the faint scent of cormorant saliva.

Then the woman brought me a pot full of oil in which to deep fry my own battered prawns.

"How will I know when they're done?" I asked.

"They turn fox-colored," she whispered and vanished into the kitchen.

"You, on the other hand, have turned tomato-colored," she told me when she came back later to clear away the dishes. I was lying sprawled out on the tatami drinking my third beer not counting the lukewarm Bavaria, and my face was bright red from two days of walking in the autumn sun. The functions board in the hotel foyer had been full of the names of guests and groups of guests who were all supposed to be staying here, but the dining room was empty all evening and I saw no one in the corridors or in the lifts.

"Are you busy?" I asked the pleasant woman.

"Oh yes," she smiled. "We're rushed off our feet."

In the night I dreamed that the house where I had grown up in London was infested with snakes. A cobra struck at my father in the garden; my mother ran sobbing into the street. And when I woke up at four o'clock in the morning and drank a can of cold oolong tea I put my head against the glass of the window and heard the first of the rain.

It was still raining when I left the hotel at a quarter past ten, having sat on the outdoor terrace drinking tea and writing notes about the cormorant fishing for an hour and realizing too late that I was wearing the hotel's indoor slippers. The receptionist turned her back discreetly when I replaced the slippers inside the glass door. I stopped at a post office to withdraw some money from my savings account. The woman behind the counter held up the withdrawal slip that I had filled out in Japanese and repeated my name and address aloud to herself, very slowly, over and over.

"Is something wrong?" I asked her.

"You've got a weird name," she said.

So names became the leitmotif of the morning. There was the beauty parlor called Trendy Hair, set back from the road on the far side of paddies, and near the Mino Country Club stood a large pink sign advertising the Hotel Merii-Go-Raando with the words Give Me Romance. It rained solidly; I walked in top gear and reached the flat little city of Mino shortly before midday. The valley had narrowed and the hills pressed in more tightly than they had at Seki. No building I saw was higher than three stories and many of the shops and houses in Mino were of dark wood and had cool stone entrances.

I went into a dark wood restaurant for lunch and watched a prim woman in a pink apron arrange pale lemon orchids in a vase beside the door.

"I like arranging flowers," she told me.

The rain was still pouring down and I was in no hurry to get on with tramping, so we talked about flowers, a subject of which I know nothing. The pink cosmos were in bloom along the river. Had I seen them? Wasn't it a wonderful name, *cosmos?* And had I noticed those wispy red flowers blooming here and there at the edge of the paddies? Yes, even I had noticed them. They were *higanbana.* That was a wonderful name, too, wasn't it? The Flower of the Equinox. And others called them Dead Men's Flowers. And still others called them the Ghost Flower. And still others the Fox Flower. And still others called them Abandoned Children. What were they called in English? I had no idea; perhaps they were some kind of amaryllis. Ah, and did I know that higanbana may not be brought inside a house?

"Why not?"

"Because it is the Buddha's law," the woman in the pink apron said seriously.

On either side of her arrangement of orchids hung two large oil paintings of no great merit which recorded Mino's claims to fame. The first painting showed an April festival in which the participants carried huge cherry-petal-like parasols made of *washi*. Washi is Japanese handmade paper (the word is written with two ideograms that mean, pugnaciously, "our paper") and the little city of Mino is so closely associated with its production that *minowashi* is a generic term for it and, in the fifteenth and sixteenth centuries, *minogami* (Mino paper) meant paper of any kind.

Paper is supposed to have been introduced into Japan in 610 by a Korean monk but that is only tradition. What is certain is that the earliest extant example of Japanese-made paper, dating to 701, is a census register for the district of Mino written on minowashi. By the thirteenth century Mino was producing paper of higher quality at lower prices than any other district in the country, and in the eighteenth century the paper sizes used in Mino became standard for all Japanese printed books. In our own century the techniques used in making minowashi have together been designated a National Treasure and, though there are now modern paper mills in and around the little city, paper continues to be molded here by hand as it has been since well before the time of the Heike.

The finest quality minowashi is made from mulberry bark. The shrubs are cropped in late autumn, the bark is removed by steaming and its inner fibers bleached by one of three natural methods: immersion in river water, burial under snow, or hanging out at night. The fibers are washed and pulped and molded into thin sheets in wooden trays manipulated by hand, and these are dried on boards in the open air. It is the fibrous nature of the finished product that makes it popular with traditional calligraphers; the irregularities and softness give it a natural appearance as well as an absorbency perfect for receiving thick globs of ink. There were no notable makers of handmade paper in the city itself, the pink-aproned woman told me; they were out in the surrounding countryside where the river water was cleaner.

"I thought that might be a papermaker's," I said, indicating the second oil painting, which showed a long low townhouse that looked mid-eighteenth century.

"No," said the woman, "that's a sake manufacturer's. It's just round the corner. You should go and have a look at it."

"You mean it exists?" I said. I had thought it was an inspiration of the oil painter's.

"Oh yes," said the woman, "it looks just like that. They make a sake called Hundred Springtimes."

"Let's have some," I said.

"Hot or cold?"

"Which is better?"

"Hot, they say."

So I sat and sipped hot Hundred Springtimes while the rain still fell beyond the doorway and the pale orchids in their vase. It was a good, rich sake, a little on the sweet side, and in my younger days (ah, younger days!) I would have ordered it cold, because that is how connoisseurs of *jizake* (local sakes) prefer to taste them, as they prefer second grade to first or special grade because in first and special grade, the connoisseurs maintain, the uniqueness of the taste has been refined away. I used to drink a lot of sake, especially on long walking trips where the memory of a particular taste became a weightless souvenir. Now I find that, if I drink sake, it adds to the insomnia that always seems to plague me on walks, so I stick to beer, predictable beer, which tastes the same whether you drink it in Hokkaido or Kyushu, in a grand hotel or on the edge of a farmer's ditch. There is no equivalent among Japanese beers, all of which are mass produced, of the widely varying local tastes of British or Belgian "real ales." The nearest you can get in Japan to experiencing that sort of regional variety is with jizake, and even jizake are becoming rarities as more and more of the sake market, which itself has dwindled under the pressure of competition from whisky and shochu, is cornered by mass-produced blends.

"Do they allow people to look round?" I asked the pink-aproned woman, nodding at the painting.

"Oh, I should think so. Just go and ask."

"You'll be lucky," snapped a fierce, unhappy-looking female customer who had come in to eat noodles and was sitting at a table by herself. "I know two people who've gone there to look round and all they've been shown is the door."

"Let's phone then," said the pink-aproned woman sweetly while the unhappy customer glared down at her empty noodle bowl. The answer on the phone was to come round to the shop, so I shouldered my rucksack and paid for my lunch and the pink-aproned woman refused to accept any money for the flask of sake I'd drunk.

It was still raining but it took me less than three minutes to find the Hundred Springtimes brewery, which was exactly as the painting had depicted it: long, low, and dark. When she had had it restored five years before, the plump woman who owned it told me as I sat in the shop sipping powdered tea, it had been terribly difficult to find craftsmen to do the roof. Terribly, terribly difficult. She too wore pink, a fluffy cashmere cardigan, and she spoke in a precise, silky voice appropriate to the purchaser of the kutani bowl in which she had frothed up my tea.

A red-haired schoolgirl from Brisbane named Angela bounced into the shop, said "Ow, 'ello!" and bounced out again, followed by the owner's daughter. They were off to buy cakes and stroll about the town. Angela was an exchange student, the woman explained. She accepted one exchange student a year, always from Australia, and Angela had stayed with her for three months. Now she was staying somewhere else and had come back for the afternoon to visit.

"They like it here," the woman confided. "They like the sense of history. They've none of their own, you see, being Australians. Sake has been brewed here on this site for 230 years. And last year our Hundred Springtimes won a prize."

"Congratulations," I said.

The woman bowed, immensely pleased, and gave me two crumbly tea-ceremony sweets and a small wastepaper bin made of washi.

While we sat talking two men came separately into the shop and asked if they could see round the brewery and the pink-cardiganed woman told them both, politely, that the brewery was not open to visitors. So I delayed asking the same question until I had finished the bowl of powdered tea, and when I finally asked, the woman sent for her head bottler and told him to give me a guided tour. He was a small man in his early forties with flecks of grey in his hair, and he was wearing a green sports shirt and gumboots.

"This is one of the people who helped us win our prize," the woman explained, glowing.

"Congratulations," I said again, and they both bowed, flushed with pleasure.

The head bottler had worked here for ten years he told me, and before that he had worked for Coca-Cola in Nagoya, an appointment for which I chided him sternly, and we had a long, quiet chuckle. Now was not a busy season in the sake brewing cycle. From the end of November through to April 10th each year was when all the real work was done. For that four-and-a-half-month period the brewery employed six male workers from Niigata and they did not take a single day off, not even for New Year. Now there were only the regular women, four of them, doing the bottling, so there wasn't very much to see, but I was welcome to see what there was.

We walked between large green tanks that had the tax bureau's precisely registered volumes carefully printed by hand on each. The tax bureau had required twenty days to do the measuring when the tanks had been installed back in 1962; filling them each with water and then siphoning it off into tiny measuring beakers that might have come from a child's chemistry set.

How much sake did the brewery produce?

Between 150 and 160 thousand *shobin* a year. A shobin is the standard-sized sake bottle and holds a little over 1.8 liters, so the brewery was producing a modest amount, most of which was sold directly to shops and restaurants in Nagoya or closer. The brewery also dealt with a wholesaler who distributed a small portion to Tokyo and then from Tokyo (ah, the wonders of the Japanese distribution system, about as rational as cormorant fishing) all the way back to Osaka.

Was it the local rice or the local water that made the sake a prizewinner?

Oh, the local water definitely. In fact, Gifu rice was too crumbly to be of much use in sake making. Instead, the brewers at Hundred Springtimes used a blend of rice from Shiga, Nagano, and Hyogo (all prefectures in central Honshu, Hyogo in particular being noted for its sake). Did I know what made the difference between the grades? Well, it depended on how much of the rice grain was used and how much was polished away before fermenting. The more of the grain that was used, the rougher and cheaper the sake. The lowest grade, second grade, used about 72 percent of the grain. First grade about 68 percent. Special grade used 55 percent as well as a superior rice to begin with. And for the grade above that, called *ginjoshu* (song brew) only 40 percent was used, and all of the rice for that came from Hyogo.

We stopped at a filtration tank and the head bottler filled a small teacup with new sake for me from the tap. It had a crisp, cold, clean taste and I asked him to join me in a drink.

"No," he said, "I don't drink alcohol," a confession I found every bit as disturbing as his having worked for Coca-Cola. It reminded me of the time I sent back a soured bottle of wine in a posh restaurant in Kuala Lumpur and had to quarrel about it with the sommelier, who was Malay. "Taste it," I kept begging him. "No, sir," he replied seriously, and we both knew that his religion and the laws of his country prevented his so much as wetting his lips with it. "The wine is fine," he kept assuring me. "That is how it is supposed to taste."

How were the changing habits in Japanese drinking affecting the sake business?

"Ah, well," the head bottler admitted, "there's not the same appreciation as there used to be. People like to think they know something about what they're drinking, but nowadays most of them don't. The other day I had to go all the way to Nagoya to apologize to a customer who'd complained about a tiny scrap of some sort of solid stuff he'd found in one of our bottles. It was probably a little bit of a paper label that had got inside during washing. Usually, if somebody complains about something, they'll accept an apology over the phone and we'll send them a couple of fresh bottles by post. But this customer demanded an apology in person. He was really haughty; the president of some small company with maybe a seat on a local committee, and he behaved as though he were the world's greatest authority on sake. So I took three fresh bottles to Nagoya in person, bowed and apologized and went through the whole rigmarole. And he wouldn't accept the sake I'd brought him. He got angry and stood there shouting about how he didn't want any of this newly brewed stuff; he wanted a properly matured vintage. I suppose he'd read some beginner's guide to wine and thought that sake matured like wine does. It doesn't, of course. It's more like beer. You should really drink sake within three months of bottling. And here was this pompous, spluttering man knowing nothing whatever and thinking he knew the lot. . . . "

Back in the shop the pink-cardiganed woman urged me to take a bottle of Hundred Springtimes away with me to drink that evening at the hot spring where I told her I was planning to stay, but the bottle she offered me was heavy and I knew I'd never drink it anyway.

"Come again when it's the busy time," said the head bottler, bowing as I left, "and bring your wife and daughter."

Then I was on the road again, passing another of Mino's sights: an old wooden lighthouse which had also been built in the eighteenth century, to guide the boats that transported washi downriver to Gifu city, and which had a tiny door and what must have been a precipitous ladder inside its pillar of curved blackened planks. Mino wore its badges of age very well; neither snobbily nor scrambling to tout them to every sightseer who got off a bus. I didn't discover until I bought some picture postcards in a stationer's on my way out of the town that the brewer's shop where I had sat drinking tea is a nationally registered "Cultural Asset" said to provide the best extant example of a style of Edo-period roof called *udatsu*. This sort of roof features an elaborately ornamented tiled ridge at either end which, as well as being decorative, was supposed to act as a fire break.

The rain had stopped and the sky was patched with high white autumn clouds. I crossed the clear, calm Nagara on an old bridge of gnarled planks and tramped on up an empty road that followed the meandering river. The mountains rose ahead, tinted with mist, and though, near Mino, the road passed a silent granite factory and a concrete factory and another factory that made toilet rolls, these soon gave way to golden paddies and small woods of strong-smelling pine and, in clumps that bent in the afternoon breeze, the equinoctial red of the Ghost Flowers. Near Tachibana Shrine the screens of a house had been drawn back to let in the autumn sunlight and a funeral meal had been laid out on tables. Black-suited men sat eating and drinking or leaning on the fence outside in the street and staring down at the shallow river. I reached the narrower road that led to Yunohora and turned along it as it wound beside a stream and through an old brick arch on which were pasted the faded advertisements for the inns.

Only one inn, the Yumotokan (Inn of the Hot-Water Source) seemed still to be in business. The pink-cardiganed woman at the Hundred Springtimes brewery had warned me that Yunohora was neither famous nor elegant; just a plain old country hot spring that had seen better days. But the woman at the inn welcomed me with no fuss, sat me in her corridor while she cleaned up my room, and briskly explained the items of my dinner in the manner of a French maître d' when she brought them in to me on their tray. This was a river trout, this was raw carp, these were horse mackerel, and these were horse mackerel's eggs. And this was an extra-special treat: matsutake mushrooms; did I know what they were? They had been gathered that morning in the hill behind the inn, the very first matsutake of the year. They had a rough, raw, earthy smell. I was allowed two minuscule slivers.

I read myself to sleep with the story of Lady Gio from the first book of *The Tale of the Heike*. Lady Gio was a dancer and, at seventeen, had become Kiyomori's mistress. For three years Kiyomori had remained in love with her. Then one day another young dancer turned up at his gate and Kiyomori's fancies changed. Lady Gio was evicted from the palace and, after a year of brooding and weeping, was recalled, but only to entertain the new mistress. Unable to bear the shame and heartache, Lady Gio, at twenty-one, had shaved her head and entered a nunnery. So had her mother, her nineteen-year-old sister, and the dancer who had replaced her in Kiyomori's affections and whom he had loved for one year; she too was seventeen. The dancer had found on a sliding door of the palace the poem that Lady Gio had written there on the day that Kiyomori abandoned her:

> *Grasses of the plain,*
> *You bloom and wither,*
> *Every one alike.*
> *The fate of all things*
> *Is to wait for autumn.*

I woke at twelve, at four, and at six. In the room across the corridor four drunk men kept a loud conversation going all night, and the only dawn chorus in the hill outside my window was the long *piiiiii piiiiii* of a hawk.

❧

My road was old and shadowed and quiet, flanked by woods and steepening hills that the sun strove to peer over. On the opposite bank of the Nagara River, half a kilometer away, the traffic on the newer highway grumbled through a string of smoggy tunnels. But on my side of the river there were no tunnels and the strongest smell was of mud mixed with straw, floating out of the cropped autumn paddies that marked the approach to a hamlet. The river water was crystal clear, every pebble on the riverbed visible even from the road. From time to time the river narrowed to flow through beds of larger stones that stretched from bank to bank, or slewed into rapids and tumbled over boulders, forcing the invisible ayu and the satsuki masu, on their way upstream from the sea in spring, to leap and struggle like salmon. But even at its narrowest the river ran fast and deep. It did not have the played-out look of so many Japanese rivers at the end of summer. And as I walked along my quiet old road while the highway traffic, freed from its tunnels, roared and choked in the blue crisp morning, I pondered the plans that the Construction Ministry and the Water Resources Development Public Corporation had laid for the Nagara River more than twenty years before and which, if realized, would put paid to its bright fast flow and the satsuki masu's struggles.

The Nagara is the last major Japanese river to remain undammed, and moves are well-advanced to dam it. The plan for a dam was approved by the government as long ago as 1968 but actual construction did not begin until twenty years later owing to opposition from local groups, mainly fishing cooperatives in the little towns and cities, whose members argued that a dam would upset the ecostructure of the river and prevent the ayu and the satsuki masu (a species found only in the Nagara) from traveling upstream, and so ruin the fishermen's livelihood. They argued, too, that it would spoil the cormorant fishing, an argument that historians at least cocked an ear to since, although now declined into a tourist amusement, cormorant fishing once enjoyed the protection of the great Oda Nobunaga (who was so impressed by it that he decreed no dams might ever be built across the Nagara) and it still enjoys the official patronage of the Imperial Household Agency.

But the Construction Ministry, during the headlong pursuit of industrial and economic growth that characterized the 1960s and 1970s in Japan, was unmoved by such objections. The purposes of the dam, it bluntly repeated, were flood control, the provision of water to industries in the Nagoya area, and (in a bid to sway the cooperatives) the prevention of seawater flowing upstream and so polluting the fishing grounds and adjacent farmland. Subsequently, opponents of the dam were able to show that salinity in the nearby paddies had substantially declined since the first government surveys were made. They also pointed out that seawater would only flow upstream in disruptive amounts if the ministry's first-stage construction plans, which called for dredging a 25- to 30-kilometer stretch of the river from its mouth, were carried out; no dam, no dredging; no dredging, no pollution. But flood control and the supply of water to industry, declared the ministry, must take precedence over ecological concerns because they placed the welfare of the general above that of the selfish particular (not to mention the welfare of the construction bosses who would organize the building, the politicians who would grow quietly richer by awarding the contracts, the banks who would furnish the loans, the gangsters who would recruit and control the labor, and other elements essential to a happy and efficiently arranged society). This argument has been similarly employed by government agencies at Narita airport; along newly planned bullet-train routes; at the site of proposed nuclear generating, reprocessing, and storage plants; and wherever else local opposition has seemed likely to interfere with money-spinning "development." One by one the fishing cooperatives succumbed to political and other pressures and, after two decades of weary confrontation punctuated by long sessions of repetitive haggling (one concession won by the fishermen was the incorporation of runs for the ayu, though these would be of no use to the satsuki masu), the cranes and bulldozers at last took up their stations on the Nagara's banks.

But the 1960s and 1970s, even in happy, efficiently arranged Japan, had given way to the 1980s, and the obsession with industrial and economic growth at the expense of all else under the sun had begun to be tempered by other considerations, including the first faint glimmerings of a grassroots concern to protect what was left of the natural environment. Previously this sort of concern in Japan had been linked to other priorities, such as an aversion to nuclear energy (Japan's famous "allergy") or an unwillingness to give up for public works land that a family had farmed for generations. Now the concern had broadened and refocused. Now it was not simply particular parcels of family land that were perceived as worthy of protection, but nature itself. And now a new set of mouths began to voice their opposition to the government's 150-billion-yen scheme for the Nagara.

By the beginning of the 1990s the Nagara River dam had become one of two issues over which Japan's fledgling environmental lobby—with aid from journalists, celebrities, and scientists, both Japanese and foreign—had run the government to a standoff (the other is the proposed new airport on the island of Ishigaki which, if built, would destroy one of the East China Sea's most extensive patches of living coral). In the intervening decades, too, the scientists, journalists, and amateur ecologists had acquired an unlikely ally within the Japanese establishment in the shape of the Environment Agency, set up in 1971 as part of the Prime Minister's Office with a director-general of cabinet rank. Both in the matter of the Nagara dam and that of the new Ishigaki airport the agency has, albeit hesitantly, sided with the opposition, urging that original plans be reexamined and calling for more detailed environmental impact studies. Though critics charge that the activities of the agency are largely cosmetic, designed to appease environmentally minded critics abroad, and that, lacking the clout of cabinet colleagues like the Construction Minister and the Minister for International Trade and Industry, its director-general can simply be overruled or browbeaten into silence, this opposition from within was a major factor in forcing both projects to a standstill.

The standstill is over, at least for the moment, and the cranes and bulldozers on the Nagara's banks are busy again, though I saw nothing of them; I had joined the river well above the dam's projected site. But they cast a shadow on the crisp autumn day, and the fishermen I passed, stretching their thin ropes across the river from bank to bank, looked, as much as the satsuki masu, like an endangered species. I asked one fisherman what the ropes were for. The fully grown ayu, the females bursting with eggs, were now on their annual migration downstream to the spawning grounds near the estuary. They were wary of these ropes, the fisherman told me, and not liking to swim under them, they would congregate behind them, so making them easier to net. It was a more practical method than using cormorants, if rather less sporting. But sportsmanship and efficiency, like undammed streams and well-stuffed bankbooks, do not form easy friendships.

3

The Space Between the Rocks

❧

In an unusual graveyard the ghost flowers grew, unusual because all the graves were wooden, roofed like little wells, and grey. And in the next-door field above the drying straw an inflatable balloon painted in primary colors like a bull's-eye served to scare away the scavenging birds. I sat for a few minutes beside three small stone statues that I had taken from a distance to be images of Jizo, the kindly, bland protector of travelers, but which turned out on closer inspection to represent a fierce three-faced goddess called Ashura. In Hindu mythology, the Ashuras (or Asuras) are pre-Aryan demons who fight eternally against Indra, the storm god and warrior king. Originally gods themselves, the Ashuras fell from grace when the Aryans took control of heaven but retained a power almost equal to that of the newer gods with whom they struggle for dominion over the three worlds. These small wayside statues depicted the feminine Ashura in her simplest, most Hindu form:

an angry scowl on each of her faces, a rod of chastisement in one hand, a Karmic wheel in the other, the only concession to Buddhism being the lotus on which she stood or sat.

I was surprised to find the primal Ashura here beside the Nagara River because my impression of her had been wholly conditioned by a long and loving acquaintance with the most celebrated of her Japanese representations, the wonderfully slender, wonderfully ambivalent eighth-century Ashura of the Kofukuji temple in Nara. The Nara Buddhists transformed the frowning demon into a protective Buddhist goddess, her six slender arms devoid of weapons, her presence devoid of threat. But in each of her faces they carved a complexity and a humanity that nothing in the Hindu depictions approaches. There is anger there, and pain, and sorrow, and disinterest, and surprise, and dumbfounded acceptance, and the peace that has come to her finally through knowledge of the Buddha. In fact, if it were not for the slightly perplexed frown with its hint of contentiousness and unease, the central face of the Kofukuji statue that stares out at you above hands joined in prayer could almost belong to the Goddess of Mercy, so unrecognizable is it as the visage of a demon—just as the fat, rollicking Buddha of the Future, arrived in Nara and Kyoto from China, became a creature of such androgynous delicacy, such compassion, such otherworldly beauty that, for all their debt to the ideas of other cultures, it is clear that, so far as the forms are concerned, the early Buddhists of Nara and Kyoto (some of whom had themselves arrived from China or Korea) concocted a pantheon all their own.

Beyond a small hamlet where white-smocked women cooed over babies and walked their toddlers in diminishing circles, the road was closed to traffic; it was being retarred. A wizened old security guard in a plastic helmet blew his whistle very loudly at the only car that had come along all morning and fussed busily and pointlessly about in the dust while the driver made a huffy U-turn that sent chunks of old asphalt crashing down onto the river bank. But I could walk along the road, the old guard told me sternly, as long as I didn't leave footprints in the tar or disturb the construction gang's miniature sandbags, so I was spared for another peaceful hour the need to cross the limpid river, now very still and turquoise-green, and join the uncompassionate highway. In the end I had to, swapping the scent of burning chaff and the tiny eggplants withered on their stalks for the roar and stink of diesel trucks, the clatter of one-coach trains along the parallel railway track, and, for the next few miles, a complete absence of anywhere to sit and rest.

I asked in a large new liquor store if there were any restaurants further along the highway. The prim proprietress and her prim female customer looked at each other with fixed grins on their faces and the proprietress, speaking through her fixed grin, said, "There's one beyond the next tunnel. Five minutes by car. You'll see the sign. It says Sapporo Ramen."

The two women primly chortled.

"Well," I said, "that's a long way on foot. I'll sit and have a beer here if you don't mind."

"I do mind," said the proprietress, still grinning, her lips tight against her even teeth. "You can stand outside and use the vending machine."

So I left, ignoring the vending machine, and an hour later had two Sapporo drafts and a plate of fried noodles as hard as oak twigs in a family restaurant with plastic tables and yellow plastic-upholstered chairs. The midday sun came scalding through the wall-sized windows and I was sweating harder when I got up from my plastic chair than I had been when I'd slumped into it.

For most of the rest of the day I was able to tramp along the empty old road across the river, where huge signboards designed to be read from the highway advertised a ski slope with a brand new "snow machine," a "sky restaurant," and a "radon center" (that is to say, a therapeutic hot spring whose waters contain, either naturally or by design, the element Rn, atomic number 86, a decay product of radium; I trudged on wishing I had brought protective clothing). The radon center was just outside the little town of Gujo Hachiman and I reached it late that afternoon in a state of such weariness that, from a distance, I mistook the word *chainsaw* for *chanson* on a shop sign, and thought I was approaching a coffee house where I could sit and be serenaded by Charles Aznavour. What I was in fact approaching was a town of a kind I'd dreamed of finding when I'd first arrived in Japan almost twenty years before, a town so extraordinary that, when I went out to stroll around it that evening, I almost forgot to limp.

Nothing revealed itself at first; just a low, flat wedge of streets squeezed between the river and the encroaching hills. The highway, as it approached the town and then skitted away from it to the west, gave no indication of its character; the outskirts were clogged with the usual gasoline stations and car dealerships, a cement factory, five-story apartments made of ferroconcrete unpainted except for their bright blue balconies, an unprepossessing ryokan near the station, an air of clutter and dreariness. I turned off the highway and walked down a street of shops towards what I supposed was the town center. A grocer I asked told me that there were plenty of ryokans further on, but I collapsed over the doorstep of the first minshuku I came to, a little short of the town center on a very noisy corner. The middle-aged woman who ran the place explained that she didn't have much food and seemed quite keen that I should go away, but she grew friendlier after I had signed her register and climbed her stairs on feet that I thought would drop off before I reached the upstairs landing. Still, when dinner was over and I had had a beer and a bath and a rest, I clopped out of the front door in the minshuku's wooden clogs and, half a minute later, stopped dead in my tracks, wondering whether, after all the time warps I had suffered in the corporate pavilions at Nagoya, a real one had finally snared me.

All but one of the major English-language guides to Japan, including my own, ignore Gujo Hachiman. It is not in the Japan National Tourist Organization's *Official Guide*, nor in Fodor's, nor in Bisignani's *Japan Handbook*. The exception is Lonely Planet's *Travel Survival Kit* in which the town merits a single paragraph which begins, "There isn't much to see here." Not much to see? Well, there are no roaming herds of wildebeest, no auroras dancing in the night, and Krakatoa is not erupting on the horizon. But what there is to see here is what almost every Westerner who comes to Japan in the first flush of oriental infatuation thinks he will find at every turn and grows bitter over when he realizes he won't.

It is a town of low, dark, wood-and-plaster buildings, paved lanes, and running water. The windows of the buildings are narrow and slatted. The lanes, too, are narrow, steeply walled, and end in dimly lanterned eating places or in small stone bridges that arch over splashing streams. It was like an Edo-era stage set, the sort they show visitors at the Toei film studios, and I half expected a director in a corduroy jacket with a megaphone in his hand to leap out from behind a pot of bamboo shouting "Lights! Camera! *Sutaato!*" There were no parked cars on the streets, no moving ones. Such shops as remained open were of the kind that cater to sightseers—a small, carefully ethnic tea house, a shop that sold woven goods, a shop that sold souvenir dolls and picture postcards—but there were no sightseers lurking among the pots any more than there were corduroyed directors. Posters in the windows of the shops depicted what I soon realized was the town's main attraction: a summer dance festival that is staged almost every evening between mid-July and early September and climaxes during the four days of O-Bon, when the dancing goes on all night.

"The tourists dance more than the locals do," a timid, visibly shaking woman told me when I went into her shop to buy some postcards. She stood in the space behind her tiny counter and her eyes flickered wildly over her stock, as though she were bidding it goodbye. I felt like a man who has emerged from a time machine to endanger the solemn procession of the years, and the woman exhibited, one after another, all the danger signs in her repertoire. "The dance is getting ever so famous," she said, the words spilling out of her mouth in a rush. "Ever so, ever so famous it is. You should see it. Oh, you really should." She was an Inca flinging gold idols at a conquistador, hoping to avoid the *auto da fé*. "Sometimes they do it in the big space at the park, sometimes at one or other of the crossroads. It's not like other festivals where you have to belong to a group to take part. Anyone can join in. You could too." And that—I considered as I left her shop and the woman fled back into the safety of her time warp—that, as much as the number of evenings on which it is staged (thirty-one this year), makes the Gujo Dance a rarity.

I was once asked by the BBC to assist in the making of a television film that would feature a Japanese dance festival. In an early fax, the British producer had explained what he wanted his film to show: Japanese people "having spontaneous, unrestrained fun." My first thought when I read this was to forget dance festivals altogether and find a massage parlor with a two-way mirror. But, alas, the narrator's commentary for the film had already been composed and it referred unequivocally to the "carefree atmosphere of a summer festival . . . the one occasion on which even Japanese hair is well and truly let down." "Here at least," bubbled the script, "they throw themselves wholeheartedly into having fun, and *giri*—the Japanese sense of duty and conformity—gives way to *ninjo*, or spontaneity." Those words revolved glumly inside my head as, having selected an ideal camera position and spent half an hour helping the crew set up, I watched three dozen policemen attach red-and-white festival bunting to two massive grey police buses with wire mesh on their windows which, ten minutes before the dancing was due to begin, were parked in positions that shut off the festival entirely from our view.

Most of the better-known Japanese festivals do not demonstrate a lack of restraint; they demonstrate the opposite: a passion for careful organization. That is not to say that the people who take part in them do not have a good time. In the end the BBC's camera was able to capture enough happy, sweaty faces to satisfy the producer and his fax. But these were not the faces of people unrestrainedly letting their hair down. These were people who had taken the trouble, months in advance, to register with a committee, and had rehearsed for many weeks. They wore costumes identical to those worn by their fellow dancers, went where and when and with whom they were told, were launched on their dance by a loudspeaker command at six-thirty sharp and were stopped by whistles at exactly half past nine. They were also people who clearly derived the main part of the pride and enjoyment they found in participation from being members of a properly organized group, not from acting spontaneously. Perhaps, I suggested to the producer when filming was over, the notion that fun requires some sort of impromptu orgasm of the ego and cannot be the result of collective deliberation is a uniquely Western one. The producer liked the phrase "impromptu orgasm of the ego," although not enough to include it in the commentary.

However, collective deliberation can have its drawbacks, and the crisp distinction maintained at so many Japanese festivals between participants and spectators increasingly results in what used to be (and ought to be) a local celebration turning into an extravagantly mounted show. Sometimes, as at the overly famous Awa Odori in Tokushima city, the show even has a paying audience who climb out of their tourist buses to sit on rows of specially reserved benches. Ironically, the words of the song which accompanies the Tokushima dance go out of their way to encourage audience participation: "The fool who watches the fool who dances is as big a fool, so he might as well dance"; but nowadays every effort is made—by organizers, stewards, tour guides, and policemen—to keep the watching and the dancing fools as separate as barricades and admission tickets can manage. Anyway, it appeared from what the trembling Inca in the postcard shop told me, and from the posters in her shop window, which showed kimono-clad crowds milling about with no discernible sense of direction, that I ought to have brought the BBC to Gujo Hachiman in August and encouraged the producer and the rest of his crew to drop their tools and shimmy.

Personally, I was glad to have arrived in Gujo Hachiman a month too late for the dancing (and since my right foot still felt as though it was about to drop off, I would have been a sidelined fool at best). This evening in early October I had the streets of the little town almost to myself. I followed a paved alley with boulders for walls and came to a small cul-de-sac where a spring of water gushed out from beside stone steps to form two rectangular pools in the road. According to the English explanation which was printed on small blue banners that hung outside each of the shops in the main street leading to the cul-de-sac, this was "The Fountain of Youth, *Sogisui*," and the banners added, "With every good wish for your happiness this holiday," as though whoever contributed the text had spent a good part of his life doing a doctorate in greetings cards. Actually, "fountain of youth" is a fanciful translation of *sogisui*; the word means something more like "water belonging to the local god," but I suppose a local reference would appear too parochial to an urban council bent on encouraging non-locals—especially youthful non-locals—to treat the town as a cross between a theme park and a palais de dance.

I liked the spring and the shops and the bouldered alleys. But more than these I liked the ordinary things: the darkness, the old wood-and-plaster houses, the absence of sightseers, the silence broken not by the grumbling of traffic but by the handheld wooden clappers that warn against fire and the splash of free-running water—things I looked for in every Japanese town, things so unworthy of preservation that in most towns they no longer exist. Most of all I liked the look of the dimly lanterned eating houses and so, though I had only just finished dinner, I lurched into one not far from the Fountain of Youth to drink a beer.

Maybe I chose badly or maybe, now that the tourist season was over and no more kimonoed dancers roamed the streets, all of the little eating houses had acquired the same air of despondency. The only other customers in the place were an untalkative young couple eating grilled frogs, and I sat next to them at the counter trying to think of something to say. The master was burly and unsmiling and had a long scar down his left cheek. He served me a beer and I asked him for a snack to go with it.

"Anything you recommend," I said cheerfully; so he seized the chance to empty most of a very old jar of pickled octopus intestines. For the young couple he grilled more large frogs' legs, sprinkling them with salt and laying them to spit and sizzle on the gas range, and then went back to sit and watch television at the other end of the counter. I didn't pay much attention to the television and it was only later that I realized that the master was watching a documentary about rehabilitating *yakuza* (members of criminal gangs) after they had finished serving prison terms. I realized this after I had managed to startle the other three people in the shop by mistaking the subjects of the program for invalids. I had caught a snatch of the commentary in which the word *rehabilitation* occurred and assumed that some sort of illness was being discussed.

"What disease are they talking about?" I said to the young woman next to me in an effort to start a conversation. She glanced past her partner at the television screen, on which was being shown a botched attempt to remove a large tattooed chrysanthemum from an ex-gangster's shoulder blade.

"Disease?" said the young woman, smiling.

"Yes," I said, "is it some sort of skin cancer?"

"You explain it to him," the young woman called out to the master of the shop, still smiling and devouring a frog's thigh.

The master got up quietly, came and stood opposite me on the other side of the counter, leaned across the spitting frogs with his scarred cheek about a foot from my octopus intestines, and snapped, "Yak'za."

Then he went and sat down again.

I initiated no more conversations. A pal of the master's turned up shortly. He had lightly tinted punch-permed hair, a black suit and a silk tie with roses on it and, after the master had cooked him a huge, oily fish, they sat at the far end of the counter and discussed matters in low voices. I was quite sure that I would be overcharged. I ordered another draft beer and started toting up the bill in my head. I won't pay more than two thousand yen, I told myself, but I bet they'll ask for five. Then what'll I do? In a yakuza film I'd once seen, Ogata Ken took off the wooden clogs he was wearing and belted his adversaries round the head with them. That was the traditional way of doing things, I reckoned, and this was a traditional town. What's more, I was wearing wooden clogs. I reached down below the counter while no one was looking and tugged at the velvet straps of my clogs to make sure they were securely fastened to the soles. The trouble was that my legs ached. And my blisters were really playing me up. I couldn't very well belt my adversaries round the head with a pair of clogs and then stand there waiting for them to belt me back because my legs were too wobbly to limp away on.

I got up to leave.

"How much?" I asked, screwing my eyes into tight little slits and glaring along the counter at the master of the shop, whose pal was frowning glumly at the remains of his fish.

"Thank you. One thousand, eight hundred yen," the scarred master said, coming towards me wiping his hands and beaming broadly for the first and only time that evening.

"Look after yourself and have a good trip," he said cheerily as I crept out of his eating place, my clogs going clip-clop on the tiles of his doorway. Round the streets the clappers that warn against fire still echoed off the paving stones. They echoed through the first ten minutes of my dreams as well; a solid crack of wood on nose.

I took my time over breakfast and watched a television program in which four young Americans temporarily in Japan to study car production assured a satisfied-looking Japanese television host how incredibly much they were learning. Then I went downstairs intending to go out and look at Gujo Hachiman in daylight and ran into the husband of the minshuku, dressed in a khaki outfit smothered in pouches and pockets stuffed with ballpoint pens, who had delayed going to work that morning so that he could tell me what to see. He was a thin man who appeared to be allergic to shaving cream, and he confronted me at the bottom of the stairs with one of the town's giveaway streetplans on which he had inked a route in red and circled the things I must be sure not to miss: the castle, the art museum, the Fountain of Youth.

Gujo Hachiman was a castle town, he explained, speaking rapidly and breathily, a purply-pink skin rash twinkling on his chin, but the castle had been pulled down at the time of the Meiji Restoration and the present tiny castle on its teetering hilltop had been built in the feudal style in 1934 as a "symbol" of the town's former glory. I should go and see it anyway. And I should go and see the art museum as well. And if I was heading up Shirotori way (I was planning to reach Shirotori that evening) I should make a point of stopping off to see the big shrine at Hakusan Nagataki where a museum houses a collection of more than three thousand cultural artifacts, including pottery painted by Ando Hiroshige. I watched the thin, spotty husband with his pockets full of pens getting worked up about Ando Hiroshige, and when he paused for breath I remarked that he seemed to be very knowledgeable. "Yes," he agreed with a curt nod of his head, "but only about things in the neighborhood." And this combination of boast and disclaimer pleased me so much as I wandered out into the street with the annotated giveaway streetplan that I followed all the red-inked lines.

In daylight the pains that the authorities have taken to make Gujo Hachiman attractive to tourists are obvious at once. Everywhere you go there are signboards and maps. The paving stones, upon inspection, look hardly more than three years old and they have been laid symmetrically in fresh clean concrete that must be swept daily and scrubbed twice a week. Their symmetry is particularly striking in the vicinity of the Fountain of Youth and on the road that leads to the art museum. The art museum itself exhibits calligraphy, hanging scrolls, tea ceremony utensils, screens with pictures pasted on them, a nice old well in a shady courtyard, and a carefully restored (not replicated) tea house. It has a fine old stone storehouse too, and a small dumpling-shaped woman at the front desk who became so excited at my appearance that I wondered how many visitors the little museum got. There was one other visitor in the vestibule when I strolled through it on my way out. He chuckled loudly when the excited woman asked me to write my name and address in Japanese in her visitors' book, even louder when I actually wrote them, and then skipped outside so that he would be in position to snap my picture as I left.

On the banks of the Yoshida River a waterwheel spun lazily; it might have been there for centuries but it looked as though it had been installed last week. And along with the posters depicting the dance was one advertising a concert to be given in a fortnight's time at the town's cultural center by the Quintetto Argentino de Arcos. I collected my rucksack from the minshuku and, before tramping off towards the foul-smelling highway, stopped in at an elaborately ethnic coffee shop. A plumpish, grey-suited man whom the staff and the other three customers reverently addressed as "sensei," interrupted a disquisition on the property market in Hawaii to remark loudly as I propped my rucksack against the leg of a rustic table, "Look, Hachiman is becoming international."

"Congratulations," I said to him and offered the assembly a small, lopsided bow. There was a rustle of muted conversation at the revelation that I spoke Japanese and another rustle when the menu appeared and it turned out that I could read it. What did I do for a living, the grey-suited sensei wanted to know. I surveyed property for a consortium of British real-estate agents, I answered. The rustle of conversation ceased and a puzzled silence settled on all but sensei.

Oh yes? And what was I doing in Gujo Hachiman?

Surveying property, I said, and bowed, and closed the menu and ordered Mocha Matari.

Surveying property? What sort of property?

Well, there were a lot of people in Britain interested in purchasing riverside houses with waterwheels.

Sensei nodded and the three other customers looked at each other, and at sensei, and at me.

And since almost all of our Scottish castles had been sold to American and Japanese purchasers, a British pension fund had asked me to recommend a Japanese castle that they might buy. Not an old one, of course, and nothing too large. A small one built in the feudal style around 1934 would be just the ticket.

A young man in a red shirt with his front teeth missing uncrossed his legs.

The woman next to him picked up and put down her tea spoon.

And I had spent the last hour drafting a proposal for the sale by auction of something called—what was it?—the Fountain of Youth.

"You are joking," said the deeply frowning sensei.

"Yes," I said with a straight face. "I am joking."

After that the mood improved and there was no further talk of becoming international.

Out once more on the banks of the Nagara the old road and the highway seemed to have spent the night exchanging souls. The highway was now less clogged with trucks but the old road was wider and straighter and busier and at times acquired the brusqueness of a modern bypass. There was more industry, more new apartments along it, and here and there a gasoline stand or a small cluttered restaurant. The river appeared to have been straightened, too, pointing up like a stretched ribbon towards the range of blue mountains I was steadily nearing, dominated by the 2,702-meter peak of Hakusan, this morning beheaded by cloud. Along the bank of the river abandoned tires had been turned into flower planters and were being investigated busily by bold crimson dragonflies. In one hamlet there was an English conversation school, a newish building roofed with corrugated tin. And across the river on the highway stood a single coffee shop called Bistro de Cafe Gear, Trad Cafe Club, Scene 1986, enough foreign names to start a Left Bank.

I crossed the river to eat lunch in a quiet sushi shop in a township called Yamato. I sat at its counter for the whole of what is usually a restaurant's busiest hour and was its only customer.

Was this the center of Yamato, I wondered. It didn't seem a very lively town.

"It isn't a town at all," explained the sushi shop master. "It's just a collection of separate villages. You could call this the center, I suppose, because this is where the town hall is. But there's nothing even resembling a town, not for another twelve kilometers when you get to Shirotori.

"Still, we've got good fish," the master assured me, casting around for something to say. "We're right bang in the middle of Honshu and we get our supplies from both coasts, from the Japan Sea side as well as from Nagoya. Not to mention what comes out of the river. And, by the way, you speak good Japanese. *Heta na Nihonjin yori jozu.* ["Better than an inept Japanese person"; a popular comment meant as praise.] How old are you?"

"How old do I look?"

"Thirty-five."

"How old are you?"

"How old do I look?"

"Thirty-four."

So, politely, we fumbled for conversation, the master and his assistant standing, smiling, behind their counter and its empty stools, ready for action that never arrived, and the master's thin mother, with silver teeth, poised by the telephone to take delivery orders, of which none came in during the hour I was there. Then I noticed a sumo wrestler's handprint on a square white board on the wall behind the master's head and asked whose it was.

"Oh, that's Konishiki's," the master said, looking round at the huge red-ink palm and fingers and at the illegible, black-scrawled Japanese signature. "He writes a good hand for a Hawaiian, doesn't he?"

"Better than an inept Japanese," I said.

"I don't think that's really his signature, is it, though?" said the assistant. "I think it's printed."

"No, that's his signature," said the master.

"I mean it's a printed version of his signature," said the assistant. "He signed one and then they copied it."

"No, surely it's his signature," said the master's mother. "Isn't it his signature?"

"It's printed," said the assistant. He licked his index finger and rubbed it lightly over the thickest of Konishiki's putative brushstrokes, and his finger came away clean.

"There, what did I tell you," said the assistant.

"Well, I'll be . . . !" said the master's mother, very pleased.

"It's printed," the master explained to no one in particular, beaming proudly round his empty shop at the ingenuity displayed on his wall.

• • •

Late that afternoon I walked into Shirotori behind four small boys who raced ahead of me screaming and looking back and daring each other to wait until I had caught up, which none of them had the courage to do. I felt like Godzilla come up to stomp all over their town, though it hardly seemed worth the stomping. Shirotori was small and squat and empty. Its chief vital sign was the sound of an interview, being broadcast through the omnipresent loudspeakers in the shopping street, with a nationally famous group of adolescent singers and dancers called the O-nyanko (Meow-Meow Girls). "Meow, meow, meow," they went as I trudged up and down in search of a place to stay and at length slumped into a ryokan where a plump, friendly woman with bold red lipstick, an unsuitably bright emerald green blouse, three strings of cultured pearls and a head of hair so solid with lacquer that you could have stood a clock on it, asked me if I would prefer coffee to tea as an offering of welcome.

"I would prefer beer," I told her.

"All right," she beamed, and brought me a can of Asahi Super Dry. "And since this is beer instead of tea, we won't charge you anything for it."

I liked the ryokan at once. The plump woman did all my washing and hung it on poles outside my window while I lay soaking in the bath. When I came downstairs she was feeding the carp in the pond in her old-fashioned courtyard. There were twenty or thirty carp, black and gold and mottled, and all as plump as their feeder.

"They eat what the guests leave," the woman explained. "Rice, pickles, anything at all."

An older woman was plucking small black berries and putting them in a large round bowl.

"Those are wild grapes," the emerald woman said. "And this—I wonder if you know what this is?"

It was a large branch covered with purple-white cocoons; the sort of cocoons from which Godzillas hatch.

"This is *akebi*," the woman said.

"Are those cocoons?"

"No, they're only berries."

"They look as if they've got huge grubs inside," I observed. "What do you do with them?"

"Oh, they're just for decoration. When I was a child we used to eat them. But not any more, no, not any more. We used to call this plant the Princess of the Mountains. Fancy eating something with a name like that."

The plump woman laughed, then laid the branch down, and her lacquered head bobbed, as hard as a mummy case.

In the morning she bustled up and down the stairs and came into my room while I was still in my underpants.

"I thought not. I thought not. Your stuff's still wet. Oh, what on earth are we going to do?"

"Have you got a plastic rubbish bag?"

She bustled downstairs and bustled up again.

"Will this do? What do you reckon?"

We stuffed my wet washing into the rubbish bag and I zipped it away inside my pack. It had been a chilly night, and the twenty-fifth typhoon of the year was meandering up the Pacific coast. The forecast was for solid rain. The woman bustled out and bustled back in.

"Here's a cup of coffee."

"Many thanks."

"And here's the bill. And here are two pens for you to take away as souvenirs. Where are you off to?"

"The Hirugano Plateau."

The woman bustled out and bustled back with a timetable.

"The bus is at 9:30. The ones after that only go half way. You'll miss it if you don't get a move on."

"I'm not taking the bus. I'm going to walk."

"Walk? What do you mean walk?"

"I told you last night I was on a walking trip. I've walked all the way from Nagoya. . . . "

"Yeah, but you can't walk from here to the Hirugano Plateau. It'd take you—why!—it'd take all day!"

When I was dressed and ready to leave, the emerald woman astonished me by going down on her knees on the tatami and assuming a formal posture of entreaty. She lowered her head and it looked from the front like a tight shiny ball of twine.

"And now I've got a favor to ask you," she said. "I wonder if you'd mind having your picture taken. You're the first foreigner who's ever stayed here, you see, and I don't suppose we'll see another in a hurry."

We went downstairs and I stood outside the doorway with the older woman who had been plucking berries. The emerald woman dragooned a passing neighbor into operating her automatic camera. She positioned the neighbor on the other side of the street, skipped back to the neighbor and looked through the viewfinder to make sure that the name of her ryokan was in the frame, skipped back to me, grabbed my arm and said, "Oooo! You're a lovely man!"

The neighbor raised the camera.

"Are you sure you can see the ryokan name?" the older woman asked, turning round to peer up at the nameboard as the camera went click.

"Take another one. Granny's spoiled it," said the emerald woman, clucking at granny and squeezing my elbow.

When the camera had clicked a second time, granny hobbled across the street, took the camera from the blinking neighbor and squinted through the viewfinder to make sure that the nameboard had been shot.

"Come again," she called.

"Come again," called the neighbor.

"Come again," beamed the emerald woman, waving as I tramped away and fingering her cultured pearls. The Meow-Meow Girls were silent this morning and the scattered shoppers who were hurrying along the street glanced up at the louring autumn sky and the locks of the approaching storm.

⁂

The old road had ended; the highway began to steepen and wind. The Nagara valley had narrowed until it was barely wide enough to contain the river, the highway, and the railway track which ploughed on for a further six kilometers and then stopped in the middle of the mountains. All three followed the loops of the valley, pressed into it like one fraying thread. I reached the large shrine near the turnoff for Hakusan Nagataki, which the rashy chinned man in Hachiman had told me housed Hiroshiges, but the treasure museum was closed. At eleven I passed the halt at Hokuno where the railway ended, and the road still climbed. The day grew cooler, the sky bleaker; spots of rain began to fall. This, in winter, was ski country, and on either side of the winding highway signboards advertised shuttered resorts. One had a Hotel Rainbow Tower complete with a French restaurant; another resort was called Heike Flats. The hills rose so steeply from the river that cultivation was all but impossible. Here and there a group of small paddies clung to a patch of what was once the riverbed, but the commoner signs of human attention were ditches and rents and craters in the woods and the mechanical excavators that made them. Three of these were demolishing an entire hillside, clanging and swinging above the road, which was protected from the landslides that threatened to bury it by a wall of pile-driven iron.

By two the river flowed thin and fast, far below the clanging excavators, the doglegging highway, and the Pension San Moritz. Every driver of every parked diesel truck napped or munched with his engine churning and the air in the laybys was as foul as in the tunnels. Most of the buildings I passed were minshukus, but all were closed until the snow. Just after two the rain began in earnest. I sheltered for about twenty minutes under the roof of a garage built onto one of the locked-up minshukus and watched the odd bus come sliding down the curve with its windscreen wipers slashing. But the rain showed no sign of letting up and in the end I pulled on my waterproof gear, spat, cursed, and tramped away. At 3:15 I came to a waterfall which, according to the explanatory notice there, was the actual source of the Nagara, but the rain was pelting solidly and a construction gang was destroying a nearby concrete wall with a pneumatic hammer so I didn't stay to enjoy the view. Finally, just after four o'clock, the road leveled out and I found that I had arrived at the Hirugano Plateau. I was puzzled to see among the first of the buildings there, an alpine church with a red tiled steeple until, wiping the rainwater out of my eyes, I found that it was a shop selling crepes. After that, the Mont Blanc Sky Restaurant, the Restaurant Bremen, the Raspberry House, and the Lodge Wide Pecker came as no surprise at all.

The Hirugano Plateau, I realized as I sloshed along the empty highway between dripping clapperboard pensions, doll's house–like shops stuffed with cuddly toys and flagpoles which alternately flew the drenched Union Jack and the drenched Stars and Stripes, was an intended paradise for the *yangu* (young). At the Hirugano Plateau the yangu could find practically all of the amenities that would have been available to them if they had stayed in their city apartments and not bothered coming to the countryside at all—pizzas, crepes, pop music, teddy bears—except that here they could experience the countryside as well and, when it snowed, the snow. It is not so surprising that the yangu should deck their winter fairylands with foreign trappings when you consider that, despite the reliability and depth of the annual snowfall in many parts of Japan, winter activities such as skiing and skating were unknown here before the last quarter of the nineteenth century, and that all such activities (with the exception of sledding, a traditional children's pastime in some country areas) were originally introduced and championed by foreigners. Skiing, for example, was completely unheard of until, in 1911, a certain Theodor von Lerch, the Austrian military attaché in Tokyo, taught it to the 58th Infantry Regiment of the imperial army stationed at Niigata. Ice skating, the winter sport at which Japan has shown most promise in international competition, was introduced earliest (in 1877 by American expatriates living in Sapporo), but it was not until round about 1910 that it began to catch on.

Eventually I plunged into one of the doll's-house–like cafes, half expecting to find it staffed by marionettes with rosy cheeks who waltzed among the tables with strings attached to their elbows and knees. But it was staffed instead by a neurotically shy woman who, when I asked her if there was anywhere to stay, made whiny noises about three or four minshukus and told me that all of them were closed.

"You mean there's nowhere at all that might take me?"

She seemed to shiver at the thought. I drank a beer while my plastic clothes made a large pool on her pink parquet floor. Then I pressed her to stop being noncommittal. Japanese people often try to avoid recommending one neighboring business over another in case word should get back to the unrecommended neighbor and imagined community harmony suffer. But I refused to believe that, even on an off-season Friday, not a single one of the lodging houses that cluttered this strip of ersatz Alps would, in return for the proper fee, offer me the facility it advertised. And the wet pool on the pink parquet floor was widening by the minute.

"You might try Irori," the woman said at last, closing her eyes and suffering agonies. "It's another kilometer up the road. There's a sign outside that goes round and round like the ones the police use when there's been an accident. Go in even if the sign's not revolving."

"And you think they'll be open?"

She shuddered and winced.

I sloshed along the road and found Irori. The sign wasn't revolving and the restaurant was empty. But a woman was standing in the doorway grinning and holding up five fingers.

"I'm Mother," she announced above the smack of the rain on my plastic hood. "And a room with two meals is 5,500 yen."

"You must have had a phone call," I said, laughing and hanging my rain gear over the backs of three of Mother's chairs.

"Of course I had a phone call," Mother said, looking wise. "Mother must be warned or else where would Mother be?"

Mother was in her fifties, and wore fashionably wide culottes under her Kitty apron. Another woman and a teenage girl were sitting in the restaurant rolling hand towels into tight little tubes but they went home at half past five and, of an evening, Mother closed her restaurant and ran the lodging house by herself. Mother was a wily, lively bird with a voice like a crow's and a face that wouldn't stay still. She gave me a graphic demonstration of the conditions likely to affect her business.

"When the snow is this deep," she told me, holding out two fingers pressed together to make a width of about four centimeters, "it's worth ten thousand yen a day. This much," she said, holding out four fingers, "is worth twenty."

"And what about when there's no snow at all?"

"Then," she said, "Mother waits."

The last two winters had both brought light snowfalls and business had been tricky. It wasn't like in the old days when you could confidently look forward to four meters and Mother would wake up on a snowy Saturday morning and do a jig of joy. "*Okyakusan wa kamisan!*" she would sing to herself, "Customers are gods!" And she would rub her hands together in a gesture that signified, in equal measure, pecuniary expectancy and prayer.

The name of Mother's restaurant-cum-lodging house, Irori, was a perfect token of the snuggliness she busied herself providing. An *irori* is a sunken charcoal hearth round which, before television and electric carpets, families used to gather in winter to grill fish and boil water for tea and, with the aid of quilted blankets, keep the cold from freezing their marrow. You still come across these hearths here and there, in rural minshukus or painstakingly ethnic restaurants where they provide city dwellers with a taste of what they like to call country living. And you can find the heavy timber versions in pricey antique shops in Tokyo and in the corporately rented city apartments of comfortable foreign bankers, converted by the bankers' comfortable wives into plant holders and glass-topped coffee tables. I looked round Mother's lodging house in vain for a glimpse of an actual irori, but she must have judged the name sufficiently cozy and the provision of snuggliness and country living the proprietor's business, not the furniture's.

The other guests at Irori that night were five golfers who arrived very late, company big shots from Nagoya with grey-flecked hair and unmuddied golfing shoes who complained that there was no spin dryer, and a landscape gardener and his two assistants. The gardener, Mr. Hatta, sat separately from his assistants and contemplated a large hand-drawn blueprint of the garden he was building. But when Mother had cleared the dinner trays away and the golfers and assistants had gone to soak themselves in the bath or compare swings or polish their shoes, Mr. Hatta invited me to join him over a bottle of *Oni Goroshi* (Demon Killer)—a rural sake from the tourist town of Takayama, grown like the town itself too famous—and gave me an impromptu seminar on the dying craft he had spent his life serving.

Mr. Hatta was fifty-seven and his son was thirty-six. His son had followed him into landscape gardening, but Mr. Hatta bemoaned his son's approach. His son was full of his own inventiveness, the worried Mr. Hatta sighed; he appeared to think that you could plan a garden off the top of your head. But a garden must demonstrate traditional principles and its designer must steep himself in these principles if he was to produce a garden worthy of the name. Mr. Hatta had followed his own father into landscape gardening and had spent five years as an apprentice in the old imperial capital, Kyoto, the undisputed center of the craft where every gardener must serve his time. After that he had gone to work for himself and then, unsatisfied, he had apprenticed himself again. He had studied flower arrangement and the tea ceremony, arts that he held to be close to his own, and he was especially proud of the license he had obtained to teach classical dance.

Mr. Hatta was a small, wiry man, dressed in a pale blue track suit; his face was brown and leathery and his fingers were like snails. With his snail-like fingers Mr. Hatta moved tumblers and ashtrays and empty bottles about the table to show me how each of a garden's elements acts as an "anchor" for the spirit it contains. These anchors were the key to Mr. Hatta's craft. Unless you understood their use, nothing would come right. The work of a landscape gardener is to recreate the whole of nature in a tiny, predetermined space. Of course, this required great imagination, of course you had to use your head as well as your hands, your instincts as well as your knowledge and training. But you must always build on the bones of tradition. That was essential; always the bones.

Mr. Hatta unrolled again the blueprint he had drawn up for his current project, a private garden consisting only of rocks and sand which would run the length of one side of a house and would cost its owner five million yen— an inexpensive garden, Mr. Hata explained, but at least the cost would enable him to use old moss-covered rocks instead of rocks heaved directly out of a river. But even if you used fresh rocks, the secret lay in how you arranged them. This sort of garden involved a comparatively simple arrangement, since it was designed to be viewed from only one side, although a certain amount of consideration must also be given to the angle from which a guest arriving at the front of the house would glimpse it out of the corner of his eye. The trickiest were courtyard gardens of the sort you found in some old houses and temples, designed to be viewed from three or four sides; these were the ones where instinct and imagination were no match for principles and anchors.

I noticed on the blueprint that Mr. Hatta's current project included a scenic waterfall. Yes, said Mr. Hatta, that smudge of ink represented a waterfall, though in reality it would just be a blue-tinted rock. In a more expensive garden of which he was particularly proud, Mr. Hatta had found an ingenious way of incorporating a real waterfall that did not require a pump but made use of the natural lie of the land. This saved the owner a hefty electricity bill, as well as demonstrating principles and anchors.

Mr. Hatta lived in the small city of Sabae in Fukui prefecture, near the coast of the Japan Sea, and he confined his business to the three prefectures of Fukui, Ishikawa, and Gifu. The homeowners who were most serious about their gardens, he reckoned, lived in Ishikawa, especially in the old castle town of Kanazawa. Some of them would spend small fortunes on a collection of proper rocks. Next came the residents of his own prefecture, Fukui, since they, too, had strong samurai and merchant traditions. And last came the people of Gifu, where he was at present working. Theirs was a farming and a peasant culture and they knew precious little about landscaped gardens except that they wanted them on the cheap. Two different prices were always agreed upon, one for the garden and another for maintaining it. Maintaining it would entail the sending round of specialists once or twice a year: in spring, and again in the autumn when they would wrap up the trees so that they resembled pyramids of straw. Lawns were extremely difficult to maintain because they needed constant attention and Mr. Hatta generally warned homeowners wanting lawns that they would have to look after them themselves. Besides, lawns were un-Japanese. I told Mr. Hatta an apocryphal story about an American tourist at Hampton Court who had so admired the lawns there that he demanded to see the head gardener and asked him for specific instructions on how to create such lawns back home.

"Well, sir," the gardener had begun, and went on to supply the American tourist with detailed information about seeding, weeding, fertilizing, and other essentials. The American tourist made careful notes.

"And then, sir," the gardener said, raising his cap and nodding solemnly as he emphasized his words, "You must roll the lawn, with a heavy roller, once a day for four hundred years."

Mr. Hatta chuckled appreciatively. Yes, he repeated, lawns were un-Japanese.

Towards the end of our anecdotes and anchors, Mr. Hatta produced a glossy brochure which he presented to me in lieu of a namecard. The brochure showed a recently opened theme park in Ishikawa. It was the brainchild of a rich philanthropist who had bought up old buildings from the surrounding countryside and shifted them pillar by pillar to his park. Mr. Hatta had designed the entire arrangement and was especially pleased with his success in incorporating elements of the existing landscape into his design instead of having them bulldozed away. He seemed quite untroubled by the artificiality of a collection of buildings, emptied of their inhabitants, uprooted from their villages, signposted, described in explanatory pamphlets, viewable only on payment of a fee. What troubled him was the reluctance of sightseeing groups to spend more than a quarter of an hour at the park. The buildings now housed traditional craftsmen—potters, glassblowers, and the like—who spent their days demonstrating endangered crafts to busloads of camera-toting tourists. But in order to fully understand what they were doing you had to watch them for a minimum of two hours. And who, these days, had that sort of leisure?

Not the five golfers from Nagoya. They were up and out by seven A.M., discussing their clubs as they waited for their chauffeur.

"Weren't you disturbed by the trucks?" Mother asked when I crawled downstairs to a breakfast of toast and jam. "They're on the road from three o'clock. Terrible din. Didn't they wake you?"

"No," I said, "the golfers woke me. I slept through the trucks. It must have been the Oni Goroshi."

I found Mr. Hatta cleaning his teeth.

"What's so special about the garden at Ryoanji?" I asked him, naming the famous rock and sand garden in Kyoto's most brochured and pamphleted Zen temple.

"The spaces between the rocks," he replied, with his mouth full of toothpaste.

After that Mother took my picture with a bright green throwaway cardboard camera. Then she got an early customer to photograph the two of us together. Then she took a whole series of pictures of me with the plump, pretty, spotty-faced girl who had been rolling hand towels the previous evening and who had turned up to work the toaster.

"This is your big chance!" Mother told her.

I left Irori at ten o'clock, striding away through the space between the rocks.

4
Pickled Culture

❧

Since the winter of the first year of Bunji [the year of the defeat at Dannoura] the offspring of the Heike had all been captured or killed. It seemed that none except those that were still in the wombs of the Heike women survived. . . . "

All of the great Heike warriors who had not died at Dannoura subsequently perished in disgrace. Kiyomori's third son, Munemori, who had succeeded his father in leadership of the clan, was beheaded together with his eldest son and their heads were paraded through the streets of the capital and hung on a sandalwood tree outside the city prison. His eight-year-old son, Yoshimune, was dragged from the arms of his former wet nurse and beheaded on the banks of the Kamo River. Kiyomori's fifth son, Shigehira, who, in a campaign against the bellicose monks of Nara, had burned to the ground the temple of Kofukuji and the Great Buddha Hall of Todaiji, was captured in battle

347

and delivered into the hands of these same warlike monks who first thought of executing him by burying him up to his neck in the earth and beheading him slowly with a saw. But more humane council prevailed and his head was lopped off in the normal way with a sword and nailed to the gate of Hannyaji Temple. "The Brahma leads a tranquil life in his palace," a priest had explained to Munemori on the eve of his execution. "But never forget that a pleasant life such as his is evanescent. How much more so is your life in this world, where everything is transient as a flash of lightning or a drop of dew. . . . "

The Heike children who had remained in the capital, down to those of the retainers and servants, were snatched from the arms of their mothers. The younger ones were drowned or buried alive; the older were strangled or stabbed. The last to be killed was Rokudai, Kiyomori's great grandson, who was captured at the age of twelve, spared until he was twenty-six, and then executed like his great uncles before him.

"And with the death of Rokudai perished the Heike forever," says their chronicle.

But though the flower of the Heike perished, we know (or think we know or are encouraged by local lobbyists to know) that the survivors—the minor clan officials, the distant relatives, the in-laws, those in the wombs of the women—made their way to the far corners of Japan and settled into legend. The Hirugano plateau is 900 meters above the sea and the watershed of central Honshu. Having reached it, if they reached it, the women could descend into hill country undisturbed by war and famine and discharge the fruit of their wombs in peace.

I was surprised, after a week of uphill slog, to find myself descending. I had not expected the road to turn down before the border with Toyama prefecture, sixty kilometers further on. But the Nagara had been replaced by the Sho River, bubbling and churning along the same downhill path that my sodden boots were trudging, and a sign at the border of Shokawa village conveyed, in village English, a cheery, cloudy "Well Come." The headwaters of the Sho were glorious; a chain of waterfalls, boulders, and green pools with the current running swift and clear below the road that followed the narrow valley. The overcast sky and the odd little iron foundry out here in the middle of more-or-less nowhere with its hoists and girders and oxyacetylene burners barely dented, for me anyway, the pleasures of this damp remoteness.

Yet much municipal effort had been expended on improving remote delights. Apart from the Well Come sign at the village border the road was lined with a complete series of explanatory notices that told you everything you might want to know about Shokawa's emblems. The village tree was a white birch (the prefectural tree was a yew) and the village flower was the summer lily that you sometimes found growing amid wild bamboo grass. A signposted park on the river bank, opened two years previously, boasted a number of signposted picnic spots. There was, of course, a "white birch picnic spot," as well as a "bamboo lily picnic spot," and there was a "relaxing picnic spot," a "beech wood," and an "oak wood," each carefully catalogued for the benefit of visiting city dwellers who might otherwise have become disoriented at the thought of having wandered into a wilderness.

Occasional gaps in the overcast brought instant warmth, which didn't last. A minshuku had a notice out touting itself as a *shizuka na yado*, a "quiet inn," but it was separated from the national highway by no more than a thin radish patch. More signboards and explanatory notices were posted wherever a "sight" loomed. A little Jurassic-era fossil, discovered in 1959, mounted on a plinth and surrounded by wire, was accompanied by a printed lecture that took me ten minutes to read. The grandest sight was two old cherry trees that stood above the spot where Irori's Mother told me she had spent her childhood, a spot now vanished beneath the lake created in 1961 by the Mihoro Dam, which, at a height of 430 feet and with a storage capacity of 379,700,000 cubic meters, is the largest rock-filled dam in East Asia. The cherry trees, according to their sign, were 450 years old and had been registered as prefectural assets five years after the dam was constructed. Their huge, twisted, moss-covered trunks and their branches, which spread from the lake to the highway, propped up on posts the size of telephone poles, presented a stark contrast to the unluckier trees, drowned and black, whose branches stuck up, unsignposted, out of the dammed green water.

The pleasures of remoteness, damp or otherwise, had not persisted long. The land that surrounded the cherry trees and the man-made lake was the dreariest and windiest place that I had so far passed on my eight-day tramp. There were no communities in this half-submerged valley; only ghosts and remembered childhoods. Spots of rain fell, very cold, and I pulled on my sweater and walked away past the long, bending bamboo grass, pale brown and fawn and wispy and dying, that clotted the sides of the artificial lake. A low cloud ceiling, no more than sixty meters above the water surface, shrouded the humps of the grey hills, and a procession of sightseeing buses from Osaka slowed as they passed the registered cherry trees, but none of them stopped and the signboards went unread.

At two o'clock I crossed a bridge into the precincts of the village called Shirakawa, a name that means "white river" but which is stained with darker colors. Go-Shirakawa, the seventy-seventh emperor of Japan by traditional count, can be said—and was said by several of his contemporaries—to have been more responsible for the chaos and ruin of the wars between the Heike and the Genji than any other figure, not excluding Kiyomori. Go-Shirakawa's short reign (1155–58) ended long before the wars began, but as the retired, or "cloistered," emperor he continued to wield tremendous power behind the scenes throughout the period of the major "disturbances" until seven years after Dannoura. He at first enjoyed the support of the Heike, then enlisted the help of a powerful monk to reduce their influence at court, then covertly exploited for his own benefit the rivalry between the Heike and the Genji, then played a large part in initiating the feud that was to erupt, after Dannoura, between the Genji leader Yoritomo and his brother Yoshitsune. No one can be certain that Shirakawa village was named for this turbulent twelfth-century monarch (it might equally well have been named for the cheerfully churning river that bubbled, before the dam, through its dreary valleys), but Shirakawa is one of the areas that claims most fervently to have been settled by the Heike, and I suppose it is possible that the low-ranking or as yet unborn Heike survivors, uninformed of court affairs and unaware of Go-Shirakawa's part in their downfall, might have remembered their former loyalty to the scheming emperor when naming their remote new home.

The road that ran through their new home was now a mess of filthy, unlit tunnels, too narrow for the hefty trucks and sightseeing buses to pass each other without scraping the tunnel walls. For miles I came across no buildings, only endless road works in progress that slowed the passage of the trucks and buses till their diesel fumes choked the damp air. Near one of the tunnels half the road had fallen away to crash into the lake, and in another, unsurprisingly, a small Buddhist saint was cemented to the tunnel wall to mark the spot where someone had died. Yet weekend motorists sped through these tunnels without bothering to turn their headlights on, so perhaps the cement mixers that lined the road were there to affix more Buddhist saints.

Eventually, and in one piece, I reached the hulking dam itself and the Mihoro Lake Center Restaurant where I stopped for a beer. The rock-filled dam was a real eyesore. Sorer still was the sight of the 215,000-kilowatt hydroelectric plant and the pylons and smaller generating plants that marred the low hills and cluttered the bends in the road. A smart young man in a waistcoat and tie served me a beer and told me that he had gone to Tokyo when he was fifteen and had stayed there for five years trying to make it as an actor. He loved films, he told me, although since the nearest cinemas were in Gifu city, 110 kilometers away, and Takaoka city, 96 kilometers away, the opportunities to indulge his love were few. After he had been five years in Tokyo his father had fallen ill and he had been pressured into returning home to work in the family catering business. It was the old story, the country boy's lament; I had heard it throughout rural Japan: the triumph of Confucian drudgery over youthful dreams and spry ambition.

"It'll be lonely here in another fortnight," the young man said, glaring out of the window at the dam. "No more tourists until the snow." And no more cinemas until the snow was gone.

The young man outlined his likes and dislikes briskly. The Japanese education system was absurd; he would never inflict it on a child of his. And my walk was absurd in a different way, a way that made him guffaw. If I was planning to spend the night at Hirose Hot Spring, six or seven kilometers further down the road, the place that offered the best "service" was the Fujiya ryokan, which the young man promptly telephoned. "I wish I could meet you again," he said seriously as I paid my bill and walked out of the restaurant to find a red minibus waiting for me, driven by an unshaven, open-mouthed man who had come from the Fujiya ryokan to fetch me and looked utterly distraught when I told him that I would walk. He waited for me at the next tunnel entrance and was puzzled and upset that I hadn't changed my mind. And he waited at the tunnel exit too, his mouth drooping, his eyes downcast. But I apologized and bowed and trudged away down the grey, fumy asphalt road, and the once bubbling Shirakawa River, suddenly drained and made sludgy by its damming, dribbled beside me like a sick dog.

Shirakawa village, I discovered from a paper chopstick wrapper that I had picked up at the restaurant, was relatively rich in folk songs though none was being broadcast from loudspeakers in the normal way of advertising culture as I trudged through the village's precincts. Most of the printed verses on the chopstick wrapper were unfamiliar to me, but in the words of one or two you could detect a hint of how the Heike might have felt on their arrival here eight centuries before. These words, for instance, from "Shirakawa Shossho":

Today there is no more living at ease;
We suffer hardships none can imagine.

Shossho appears to be a dialect variant of *shuse*, meaning a successful position in life, the loss of which must have haunted the Heike long after the fruit of their wombs had grown to rustic manhood. And this verse from "Shirakawa Wajima":

These mountains too deep even for birds to penetrate,
Though those who live here think them their capital.

Wajima is a small city near the tip of the Noto peninsula, a limb of Ishikawa prefecture that reaches far out into the gloomy Japan Sea. The city is famous for its lacquerware and the name of this song is thought to derive from the expeditions that Wajima craftsmen made deep into the Gifu mountains to collect raw sap from the lacquer trees that grow wild here. Collecting sap was a slow and arduous business and the men from Wajima might spend as long as four years among the mountain dwellers of Shirakawa, time enough to observe their plight and the style of life they made from it. In the song the word for *capital* is *miyako*, a virtual synonym for the old imperial city of Kyoto in which the Heike had risen to wealth and power, and from which they had been driven by fire and sword, their children betrayed and slaughtered.

Below the rubbly Mihoro Dam, next to an incongruous sign that warned of the comings and goings of dump trucks, I stumbled across the first example of a registered "sight" that I was to see a lot of during the next three days. Shirakawa village and the neighboring region called Gokayama (Five Mountains), which contains the settlement of Taira, the destination of my trudge, are famous for having preserved a style of architecture known as *gasshozukuri*, which literally means "built like hands placed together in prayer." This term describes the very steep slope of the thatched roofs of these old plank buildings, a style intended to protect them from the heavy snows that are a feature of the region. The example that stood below the dam, and that was signposted in village English (Old The Toyama's Folk Building), was a five-story farmer's house, built in 1827 and therefore, by Japanese standards, ancient. It had belonged to the Toyama family who had farmed the surrounding countryside. But the steepness and close encroachment of the mountains had so reduced the amount of arable land available to the Toyamas that they had not had the option, common in flatter, more cultivable regions, of setting up their second and younger sons in branch families with separate dwellings. So father, mother, eldest son and family, uncles, aunts, brothers, sisters, nephews, nieces, and grandchildren had all lived together under this one steep roof—more than forty people in all—and the unusual size of the building (22 meters long, 13.3 meters wide, and 14.5 meters high) amply reflected its occupancy.

Though the house has five stories, only the ground floor and what might loosely be called a mezzanine were available for human habitation. The upper floors were used for storage and for the raising of silk worms. These stories could not have been lived in in any case since chimneys appear to have been unknown to Japanese builders of the time and the great amount of thick oily smoke generated by the vast ground-floor hearth was allowed to find its way through gaps in the upper floors and escape finally through the thatch. I wonder the silk worms didn't choke to death.

It is often said in connection with traditional architecture that, like the mother of Irori, most Japanese people have no trouble tolerating the winter cold but are driven barmy by the summer heat. Thus, the gaps and cracks in a house's walls that result from the warping of ill-seasoned timbers or the wearing and tearing of paper screens or—dare one say it?—insufficient skill on the part of the builders tend to be regarded as blessings, and the draughts that swirl and eddy through such cracks at the height of summer are greeted with relief. In some parts of Japan, particularly in the north and in areas that face the wild Japan Sea, these draughts—which by November have turned to blasts—are partly suppressed during the winter months by the charming expedient of wrapping the entire building, or at least its lowest story, in a flexible overcoat made of woven straw that will not be removed until May. From the displayed photographs and sketches of gasshozukuri in winter I gathered that this was also a practice in the mountains of Shirakawa, and in the huge dark downstairs of the Toyama house I shivered at the thought of snow.

Needless to say, the Toyama house has been designated an Important Cultural Property and made the responsibility of the village authorities who have turned it into a museum. As its explanatory English pamphlet notes, "the house is so spacious and dimly lighted inside that it is not fit for our modern way of living." It is fit only to remind us of what "the real Japan" was like once upon a time and to provide visitors with an opportunity to go "oooh" and "ahhh" and "*natsukashii*" ("that brings back memories!") at the sight of battered old farm implements that they have no idea how to use. I paid the 210 yen entrance fee and spent an hour sitting at the beautiful old hearth that still smelled of charcoal ash, under thick black beams that oozed a stink of oil and fish and radish and smoke.

It was after five when I reached Hirose Hot Spring, whose buildings sparsely lined the single road I had been trudging along all day. The ryokan that had been booked for me was the last building on the left and I received a friendly, unfussy welcome from the owners' nineteen-year-old daughter who gave me a little toy pair of clogs and said, "You've had a tiring time."

"This is a nice old place," I said.

"Too old," she replied with a little grimace, and showed me the sights in the downstairs corridor, which included two stuffed brown bears and a framed picture of the supposedly glamorous daughter of a lousy screen actor well-known for his portrayal of gang bosses. I once also saw him portray a junior high school teacher whom he endowed with all the mannerisms of a gang boss. In the picture, which had been taken to advertise the hot spring, his daughter was sitting in the outdoor bath with no clothes on in the snow. She and her crew had flown down from Tokyo to Toyama, had then driven up here by car, spent three hours snapping and being snapped in the bathtub, driven down to Toyama again, and flown back to Tokyo, all in the same day. The owners' daughter cited this itinerary as a perfect instance of pottiness. Then she showed me another framed picture which featured the lousy screen actor's daughter posing with the local headmaster who, as soon as he heard that a celebrity was due, had grown extremely lively and insisted on being included in the shoot. The owners' daughter, whose headmaster he must once have been, thought this was an even clearer instance of pottiness. And then, not thinking it potty at all, she showed me a third framed photograph of bulldozers constructing the Mihoro Dam, admiring the rubbly eyesore as though it had set a permanent seal of loveliness on the landscape.

I went and sat in the outdoor bath, vacated now by actors' daughters and occupied only by two young men with brusque manners and gruff speech, policemen rather than gang bosses. They were drinking lumpy white *doburoku* (unrefined sake), apparently the tipple of the region since a poster in the ryokan's entrance hall advertised a doburoku festival, due to take place in a few days' time: all the unrefined sake you could drink for free so long as you didn't keel over. The gruff young men were sipping their doburoku out of elegant red lacquer cups and after some hesitation they offered me some. It had a fruity taste, I remarked appreciatively. No, not at all, it was made from rice, said one of the young men as though instructing a creature who had just fallen out of the moon. Shortly after that the policemen went away and I had the bath to myself.

The bath was a rocky pool on the opposite side of the highway from the ryokan, connected to it by a footbridge. It felt a little like bathing on a race track. Next door was an all-weather tennis court that had been advertised for miles back on placards along the highway; I had feared some sort of hulking sports center. But the ryokan was old and dark, full of the twisting corridors and sighing stairs that give a building character and a traveler, oddly, a sense of not belonging. This is my home, the daughter had told me with a little grimace about its age; certainly it wasn't mine. The outdoor bath was not very hot, so out of curiosity I recrossed the footbridge and transferred myself to the wooden indoor tub. The water at Hirose Hot Spring comes out of the ground at 90 degrees centigrade and is cooled in stages before it reaches the tubs. The distance it must travel to the outdoor bath cooled it more than comfort required, but the indoor bath was almost too hot to sit in. I stuck it for five minutes and then lounged on the scalded rim, faint and staring at the steamed-up windows.

A middle-aged guest came down for a dip, got into the tub, said "Ouch!" and got out again. "Are you alone in there?" asked a female voice from the other side of the peeling plaster wall. "No, I'm not alone in here," said the guest. "There's—you wouldn't believe it—a gaijin!" And to me in English, "Once more let's challenge!" The guest plunged in, said, "Ouch! Ouch! Ouch!" and jumped out after thirty seconds.

Dinner included a mixture of chopped-up vegetables in fermented bean paste which were grilled over paraffin wax on a dried magnolia leaf. It took a lot of effort, the owner's wife explained, to find fallen leaves the right size and to wash them. I must be careful to see that the leaf didn't char. I fell asleep and burnt the leaf to a black lump, and the rain that came down from the early morning pounded the outdoor leaves where they had fallen: soggy dinners for a fortnight.

The rain had not let up by breakfast (fermented bean paste, slightly damp leaf) and I sat for an hour in the outdoor bathtub with the rain streaming down my face, trying to get warm. I spent another hour chatting up the owners' daughter, twenty minutes stuffing my damp clothes into the plastic rubbish bag she had found for me, and finally set off at half past eleven through a teeming downpour that was turning to sleet. Cold and swearing, I trudged along the highway and, since it was a Sunday, spent a great many minutes cowering out of the way of sightseeing buses. On the north-facing slopes the wind drove rain into my eyes and mouth and ears and neck, and by the time

I reached the picturesque thatch-roofed valley which my map called Shirakawa Gassho Village and which squatted under the second of the Sho River's famous eyesore dams, I was in no mood for sights. Of the first four gasshozukuri buildings, one was a museum, one was a souvenir shop, and the other two were restaurants. I tumbled into the first of the two restaurants, stripped off my dripping plastic trousers, and sat in a widening pool of rainwater at a table with seven elderly Australians.

The Australians were a retired policeman, an engineer, a sheep farmer, their wives, and a plump, mole-faced, plummy woman who sounded exactly like Margaret Thatcher and told me that she had been born in Rugby, England, but had lived in Australia for forty-two years. She admired "Japanese discipline," she explained. There was too much slacking and striking in Australia. It took me ten minutes to attract a waiter.

The sheep farmer, who was sitting on the other side of the plummy woman, beckoned me over to chat with him. "They told us to be on the lookout for wildlife," he said, winking at the retired police officer while the entire party took stock of my appearance. The farmer was fat, wore a soggy rabbitskin hat, and was keen to tell me about the war. "I was like James Bond," he told me grinning. "I had a license to kill Japs. . . . "

"Mind you," he said seriously, "I reckon they're a friendly bunch. Even when we were fighting 'em I reckon I understood 'em better than most Australians do. The Jap soldiers lived a lot more rugged then we did, so naturally they treated their prisoners worse. You're lucky; you weren't even a gleam in your dad's eye. And what do you do here, if you don't mind my asking?"

"I'm a writer," I told him through a mouthful of hot noodles.

"You're just the gent I've been looking for," he said and clapped me across my wringing wet shoulder blades. "Maybe you could help me with a little project."

I groaned. The mole-faced woman removed from between her lips the rosy stone of a pickled plum and glared at it with Thatcherite distaste. The sheep farmer took out of his jacket pocket a crumpled letter in a painstaking hand addressed to the editor of the *Japan Times*.

"You could tart it up a bit," he suggested, and gave it to me to read. The letter was about a Japanese driver whom the farmer had met in North Borneo five weeks after the war had ended. The farmer was keen to trace the driver so that they could have some sort of a reunion. The letter went on for two ballpoint-penned pages.

"It's fine as it is," I told the farmer, "it doesn't need any tarting up."

The farmer's wife, who was sitting with the other wives on the retired police officer's side of the table, said to her husband, "You ought to try this," and held out a chopstick with a glob of fermented bean paste on its tip. The farmer looked at it quizzically, as though it had just been fished out of his sheep dip, and his wife said, "Use your finger." The farmer took the chopstick from her, licked the tip of it with his tongue, and said, "It doesn't beat Vegemite." His wife took back the moistened chopstick with a pucker of Thatcherite irritation and attempted to remove her husband's saliva from it by dunking it in her tea. "Quite tasty really," the farmer said and got up and went to the lavatory. When he came back he spent several minutes assuring me that, despite occasional rumblings from the Australian immigration authorities, Asians could be decent chaps.

"There's one or two quite fine Asians in Perth," he told me. "Doctors and so on; brainy blokes." His license to kill, he mused solemnly, had expired long ago.

"How are you enjoying your trip?" I asked him.

"The countryside's very nice," he said and we both stared through the window at the blinding rain. I felt a twinge of pity for the seven Australians and their Japanese-American guide who had been born in the United States, been brought back to Japan at the age of ten when war had broken out, had lived in Nagoya for the past forty-seven years, and still carried an alien registration card, which she drew from her handbag and proudly flourished. They had come to these thatch-roofed valleys between times. A fortnight ago it had been blazing summer; in a fortnight's time the hills would be a riot of scarlet and crimson and umber-flecked gold. Now all they had was the teeming rain, and as I pulled on my sodden plastic trousers, the farmer said, "Now, mind, if you're ever in Perth . . . "

I saw nothing that afternoon nor wanted to. All I wanted was to get myself dry. At a quarter to four I waded into the touristy village of Ogimachi where forty Honda motorcycles were lined up outside a thatch-roofed coffee shop, and asked at the first ryokan for a room. The only room free, the okami-san told me with an elaborate apology, was one that overlooked the highway, but I would have accepted a cubicle in a public lavatory as long as it meant getting out of the rain. In fact, during my impoverished student days, I had spent one or two nights in a public lavatory and it wasn't half as bad as it sounds. At any rate, the ryokan in Ogimachi was far more comfortable than that, and, what's more, Bruno Taut had stayed there. Bruno Taut stayed here you know, said the okami-san as she showed me to my room. Bruno Taut stayed here, said the Ogimachi pamphlet that I found among the comic books under the television stand. Who the fuck was Bruno Taut, I wondered, hoisting my stinking clothes out of their rubbish bag and arranging them around the walls.

Bruno Taut (1880–1938) was a German architect who came to Japan in 1933 to escape the Nazis (an interesting choice of destination) and spent the next three years here. During his stay he became a champion of some of the forms of traditional Japanese architecture. He especially admired those forms that he felt demonstrated a simplicity of line and a sensitive use of natural materials (despite his own reputation for a "progressive" use of steel and glass) and he waxed particularly enthusiastic about the seventeenth-century Katsura Detached Palace in Kyoto, an example of what he called "emperor art," while at the same time pouring Teutonic scorn on the extremely ornate style of Toshogu Shrine at Nikko, which he called, disparagingly, "shogun art." He was also, it seems, an admirer of gasshozukuri and, in his more fanciful flights of enthusiasm, compared the "uniqueness" of these rough thatched buildings to the Katsura Palace and the Grand Shrine at Ise, comparisons that might, in 1933, have been taken for instances of lese majesty and sacrilege, did not Japanese people nurture the highest regard for visiting foreign intellectuals who say nice things about them and their artifacts.

Bruno Taut made an appearance, though only as a respectfully intoned name, in the videotaped television documentary that all the guests at the ryokan were required to watch as we ate our communal dinner. The ryokan had a large video screen that descended heavily from the dining room ceiling and was revealed when purple curtains parted—a touch of drama that fostered my growing suspicion that I had wandered not into a village but into a theme park. The videotaped program was an old one and the high point of the entertainment for me was its interruption by an urgent newsflash announcing that British troops had landed in the Falkland Islands. Otherwise the program showed the rethatching of one of the area's gasshozukuri houses, a massive operation involving perhaps a hundred volunteers, whom a master thatcher ordered about through a red plastic megaphone. A gasshozukuri roof requires rethatching every three or four decades and the area aimed to do one a year, but even this modest program was threatened by the dwindling number of thatchers and the rapid extinction of their craft. Within the next few years, the narrator predicted, all the gasshozukuri buildings in the area would disappear except those singled out for special protection by the prefectural government.

The dinner companions with whom I contemplated this slow disappearance of a nation's treasure, recognized and admired by Teutonic architects but looked on indifferently by the nation's own with the wherewithal to prevent its vanishing, were four youngish people from neighboring Nagano prefecture who insisted on dragging my table, which had been set up in splendid isolation, over next to theirs so that we could all be "friends." They were two men and two women whose exact relationship with each other, if it extended beyond "friendship," I never fathomed.

"We're all good friends," they chirruped as they rearranged my dishes and chopsticks. "He's my good friend and I'm her good friend and now you're a good friend of us all."

I spent the first five minutes in their company fearing that I had fallen in with a group of born-again religionists who were going to sod up my plans to drink beer. Once, shortly after I arrived in Tokyo, I emerged from the shower in my apartment stark naked to find two quite pretty young women, whom I had never set eyes on before, standing in my kitchen. Unimpressed by my nudity, they announced that they had come to cook my lunch and proceeded, while I hurriedly pulled on trousers, to do this from ingredients they had brought with them in a shopping bag. You're on to a good thing here, I thought to myself when, over the lunch which they had cooked me and in the eating of which they refused to join, the two young women went on and on about what good friends the three of us were going to be. But as soon as I had finished eating lunch, they insisted that I accompany them to a local gathering, held at a "good friend's" nearby flat. This, after a couple of guitar-accompanied songs of the "We Shall Overcome" type, turned into a tirade against all things foreign delivered by a man with a badly scarred face who said that he had been born in Hiroshima to a nodding, smiling neighborhood group which I finally recognized as a chapter of the lay Buddhist organization called Soka Gakkai. After this taste of international friendship I made sure, whenever I went into my shower, that the front door was locked.

But the four ryokan guests from Nagano showed no sign of being born again or of wanting to sing songs or deliver tirades, and joined me with lay enthusiasm in polishing off eight large beers.

"Aren't Japanese people splendid!" said the man sitting next to me who had small grey flecks in his hair. "We're so kind and welcoming! We make friends with *anyone!*"

What did he do for a living, I wondered in order to change the subject.

"I run a pork cutlet restaurant," he laughed, and his friends, too, found this irresistibly funny. "I don't look as if I run a pork cutlet restaurant, do I?"

And what were he and his friends doing in Shirakawa?

They had come to play tennis on the Fujiya ryokan's small court, which they had booked for the following morning. And when I joined them at breakfast the following morning the restaurateur with grey-flecked hair was into his second pre-tennis beer. There were videos at breakfast too; one about a local lion dance supposed to date from the time of the Heike, and another about shoveling snow off thatched roofs. I watched these but I didn't linger, and I didn't join the tennis players in their warm-up beers. I was out by nine to look round the village, or the theme park; it was no simple matter to say which.

True, there were villagers about, or people who looked like villagers are meant to look. They were mostly elderly, as villagers are, and they all wore straw hats and had straw packs on their backs and were willing to oblige youthful photographers with throw-away cameras and middle-aged photographers with cumbersome tripods by standing under some picturesque eave and gazing in the direction of Mount Hakusan. Some of the village houses, too, were lived in. Billows of steam came off sodden thatched roofs as the morning sun did its best to dry them, and looked to the casual eye like smoke from hearths, so that even the pretend houses appeared to be inhabited. The pretend houses were souvenir shops and restaurants and coffee bars, all seen by the visitor to their best advantage from the Ogimachi Viewing Point, a specially constructed sightseeing platform toward which, after snapping straw-hatted villagers, the photographers all made their way. But rice straw dried in stooks by the roadside and the morning sky, blue and breezy, made a stroll round the paths a pleasant exercise, even to one who had come equipped with neither camera nor tripod nor the willing suspension of critical appraisal upon which theme parks rely. I was reminded, strolling round the breezy paths, of why I had come to Japan in the first place—not in search of the coyly picturesque but of something I had thought might be living and was dead.

What had brought me to Japan in the first place, almost twenty years before, was theater; in particular the form of theater called Noh. I had studied drama as a degree subject at Birmingham University—a fatal mistake, I now believe, since drama is a practical art like thatching, and to turn it into an academic discipline, or at least to do this before one has properly mastered the practical essentials, is to imperil both a love for it and the will, as well as the competence, to pursue it as a vocation. I had always believed that theater was my vocation, a belief that arose out of love. But by the time I had spent three years trying to work out to what extent narrative was essential to dramatic tension, and whether Brecht or Artaud or Stanislavski or Grotowski was the One True Prophet who held the Tables of the Law, my love had turned to something like impatience and my aptitude for the practice of theater to a woeful fondness for grandiloquent theory.

My favorite grandiloquent theory was that, in order to survive the competition of film, television, and other newfangled media (which it actually showed every sign of doing whether I spun grandiloquent theories or not), live theater must make a return to its "roots." These roots, whether in the West or the East, were religious. I did not believe that modern theatrical performances should resemble church services but I did believe that, if they were to realize their fullest potential for "involving" (a dangerously theoretical notion) their audience, they must contain strong elements of celebration and ritual. The ancient impulse that brought performer and spectator together was shared belief—in God, or the preeminence of Athens, or some similar communal creed. The duty of those who worked in modern theater (I insisted to anyone daft enough to listen, including a committee of the Arts Council from whom I spent six months failing to obtain a grant) was somehow to resurrect this impulse. Well and good, but how?

In my postgraduate year I directed plays, in the university and in local theaters, which could be made to contain strong doses of ritual and which seemed to me to celebrate something—though it was usually hard to say what this something was. All of the plays I directed were classics; tragedies rather than comedies. I directed *Doctor Faustus* with a huge pentagram for a set, Racine's *Phaedra* in what I fondly thought was medieval Japanese costume (arguing, when challenged, that the spareness of line and color—"like ink paintings"—mirrored the famous spareness of Racine's verse). I directed *Hamlet* in the Bad Quarto text ("But you lose all the poetry!" squirmed Professor John Russell Brown, later dramaturge to the National Theatre, bursting with irritation at the fact that my production and not his was representing Britain at a festival in Belgium) with a backdrop of two huge playing cards, the King and Queen of Spades (death, chance, special providence, king of shreds and patches, all that). I directed Sophocles' *Oedipus Tyrannus* and *Oedipus Coloneus* in one long evening in a stone circle near Edgbaston cricket ground, complete with altars labeled Alpha and Omega and an obliging sun (the real one) that sank nightly over the action at the very point when Oedipus put out his eyes.

Then, when I was beginning to run out of familiar masterworks that might be squeezed into my scheme of things, I came across Donald Keene's *Anthology of Japanese Literature* in a second-hand bookshop in Malvern. At university the Japanese arts had interested me in a vague sort of way. I had been to exhibitions of woodblock prints, bought a book on Japanese architecture, and had had to partly carry my lapsed Catholic girlfriend out of a Birmingham cinema at the end of a showing of Shindo Kaneto's *Onibaba*, because when the old hag in the demon mask leapt over the pit that she was supposed to die in crying, "I am a human being!," my lapsed Catholic girl-friend fainted. This event provided me with sufficient encouragement to pursue my interest in the Japanese arts, so I bought the anthology despite its costing twenty-one shillings and found in it translations of four Noh plays, which I read with mounting excitement.

The Noh theater dates from the fourteenth century when, out of a hodge-podge of ancient literary texts, folk dances, and religious or semi-religious rites, a father and his talented son, both actors, concocted a highly sophisticated dramatic form that appealed at once to the ruling classes with their newfound interest in Zen Buddhism and was to remain a highlight of officially sanctioned Japanese culture down to the present day. A small cast of actors or dancers, a chanting chorus, and three or four onstage musicians portray events from legend or from, say, the Heike saga in a manner that exquisitely emphasizes the sense of evanescence, resignation, and inevitability that pervades *The Tale of the Heike*. Typically, a wandering monk encounters a mysterious stranger who alludes to long-past events in a manner that eerily suggests first-hand experience. Then, after a short interlude, the stranger reveals himself to be, for example, the ghost of a young samurai and performs a dance to celebrate the circumstances of his life or death and to exorcise his sorrow.

Masks and elaborate robes, a sparsely decorated stage, a short, poetic text capable of almost infinite expansion through the introduction of ritual movement and gesture, a subtle melding of past and present, an absence of anything so vulgar as narrative tension, a simple theme that reinforced an understanding shared by performer and spectator—all these fed my freshly graduated sensibilities like manna from Heaven. Within days of reading them I had determined to stage productions of two of the plays in the anthology, one called *Uto*, translated as "The Birds of Sorrow," in which the ghost of a hunter reenacts the trapping and killing of birds that have condemned him to the Buddhist Hell, and another called *Aya no Tsuzumi*, translated as "The Damask Drum," in which the ghost of an old gardener who committed suicide out of unrequited love recalls the cruel trickery of which his infatuation made him victim.

I had never seen a Noh play performed but that didn't matter. I was not interested in trying to copy a performing style; I was interested primarily in the fact that here in a form of drama still apparently alive and well in present-day Japan resided all the elements that I believed live theater required to secure its role in modern society, not least an unbroken connection with its "roots." I staged the plays as modern dance dramas with six female performers dressed in leotards and tights. We used masks, a bare stage, small percussion instruments that the dancers picked up, played, and discarded in the course of the action, and a great deal of mime and ritualized gesture which we made up as we went along. The year in which I did all this was 1970, the same year in which a highly publicized international expo was being held in Osaka, mildly contributing to the passing interest shown by a handful of British intellectuals (such as the manager of Better Books in the Charing Cross Road who sponsored our London performances) in things Japanese. The *Mainichi Shinbun* sent its London correspondent to review my Noh plays (he spent the evening smiling smugly), and I subsequently found myself being asked to give talks on Japanese theater at British universities.

At which point even the freshly graduated I was forced to stand still a minute and take stock. Not only had I never seen a Noh play performed, I had never heard either chant or music, I knew nothing of the history or techniques of Noh nor about any of the 240 or so plays in the repertoire other than the four that I had read in translation. But I was hooked; hooked so firmly that I decided to travel to Japan—a much more adventurous decision in 1970 than it is now—in order to see the Noh for myself. An Arts Council grant having failed to materialize, I had no money for such a trip. So I signed a contract with a London-based language school to teach English in Tokyo for two years (I anticipated breaking the contract and going back to England after one), in return for which I was given an air ticket and allotted a four-and-a-half-mat room in Ikebukuro furnished with a refrigerator and an electric fan.

I arrived ninety-seven days before Mishima Yukio stuck a sword into his belly and had his head lopped off in an office at the Ground Self-Defense Force's headquarters in Ichigaya. Tokyo struck me as a lively place. In between teaching English conversation (not English, which is taught by properly qualified Japanese senseis who do not speak a word of it), I spent much time at Tokyo's principal Noh theater, the Kanze Kaikan, where, after a brief spell of innocent awe, I was assailed by disillusion.

Now that I had seen it in the flesh, it was no longer so easy for me to say, as I had cheerfully said to my cast of dancers in the Charing Cross Road, that the Noh theater is a living force. So culturally edifying is the Noh that great pains have been taken to pickle it. Like much else in Japan that is deemed worthy of awe, the Noh has been stripped of any connection with life as it is actually lived and frozen into a fossil. Far from actively "involving" modern spectators, it haughtily ignores them. Its outward forms have remained as unchanged as possible since the time of its fourteenth-century founders (the most important change, an unplanned one, is that the pace of the performances is far slower today than it can possibly have been in the fourteenth century owing to the exquisite care and precision with which the original steps and gestures have been mimicked down the generations). The result is not so much that we feel that we are participating in a live experience as that we are receiving a lesson in the history of aesthetics. It is rather as if all modern productions of Shakespeare's plays in England were mounted on replicas of the Elizabethan stage, in Elizabethan costumes and in the broad Devonian dialect which spoken English in Elizabethan times is thought to have resembled. This procedure would certainly be of interest to a small band of antiquarians, and it is also likely that professional directors could learn some important lessons about stagecraft from it (as, indeed, were learned when William Poel and Harley Granville Barker championed a revival of Elizabethan staging techniques for Shakespeare in the earlier part of this century). But if every performance without exception were staged according to such antiquarian yardsticks, Shakespeare would very soon forego all claim to the attentions of any other segment of society. Scholars and "connoisseurs" might twitter with satisfaction but anyone interested in the content and meaning of the plays beyond their outward forms, anyone in search of shared beliefs or the salvation of theater in modern times, or simply an entertaining evening out, might as well go hang.

The performers of the principal roles—the *shite*—whom I went to see at the Kanze Kaikan were mostly men in their sixties and seventies playing teenagers or young unmarried women. Verisimilitude is of no importance in the Noh, and the most respected of these performers, some of them officially designated by the government as Living National Treasures, more nearly resembled Dying National Treasures. The members of the audience, too, were mostly middle-aged or old, obviously well-heeled and with a lot of leisure time to dispose of. By far the majority came not in search of revelation or catharsis or pleasure, but because they belonged to study groups. Prominent among them were the parties of elderly kimonoed ladies who attended weekly chanting lessons and spent entire afternoons at the theater with their heads buried in the elegantly calligraphed play texts that they had brought with them, never raising their eyes to look at the stage. Those who did not follow such texts, or did not belong to study groups, tended to disregard the language altogether and to fix their attentions on the music and dance. One reason for their doing so was that the language of Noh, like everything else connected with it, is fourteenth-century and, especially when chanted through a mask with no mouth opening by a Dying National Treasure, is about as comprehensible to a cross-section of modern Japanese society as an oral rendition of Beowulf in the original would be to a cross-section of modern British society.

Soon I began to find the museum-like atmosphere in the Kanze Kaikan stifling and I went there less and less frequently, although I did not altogether lose my interest in Noh and thought hard about how to sustain it. I decided that, instead of merely paying to watch the plays, I must acquire a practical knowledge of one or other of their constituent arts: music, chant, or dance. Since, when I arrived in Japan, I spoke not a word of Japanese, much less read fourteenth-century literary texts in elaborately illegible calligraphy, chant appeared to rule itself out. Lessons in *shimai*, or dance, I discovered after a couple of tentative enquiries, were very expensive and concerned themselves exclusively with the perfecting of *kata*—outward forms—with no reference whatever to meaning or message or grandiloquent theories about "roots." That left music, and by a happy coincidence one of my English conversation students, a young woman for whom I had conceived an infatuation, turned out to be taking lessons in the *kotsuzumi* hand drum, which is an important— arguably the most important—part of the Noh's instrumental ensemble.

The young woman was happy to let me accompany her to her kotsuzumi class (her mother was less happy), where I was introduced to her teacher who agreed to give me lessons. So once a week for the next few months I knelt formally for forty minutes at a stretch on the tatami floor in front of this teacher, my knees, calves, and thighs on fire, struggling to disentangle the drum from its wrapping cloth, to grip it properly with the fingers of my left hand and to position it at the correct angle on my right shoulder. No further steps—such as actually producing a sound from the drum—could be contemplated until I had mastered these niceties of form. Once or twice I ventured to ask in painfully rudimentary Japanese a question about the rhythmic structure of the Noh. The teacher frowned. The young woman who had introduced me to the art (and for whom my infatuation was fast proving subject to the eternal evanescence) blushed. The three or four other pupils present giggled quietly among themselves and whispered to each other things like, "It's so difficult for a foreigner to understand. . . . " But understanding played no part in the proceedings. "The little finger of your left hand is at the wrong angle," the teacher would say sternly and I would rewrap the drum in its embroidered cloth and start all over again.

Eventually, after almost half a year of this, the teacher announced that she intended me to take part in a forthcoming public recital featuring her and her school. By this time I had been permitted to tap the drum twice. No, I protested, I could not do that. I had not the faintest idea of what I was supposed to be up to. Nevertheless, the teacher insisted, I would make my stage debut three weeks hence—her only foreign pupil—and she would procure me a formal kimono for the occasion. No, I said more firmly, I did not yet comprehend the art and had no desire to subject myself to the scrutiny of an audience. That's as may be, said the teacher with impeccable politeness, but I would do as I was told. "It's so difficult," murmured the pupils among themselves, "for a foreigner to understand. . . . " No, I said, swivelling on my tormented knees, it was not because I was a foreigner that I found things difficult. It was because I had been taking lessons in this sodding drum for five months whereas they had been taking them for an average of fifteen years. What's more, I had not yet been permitted to so much as glance at a musical score. I had no idea how to read the notation, I had not rehearsed with any of the other component elements in a Noh ensemble—flute, stand drum, and so on—and I would present a ridiculous spectacle if I appeared thus unprepared on a public stage whether I was dressed in a borrowed kimono or not. Well, if I didn't agree to her proposal I could always discontinue my studies, suggested the teacher sweetly. So that's what I did. I never touched a kotsuzumi again. Nor did I ever touch the young woman who had introduced me to the class and whose lessons in English conversation terminated at about the same time as my lessons in the music of the Noh.

I emerged from this reverie of twenty years past and landed back in the present in front of one of the thatched souvenir shops in Ogimachi looking at a pile of brand new *bin-zasara* that had been manufactured for sale to tourists. The bin-zasara is another ancient musical instrument, one used not in classical arts like the Noh but in folk performances like the country kagura staged during shrine festivals as entertainments for the gods. It is a sort of rattle, long and curving, made of a hundred or more small flat pieces of wood connected together by a string. Gripped in both hands and shaken briskly, it produces a sharp sound somewhere between the sliding of cracked tiles off a roof and the hissing of a large snake. I picked up one of these rattles and shook it, reflecting that mastery of the bin-zasara may not require fifteen years of study and that, having learned to grip it correctly, the aspiring rattlist may be allowed to shake it in less than five months after commencing lessons. It is a much simpler instrument than the kotsuzumi. Perhaps it requires only four months.

I tramped out of picturesque Ogimachi unable to make up my mind for certain whether Japan's signposted fossil culture disappointed and infuriated me or whether I should simply be grateful that the Noh and gasshozukuri villages had not vanished altogether. Was it better for an art to die and be decently buried or to die and be pickled in formaldehyde? The latter was definitely more profitable, I thought; the bin-zasara sold to tourists cost as much as five large dinners.

5
Ghost Roads

H akusan's peak was white with autumn snow and the day, though sunny, was cool. A little way out of Ogimachi I passed a tea house, two-thirds of whose thatched roof had been replaced by sheets of purplish brown tin. That's the way they all will go, I mumbled. The tea house was called Dream.

My road began to plunge through a series of long, unlit tunnels, most of them skirted by the ghost of an older road which I followed whenever the nettles permitted.

This ghost road, too, wound through tunnels, narrow, damp, pitch black, and broken, where I found stacks of eulalia grass stored for thatching and trod timidly in fear of snakes. Twice I glimpsed the river and each time its banks were scarred with a battered gravel factory or a new sky-blue cement works. Abandoned sheds, once villages, occasionally nudged my tangled road while the river dropped more and more steeply away and, in the tunnels, I shivered with cold. Heavy rockfalls here and there had destroyed what was left of the road's hard surface and beside the broken cliffs and mounds of rubble pebbles were piled for prayers. I scrambled over these pyramids of scree, and thorns tugged at my sleeves. My legs were stiff to the thighs from rain and the scrambles left me breathless. At about midday the tunnels ended, the ghost road merged again with the living one, and I marched through the last little hamlet of Gifu where acorns lay on straw mats beside the highway and the hum of a generating plant was the only man-made sound.

Now began a series of seven suspension bridges, collectively advertised as a "sight." Far below the river trickled brightly through twisting gorges that would have rendered the fleeing Heike invisible even to the kites. Water tumbled down the steep sides of the gorges and midway across the second of the signposted "Seven Bridges of Hida" I left Gifu and entered Toyama prefecture, where I was welcomed by another generating plant and a tatami-sized patch of rice. In the middle of the third bridge I entered Gifu again; in the middle of the fourth I stepped back into Toyama; on the next I returned to Gifu and so on until the sixth was behind me and Toyama began in earnest with a set of jerry-built dormitories for workmen constructing another dam.

On the other side of the seventh and last Hida bridge lay the village of Upper Taira whose first sign of life was a sprawling complex of noodle restaurants and souvenir shops selling miniature thatched houses and touting its folksiness with songs broadcast through loudspeakers arranged on poles all round the bus park. Further on stood a gasshozukuri house that had been converted into yet another museum, surrounded by coffee shops and stalls selling baskets and more loudspeakers trumpeting the region's musical heritage courtesy of Panasonic. Outside an actual dwelling a motorcyclist stopped to take a picture of an old woman spreading acorns on a mat. "May I take your photograph?" he asked her nervously. "Please," said the old woman and, while the motorcyclist was unpacking his camera, she disappeared into her house, reemerged with two cats, one under each of her wiry arms, and settled herself and her pets on a fire hydrant well away from her acorns and mat to be photographed doing a V-sign. The defeated motorcyclist muttered and snapped.

Further still, in a valley to the left, well below the sightseers' highway, stood a whole hamlet of gasshozukuri houses that had been registered en bloc as a cultural asset. The hamlet was called Suganuma (Sedge Swamp) and I might have given it a miss except that my rain-stiffened legs were on the point of collapse; my arms, wrists, and neck were itching from the thorns and nettles; and I noticed by shading my eyes and squinting that one of the thatched houses in the hamlet had a board up that read Minshuku. So I left the highway at half past three and tramped down into the valley, pausing to visit Suganuma's pair of small museums, in one of which, completely alone, I viewed a collection of straw raincoats and farm implements to the accompaniment of a taped commentary with folk songs which the elderly custodian switched on for me the minute I had finished buying my ticket, and in the other of which was a video game where I pointed a fake musket at a bulls-eye target ("Aim low," a second elderly custodian advised) and, if I scored, was treated to a thirty-second film clip of rival samurai armies blasting each other to mincemeat. My legs were wobbling when I stumbled up to the entrance of the house that advertised itself as a minshuku, hauled back the dusty plank door, and shouted a loud hello.

A woman with a baby strapped to her back and a face like a half-awake dog appeared.

"Have you got any rooms free?" I asked her.

The dog-faced woman stared at me without answering. The baby on her back caught sight of me round the side of the woman's neck and started to cry.

"I mean, you know, I'd like to stay the night. . . . "

The woman stared. The baby grizzled.

"If that's all right. If you've got a room, I mean."

"Will anywhere do?" the dog-faced woman snapped.

"Oh, yes, anywhere at all will be fine."

She stared at me. The silence deepened.

"How many of you are there?"

"Just me."

Stare. Sniffle. Hiccup.

"You'll have to share."

"Well, yes, all right . . . "

"With a lot of people."

Stare. Silence.

Finally, when it looked as though the only alternative to turning round and limping away was to shove the dog-faced woman bodily out of the doorway, an old man bobbed out from behind a screen rubbing his hands on a bloodied apron.

"Welcome," he said.

"He's by himself," the dog-faced woman hissed.

"That's all right," said the old man, pushing her halfway out of the dirt-floored entrance hall. "Welcome. Welcome. Welcome."

"It's seven thousand yen," the dog-faced woman snarled.

"That's if you have the pheasant stew," said the old man. "I'm making it now. It's the specialty of the house. Otherwise it's four thousand, eight hundred yen."

"Well, all right, I'll have the pheasant stew."

"There's only one of you?"

"Yes."

"I see."

"Can I come in now?" I said, starting to unhitch my rucksack. The old man pushed the dog-faced woman further back inside the dim house. The baby wailed. I took off my boots.

"Welcome," the old man said. "Welcome." The dog-faced woman stared at me as though I had come to murder her firstborn.

Once inside I saw what the woman had meant by having to share. The interior of the house was still in its original state, one huge room undivided by screens, and anyone staying the night had two choices: to bed down with whoever was kipping downstairs or with whoever was kipping upstairs in the only other habitable space, now free of suffocated silk worms. I was directed upstairs, where it turned out I would be kipping with the elderly owner of a Ginza coffee shop who had arrived without a reservation five minutes after I had and been admitted much more briskly. His first grandchild had just been born, he told me proudly as I hung my still-damp clothes over the gnarled beams below the thatch. His son was a doctor, studying gastrology in Paris. Japan's gastrological research was now on a level with that of the

United States, so anyone who wanted to get ahead went to Europe, especially to Paris, he explained. Paris was so advanced.

Was the coffee-shop owner taking a few days off work, I asked, wringing rainwater out of a shirt.

Oh, he didn't do much in the way of work. In addition to owning a coffee shop in the middle of the world's most expensive square kilometer of commercial real estate, he owned an apartment building in the up-market Tokyo district of Azabu which he rented out to corporations that employed foreign stockbrokers and the like. No, he didn't have much work to do.

As dusk fell the other guests began arriving: a young couple from Gifu city, the boy a travel agent, the girl a student; four newsagents from Osaka; and three smiling young women so shy that no one had the heart to ask them where they came from or what they did. At six o'clock we ate our fatty pheasant stew and at seven we shifted to sit round the smoky hearth. I drank a beer; the family's children gathered to ogle a massive color T.V., one six-year-old girl kneeling formally on the tatami with her hands clasped delicately in her lap. Two plump old women plonked down to sit with us, stretched their legs out till their bare brown toes were half a centimeter from the glowing charcoal, and then fell jointly into a coma. The newsagents drank shochu; the coffee-shop owner assured us of the advanced level of gastrological research in Paris. The old man, having removed his bloodied apron, started to grill oily char on bamboo skewers over the hearth. The shy young women withdrew and went to sleep in a corner.

"Wake 'em up," shouted the old man, "The char are done. They'll miss 'em." But no one stirred around the smoky hearth. The char oil hissed. In different parts of the rustling house middle-aged women strapped sleeping babies to each other's backs, and the comatose older women with their brown toes almost touching the smoldering embers scratched their crotches and began to snore.

"They used to make gunpowder in this village," the old man said to no one in particular. "All of 'em were in on it. It was a regular industry." That explained the video game and the samurai armies blasting away with muskets, I observed.

"Ah, it's nice to have a bit of knowledgeable company. I don't know what

I'd do without it. In winter, you know, we don't heat the upstairs so there's a limit to the number of guests we can put up. They have to lie in the center of the floor so the heat from the downstairs hearth'll rise and warm their backs."

And the smoke'll suffocate them in their sleep, I thought. The dog-faced woman appeared, grinding her teeth.

"Can I have another bottle of beer, please?" I asked her.

"I've brought your bill," she snapped, and thrust a dirty scrap of paper into my hand. I squinted at it in the dull glow of the neon tube that was screwed, between five sticky fly papers, to the timber canopy over the hearth. From a black chain the thickness of a fist hung a spoutless iron kettle.

"You want me to pay now?"

"Yes."

"What, for the accommodation and dinner and everything?"

"Yes."

I chuckled and fished my wallet out of my jeans and found that it contained nothing smaller than a ten-thousand yen note.

"I've no change for that," the dog-faced woman snapped.

"I'm sorry; it's all I've got," I said.

The four newsagents looked at each other, drained their shochu glasses quickly, stood up, bade the old man a polite goodnight, and vanished into a distant corner.

"Never mind, never mind," the old man said. "He can pay in the morning like everybody else." The dog-faced woman stared at me and didn't move. The sniveling baby had been transferred from back to back and had finally gone to sleep strapped to the old man's.

"I'm going to phone Tokyo," I said.

The dog-faced woman followed me out to the phone in the kitchen and stood watching me while I made the call. When I had finished I put the receiver down and waited for the operator to call back and tell me the time and charges, but as soon as the phone rang and I picked up the receiver, the dog-faced woman snatched it out of my hand.

"Two hundred and ten yen," she said, staring at my face. I paid her out of the loose change I had in my pocket.

"Here, let's have some shochu," said the old man when I joined him back at the dim hearth. The plump old women were still comatose, roasting their toes against the dying charcoal, but everyone else, including the coffee shop owner, had gone into the far recesses of the building to sleep.

"Don't give him any more to drink," said the dog-faced woman who had followed me from the kitchen, but the old man ignored her and she shuffled away. And when the old man asked me how old I was and I told him that I was forty-two, he called her back to bring larger tumblers. Forty-two is an auspicious age. We sat and toasted the spoutless kettle.

"How did you like the pheasant stew?" the old man wanted to know.

"It was fine," I said. It had tasted like fatty chicken.

"It's our specialty," he told me proudly. "They phone in orders from all over the place. We've got four people stopping in for lunch tomorrow."

"You work hard," I said. The old man reached over and refilled my tumbler from the half-empty bottle.

"There's a pile of stuff to fret about," he said, more to himself and to the sleeping women than to me. He shrugged his shoulders gently and the troubled baby sighed in its sleep. "There's the thatch'll need redoing soon. It's near enough twenty year since it was done, and after thirteen or fourteen it gets ragged. Nowadays some of the places on the pamphlets get volunteers from the cities to help. You should see 'em!" he laughed. "Especially with the snakes."

"Snakes?" I said, feeling a draught through the wall.

"Oh, yes," said the old man. "They nest in the thatch. It's their home as much as it is ours. No one in these parts worries much about snakes. But city folk take 'em for the very devil."

I told the old man how I had once killed a cobra on the lawn of my mother-in-law's house in Penang. It had come up from the river for the small frogs that invade the garden after a rain. My mother-in-law's alsatians had gone for the cobra and one of them had managed to sink a tooth into it so that within half a minute the wound on its back was alive with tiny red ants. The cobra was livid, knowing that it would die. It stood stiffly alert in the middle of the lawn, waiting for me to come within range of it, recognizing in me, not the ants or the dogs, the agent of its death. And for fifteen minutes we performed a silent ballet while the dogs watched entranced and panting in their cages, the cook stood with her hands clasped to either side of her head, and my wife leant against the doorway that led into the cool house aiming a Japanese camera. Finally the cobra lowered its body to the clipped grass in weariness and disgust, and I took two steps towards it and killed it with a parang.

"I didn't want to kill it," I explained to the old man, who was gazing at the sputtering kettle. "But the ants were in the wound, you see; they would have tormented it to death."

"Aren't you cold?" the old man asked me suddenly. "How can you sit there with your sleeves rolled up?"

"Oh, I'm used to the cold," I laughed. "I'm from England."

"England," said the old man, gazing at the kettle. "It's cold there, I know. It's near the South Pole."

"Go to bed," ordered the dog-faced woman, appearing from the kitchen to cast a long shadow over the dying charcoal. "It's ten o'clock. I want to sleep."

The old man said nothing, gazing at the kettle and shrugging his shoulders up and down while the baby sighed, strapped to his back. So I drained the last of the shochu from my tumbler and climbed the stairs to where my futon had been laid out beside the snoring coffee-shop owner. For hours I tossed in an uneasy sleep and in my dreams whole nests of writhing avengers fell out of the thatch onto my face.

At seven a loud orchestral jingle woke the entire drowsy village and at ten past seven the same loudspeaker began broadcasting community announcements about two meters from the gap in the thatch that was nearest my head. I went out for a walk before breakfast. The footpaths between the thatched houses had all been smoothed and concreted for sightseers but, once the community announcements had stopped, there was little trace in Suganuma of the theme park atmosphere that had haunted Ogimachi. There were no coffee shops or restaurants other than my minshuku where pheasant stew that tasted like fatty chicken was available at lunchtime to travelers who had phoned; there were no souvenir shops, no viewing platforms, and the small gunpowder museum had all the appearance of a private dwelling until you got close enough to hear the videotaped carnage. The hills surrounding the village were so steep that from the air the thatched houses must have looked like tea leaves at the bottom of a deep cup, but all of them seemed lived-in.

For breakfast the old man, who had donned his all-day uniform of a blood-ied apron and was already busy chopping up fowl, gave me an egg with a hole punched in it through which I could suck the yolk. He gave one to the Ginza coffee-shop owner too, who peered at it nervously while he brushed his teeth.

"Cold, isn't it?" said one of the plump old women who had spent the night with her toes to the faded embers. And the dog-faced woman, bottle-feeding the baby, stared up at me and gave me the adumbration of a smile.

"I'm sorry I was rude last night," she said. "But your face is still red this morning."

I flashed her an over-generous grin and spent three minutes trying to puzzle out what on earth she had just said.

"I thought you was drunk," she explained at last, "when you turned up at the door with a red face like that. I thought you was going to cause trouble. But you've got a red face all the time."

No, I said solemnly, it was just that I had spent two weeks hiking in the autumn sun.

"It's because your skin's so white," she said. "It's bound to get you in trouble running about with skin as white as that." And the primitive half-smile crept back onto her face. Still, mine was the first bill she presented before shushing us all out at half-past eight.

"Come again," she said, and the strapped baby, craning to see me round her bobbing neck, set up a howl that vied in decibels with the community announcements.

It was a hopelessly beautiful morning, crisp and cold and the sky a soaring blue. On the highway I found large signboards urging the future construction of a bullet train to bring "a new world to Toyama," but the present world seemed in comfortable repair. There were road signs with careful English translations and neat, coddled flowerbeds in which, at measured intervals, the scarlet sage was labeled. Further on, where the highway crossed the slow, green river an older road was labeled in Japanese, The Folk-Song Lovers' Hiking Path and another sign (the prefectural authorities must have solved the rural employment crunch by recruiting an enormous number of sign-writers) said in English, Gokayama Scenic Route: Traditional Folk Music Region.

Toyama has always struck me as a prefecture that takes pains to impress upon the natives of other, inferior prefectures that it is all right, thank you very much, and what a shame they aren't privileged to live here. Like the genteel, insecure English middle classes, it wants you to admire its serviettes. Years ago, when I walked the length of Japan, I came to Toyama out of the no-nonsense north and at once began recording differences. Elsewhere family graves had been marked by simple headstones; in Toyama they were more like public cenotaphs. The bus shelters in Toyama were equipped with dust-pans and brushes and the toilets in the coffee shops had pink fluffy seat covers. Entering Toyama from neighboring Niigata was a little like crossing the border between Yugoslavia and Austria circa 1960, emerging from a land where workers in shabby raincoats had calluses on their hands and feet into one in which closely shaved citizens ate cream-filled pastries, consulted pocket watches, and kept their jewelry in bank deposit boxes. The coddling of roadside flowerbeds and the labeling in two languages of regions and routes seemed entirely characteristic of Toyama, but how would it deal with a Folk-Song Lovers' Hiking Path? With the usual loudspeakers in the trees, I supposed, and members of the local Lions Club dressed in knickerbockers and Tyrolean hats with feathers playing accordions under the boughs.

In the event, however, there was nothing to distinguish the Folk-Song Lovers' Hiking Path from any other unfrequented rural road. As a folk-song lover I felt a pang of regret, like arriving to find one's favorite pastry shop all out of apple strudel. I trudged along the empty route for an hour or so, past a couple of thatched houses that had been turned into restaurants, both of which were closed, and a stately hawk in a tall pine tree, whose shrill *piiiii* . . . was the closest thing I heard to music. A woman sweeping out her porch and dusting the plaster badgers in her yard told me that there was no point in my going any further because the road soon lost itself in the hills and that I had better rejoin the highway by crossing the river at the first available bridge. This I did, squeezing past a gang of workmen with dump trucks and a drilling machine, and at 11:30 I found myself, according to the umpteenth carefully lettered sign, on the edge of the village of Taira, whose name, resonant of the Heike and their history, had set me off on this two-week tramp.

The first thing I saw on rejoining the highway was another gasshozukuri house converted into a museum and a large cloth banner stretched across the road in front of it announcing that this area was The Home of the Kokiriko (a different, more colloquial name for the bin-zasara rattle) and a poster which informed me, in case I had come all this way to take part in it, that the annual Kokiriko Festival had been held a fortnight before so I had missed it. I drank a beer in a restaurant where the owner spent all his time demonstrating the kokiriko to noodle-slurping lunchers and then left my pack behind his counter and strolled back to look at my sixth or seventh thatched museum.

This one, formerly the house of a family called Murakami, was by far the oldest I had come across. It was built, according to the three-page English-language pamphlet I was handed (Toyama really does try hard) in 1578, well before Japan settled down to being a unified nation-state and at least ten years before William Shakespeare wrote his first play, in a style that reflected the samurai status of its owners (that is to say, it had space for guests). It was constructed, as are all original gasshƒzukuri dwellings, without the use of nails or dowels, the place of these items being taken by ropes and a method of rigidly tensing them. It was as dark and smoky, as cluttered with old farm implements collected to bemuse fee-paying tourists as any of the other houses-cum-museums I had been in, and it also boasted a resident artist: a man in a beret who sat at a downstairs table doing quick impressionist ink paintings of thatched roofs and misty mountains that he sold to the same fee-paying tourists at three thousand yen a go.

The owner of the restaurant where I had drunk my beer, advised me, between bursts of demonstrating his rattle, to make for Aikura, which he called "the heart of Taira." Aikura (literally, "a gathering of storehouses") was another hamlet full of thatched museums and souvenir shops and coffee bars and minshukus, where I might be able to stay the night and where, if I was lucky, the restaurant owner told me with what I took to be an attempt to wink, the villagers might perform a dance. So I left the highway and set out along a steep, unsurfaced, rubbly path that skirted a grim kilometer-long tunnel and brought me into Aikura the back way. In the half hour that it took me to climb the path the sky grew fiercely overcast and by the time I rejoined the paved road at the hamlet and tramped past the bus stop and the taxi stand, the entire landscape looked like an ink painting.

Some sort of a festival seemed to be in progress. A couple of stalls had been set up along what could only be the hamlet's main street and several sallow-faced young men were selling sticks of mashed rice dipped in beanpaste sauce. What was going on, I asked them. Nothing, said one of the young men. It was always like this on a Sunday afternoon. And this evening there would be a school outing to cater for. On weekends they were run off their feet.

"I was hoping I could stay," I told him, noticing that his mashed-rice-and-beanpaste-sauce stall doubled as an information center, so the young man called his mother, who came out of the thatched house behind the stall rubbing her hands on a spotless apron and told me that everywhere was full.

"What a pity!" she exclaimed. "What a pity! What a pity! And there's going to be dancing and everything. But we've got two hundred and fifty schoolchildren arriving in an hour or so to stay two nights, and all the gasshozukuri places are full."

"What about the places that aren't gasshozukuri?" I asked. Well, there were a couple such places, the woman admitted, and of course no one stayed in them if the thatched places had space, but she'd phone them for me if I liked. Which she did, but there was no reply.

"Oh, what shall we do? What shall we do?" she said brightly, bobbing and pursing her lips, and I knew from her tone and from the motherly way in which she kept clucking and cocking her head that she would find a solution, without a doubt, so long as I looked lost and said nothing.

"Go away for forty minutes," she told me. "You can leave your pack here and look round the museums. Then, if there's still no reply at the minshukus, I'll phone the two ryokans down in the valley for you and you can come back up for the dancing by taxi."

So I wandered round the two houses-cum-museums, where the same bemusing farm implements stood gathering dust in smoky corners and the same tape loops droned out their explanations of how gunpowder and paper were made in the old days to a background of the courtly sounding "Song of the Kokiriko," accompanied by drum and flute and rattle:

On yonder hill the bulbul cries,
Its voice low, its voice high;
We wake to cut the morning grass,
To cut the morning grass.

In one of the museums I found a map displaying forty-eight different locations, ranging from the far north of Honshu to southern Kyushu, where the Heike are reputed to have settled after their flight. Prominent among them, naturally, was the spot upon which I was standing. Outside, a solitary woman in a pink smock and black elbow-length rubber gloves stood in a field bundling up her straw like an illustration to the museum's tape loop, completely oblivious of the tourists who were aiming their cameras and munching their rice-on-sticks. Aikura was an in-between attraction, less daintily picturesque than Ogimachi but much more a registered "sight" than Suganuma. And the inhabitants of Aikura—not only the bobbing mother—seemed brisk and well-mannered and distinctly middle-class. Perhaps, this being Toyama prefecture, the authorities had sent them on an etiquette course.

When I got back to the mother at the stall, there was still no sign of a place to stay. Both the non-gasshozukuri minshukus had been rung again and at both there was still no one answering the phone. Now the ryokans in the valley were rung, but one was full and the other was closed.

"What shall we do? What shall we do?"

I bought a stick of mashed rice and beanpaste sauce, sat on the wall in front of the mother's house, and munched it contentedly. Buses full of school children began to arrive. I watched them park and the kids climb down and begin kicking up the dust in the village street.

"Of course . . . there's always . . . one thing we could try. . . . "

I looked up brightly and nibbled my rice.

"You see, it's not an especially big school. I mean, there's only two hundred and fifty coming. Some weekends we get four hundred and then every minshuku's so chock-full you can scarcely squeeze in through the doors."

"Ha ha ha," I said, striving to enjoy the vision of a minshuku full of dust-kicking school kids.

"But what I'm thinking is, the smallest gasshozukuri place right at the end of the village is only booked to take thirteen high school girls. . . . "

"Thirteen high school girls," I said. "Well, well."

"And, since that's not as many as they'd normally take, they could probably put you in the room upstairs. . . . "

"The room upstairs."

"If you didn't mind."

"Oh, I wouldn't mind a bit. No, no. It would be nice to sleep so close to the thatch. And I'd hate to have come all this way and miss the dancing. Thirteen high school girls. Well, well."

So without any more fuss, or any sign that the arrangement had not been settled from the moment I strolled into the hamlet, I was directed to the last gasshozukuri house on the street where a gentle couple in their seventies welcomed me and carried a *kotatsu* (a table with an electric heating element fixed underneath it) to the attic room where I would sleep, to ward off the October chill. The room was a disappointment after the snake-infested thatch of Suganuma. All of the beams and the thatch itself had been hidden by formica boards printed to look like wallpaper. I had no sense whatever of being in a house that, according to the old man who wore a thick bandage round his neck, had been occupied by his family for three hundred and twenty years. He was the tenth generation head and reckoned that the house itself predated his family's occupancy of it by about eight decades, which would make it contemporary with the rise of Hideyoshi and the expulsion of the Jesuits from Kyushu, with *Love's Labors Lost* and *The Comedy of Errors*.

The downstairs living room that housed the hearth was littered with bits of rice crackers, torn stuffed toys, and cellophane packets, and no attempt was being made to tidy it for the thirteen schoolgirls whose arrival was imminent. The old man's eight-year-old grandson and a friend of similar age and persuasion ran up and down the stairs between my fake wallpapered room and the cluttered hearth shouting facetious things at me in the Janglish they had picked up from television commercials while their mother encouraged them in their adventures by shouting out every ten seconds or so from the kitchen, "Talk to him! Go on and talk!"

The schoolgirls arrived while I was in the bath and, when I emerged in my yukata to a chorus of "Ehhh"s and "Ahhh"s and "Oooo"s, I was shunted straight upstairs.

"Can't I eat at the hearth with everyone else?" I asked, but the old man smiled and looked down at his feet.

"You see, it's the first time we've met you," he said shyly. So my dinner was brought up to me on a tray and I ate it alone, enclosed in formica.

At eight o'clock I pulled on my jeans and sweater and a pair of the min-shuku's plastic sandals and made my way in the company of two hundred and fifty high school students from Yokohama to the space in front of the village shrine where we were to watch an exhibition of folk dancing. I counted four male teachers among the crowd but they all kept as far away from me as they could and lowered their eyes whenever I looked at them. There was a female teacher, too, who by some calamitous oversight found herself standing next to me for the duration of the performance but managed to pretend that I wasn't there.

The dances were explained to us before they began by a man with a micro-phone, whose suit the lantern light turned a shade of rusty pink. Most of the students paid him no attention and the girls around me chatted throughout his explanations and the songs that followed but their teachers made no effort to silence them and continued to stare at the ground.

This hamlet of Aikura, the man told us, contained twenty-three gasshozukuri houses and had been registered as a National Cultural Asset in 1970. It was as famous for its folk songs as for its architecture and all of the songs and dances that we would witness tonight were Intangible Cultural Assets. The Heike had certainly settled here following their long flight from the capital, and it was to them that the village owed its traditions and its songs. The songs we heard were all scratchy recordings and the dances were per-formed by young people of the village, the high-school-aged girls in orange kimonos staring rigidly over the heads of their audience in an agony of shyness and the young men who had operated the mashed rice stalls, some wearing swords and formal hakama embroidered with the Heike crest and some in lemon yellow kimonos and steep straw hats with plumes that hid their faces, dancing with more assurance than the girls, with strict rhythm and fine aloofness. The *sasara* used in the "Song of the Kokiriko" each had one hundred and eight wooden teeth, the same as the number of earthly sins that are tolled away by the bells of temples—like the Gion bell—each New Year's Eve. Why, the sasara is so much a part of our native culture that it is used today in jazz combos, explained the man in the rust-pink suit to the restless, dust-kicking Yokohama students. And after thirty minutes and six dances we dispersed, the students slowly and the teachers as though occupied with suddenly remembered errands, back to the dimness of our hearths and formica and the country tedium of our thatch.

Did the Heike ever come to Taira?

The road that had brought me here, to an extent almost unique in today's Japan, had taken me through towns and villages where old traditions had died hard or been painstakingly revived. There had been Seki, famous since the twelfth century for its swordsmiths, now reduced to supplying the nation with safety razors, and the Punch-and-Judy cormorant fishing on the Nagara River nearby. There had been Mino with its handmade paper that predated the Heike by perhaps four centuries, and the old sake brewery that took such pride in the award it had won and in its elaborately tiled roof. There had been the film-set town of Gujo Hachiman with its two-month summer carnival, its Fountain of Youth, its waterwheel. There had been the landscape gardens of Mr. Hatta. And in and around remote Gokayama there had been the thatched villages that resembled theme parks, with their museums and hearths and folk traditions, some of which (like the sasara rattle and the dance that accompanies the "Song of the Kokiriko," performed for restless city schoolkids) had a pedigree that undoubtedly stretched back beyond the Heike and their battles.

Yet none of these traditions and remains, with the possible exception of the dances, can conceivably owe its existence here to the flight through these hills of the clan that scattered after Dannoura. No fleeing courtiers in flat-bottomed boats can have paused three days out of Nagoya to set up a workshop for forging swords or, further upriver, busied themselves, while their pregnant women fretted and quailed, building landscape gardens with water-falls or organizing a communal dance. But in the minds of most of the week-end tourists who visit these old towns and hamlets, the past is a generously amorphous fog. What is old is old; there is no need to bother oneself over-much about causes and results. The Heike used swords and rattles, didn't they? They danced, they may well have caught their fish with birds on strings that resembled little Nessies. All history, even—or rather especially—the recent history of the 1930s and 1940s, is a tangle best left for the senseis to unravel. These dances, these hamlets, they are mannerly and fine; they are laudable; they are Japanese.

As to the specific claim that Heike survivors settled in Gokayama, it is pos-sible that they did and arguable that they didn't. That the area would have afforded them a perfect hideaway is obvious, especially if you have taken the trouble to walk there and seen the height of the hills and the dizzying twists of the gorges. As late as the 1920s Gokayama was accessible only on foot, over a single seven-hundred-meter-high pass; no electricity reached it until Hirohito's reign. The population of the region in medieval times is said to have been almost as large as it is today, and there are records to suggest that fugitives from the wars between the southern and northern courts in the mid-fourteenth century made their way here too, as perhaps the Heike had done a century and a half before them, giving the region a reputation for harbor-ing those with whom history has played false.

Nor did Gokayama's remoteness remain entirely the fault of geography. In the late sixteenth century the area fell under the dominion of the Kaga clan whose seat was the city of Kanazawa on the Japan Sea coast. The vil-lages on the east bank of the Sho River were used by the Kaga lords as places of exile; and thus it was policy to keep them remote. It was also at the insti-gation of Kaga that the villages on the west bank, like Suganuma and Aikura, were encouraged to manufacture gunpowder for use by the clan armies, as well as paper which was used for making the scrip that served the clan as cur-rency. These semi-secret practices, too, made it essential that clan authori-ties keep the region artificially isolated by operating a strict control of the flow of people who went in and out of it. In an area so conspicuously and completely separated from contact with the wider world it is natural that stories should have developed that harped upon this officially sanctioned remoteness, that sought to exploit it in imaginative ways, and that visualized it extending back in time far further than the advent of gunpowder and scrip.

But at the time of the Heike diaspora, Gokayama was not owned by a clan. Rather it was temple property; it belonged to Kofukuji Temple in Nara, which, five years before the battle of Dannoura, had been burned to the ground by the Heike under Taira-no-Shigehira, who had in turn been beheaded by the temple monks. It is puzzling to imagine the Heike survivors seeking refuge on land that was owned by some of their least forgiving enemies. No doubt news traveled slowly between the great center of Buddhist power and these remote, snow-flecked, windy hills, or perhaps the Heike survivors reasoned that, since Shigehira had paid with his life for destroying temple property, they had at least a vestige of a moral right to pluck some advantage from his death.

These thoughts came and went as I strolled back along the dark, crowded street of Aikura, ignored by the teachers who hurried along with their lips pursed and their eyes fixed on the ground and hailed or chortled at by the jean-clad kids, and I felt a niggling in my stomach. Perhaps it was something I had eaten . . . or perhaps I had drunk too many beers. Perhaps the climb over the spine of Honshu had tired me more than I imagined. Perhaps I was experiencing the beginnings of a chill.

Lying awake in the formica-walled attic of a house that had been built in the year of the Spanish Armada, I listened while the city kids congregated on the corners, making dates and swapping jokes and wondering aloud how on earth they were going to survive a whole Monday of boredom gathering bracken and weaving straw in this end-of-the-world place they had been brought to in buses by their busy, downcast minders. At nine I heard a wooden flute, but it was only the beginning of a recorded announcement warning the village and its guests against fire. The niggling in my stomach persisted, but it would be another twenty-seven months before they found the cancer in my gut. In the end it was the sound of the sasara in my head that I fell asleep to on this last night of my walk: a harsh sound with a whispering cadence, caught between a crack and a sigh, like something scurrying through an autumn wood.

About Alan Booth

Born in 1946 in London's East End, Alan Booth, by the age of 10, had already read most of Shakespeare's works. He studied drama at Birmingham University and went on to join the London Shakespeare Center where he worked as both actor and director.

Booth went to Japan in 1970 because of his interest in theater as ritual—an idea very much in vogue in the 1960s—and studied the Noh theater. As time passed however, Booth grew increasingly disenchanted with Noh, but more and more fascinated by the country in which he had now made his home; he also began to realize his true vocation as a writer. For two decades, he contributed regularly to various English-language publications in Japan with commentaries on Japanese films or socio-political issues. During this time, he also became fluent in Japanese and extremely adept at singing classic Japanese folk songs, *enka*, endearing him to his Japanese hosts.

What Booth has become most well-known for, and perhaps what he enjoyed best, was traveling to remote corners of the country, visiting rural inns, meeting the local folk, drinking bottles of beer with his hosts, and then using his adept, witty writing style to chronicle the events. His 1986 work, *The Roads to Sata*, has become a classic, immortalizing his epic journey on foot from the northern tip of Hokkaido to the southern tip of Kyushu.

Booth died in 1993 of colon cancer and is survived by his wife, Su-chzeng, and their daughter, Mirai. *Looking for the Lost* was originally published posthumously in 1994.

KODANSHA GLOBE

International in scope, this series offers distinguished books that explore the lives, customs, and mindsets of peoples and cultures around the world.

To order, contact your local bookseller or call 1-800-788-6262 (mention code G1). For a complete listing of titles, please contact the Kodansha Editorial Department at Kodansha America, Inc., 114 Fifth Avenue, New York, NY 10011.